Supreme Democracy

Supreme Democracy

The End of Elitism in Supreme Court Nominations

RICHARD DAVIS

OXFORD

UNIVERSITY PRESS

Oxford University Press is a department of the University of Oxford. It furthers
the University's objective of excellence in research, scholarship, and education
by publishing worldwide. Oxford is a registered trade mark of Oxford University
Press in the UK and certain other countries.

Published in the United States of America by Oxford University Press
198 Madison Avenue, New York, NY 10016, United States of America.

Cataloging-in-Publication Data is on file at the Library of Congress
ISBN 978–0–19–065696–6

1 3 5 7 9 8 6 4 2

Printed by Sheridan Books, Inc., United States of America

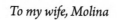

To my wife, Molina

CONTENTS

The Transition toward Democracy 80

Presidential Selection 104

The Changing Role of the Senate 133

Presidential Management 169

Conclusion

ACKNOWLEDGMENTS

Many have helped to make this book possible. The College of Family, Home, and Social Sciences provided research grants to facilitate research assistance and travel. The library staffs at the following institutions helped facilitate this research: The Manuscript Division of the Library of Congress, the U.S. Senate Historical Office, the Lyndon Johnson Presidential Library, the Richard Nixon Presidential Library, the Ronald Reagan Presidential Library, the William J. Clinton Presidential Library, the George H. W. Bush Presidential Library, the George W. Bush Presidential Library, the John F. Kennedy Presidential Library, the Dwight D. Eisenhower Presidential Library, the Harry S. Truman Presidential Library, and the Center for Legislative Archives at the National Archives.

I appreciate those who were willing to give interviews—in person or over the phone. Also, several research assistants provided invaluable help in locating materials: Desiree Anderson, Caitlyn Bradfield, Adam Duncan, Trevor Finch, Lynn Farnell, Kayla McGill, Jennica Peterson, and Katelyn Tietzen. Mel Thorne and the Faculty Editing Service at BYU provided the index.

My thanks, especially, to my wife, Molina, for her patience as I spend too many hours in front of a computer or away rummaging through archives.

Introduction

When US Supreme Court nominee Elena Kagan sat down at the witness table in room SH-216 of the Hart Senate Building for her confirmation hearing on June 28, 2010, her testimony was seen live on major cable news networks. Her appearance before the Senate Judiciary Committee was major news for three days on television, radio, newspapers, and the Internet. Twenty-three witnesses followed Kagan to testify in behalf of, or in opposition to, her confirmation. Although little was found to disqualify her, this confirmation process took slightly under three months and 37 senators voted against her confirmation.

Her predecessor had a very different experience. Kagan replaced John Paul Stevens, who had been confirmed in 1975. Stevens's testimony, which was not televised, took only one day. Only four individuals showed up to testify regarding Stevens's nomination. His confirmation process took three weeks and he was confirmed unanimously.

The Supreme Court nomination process has changed dramatically in a generation—Stevens to Kagan. Over the past half-century, television, the Internet, the influence of image-making, the growing role of interest groups, and the new salience of public opinion has transformed the way Americans select the people who sit on the US Supreme Court. The change has been part of a wider evolution of the presidential appointment and Senate confirmation processes.[1] But the irregularity of Supreme Court nominations as well as the status of the Supreme Court itself has made developments in the Supreme Court nomination process particularly important for the nation. Moreover, the Court's own expected distance from partisan politics and media image-making has created greater tension in these processes than executive branch appointments or lower-level judicial vacancies.

There is no question that Supreme Court confirmation hearings have become major television events on cable news channels, blogs, and Twitter; White House image-making characterizes nominee announcements and confirmation campaigns (along with interest group–generated news stories, typically in opposition); and public opinion has acquired a new importance as polling organizations regularly survey citizens on their views about whether they view a nominee favorably or unfavorably and whether he or she should be confirmed.

To be clear, the basic framework for the judicial selection process set out in the Constitution is still intact. The president still nominates and the Senate confirms, or not. Ultimately, those two acts are the most important parts in the process, even in today's changed nomination process.

Rather, the change has come particularly in who else is involved at both the presidential selection and Senate confirmation stages and what roles they play in the functioning of the process, as well as its outcome. Interest groups, the media, and the public now affect the process in ways they did not more than 50 years ago. These external players are important because of the effects they have today on how the president and senators carry out their constitutionally assigned tasks and, ultimately, on who sits on the Supreme Court.

With the involvement of these additional players, the nomination process has taken on the trappings of a major event in American politics. Presidential nomination and Senate confirmation are now accompanied by protracted public consideration of candidates, including much-discussed short lists and presidential interviews of top candidates; detailed staging of the president's announcement of a Supreme Court nominee; White House orchestration of the confirmation process; extensive public Senate deliberation through courtesy calls, nominee questionnaires, and Senate Judiciary Committee hearings; released reports by interest groups scrutinizing the nominee's record; and, in some cases, saturation media coverage. Lloyd N. Cutler, a former White House counsel, once remarked: "We're getting perilously close to electing a Supreme Court Justice."[2] Indeed, the process has been compared to an electoral campaign albeit one without ordinary voters.[3]

The Debate over the Nomination Process

The evolution of the Supreme Court nomination process has produced extensive debate over how nominations should be conducted today. The cleavage in opinion is not over whether change has occurred. All involved acknowledge that features of the process have been significantly altered. It is over what this change means.

Is today's process an improvement in terms of press and group scrutiny, public involvement, and accountability through increased transparency? Or is it a degradation of the process? Does it harm the nominees as justices, the Senate as an institution, or even the Court itself? Or is it good for the Court for justices to endure this public gauntlet?

Some commenters have lamented today's nominating process. They argue that nominations have morphed into something unrecognizable compared to the dignified process the Framers intended. For example, former US Solicitor General Theodore Olson has called the Senate confirmation process "much like the ancient practice of trial by ordeal—capricious, barbaric, and savage."[4] A blogger specializing in legal topics, pointing to opposing groups' treatment of Robert Bork, explained that their campaigns "legitimated scorched-earth ideological wars over nominations at the Supreme Court."[5] While chair of the Senate Judiciary Committee, Joe Biden decried the emphasis on less relevant aspects of a nominee. Biden argued that "the nation is enriched when we explore their jurisprudential views; it is debased when we plow through their private lives for dirt."[6]

Indeed, the nomination process has taken a dramatic turn to the personal. When Judge Robert Bork was nominated in 1987, the records of his rentals from a video store were obtained by journalists and publicized.[7] In 2005, during Judge John Roberts's confirmation process, reportedly, the *New York Times* assigned a reporter to investigate the adoption of Roberts's children.[8] Of course, the second round of confirmation hearings on Judge Clarence Thomas revolved around his personal relationship with law professor Anita Hill.[9]

Supreme Court nominations, like other personnel appointment processes, may easily center on personality. After all, the appointment is about an individual. The issues raised throughout the process become focused on the merits and qualifications of a person. The culmination of the process is, ultimately, a change in personnel. It is no surprise, then, that appointment processes are referenda on a particular individual.

Moreover, for media purposes, personalization simplifies the battle. Personalization makes extending the scope of the conflict easier, particularly as public opinion becomes involved. In an era of celebrity politics and culture, the public can more easily relate to an individual than to an issue or set of issues. As two scholars of the process have noted, "By this personification of issues in single individuals, the media, particularly television, can take a heretofore obscure part of the American political process and elevate it in the public consciousness."[10]

The conflict is not just personal; it also is directed at the nominee's ideology or supposed ideology. Since each Court appointment potentially affects the direction of the majority, the nominee's views about issues before the Court become important to players in the process. Open discussion about ideology was rare for most of the history of the Supreme Court nomination process. In recent years, it appears to have become the primary topic.

Moreover, the rhetoric of the process of discussing ideology has acquired a darker, more extremist tone as opposing ideological groups seek to confirm or reject a particular nominee based solely on ideology. In the Bork nomination, more than 300 interest groups formed an anti-Bork coalition that portrayed him in an advertising and publicity campaign as anti-labor, anti-women, racist, and backward. In 1990, Molly Yard, at that time president of the National Organization for Women, charged that nominee David Souter was "almost Neanderthal" and that the confirmation was life or death for women: "You're literally talking about women's lives. That's what's at stake." As a nominee, Judge Sonia Sotomayor was billed as a racist by opponents because of her claim that a "wise Latina" would reach a better conclusion than a white male.[11]

The public tension over nominees, fueled by interest groups, has affected the nominee's approach to public statements during the confirmation process. Until the latter half of the 20th century, nominees rarely spoke in public about their own confirmation processes or even the prospect of being nominated. But now nominees spend days testifying in front of members of the Senate Judiciary Committee, and, through the extension of the media, the nation at large. The expectations for public explanation of the nominee's views, including ideological positions, clash with the realities of confirmation politics. One blogger complained that the confirmation process rewards disingenuousness rather than candor. "There is no debate. There is no discussion. Now it's all litmus tests while the nominee smiles and nods and tries to tell people what they want to hear until they get a lifetime appointment and nobody can stop them."[12]

On the other hand, some scholars and observers of the new process paint a brighter picture. They even praise the sometimes raucous nature of the confirmation process today. According to that school of thought, these changes have been beneficial by opening the process beyond its traditional insular roots. Rather, they argue, the process should be transparent and engage the public. Through such engagement, the public can weigh in on those who sit on the Supreme Court and make important decisions affecting ordinary Americans' lives.[13]

The former group suggests that nominations should be above politics. They seem to operate on the premise that judicial selection works best when it is conducted by elites such as the president and the Congress, and the inclusion of other players demeans the process. The latter camp, conversely, suggests that politics has always been a part of the process and cannot be magically divorced from it. Indeed, rather than causing nominations to be more political, the newly configured process merely makes that political component more transparent than before.[14]

To ameliorate the vices of the system, scholars have advocated a variety of reforms. One is term limits that would lead to regular confirmation processes.[15] The most common suggestions target the committee hearings.[16] Stephen Carter and Ronald Rotunda have argued that senators should not ask questions about ideology, even if phrased as judicial philosophy.[17] Christopher L. Eisgruber believes such questions are appropriate, but they should not be phrased to exact commitments from justices on future cases.[18]

Another topic of debate, and one that overlaps somewhat with the preceding battle lines, revolves around who should play the dominant role in the appointment process. On one side are the advocates of presidential dominance who argue that the constitutionally designated appointment power rests with the president. Therefore, the presumption of confirmation should exist on the part of senators, save extenuating circumstances.

However, the other side argues for a more equal distribution of power between the White House and the Senate. This group views the Senate as an equal player in appointments rather than an occasional check. Therefore, the Senate should be aggressive in scrutinizing Supreme Court nominations rather than rubber stamping presidential choices.

Not surprisingly, where one sits influences where one stands on this issue. Presidents and executive branch officers, such as advisers to presidents and Justice Department leaders, tend to support presidential dominance while senators and their staffers are proponents of the second approach. And those roles can change within a person's career. For example, while he was a US senator, President Barack Obama voted against John Roberts and Samuel Alito, stating his opposition to their judicial philosophies and arguing that the Senate should examine a judicial nominee's "philosophy, ideology, and record" even while acknowledging their qualifications for the position.[19] In the case of Alito, Obama even joined a failed Democratic filibuster attempt.

However, as president, Obama was on the other side of the process when he chose two judicial nominees—Sonia Sotomayor and Elena Kagan. In announcing Sotomayor's nomination, he emphasized her qualifications as a reason for confirmation. In both Sotomayor's and Kagan's announcements, he urged the Senate to "act in a bipartisan fashion" and to do so "as swiftly as possible."[20] Later, during the process to replace Justice Antonin Scalia and in the midst of the Senate Republican majority's intransigence on considering an Obama nominee, Obama's press secretary admitted "that is an approach the president regrets."[21]

A Changing Nomination Process

The US Senate has handled 160 Supreme Court nominations since 1789.[22] A majority of senators confirmed those nominees in 119 cases or 74 percent of all the nominations. That means one of four presidential nominations did not end in confirmation. It would appear that, over time, presidents have a 25 percent chance of not getting a nominee through. Of course, such an aggregate conclusion ignores changes over time.

The Supreme Court nomination process has evolved over time, but not necessarily in a linear fashion. The 19th century was characterized by frequent battles between the president and senators over Supreme Court confirmation. However, at the end of the 19th century and through most of the 20th century, that tension dissipated. Between 1894 and 1967, only one nominee was rejected by the Senate. One scholar writing in 1941 concluded that "the confirmation process has become of diminishing significance." He predicted that "the days of equal participation by the Senate with the President in choosing Justices, typified in the Grant administration by the rejection of three appointees and lengthy consideration of another, is apparently gone forever."[23]

As will be discussed below, the Senate's approach to Supreme Court confirmations began a gradual transition toward increasing aggressiveness. However, there was a significant difference from the 19th-century practices. While in the 19th century the battle was largely between two institutions—the executive and the legislative—by the end of the 20th century and beginning of the 21st, the sphere of engagement was broad; it included interest groups, the media, and even the public. The visible changes—referral to the Judiciary Committee, the practice of regular Judiciary Committee hearings and deliberation, nominee and witness testimony, and floor debates and recorded votes—all marked an increasingly public process. These additions to the process meant lengthier deliberation by the Senate. The period from the president's nomination to Senate Judiciary Committee hearings (once they were instituted) to a vote by the Senate Judiciary Committee to a vote by the full Senate has expanded considerably over time. (See Table 1.)

The conventional wisdom is that the Senate became more aggressive in the latter half of the 20th century and therefore more prone to reject nominees. The cases of Justice Abe Fortas, Clement Haynsworth, G. Harrold Carswell, and Robert Bork are examples, although Fortas was never actually voted on by the Senate but withdrew when a filibuster blocked a confirmation vote. There is some accuracy to that conclusion, but only depending on the standard for comparison.

Even with greater interest group, media, and public involvement, the period of greatest rejection was not the most recent one but the 19th century. Most of those nominations not resulting in confirmation over the course of American history occurred in the 19th century. Twenty-four of the 41 unsuccessful nominations (i.e., withdrawn, postponed, rejected, or not even acted on), or 58 percent of the total of failed nominations, occurred in the 19th century. Obviously, the high number of unsuccessful nominations lowered the successful confirmation rate in the 1800s, which was 63 percent.[24] By contrast, the rate in 20th century was 88 percent, and in the latter half of the 20th century it was 78 percent.

Table 1 **Confirmed Justices: Average Number of Days to Confirm by Time Period***

Date	Number of Justices Confirmed	Average # of Days per Justice
1789–1809	16	2.56
1810–1830	6	8
1831–1850	9	11.56
1851–1870	10	12.3
1871–1890	11	24.91
1891–1910	12	8.33
1911–1930	10	24.1
1931–1950	13	12.62
1951–1970	11	57.91
1971–1980	3	38.6
1981–1990	5	94.3
1991–2000	3	75.7
2001–2010	4	89.25

*Includes only those nominees confirmed by the Senate

Sources:

Davis, Richard. *Electing Justice: Fixing the Supreme Court Nomination Process*. New York, NY: Oxford University Press, 2005, table 2.1, p. 67.

"Remarks by the President and Solicitor General Elena Kagan at the Nomination of Solicitor General Elena Kagan to the Supreme Court." The White House. May 10, 2010.

"Remarks by the President Announcing Judge Merrick Garland as His Nominee to the Supreme Court." The White House. March 16, 2016.

"Remarks by the President in Nominating Judge Sonia Sotomayor to the United States Supreme Court." The White House. May 26, 2009.

"U.S. Senate Roll Call Votes 109th Congress—1st Session." United States Senate. September 29, 2005.

"U.S. Senate Roll Call Votes 109th Congress—2nd Session." United States Senate. January 31, 2006.

"U.S. Senate Roll Call Votes 111th Congress—1st Session." United States Senate. August 6, 2009.

"U.S. Senate Roll Call Votes 111th Congress—2nd Session." United States Senate. August 5, 2010.

Wooley, John, and Gerhard Peters. "Presidential Audio/Video Archive—George W. Bush." The American Presidency Project. July 19, 2005.

Wooley, John, and Gerhard Peters. "Presidential Audio/Video Archive—George W. Bush." The American Presidency Project. October 31, 2005.

That last figure was considerably lower than rates for the 20th century as a whole (and therefore much lower than for the first half of the 20th century where confirmation was almost guaranteed), but also much higher than confirmation rates in the 19th century.

It is true that the Senate has become somewhat more likely to oppose nominees in the latter half of the 20th century. Yet the confirmation rate during that period was still slightly higher than the rate over the history of Supreme Court nominations. By comparison with the Senate's historical record, nominees were more likely to be confirmed in the latter half of the 20th century than in the history of Supreme Court nominations generally.

Another piece of evidence is the difference in the margin of victory for a nominee. If the Senate has become more aggressive, one would assume the vote totals for confirmation would decrease, meaning more "no" votes on the nominee. The increasing partisanship of the Senate in recent years would suggest that hypothesis. However, Paul M. Collins Jr. and Lori A. Ringhand have demonstrated that while it is true that the average number of senators voting for confirmation is lower today than in the early 20th century, the number has actually increased slightly over time throughout the history of Supreme Court nominations. That means recent nominees enjoy larger vote totals than those in the 19th century.[25]

One piece of evidence supports the conventional wisdom. The second highest rate of non-confirmation occurred in the 21st century. Of the first six presidential nominations of the 21st century, only two-thirds ended in confirmation. With a confirmation rate of 67 percent, that period looks similar to the 19th century. That would suggest a much more aggressive Senate role in vetting Supreme Court nominees than existed even in the latter half of the 20th century.

However, those statistics are somewhat deceptive. The nomination of John Roberts as an associate justice was withdrawn only because it was converted into a chief justice nomination. Discounting that, the confirmation rate was 80 percent, with only the Harriet Miers nomination failing. Even then, the Senate did not reject Miers; she withdrew 20 days after being nominated, which was early in the process of Senate consideration. Indeed, the Senate Judiciary Committee had not yet held hearings on Miers's nomination. On the four nominations where a vote occurred, the Senate confirmed in each case.

The actual rejection rate is even lower due to a president's tendency to withdraw a nomination rather than face possible (or likely) rejection. And in five cases, the nominee declined the nomination before a Senate vote. Of those 160 nominations, only 12 (or 7 percent) resulted in a negative Senate vote. Actual Senate rejection through a negative vote has been a rarity in American political history. It has been no more common in the past 50 years than it was for the whole history of Supreme Court nominations.

Discounting those justices who eventually were confirmed or declined before a Senate vote occurred, the overall confirmation rate has been 81 percent. In other words, when the Senate actually had to make a choice—decide yea or nay on a nominee or take no action at the time—they voted negatively only 19 percent of the time. And those outright rejections were more common in the 19th century. Of the 24 cases when the Senate voted no, postponed the nomination, or took no action at all, 17 occurred in that century.

Why more rejections then? One explanation may be a sense on the part of those involved that once begun, the process should be completed. This could have been the attitude of not only the president, who may have felt the nomination was out of his hands once it had been made, but also of the nominee and individual senators.

It also could be that the outcome was less likely to be known prior to a vote. The lengthy process of confirmation known today was largely unfamiliar to 19th-century government actors. Senators would have been less likely to declare their intentions in Senate Judiciary Committee hearings, through press statements to constituents and the nation, or in speeches during floor debate on nominees. For example, it may seem unusual today that John Rutledge, the first Supreme Court nominee to be rejected by the Senate, did not withdraw rather than face likely rejection. Could he not have predicted his rejection by a vote of 14–10, and therefore avoided it? Yet, apparently two weeks following the vote, Rutledge still was unaware that he had been rejected. Given the difficulties of transportation and communication, it may not have been possible to assess the outcome in advance.[26]

However, another explanation is that attitudes toward the Supreme Court transformed. In its early years, the Court was perceived as a political institution. Early justices made political speeches, a practice that led to Samuel Chase's impeachment in 1803. And some, using pseudonyms, wrote essays for newspapers of the day, thus linking them closer to political issues and parties than would be true in subsequent periods. Moreover, some justices rotated off the Court because of the drudgery of circuit-riding, a practice that diminished the commitment to the Court even by its own members. Finally, the tendency of some justices, such as John Jay, John McLean, Salmon Chase, and Stephen Field, to use the Court as a launching pad for political careers did not enhance the image of the Court as an independent, non-political body.[27]

Some scholars have pointed to a highly partisan period in the 19th century that spilled over into judicial nominations.[28] The Supreme Court was still acquiring a role as a third co-equal branch. Chief Justice John Marshall was seeking to provide the court with independence and significance in national government. During the 19th century, the Court was drawn into the controversy over slavery, virtually ignored by President Abraham Lincoln, and crippled by the Civil War and its immediate aftermath as the Radical Republicans in Congress took control of Reconstruction.

One practice in the 19th century that is uncommon today is the nomination of justices when a president was in the last months of a term. In several cases during the 19th century, presidents attempted to win confirmation of Supreme Court nominees when they were lame ducks due to their loss of re-election bids. Presidents John Quincy Adams, John Tyler, Millard Fillmore, and James Buchanan all presented Supreme Court nominations while they were lame-duck presidents and faced Senate rejection or a postponement or tabling that was tantamount to rejection.[29]

Today, the period between the general election and the inauguration of a new president is shorter, thus allowing less opportunity for a vacancy to occur and a president to attempt to fill it. And the precedent of presidents losing such battles has signaled to future presidents the futility of such action. The most recent example of such an effort was President Barack Obama's failed nomination of Judge Merrick Garland in 2016. Prior to that, it was President Lyndon Johnson's attempt to confirm Abe Fortas as chief justice before Johnson left office.

Has the Senate Become More Aggressive?

What caused the conventional wisdom that the Senate has become more aggressive, if not in the rejection rate, then in treatment of nominees? Perhaps an initial question is: When did the perception begin that the Senate was adopting a more assertive role in nominations? The conventional wisdom points to the nomination of Robert Bork by Ronald Reagan in 1987. However, there is greater evidence for an earlier change—the 1960s. (Even then, gradual change occurred over the late 1940s and 1950s.) The Fortas nomination was the first to feature a filibuster and cloture vote (failed) and led to the withdrawal of the nominee. The Haynsworth and Carswell nominations in 1969 and 1970 were the first in more than 70 years with a rejection of two successive nominees for the same position. In the early 1970s, some scholars were beginning to question whether the Senate was acquiring a new (or renewed) role in the confirmation process that contrasted sharply with its role in the previous 70 years. The staples of current confirmation processes—partisan votes, multi-day confirmation hearings, lengthy time periods between nomination and a confirmation vote—were emerging in the 1960s and early 1970s.[30]

Several aspects of the Bork confirmation process seemed to set it apart as a landmark change in the Senate's approach to Supreme Court nominations. One was the length of the confirmation hearings. Bork himself testified for five days, which, until that time, was the longest period that any nominee had sat before the Judiciary Committee.[31] Another was the number of witnesses who sought to testify for and against Bork. Still another was the intense lobbying of senators undertaken by interest groups. And still another was the extent of reference to public opinion as a measure of whether Bork should be confirmed.

Since the Robert Bork nomination, the Senate confirmation process has been the object of scrutiny by scholars. Some have analyzed individual nominations, such as those of Bork or Thomas, while others have concentrated on the process generally.[32] Specifically, the debate has centered on whether the confirmation process should be reformed and, if so, to what ends?

Scholars have not been the only players in this scrutiny of a new process. Journalists have examined the processes they have covered to determine what went wrong with the Bork and Thomas nominations.[33] And, to a greater extent than ever before, politicians have weighed in to recommend process revisions involving the Senate role in judicial selection.[34]

All of this attention to the process would suggest something significant has happened. It seems that the Bork nomination has altered the Senate's role in the process to make it a more engaged partner in judicial selection. As a result, we should expect not only greater Senate scrutiny but also a heightened willingness to reject nominees. Yet, one important piece of contrary evidence undermines that conclusion. Since the Bork nomination, only one nominee has been rejected by the Senate. By comparison, in the 19th century, there was no 30-year period when the Senate did not vote to reject or postpone (tantamount to rejection) at least two (and sometimes more) nominations.

One conclusion, then, is that the increased assertiveness comes in the process and not necessarily in the outcome of the vote. It is true that votes are closer than they were in the earlier part of the 20th century. Robert Bork was defeated by a vote of 58 to 42. Four years later, the Senate nearly rejected another nominee, Clarence Thomas, with a narrow 52–48 vote for confirmation. But, as mentioned earlier, the rejection rate is no worse than in the 19th century.

The Bork and Thomas nominations led to the conventional wisdom that the Senate has now adopted a more active role as a partner in the judicial selection process. These two high-profile processes—one that nearly resulted in a rejection and the other that actually did—not only featured a large number of negative votes but also looked significantly different from almost all other confirmation processes in the 20th century. Thomas's confirmation process included two sets of hearings that stretched over 11 days and included seven days of testimony by Thomas. Coupled with the length of the Bork testimony, it was clear the Senate was more actively scrutinizing nominees.[35]

Indeed, even without a higher rejection rate, something has clearly changed in the way Supreme Court nominations occur, particularly in the Senate confirmation stage. One measure is the length of time from nomination to confirmation. The Senate takes much longer to move to a final vote than was true prior to 1968. The time between nomination announcement and hearings is measured in weeks or months rather than days. (See Table 2.)

The hearings themselves are more elongated. The number of witnesses appearing to testify at hearings is much greater than was true prior to 1968. With courtesy calls, the hearings, and preparations of background materials for the committee, the expectations placed on nominee participation in the process

Table 2 **Historical Expansion of Time of Senate Consideration of Nominees: 1816–2010**

	Average Days until First Day of Hearings from Nomination	Average Days until Senate Judiciary Committee Votes from Nomination	Average Days until Full Senate/President Action from Nomination
1816–1830	0	8	18
1831–1850	0	16.11	29.94
1851–1870	0	6	13.88
1871–1890	1	18.20	22.86
1891–1910	0	8.75	11
1911–1930	2.62	18.54	22.62
1931–1950	5.07	10.14	12.93
1951–1970	21.31	38.36	55.33
1971–1980	11.33	25.67	37.67
1981–1990	39.33	57.83	74.83
1991–2000	49.33	60.33	71.33
2001–2010	39.25	54.75	53

Sources:

"PN1059—Nomination of Samuel A. Alito Jr. for Supreme Court of the United States, 109th Congress (2005–2006)." *Congress.gov*. United States Congress, n.d. Web. Accessed August 17, 2016.

"PN1768—Nomination of Elena Kagan for The Supreme Court of the United States, 111th Congress (2009–2010)." *Congress.gov*. United States Congress, n.d. Web. Accessed August 17, 2016.

"PN506—Nomination of Sonia Sotomayor for The Supreme Court of the United States, 111th Congress (2009–2010)." *Congress.gov*. United States Congress, n.d. Web. Accessed August 17, 2016.

Rutkus, Denis Steven, Maureen Bearden, and R. Sam Garrett. *Supreme Court Nominations, 1789–2005: Actions (including Speed) by the Senate, the Judiciary Committee, and the President.* New York: Nova Science, 2007.

have reached levels unheard of prior to the 1970s. Floor debate also can be protracted rather than perfunctory. Indeed, today, the possibility of filibuster looms over nominations.

A Gradual Evolution

The Bork nomination, particularly, has been identified as the moment when judicial nominations became pitched battles between groups and the White House. Indeed, characteristics of the Bork nomination were novel. The broad coalitions of groups, paid television and newspaper advertisements, and the length of the nominee's hearing testimony were new.

However, a process 19 years earlier also was pivotal. The failed nomination of Abe Fortas as chief justice featured the first filibuster of a Supreme Court nomination. Its success was another climactic moment as the norms of the Senate (the filibuster as a symbol of the Senate's distinctive individualism) coincided with the partisan interests of a minority seeking to forestall a nomination by a lame-duck president in order to change the direction of the Court. That failed nomination then affected the next several nomination processes as Republicans (particularly in the Nixon administration) battled Democrats who sought to thwart an attempt to overturn Warren Court decisions.

As crucial as those two events—the Fortas and Bork confirmations—were in the transformation of Supreme Court nominations, there have been several pivotal moments in the evolution to the current process that led up to the Fortas and Bork nominations and influenced Supreme Court nomination processes both pre- and post-Bork. These moments featured significant deviations from a process that had prevailed, with only unusual exception, for most of the Court's history.

One such moment was the institutionalization of Senate Judiciary Committee hearings. The Senate Judiciary Committee began to establish its preeminence in the judicial confirmation process in the 1940s. Earlier hearings were sporadic. Moreover, even as they became more regularized in the 1940s and early 1950s, they were originally pro forma.

Not only did hearings become standard, but so did the nominee's participation. Initially, exceptions were made for various types of nominees such as sitting and former senators or chief justice appointees such as Harlan Fiske Stone (1941), Fred Vinson (1946), and Earl Warren (1954). However, by the mid-1950s, exceptions were no longer allowed. Every nominee was expected to appear before the committee and answer questions posed by committee members. This included justices in recess appointments, such as William Brennan in 1956 and

Potter Stewart in 1959, as well as sitting justices who had been nominated to be chief justice. In 1968, Abe Fortas became the first sitting member of the Court not in a recess position to testify at his own confirmation hearings.

Another, and related, moment was the role of public opinion in the confirmation process. That became evident in the aftermath of the *Brown v. Board of Education* decision in 1954. Not only did certain southern politicians, law enforcement officials, and judges refuse to enforce the Supreme Court's landmark decision, but southern senators also began to take the occasion of the now-standard hearings to quiz potential justices on how they interpreted the *Brown* decision. These efforts were not intended to scuttle nominations so much as they were designed to express public sentiment toward *Brown*. Southern Democrats used the occasion to reflect their constituents' concerns over desegregation. These were early indications of how public opinion was seeping into the judicial selection process in an unprecedented way.

The Warren Court's subsequent decisions regarding freedom of speech, school prayer, reapportionment, and the rights of the accused fueled suspicions that the Supreme Court had become an activist policymaking body that was quick to overturn political institution decision making. That perception, then, animated conservative Republicans who were, like their southern Democratic colleagues, bombarded with letters in opposition to Supreme Court decisions. Senators, in turn, voiced those concerns to nominees who might affect future Warren Court decisions.

Southern Democratic and conservative Republican senators' use of hearings to challenge nominees became a method adopted later by liberal senators as they faced nominees appointed by conservative administrations. Nominees like Clement Haynsworth (1969), G. Harrold Carswell (1970), and William Rehnquist (1972) were challenged by liberal Democratic senators on their views regarding civil rights decisions. The practice had been legitimated by both sides.

For the most part, conservative senators relied on verbal queries rather than actual votes in opposition to nominees. Two exceptions were John M. Harlan and Potter Stewart, who both received dissenting votes from southern Democrats— 11 for Harlan and 17 for Stewart. Yet, others through the 1950s and early 1960s were confirmed by voice vote.[36]

However, by the late 1960s, after a string of Supreme Court decisions provoked discontent and anger among their constituents, senators' actions moved beyond questioning. Eleven senators voted against Judge Thurgood Marshall's confirmation. But another 20 senators did not show up to vote. The reduced number of "yes" votes for a Supreme Court nominee was a signal that southern Democrats were taking more direct action than merely lobbing critical questions. They were willing to vote negatively, or at least not vote positively, for a nominee who was not popular with their constituencies, even if that nominee had been selected by a president of their own party.

Still another change was the introduction of outside groups in the process. The first such group was the American Bar Association (ABA). The ABA's formal role began when the Senate Judiciary Committee solicited its evaluation of the nominee. That act suggested that senators were not adequate judges of the merits of a potential Supreme Court nominee and wanted external assistance in gauging judicial competence. Later, for several decades, presidents offered an exclusive role for the ABA in the vetting of Supreme Court nominees. The ABA's involvement gave non-institutional players a formal role in a process that had been limited to institutional players. That opening led other groups—not necessarily those primarily concerned with legal matters—to become involved in a process that was gradually expanding to include them.

Yet another seminal moment was the decision to broadcast Senate Judiciary Committee hearings. By 1981, when Sandra Day O'Connor was nominated by President Ronald Reagan, televised coverage of Congressional committee hearings was common. Some, such as the Army-McCarthy hearings and the Kefauver hearings on organized crime, had occurred 30 years previously. But Supreme Court confirmation hearings had not been televised previously. Public interest in the first female justice helped stimulate interest in televising O'Connor's hearings.

Then, with the Bork and Thomas nominations, a culture of public scrutiny emerged that formalized a shift in attitudes about what constituted an acceptable review of a Supreme Court nominee. As the preceding discussion has demonstrated, that democratization did not suddenly appear at the Bork nomination. Certainly, it took a major leap at that moment. But this democratization trend had a longer and more complicated history than a single nomination. If anything, the Bork nomination was a symptom of the trend that had already been occurring for several decades prior to 1987. Nor was it initiated with the Clarence Thomas nomination. Undoubtedly, that nomination was unmatched in the number of days a nominee testified in front of the Senate Judiciary Committee as well as the extent of media and public attention to the nomination—not to mention the tone of the coverage, which focused at an unprecedented level on the private life of the nominee.[37]

An example of an attitudinal change that has become a factor in the evolution of the Supreme Court nomination process is the question of the ethics of certain tactics. These include the aforementioned use of private information about a nominee, the disclosure of words said or acts committed by the candidate in the past that are employed to embarrass the nominee today, and the reliance on shrill characterizations of nominees by interest group spokespersons that are intended to undermine public confidence in the nominee. Even some partisans have become dismayed at the bitterness. Following the Thomas nomination, Biden lamented: "Both sides are so self-righteous that it truly is the ends justify the means."[38]

These moments individually did not significantly alter the nomination process. However, the cumulative effect has been to transform the process toward democratization. Much like presidential elections, other confirmation processes, the electoral role in the determination of public policy through voter initiatives, and the public role in the determination of high-profile public policy by Congress, Supreme Court nominations today, as opposed to those occurring in the past, are processes featuring a broad array of players—both internal and external—and are conducted much like other political processes in a democracy.

The Democratization of Supreme Court Nominations

For most of the nation's history, Supreme Court nominations were elite-driven processes, as outlined in constitutional provisions. The major players were the president, who possessed the appointment power, and senators, who checked that power through their "advise and consent" role. It was not coincidental that the primary roles were allocated to the least democratic institutions of the new government, save the Court itself. Neither the executive nor senators were chosen directly by the people. And no role was provided for the House of Representatives or state legislatures or any legislative body more closely linked with the public.

Rare exceptions to this role occurred as the media, public opinion, and interest groups acted to shape particular nominations such as those of Alexander Wolcott (1811), Roger B. Taney (1835), Louis Brandeis (1916), and John J. Parker (1930). But those were exceptions to the rule.

These constitutionally assigned players dominated the two stages of the process—presidential selection and Senate confirmation—for most of the history of Supreme Court nominations. Presidents sometimes even acted alone in the presidential selection stage without involvement by others beyond the administration. Similarly, Senate confirmation at times occurred in a matter of a few days or, on occasion, even hours.

The predominance of these players was reinforced by two factors. One was the lack of set timetables for consideration of vacancies. Presidents could decide immediately on the occasion of a vacancy, as did Herbert Hoover when he nominated Charles Evans Hughes to replace the ailing William Howard Taft as chief justice on the day of Taft's retirement; and as did Franklin Roosevelt when he announced Harlan Fiske Stone's chief justice nomination on the day Hughes retired.[39]

Similarly, senators were not bound by any time requirement to deliberate on a nomination. They could take hours or months, as they desired. Alternatively, to prevent interference from others beyond the Senate, action could occur quickly before opposition could be mobilized.

Still another aspect was the lack of transparency in the processes of presidential selection or Senate confirmation. Presidential selection occurred in private, as it largely still does today. The Senate ostensibly is more public than the executive. Yet, the slow evolution of processes of consideration of nominees meant that for most of the Senate's history there was no formal procedure as exists today. Committee hearings were infrequent; even committee consideration was sporadic. The Judiciary Committee did not necessarily take stewardship over a nomination. Other ad hoc committees could do so. When the full Senate considered a nominee, it did so in executive session until 1929. The public and press were excluded from even observing the Senate's debate over a nominee.

Those factors that advantaged elites have disappeared over the past 60 years. Informal timetables have been established. Presidents still deliberate outside the public view, but, in the age of a 24-hour news cycle and rapid response by the White House to events, they have become the object of media criticism when the process of selection drags on beyond a matter of weeks. Moreover, various external players seek to affect the process—both internally and externally. And the Senate also has adopted a minimum timetable of two to three months. No longer can presidential nominations be approved in a matter of days.

A demand for transparency has replaced opaqueness—both for the presidential selection and the Senate confirmation processes. Groups, the media, and the public demand more accessibility to the process—both to become informed and to become effective in shaping its outcome. Interest groups seek time to review a nominee in order to weigh in before Senate action, or even presidential selection. Journalists need time to investigate nominees' backgrounds. Senators seek public response as media information emerges.

Primarily, opposing senators want time for information, particularly controversial information, to emerge. They seek to stop the momentum of a president's announcement, which, for many years in the 20th century, led to rapid consideration and votes based on a widespread presumption of confirmation of nominees. When the opposite party controls a Senate majority, the timetable can be elongated to allow even more time for the opposition to generate negative information and build a coalition of opponents.

The democratization of Supreme Court nominations is not unique to the Supreme Court nomination process. Scholars have demonstrated similar trends in executive branch and lower federal judicial appointments. Judicial selection for appellate judges also has been affected by groups anxious to shape personnel appointments in circuit courts. These confirmations have become battles between competing groups. Presidential appointments now take longer. The confirmation rate has fallen sharply, and even those who are confirmed endure agonizingly long processes that stretch from months into years.[40]

The Purpose of This Book

The gradual changes in the Supreme Court nomination process over a lengthy period (pre- and post-Bork) have not been explored sufficiently. This book describes the democratization of the Supreme Court nomination process from its elite roots to its current democratic nature. It also discusses how institutional players—the president and the Senate—are affected by that democratization. How does the process operate today in a modern era of television, group power, and the influence of public opinion? How do institutional players operate in a process that no longer includes just them but also is shaped by groups, the mass media, and public opinion?

The first two chapters focus on the traditional process. The first chapter explains the underpinnings for the elite-driven process as defined by the Constitution. How did the Framers envision the roles of the president and the Senate? How were early precedents set that influenced institutional practices? The next chapter then describes how that constitutional plan evolved into the traditional process that governed Supreme Court nominations for most of the history of the nation.

The third chapter documents changes in the traditional process that affected both the president and the Senate. These were societal developments and institutional adaptations that opened the process to greater involvement by external players. This chapter examines the growing role of interest groups and media outlets, as well as the expectations of public involvement in the Supreme Court nomination process.

The following three chapters analyze the effects of democratization on the two stages—presidential selection and Senate confirmation. The first of this set reviews the current presidential selection process, describing how the democratization of the process has shaped the approach of presidents to deciding on Supreme Court nominees. The second moves to the Senate and demonstrates how senators interact with democratic forces in the process of decision making. The third chapter of the set focuses on how presidents seek to manage nominations in a democratic environment.

The concluding chapter offers a summary of the arguments of the book. But it also discusses predictions about the future of nominations in a democratic era. Additionally, it reviews and suggests reforms intended to maintain the integrity of the process in a tension-filled age.

Constitutional and Early American Political Underpinnings

The US Constitution is a parsimonious document, particularly compared to other governing charters around the world. It contains only slightly more than 4,000 words in its original form. By comparison, the Spanish Constitution, adopted in 1978, has more than 18,000 words, while the German Basic Law, passed in 1948, has over 21,000.

Given the sparseness of the US Constitution, it is no surprise that its treatment of the role of the judiciary is similarly spare. Article III establishes the judicial branch as "vested in one supreme court, and in such inferior Courts as the congress may from time to time ordain and establish." And it provides for a term of "good behavior," meaning a lifetime appointment, except in unusual cases. But only a brief mention in Article II, Section 2, describes judicial selection. That section of the Constitution grants the president power "by and with the Advice and Consent of the Senate, to . . . appoint . . . Judges of the Supreme Court."

As the delegates in the 1787 convention drafted such language they left vague what terms like "appoint" and "advice and consent" actually meant. Did this mean actual shared power between the president and the Senate? Must the president actually consult senators for their advice before making an appointment and seeking their consent? Or was it just a phrase that meant "approval?" If the former, how would that happen? Should the president send a list of potential nominees and ask the Senate to choose from among them? Should the president call in senators and ask for their opinions on who should be nominated?

The answers to these questions have been debated for many years by scholars. Henry Abraham has argued that the role of advice and consent by the Senate should primarily focus on the merit of the individual nominee.[1] Lord Bryce believed the Senate role was limited to checking the president from appointing unfit persons.[2] Other scholars have been strong defenders of a more expansive interpretation of the advice and consent role. Charles Black contended that senators had no obligation to follow the president's lead and, in fact, had a duty to assess whether a nominee's position on the Supreme Court would be harmful to the nation, not because they were not meritorious, but simply because their positions on issues would be deleterious. Similarly, David A. Strauss and Cass R. Sunstein have argued that the Constitution "contemplates a more active role [for the Senate] than simple acquiescence whenever a nominee is not deeply objectionable."[3]

Those who actually play a part in the process, particularly presidents and senators, also have sought to answer the question of what "advice and consent" really means. Presidents who have spoken publicly on the topic have claimed the preeminent role in the process. In lobbying for one of his nominees, President Richard Nixon wrote a letter to Senator William Saxbe (R-OH) asserting the president's primary role as opposed to a secondary one for the Senate. Nixon insisted the nomination revolved around "the constitutional responsibility of the President to appoint members of the Court—and whether that responsibility can be frustrated by those who wish to substitute their own philosophy or their own subjective judgment for that of the one person entrusted by the Constitution with the power of appointment." Nixon went on to claim that if "the Senate attempts to substitute its judgement as to who should be appointed, the traditional constitutional balance is in jeopardy and the duty of the President under the Constitution impaired."[4]

More recently, President George W. Bush complained that "the 'advice and consent' clause of our Constitution has been subjected to serious abuse. Members of the Senate seem to embrace the 'advice' part. It's the 'consent' part that seems to be the problem."[5]

In turn, some senators have expressed their individual perspectives on what the phrase "advice and consent" really means, particularly in response to presidential assertion of power. For example, Senator Robert Griffin (R-MI), who was the leader of the filibuster of Abe Fortas as chief justice in 1968, countered the view that the president's role should be dominant in the process. He contended that those "who suggest that the Senate's role is limited merely to ascertaining whether a nominee is qualified in the sense that he possesses some minimum measure of academic background or experience" are wrong because that view "does not square with the precedents or with the intention of those who conferred the 'advice and consent' power upon the Senate."[6]

Another senator, Charles Goodell (R-NY), in announcing to the press his opposition to a Nixon Supreme Court nominee, explained that while the president has the right to appoint anyone he wishes, the Senate "has its own duty under the Constitution. Each member of the Senate must exercise his individual judgment, and base his decision upon the most careful scrutiny of the qualifications of the nominee, and a searching inquiry as to whether the best interests of the nation will be served by confirmation."[7]

Goodell's statement suggests senators do not have a role of rubber stamping the president's choice or deferring to the president in filling seats in the third branch of government. He also specifically reserves the right of a senator to vote negatively toward a nominee if a senator feels so inclined after scrutinizing the nominee's qualifications. And perhaps the most important point that has become controversial during the past 50 years has been his suggestion that merit may not be the only qualification senators should consider, that is, that senators have a responsibility to determine what is in "the best interests of the nation." The scope of that decision making may range over other traits such as the nominee's judicial philosophy, temperament, ideology, or even attitudes toward a particular issue.

Others have emphasized the "advise" piece of "advise and consent." Senator Orrin Hatch (R-UT) has written that the Senate has the responsibility to advise a president on nominations in addition to giving or withholding consent. And Senator Paul Simon (D-IL) suggested the Senate pass a resolution stating that the "advice" section of the constitutional responsibility of the Senate "has not been exercised by the Senate" in recent times and therefore the president should engage in "informal, bipartisan consultation with some members of the Senate" before a name is submitted formally to the Senate.[8]

On the other hand, historically, not all senators have favored an activist Senate role, a fact that has strengthened the president's hand in the nomination process. Senator George Cabot (F-MA), a senator in the 1790s, remarked that the Senate should confirm a presidential nominee for the judiciary unless the individual is "positively unfit for the office, and the public duty not likely to be performed by him." Cabot believed that were senators to act otherwise, the result would be the wresting from the president "altogether the essence of the nominating power, which is the power of selecting officers."[9]

Yet, senators' approaches to the president's power vis-à-vis the Senate's typically have a partisan tinge, that is, the Senate displays assertiveness when a nomination emanates from an opposition party president while becoming quiescent when their own party's president offers a nomination. The difference becomes apparent when Democrats and Republicans on the Senate Judiciary Committee suddenly switch positions in aggressiveness of nominee questioning depending on which party's president is nominating.

Senators can make the point that the appointment of judges should be considered separately from presidential appointment of other officers in government such as cabinet officials, directors of agencies, and members of various boards and commissions. The vast majority of those appointments exist at the pleasure of the president in the sense that a resignation can be requested at any time. Moreover, presidential appointments resign at the end of a president's term anyway since their own terms in office in practical terms end with that of the president who appointed them.

However, the language of the constitutional appointment power provision does lump together judges with others when stating that the president "with the Advice and Consent of the Senate shall appoint Ambassadors, other public Ministers and Consuls, Judges of the supreme court, and all other Officers of the United States." The fact that the language does not distinguish between those officers who can be replaced by the president and those who cannot may lead to a broad interpretation of the president's appointment power covering all of a president's appointments and not just those relevant to the executive branch. It is true that Article III provides that judges may serve life terms, which clearly separates executive and judicial appointments, but, over the course of history, individual senators' approaches to appointments have corresponded more closely to Cabot's view.

The range of interpretation of role could have been prevented by more guidance from the convention delegates about the nature of the Senate's role vis-à-vis that of the president. They may not have anticipated that debate over their wording would continue more than two centuries later. Nevertheless, regardless of their intent or lack of foreknowledge, they had to get a constitution written and agreed to. Vagueness was a way to solve problems. And one of those recurring problems during the convention was answering the question of who would choose judges.

Yet, their haste has had perhaps unintended effects on the process. The paucity of detail about the process has provided presidents, as well as senators, with flexibility in approaching the task of nominating and confirming Supreme Court justices. Presidents have varied in their interpretation of the task in areas such as the method of deciding on a nominee, the timing of appointments, reasons for making a certain appointment, and even the expression of those reasons.

Some presidents, particularly recent ones, have undertaken extensive background searches and interview processes to find a nominee. Others have decided on one person early on and acted accordingly without any additional scrutiny of a nominee. In 1930, President Herbert Hoover named Charles Evans Hughes as chief justice only five hours after receiving the resignation letter of Chief Justice William Howard Taft.[10] Other presidents have been nearly as rapid. George H. W. Bush wasted little time in deciding on Supreme Court nominees. In 1991, Bush took only four days to announce a replacement for Justice Thurgood Marshall. The year before he had made up his mind in only three days. But President John F. Kennedy worked even faster; he decided on one nominee in two days and the second in only one.[11]

In contrast, President Bill Clinton took three months to decide on Judge Ruth Bader Ginsburg in 1993. But other presidents have elongated the process even further. In 1910, President William Howard Taft did not decide on a chief justice nominee for more than five months; and in 1939, President Franklin Roosevelt took six months. In terms of timing, the Constitution does not require the president to fill a vacancy in a certain time frame. (Nor does it mandate timely Senate action either.)

Another difference in approach is the reasoning for the appointment. The rationales for presidential appointment—stated or unstated—vary considerably from president to president. In some cases, the merit of the appointee was preeminent in public announcement as well as behind-closed-doors consideration. Nominees like Oliver Wendell Holmes Jr. (1902) and Benjamin Cardozo (1932) were widely considered eminent jurists who belonged on the Supreme Court. Presidents responded to that sentiment.

Yet, merit is only one factor, and, seemingly, sometimes not an important one. Another, at times, has been cronyism. Of President Harry Truman's four Supreme Court nominees, all were personal friends from the Senate or members of his cabinet. President Lyndon Johnson's nominations of his old friend and frequent adviser, Abe Fortas, as an associate justice in 1965 and then as chief justice in 1968 were criticized at the time for cronyism.

For still others, a nomination may be the fulfillment of political promises. President Dwight Eisenhower promised California Governor Earl Warren an appointment shortly after Eisenhower was elected in 1952, although there is speculation that Eisenhower may have talked with Warren about an appointment when Warren was running against Eisenhower for president at the 1952 Republican National Convention.[12] While a candidate, President Ronald Reagan promised that one of his first appointments to the Court would be a woman.[13]

Clearly, a major force for many presidents has been ideological compatibility. In some cases, that litmus test was explicit. Franklin Roosevelt demanded adherence to the New Deal and was reluctant to appoint Joseph Robinson, the Senate Majority Leader, who had been a strong supporter of the Court-packing plan but was considered too conservative by many New Dealers.[14] Richard Nixon sought strict constructionists, particularly from the South.[15]

Another point of extreme variation has been any expression of a stated reason for an appointment. Initially, presidents offered no explanation to accompany an appointment. When President George Washington sent his first six Supreme Court appointments, he merely listed the names of the individuals. There was no commentary.[16] Today, in an age of press conferences and news releases, as well as heightened public interest in the Supreme Court nomination process, presidents and their surrogates offer expansive public explanations for their appointments. When nominating Sonia Sotomayor in 2009, Barack Obama took most of a 40-minute press conference to outline his decision-making process, review his selection criteria, and describe how Judge Sotomayor met those criteria.[17]

The various approaches to these aspects of the task are driven by precedents set by previous presidents but also relate to an individual president's interpretation of how this task affects the president's and the administration's goals as well as the individual's personal decision-making and presentation style. The brevity of the Constitution's description of the process of judicial selection provides the opportunity for presidents to place their own particularistic stamp on the process during their incumbency. Even to the extent presidents have set precedents, as will be discussed later, no succeeding presidents are bound by those precedents because the Constitution does not require them to be.

The executive is not alone in interpreting and re-interpreting the vague language of the Constitution to fulfill this function according to institutional and individual imperatives. The Senate also is given no direction by the Constitution in its "advise and consent" role. How does the Senate go about doing this? What are the procedures it should follow? How much vetting of a nominee should the Senate do, and in what form? None of these are spelled out in the Constitution. All have been determined by the Senate as an institution over time and can be altered by the Senate at any time a majority (or in some cases, super-majority) so chooses.

Not only is the institution not bound by constitutional strictures, but senators also possess enormous latitude in each individual's particular approach to the task of voting for or against confirmation. Since there is no constitutional (or even statutory) direction on how senators undertake the task of individual decision making, they can approach this responsibility as they see fit. Indeed, the process of decision making is hardly uniform. Some senators make quick decisions about a nominee, typically based on the senator's relationship with the president. They may even announce their intent to vote for or against a nominee immediately following a presidential announcement, or sometimes even while a president is contemplating appointing a particular nominee. On the other hand, others act more deliberately and carry out an extensive personal vetting process that relies on examination of the record and consideration of the merits of the nominee. The Constitution prescribes no process or set of standards for Senate action.

In similar fashion to presidents, the reasoning senators use, and communicate to others, can vary. Support may be due to ideological compatibility with the nominee or partisan ties to the president or merely a sense that constituents favor confirmation. Opposition could be partisan, ideological, or constituent-based, or it could be an attempt to embarrass an opposition-party president. Clearly, several reasons may justify a yea or nay vote in the senator's mind. Senators are not bound to consider one reason over another since there are no restrictions on how they decide.

All of this variance derives from constitutional vagueness that grants the constitutionally prescribed players—the executive and the Senate—unusually broad flexibility in carrying out their assigned roles in judicial selection. Due to the vagueness of the Constitution regarding judicial selection, the process has been able to adapt and evolve over time, a phenomenon that would have been more difficult with a more detailed prescription of the process. Therefore, the rules and practices of the Senate and the traditions and current needs of individual presidents have acquired a greater importance in the process than might otherwise have happened if there had been greater specificity. And those traditions and practices, since they are not etched in constitutional stone, are fungible.

All of that vagueness and adaptation has allowed for democratization to occur in the judicial selection process. Specific provisions that bound future generations would have made democratization more difficult since change would have needed to be instituted through amendment rather than adaptation. The process would have been less susceptible to historical development.

Interestingly, democratization initially was not built into the judicial selection system, although it was considered. The Framers' initial approach was a somewhat more democratic process that might have produced greater democratization more quickly than the one they eventually settled upon. But over the course of several weeks, the Framers ultimately went in a different direction.

The Framers and Judicial Selection

As the convention delegates who were gathered in Philadelphia in May 1787 began to address the issue of how the members of the judicial branch were to be selected, they did not begin with a blank slate. They drew on the models of judicial selection existing in the former colonies and currently in the states. Indeed, in some cases references to these models were explicit as delegates raised examples from their own or other state government structures.[18]

During the colonial years, judges generally were appointed by the royal governor. Once the states were independent, they rejected that model of executive control. Instead, they adopted systems designed to check executive power and maintain judicial independence from the executive.[19] Most states opted for legislative control of the judicial nomination process.

The Framers were most familiar with this model of legislative selection of judges, and those who gathered in Philadelphia generally preferred it over executive control. As Ruth Bader Ginsburg stated, the "Framers were a suspicious lot."[20] They worried about strong executives, like King George III, who would arrogate power and establish a dictatorship.

Therefore, their default process as they began deliberating judicial selection was legislative, not executive, control. The Virginia Plan, proposed early in the convention, provided that a "National Judiciary be established to consist of one or more supreme tribunals, and of inferior tribunals to be chosen by the National Legislature."[21]

Yet, the Framers also were concerned about legislative power. As Ginsburg has noted, some of the Framers "distrusted assemblies of men."[22] The Framers had seen some state legislatures become tyrannical in their respective states. Most states limited the powers of their governors, thus making them weak in comparison with the state legislature. Another indication of weakness was the brevity of a governor's term. With the exception of New York, Delaware, and South Carolina (which had two- or three-year terms), state constitutions provided only a one-year term for the governor.[23] Moreover, the newness of a national executive meant the new Congress might overwhelm the executive and blunt the Framers' efforts at achieving the appropriate balance of power between the two.

These fears about legislative dominance of the new federal government carried over into their deliberations about the judicial selection process. Their debates reveal a gradual movement away from the idea of exclusive legislative power over judicial appointments. Even though Virginia delegate James Madison was one of the architects of the Virginia Plan, he became wary of legislative power, and when the convention seemed headed toward legislative appointment he suggested the convention leave the issue of judicial selection to later discussion instead of immediately adopting the idea of selection by the legislature.[24]

Caught between the disadvantages of executive appointment (dictatorship) and legislative appointment (tyranny of the legislative branch), the Framers commenced the search for another model. Eventually, they found it in several existing state constitutions that had sought to divide power between the two branches. Three states (New York, Massachusetts, and New Hampshire) shared judicial appointment power between the executive and legislative branches. Pennsylvania also split power, although slightly differently: The president of Pennsylvania held judicial appointment power, but was checked by an executive council. New York and Massachusetts both gave the appointment power to the governor, but checked that power by requiring the governor to obtain the "advice and consent" of a separate council.[25]

Debates at the Constitutional Convention

The movement toward an attempted balance of power between the executive and the legislative branches did not emerge immediately. Alexander Hamilton, a delegate from New York, was the first to suggest that the executive nominate justices but the Senate possess the power to confirm or reject. However, the convention ignored his proposal.[26] On June 5, 1787, James Wilson of Pennsylvania questioned the conventional wisdom of legislative power and moved that the judiciary be appointed by the executive and not the legislature. According to James Madison's notes, Wilson argued that

> experience shewed the impropriety of such appointmts. by numerous bodies. Intrigue, partiality, and concealment were the necessary consequences. A principal reason for unity in the Executive was that officers might be appointed by a single, responsible person.[27]

But Wilson was opposed by John Rutledge of South Carolina, who felt the Pennsylvania delegate's proposals appeared too much like monarchy. Benjamin Franklin said he opposed appointment by either the executive or the legislature. Instead, perhaps in a spirit of levity, he offered the Scottish model as worthy of emulation. In Scotland, Franklin explained, the nomination was made by lawyers, who tended to nominate "the ablest of the profession in order to get rid of him, and share his practice among themselves." Franklin concluded that such a process always secured the best choice for a judgeship.[28]

James Madison also opposed Wilson's proposal, but simultaneously disliked the idea of the legislature, as a whole, making the appointment. Madison felt similarly that the odds were great that judicial appointments would be the product of deals among members. He also worried that the legislators would be too biased in their deliberations on judicial appointment, particularly since, Madison argued, many of them "were not judges of the requisite qualifications" for membership on the Supreme Court. However, Madison also opposed Wilson's recommendation because he did not want to vest that much power in the executive branch. Instead, his suggested compromise was for the Senate, a smaller and more deliberative body, to make judicial appointments.[29]

On June 13, the convention took up a report of the Committee of Whole on the Virginia Plan and again debated the appointment of judges. Two delegates moved to add language that made the judges subject to appointment by Congress. Madison objected on the grounds that the result would be the appointment of inferior judges. He moved that the "second branch of the legislature" or the Senate, appoint the judiciary. The convention agreed to the resolution.[30]

Two days later, when a group of delegates proposed a more limited reform termed the New Jersey Plan, they included a provision that the Judiciary, which was more modest in form than envisioned in the Virginia Plan, would "be appointed by the Executive."[31] However, the New Jersey Plan could not command a majority of the delegates. Nor was the specific proposal for presidential appointment accepted.[32]

The issue of representation, not judicial selection, dominated the convention in the ensuing weeks. It was not until July 18 that the convention once again debated who should appoint judges. Nathaniel Gorham, a delegate from Massachusetts, felt the Senate was too large a body and senators would not feel personally responsible, as would an executive, for making good choices. He recommended that that the president nominate "with the advice & consent of the 2d branch." He pointed to his own state as an example of the success of that model of judicial selection.

Reaction from the convention was mixed. James Wilson supported Gorham's proposal, although he admitted a personal preference for executive appointment alone and then made a motion to that effect. Virginia delegate George Mason opposed Wilson's motion on the grounds that if the judges had a role in trying an executive who had been impeached, then those same judges should not be appointed by him. Mason's concern indicated the interlocking nature of the provisions of the Constitution the Framers wrestled with. And the judiciary, although ostensibly separate from the other branches, was connected to the legislative and/or the executive through the selection process.

While Gorham argued for Wilson's motion, he was opposed by Roger Sherman of Connecticut, Edmund Randolph of Virginia, and Gunning Bedford Jr. of Delaware. Sherman argued that the Senate "would of course have on the whole more wisdom" than the executive and that there would be less intrigue among candidates for appointment than would be true of the executive. Wilson's motion to make appointment of the Supreme Court a function of the president ultimately was defeated. Then, Gorham proposed again that "the Judges be nominated and appointed by the Executive by & with the advice and consent of the 2d branch." However, his motion also was defeated, although more narrowly; the vote was 4–4 with Georgia abstaining.[33]

Then, Madison offered a compromise that suggested how far he had traveled on this issue in six weeks. While he initially supported the Senate's exclusive role, now he was supporting a plan to make the Senate a decidedly secondary player. He proposed that the judges would be nominated by the president, an act that would go into effect unless two-thirds of the Senate voted no. In defending his proposal, Madison argued that the Senate had now been differently constituted than it was before the Great Compromise. Nevertheless, Madison's shift toward executive power was a major development that ultimately impacted the Constitution's treatment of judicial selection. However, none of that was obvious at the time. In fact, further debate on Madison's motion was postponed.[34]

Discussion of Madison's motion was taken up again on July 21. Madison explained that his motion would lead to the selection of better judges than if the Senate acted alone. The individual senators would be able to make appointments for the wrong reasons and "might hide their selfish motives under the number concerned in the appointment." If the president made a bad appointment, two-thirds of the senators would recognize it and "join in putting a negative on it." Moreover, Madison argued, the Senate, as representative of the states and with an equal vote for each state, would lead to rule by the northern states, which would possess a majority in the Senate.[35]

Madison's motion provoked debate among the delegates, who varied in their preferences. Some wanted the executive to decide, while others preferred the Senate. Gouverneur Morris of Pennsylvania supported Madison's motion. He suggested that the executive would be more competent for the task of making good appointments to the federal bench because of the national character of the office. The president would have better information about potential nominees and would lack the parochial interests of the senators, who represented individual states.

But Madison's proposal ran into immediate opposition. George Mason feared that Madison's motion gave the president too much power. He felt that even though the Senate had a role, in reality the power would rest primarily with the president. Gorham believed the senators would be too parochial, while Edmund Randolph of Virginia countered that the Senate role would assure broad geographical representation in the judiciary. New York delegate Elbridge Gerry objected to the two-thirds requirement in the Senate, which led Madison to revise his motion to allow rejection on the basis of a simple majority.[36]

The delegates finally voted on Madison's motion "that the Judges shall be nominated by the Executive" and that such appointments would go into effect unless rejected by the Senate. But the motion was defeated 3–6. That motion was replaced by another motion that the "Judges of which shall be appointed by the second Branch of the national Legislature." That motion passed 6–3.[37] As a result, when the Committee of Detail reported to the full convention on August 6, its draft included this clause: "The Senate of the United States shall have power to . . . appoint Ambassadors, and Judges of the Supreme Court."[38]

However, over the next four weeks, sentiment in the convention seemed to shift away from the legislative supremacy advocates. One factor must have been the element of time. The convention was close to wrapping up. Yet, there were still issues to be resolved, including this one. But another was the composition of the Senate. While the Virginia Plan had envisioned a Senate that was controlled by the people, the Great Compromise had created a Senate that was beholden to the state governments. Half of the national legislative body would be state controlled. States would exercise that power to affect the judicial appointment process toward their own interests. A check was necessary on that power, which could be accomplished by making the executive the nominator and granting the Senate the more limited power of "advice and consent."[39]

The amount of trust Madison placed in the executive, and distrust for even the Senate, was surprising given that Madison himself had been instrumental in drafting the Virginia Plan that gave the legislature (not just the Senate) the power to determine judicial appointments. That plan had allocated no role for the executive. Over a few months, Madison had turned from a delegate accepting exclusive legislative role to one advocating near exclusive executive role. That role would have been near exclusive because obtaining a two-thirds majority against a nominee would have been extremely difficult. In fact, only one Supreme Court nominee (Alexander Wolcott in 1811) has been rejected by a two-thirds vote.

Madison's basic concept of executive initiation accompanied by a Senate check was approved by the delegates. Gouverneur Morris, who was a member of the Committee of Eleven responsible for dealing with the remaining knotty issues, expressed the sentiment that appointment by the president with the advice and consent of the Senate would mean that "as the President was to nominate, there would be responsibility, and as the Senate was to concur, there would be security. As Congress now make [*sic*] appointments, there is no responsibility."[40]

However, the power of the Senate to check the president was enhanced by the final suggestion of the Committee of Eleven. On September 4, the Committee of Eleven recommended the draft be altered to read: "The President . . . shall nominate and by and with the advice and consent of the Senate shall appoint . . . Judges of the Supreme Court."[41] Three days later, the delegates once again took up the question of presidential powers, including appointment. While approving the president's power to make treaties with the advice and consent of the Senate, the body then went on to the appointment power. The delegates agreed that the president should appoint executive officers, including ambassadors. When the term "Judges of the Supreme Court" was added, there was no debate. The final vote was opposed by only two states. As the convention was rushing to a conclusion, it finally established the president-Senate coordination that exists today.[42]

The movement away from the Congress appointing judges (including justices) toward the executive playing a dominant role had become gradually more attractive to the delegates. They began to share Madison's greater concern about the recklessness of Congressional decision making in this regard. That movement was a step away from public involvement through the public's direct representatives—the members of the House of Representatives. The plan that was emerging was cutting out those individuals closest to the public. Instead, the two players remaining would be those most distant from the people. Under the new government, neither senators nor the president would be directly elected by the voters. Only the House of Representatives would be, and they would hold no power in the process.

Judicial Selection in the Constitutional Ratification Process

Even with delegate approval, the Constitution still needed to survive the ratification process, which was far from a certainty. However, the success or failure of ratification did not hinge on judicial selection. That aspect of the new government's design was a minor point in the document and engendered almost no discussion or opposition.

Federalist essayists did not expend much energy discussing judicial selection. More specifically, the authors of the *Federalist Papers* also spent little time discussing the judicial selection process. Such a discussion is combined with the appointment of other federal government officials in numbers 76 and 77. In the numbers on the Judiciary, Alexander Hamilton felt more need to explain the provisions that guaranteed independence of the judiciary without establishing judicial dominance than how judges would be appointed and confirmed.

Hamilton did offer an explanation as to why judicial nomination did not conform to the practices of most states at the time in granting such power exclusively to the legislature. He argued that housing the nomination power in the president would be more beneficial to the judiciary because the president would be a better judge of the match between the qualities of an office and the individual who could best serve. Moreover, the president would be less likely than legislators to respond to personal considerations such as rewards to individuals through such posts. As Hamilton puts it in *Federalist 76*: "A single well-directed man, by a single understanding, cannot be distracted and warped by that diversity of views, feelings, and interests, which frequently distract and warp the resolutions of a collective body."

However, Hamilton contended that some check of the president's appointment power was necessary to prevent abuse of the executive's power. At the same time, the check could not be so powerful that the executive's appointment power would be meaningless. Hamilton expressed his satisfaction that the check incorporated in the Constitution was just right to achieve that balance.

Hamilton also explained why the Senate had exclusive power in the legislative branch. Reflecting the contemporary view that the Senate would be more removed from public whim, Hamilton termed the House as "so fluctuating and at the same time so numerous" that it would be unfit to play a role (*Federalist* 77). This view of the House did not lead to objections on the part of most anti-federalists since they generally favored the Confederation Congress, which was more akin to the Senate than the House anyway. Nor did anti-federalists object to the Senate's greater power over the House, although they did think the Senate was too independent of public opinion.[43]

Hamilton felt obliged to expound how the balance between the executive and the legislature would occur. For example, in a prescient explanation, Hamilton contended that the Senate would possess strong disincentives to simply reject the president's nomination because he could easily appoint another who would be no more acceptable to the senators:

> The Senate could not be tempted, by the preference they might feel to another, to reject the one proposed; because they could not assure themselves, that the person they might wish would be brought forward by a second or by any subsequent nomination. They could not even be certain, that a future nomination would present a candidate in any degree more acceptable to them; and as their dissent might cast a kind of stigma upon the individual rejected, and might have the appearance of a reflection upon the judgment of the chief magistrate, it is not likely that their sanction would often be refused, where there were not special and strong reasons for the refusal. (*Federalist* 76)

History has borne out Hamilton's prediction. The Senate has not rejected someone because of preference for another particular nominee. Confirmations have been waged over that specific nominee and not over whether the president would appoint a better nominee if the one before the Senate was not confirmed.

Anti-federalists aimed their attacks on various features of the new Constitution, but judicial selection was not one of them. This may seem surprising because the judiciary itself was an object of severe criticism by opponents.[44] The power of the judicial branch occupied their interest far more than who actually served there and how they got there in the first place.

The lack of connection between the people and the judges did not become a theme of discussion about the new Constitution. Only one anti-federalist objected to the judicial selection process. His concern was based on the distance between the people and their judges because the Constitution "deprives the inhabitants of each state of the power of choosing their superior and inferior judges."[45] His voice was an isolated one.

Similarly, ratification conventions in the various states did not dwell on judicial selection. Some debated the president's appointment powers generally. In the Virginia ratifying convention, George Mason opposed the Constitution because it allowed the Senate to play a role in the appointment process, thus "dangerously blending the Executive and Legislative powers."[46] However, James Wilson told the Pennsylvania convention that such blending was not only acceptable but hardly unusual since several states, such as South Carolina, North Carolina, New Jersey, and Georgia, had constitutional provisions mixing powers of the executive and judicial.[47]

The delegates at various ratification conventions speculated on what the "advice and consent" process would look like in reality. Some argued that the president would be compelled to do the Senate's bidding. In North Carolina, Samuel Spencer argued that the president would be bound to accept the Senate's nominee because the Senate would reject all those the president proposes. However, James Iredell did not agree, responding that the "Senate has no other influence but a restraint on improper appointments."[48]

Interestingly, one critic of the appointment method was prescient about the future controversy regarding the Senate. John Adams, who was minister to England at the time, supported the Constitution generally but believed the president alone should appoint. Adams predicted that if the Senate did not reject appointments, "they will be censured and ridiculed for their servility; if they do use it, they will incur the resentment of the Executive and also of disappointed candidates."[49]

When the new Constitution was ratified, the new federal judicial branch could be formed. The Federal Judiciary Act of 1789 set the number of justices at six. Now, the theoretical judicial selection process became reality as George Washington faced the responsibility of being the first president to nominate Supreme Court justices and set the precedents that might affect judicial selection for years to come.

Effects on Process Evolution

This review of the historical underpinnings of the judicial selection process leads to some important conclusions about the origins of Supreme Court nomination processes. One is the Framers' lack of much attention to the issue of judicial nomination, particularly compared with many other new government components. There was a consensus that a judiciary should be formed and that it should have certain powers. And, for most of the period of the convention, they were in general agreement about one important aspect of the judiciary—who would select the judges. It would be the legislature's role.

The historical record is vague about how the advocates for greater executive power eventually tipped the convention away from the conventional wisdom of an exclusive legislative role. Their repeated attempts to inject the executive into the process finally bore fruit as the convention reached its conclusion. Perhaps the victory was due to the element of time, that is, the ability of the executive proponents to wear down the opposition and then make proposals at the end of the convention. Perhaps the argument for yet another check and balance won the day over single institutional control.

The Framers' deliberations and ultimate conclusion could lead to opposite inferences about Framer intent. One would be that the Framers' support for legislative control through most of the convention was a signal that they believed the Senate should be a major force in the process rather than merely a secondary institution. That conclusion clearly tilts toward those advocates of an aggressive Senate role in the process. As David A. Strauss and Cass R. Sunstein argue, the Constitution "provides that there will be senatorial 'advice' before the fact. It ensures that no nominee may serve without senatorial 'consent.'" Therefore, "the Senate should now assume a self-consciously independent role. It should insist on its constitutional prerogatives."[50]

On the other hand, the Framers' ultimate rejection of Senate exclusiveness suggests they believed the executive was the safer, wiser place for making judicial nominations, particularly given the Senate's connection to state legislatures through the senator selection process. Clearly, that was the argument of certain delegates such as Alexander Hamilton, James Madison, and James Wilson. Therefore, as a rejection of the original proposal accepted by the convention that the legislature nominate and select judges, the final agreement by the delegates suggests that delegate views had shifted from legislative preeminence to executive dominance, albeit with a check intended to prevent an abuse of that power by the executive. Yet, the Senate's role is not pro forma. When the legislature was choosing judges, there was no executive check included. Therefore, the delegates seemed more concerned about executive abuse than they did abuse by the legislature.

The questions for today remain. Is the Framers' concern about executive abuse lessened today? Should the Senate abandon any role because of the rarity of historical examples of presidential appointments of a corrupt character?

On the other hand, there is no indication from the record of the convention that the delegates felt the Senate's check should be broadened to include ideology. But neither is there any discussion of the executive using such power to impose a particularly ideological perspective on another institution of national government. The question of whether ideology should play a role for either player in the process clearly was not settled by the Framers.

Obviously, the Framers' intent has informed the debate over constitutional roles for the president and the Senate in the judicial selection process, as both sides have pointed to their respective interpretations of that intent. But it has not dictated the debate's resolution because presidents and the Senate have adopted their own approaches and procedures over time. The vagueness of the actual language and the differences among the Framers themselves offer some support to both sides.

The Non-Democratic Court

Tying Supreme Court justices or other federal judges to the public through a democratic judicial selection process involving direct judicial elections was never an option for the Framers. The next closest alternative—the appointment by those directly elected by the public—the House of Representatives—was part of the Virginia Plan, although that power was shared with the less democratic upper house, which would be selected by the lower house. The inclusion of the House of Representatives—the body directly elected by the people—would have reduced the distance between judges and the people and increased the role of the public in the decision-making processes of judicial selection.

But the Framers gradually rejected that role. Part of the explanation lies with the Great Compromise whereby the Senate now took on a different composition—representative of the states rather than the people. However, perhaps a greater reason was the fear of legislative dominance over the executive that was pervasive in the debate about power between the legislative and executive branches. The checks proposed by some delegates primarily targeted the legislative branch. The specificity of powers for the legislative branch limited that branch's future role, while the executive's power was left vague, undefined, and susceptible to future expansion.

That fear of legislative dominance was a concern about the power of direct democracy in the new government. Hence, the importance of creating distance between ordinary people and the judges who should uphold the law regardless of public sentiment. That would have been particularly true with the justices of the Supreme Court who would become the interpreters of the Constitution. Undemocratic institutions operated best, they might say, that were least affected by democratic ones and the voters who are represented by such democratic institutions.

Eventually, the Framers' plan for separation would be undermined as democratic forces sought greater role in all processes, including those involving judicial selection. Democracy would begin to reshape elections, policymaking, and personnel selection within the executive branch. By the 20th century, presidents and senators would be affected by those forces and become increasingly responsive to the very public that the Framers sought to distance them from. Gradually, judicial selection would follow.

The Traditional Process

When George Washington considered whom he would appoint to the first Supreme Court and how he would do so, he settled on people he knew personally and made the decisions by himself. Most of his initial appointees had served with him as delegates to the Constitutional Convention.[1] He did not need much advice from others about his choices. In his mind, the decision was his to make.

In accordance with the Constitution's provisions, the non-democratic nature of the judicial selection process emerged quickly. The first president, George Washington, did not interpret the Constitution as including groups, the media, or the public in the decision-making process regarding judicial nominations. There was no effort to float names in the press to gauge public reaction. The president or his staff did not visit with various interest groups to determine their views. Given the Constitution's provisions regarding the process, and Washington's own embrace of the process outlined in the Constitution, those types of actions would have been superfluous to the implementation of the judicial selection process.

Before he made decisions about the Supreme Court, Washington did consider the need to obtain senatorial advice on matters of joint responsibility through the "advice and consent" clause. To that end, in August 1789, less than four months into his term, Washington decided to seek the Senate's advice on a treaty with the Creek tribe. The new president came to the Senate chamber and presented the proposed treaty to the assembled senators. Apparently, Washington expected the Senate to discuss the treaties at that moment, and perhaps even approve them quickly, while he was present. However, when a motion was made to refer the treaty to a committee, Washington opposed it. He did return to the Senate later but was similarly dissatisfied and determined that he would no longer officially seek the Senate's advice.[2] Rather, he determined that "advice and consent" would come following his decision-making process, not during it. In other words, the Senate's role would be limited to consent or not.

His decision not to seek an advisory Senate role shaped the relationship between the president and the Senate generally, including judicial selection. Washington and subsequent presidents have acted alone on Supreme Court nominations, determined to make nominations without formal Senate advice. When, one month later, Washington submitted his first six nominees to the Senate for confirmation, he did not go to the chamber formally to solicit opinion.[3] Although many subsequent presidents have counseled with senators privately and individually (or in small groups), no other president has deviated from that pattern of interpreting "advice and consent" as a feature antecedent to presidential selection.

For its part, unlike Washington's reaction to "advice and consent," the initial Senate reaction to Washington's nominations did not set a firm historical precedent. The Senate immediately consented to all of his first six nominees (to fill the original Court) and, over time, all but one of Washington's subsequent nominees. That is a record of confirmation success for Supreme Court nominees not likely to be matched again in US history. (Franklin Roosevelt came closest with nine successful nominations in 12 years.) Only 11 of Washington's nominees actually served on the Court. Nevertheless, Washington, over eight years, basically selected a justice for every seat on the Court twice.

The rapid turnover in the early years of the Court's history was the result of poor working conditions as well as a lack of prestige for the new institution. Indeed, the Court had little to do in its early years as a joint body since the Supreme Court initially handled a paucity of cases. Plus, the first justices rode circuit twice a year, which required them to travel around large geographical areas to preside at trials. Such travel cut into their own law practices and took them away from home to travel on poor roads and to take lodgings in taverns and inns around the circuit.[4]

Service on the Court was not a coveted position, and some justices left after only a few years to do other things. John Jay became governor of New York and John Rutledge resigned to serve on South Carolina's Supreme Court. Thomas Johnson simply could not stand the circuit-riding; he later served on a District of Columbia court.[5] The average tenure on the Court for the original six justices was under seven years. By comparison, the average tenure for more recent justices (from 1969 to 2008) was closer to 21 years.[6]

The demands of Court service, particularly the circuit-riding, as well as the inability of the Court to become a co-equal institution during its first decade, led John Jay to decline a second appointment as chief justice in 1800. Jay called the Court lacking in "energy, weight, and dignity" as well as in the "public confidence and respect which as a last resort of the justice of the nation, it should possess."[7] That assessment is ironic as Jay was initially interested in serving on the Court because he felt this new institution would be instrumental in handling critical issues facing the new nation, such as boundary disputes, Revolutionary War debts, and the relations between the state and federal governments. But a decade later, Jay had concluded that "the Efforts repeatedly made to place the judicial Department on a proper fitting have proved fruitless."[8]

As the first chief justice, Jay could speak from experience. Jay was an attorney, but he also was a politician and diplomat. Indeed, most of his service to the new nation had been in foreign affairs. He had served as a US peace commissioner to negotiate the end of the Revolutionary War, minister to Spain, and secretary of foreign affairs for the Confederation government. But he also was president of the Continental Congress and a co-author (with James Madison and Alexander Hamilton) of the *Federalist Papers*, the most prominent essays supporting ratification of the new Constitution. Yet Jay's appointment was not wholly political. Jay was a respected lawyer and had served as chief justice of the New York Supreme Court.[9]

Washington's picks reflected his approach to the role of the Supreme Court and those who should serve on it. For him, the Court was both a legal and a political institution. His nominees reflected that approach: His choices included those who had both legal and political experience. If anything, as mentioned above with the preference for those who had been 1787 convention delegates, Washington placed a priority on men who were qualified through legal backgrounds but also had played prominent political roles in the states as well as in the formation of the new nation. For example, Jay had less legal experience than others who sought the position of chief justice, but he was well known throughout the nation.[10]

Eight of Washington's appointees had served as judges in their respective states but they also had significant public service records. Washington particularly favored individuals who had been involved in the Revolution and Confederation government. Six had been in the Continental Congress.[11]

Washington also set the tone for the judicial selection process by incorporating other criteria besides merit into the decision-making process. One was personal friendship. Washington preferred individuals he knew personally. Since he had been involved in the Revolution, was familiar with the players in the Continental Congress as well as the Articles of Confederation government, and had presided over the Constitutional Convention, Washington knew many potential nominees. Most of those he appointed he had worked with in some way during his career. George Washington held friendships with most of his nominees from their service in the Revolutionary Army, the Continental Congress, or the Constitutional Convention.

Other early presidents continued the appointment of friends and close acquaintances. When John Marshall was nominated to be chief justice he was serving as Adams's secretary of state, and President James Monroe's only Supreme Court appointment was a cabinet member. And most of President Andrew Jackson's appointments were personal friends.[12]

Another important criterion was geography. Washington wanted the Supreme Court to represent the geographical breadth of the United States.[13]

When he nominated James Iredell of North Carolina, he noted that Iredell was "of a State of some importance in the Union that has given no character to a federal office."[14] According to Henry Abraham, Washington's appointment of Jay, a New Yorker, was geographically based: New York played a strategic role in the new nation, but it only narrowly ratified the Constitution (30–27) and was the 11th state to do so.

The extent to which geography played a part is shown in the regional makeup of the Court during Washington's presidency. His first six appointments drew from six different states—one from New England, three from the mid-Atlantic, and two from the South.[15] By the time of his last appointment in 1796, Washington's 14 nominations had included individuals from nine of the 15 states.

Yet another criterion was adherence to the Federalist philosophy. With one exception, Washington's picks were strong proponents of the Constitution. They took the Federalist side in the ratification process and continued generally to support Washington's view of government, which came to be represented by the Federalist Party. Washington even appointed the most openly partisan justice in the Court's history. Samuel Chase, who already held a reputation as an outspoken partisan, was nominated and confirmed in 1796. Chase later became the only Supreme Court justice to date to be impeached by the Senate, a distinction that resulted from his partisan statements on and off the bench.[16]

Washington's ideological approach was continued by John Adams: His three appointments were solid Federalists. As the first partisan transfer of power in US history, the election of Thomas Jefferson raised the question of whether judiciary appointments would reflect that partisan change. George Washington and John Adams had set partisan tones by appointing Federalists. As president, Jefferson also adopted a partisan stance. One critical trait for a nominee in Jefferson's mind was adherence to Republican principles. He insisted that his Supreme Court appointments be loyal Republicans who could counter the influence of the Federalists on the Court.[17]

Jefferson also followed Washington's and Adams's lead in preferring certain background traits. Jefferson continued their practice of appointing individuals with political as well as legal backgrounds; two of his three appointments had previously served in their respective state legislatures. Additionally, Jefferson adhered to the rule of providing geographic diversity for the Court. His first appointment was a South Carolinian because there was no representative on the bench from that circuit at the time.[18]

Still another precedent was the use of a Supreme Court appointment to solve a president's political dilemmas. John Jay's appointment dealt with the problem of accommodating two dominant personalities—Thomas Jefferson and Alexander Hamilton. While rumors circulated at the time that Jay could be appointed to State or to Treasury, it was apparent that either Jefferson or Hamilton would be excluded if Jay took one of those positions. When Jay asked Washington to appoint him chief justice, he was solving Washington's personnel conundrum by allowing him to appoint both Hamilton and Jefferson to new, important positions in the government.[19]

Already in the administration of the first president, the traditional process of Supreme Court appointments emerges. Merit played a role, but so did other components of selection criteria—political needs, ideology, geography, and friendship. By not selecting the best legal minds or the most prominent judges, Washington was admitting the hybrid nature of the Supreme Court—both legal and political—as well as setting precedents for future presidents.

The process also began to take form as presidents viewed their role as solitary. "Advice" from the Senate only really meant consent. Therefore, the Senate held a formal second role rather than a shared part in presidential selection.

Moreover, the initial process was limited in its connection with democracy, even representative democracy. The president and the Senate carried out their roles without involvement by other players, including the House of Representatives or the state legislatures. Interest groups and the press, and particularly the public, generally were unimportant.

Presidential Selection

The precedents of the early presidents established a particular process that continued for most of the history of nominations, and, essentially, still exists today. The first stage of that traditional process is presidential selection. In explaining the traditional process, it is important to examine two features of that stage. One is the presidents' criteria for selecting nominees and the other is the process by which they do so. Both have common elements, but the application for each presidency varies widely from that of other presidents, with some aspects of the process becoming more important and some decision-making criteria outweighing others.

Selection Criteria

Merit

The criterion considered most fundamental to presidential selection is merit. Supreme Court justices are expected, by elites, to be competent in their roles. They carry specialized responsibilities beyond those accorded government officials generally. This requires an advanced knowledge of the law not expected for presidents or members of Congress. Indeed, since law schools have become the standard means for legal training, justices have been expected not only to have graduated from them but, for the most part, also to be alumni of the most prestigious of these schools.

Merit has been an important criterion for the Senate in assessing whether someone belongs on the Court. When the merit of the nominee has been questionable, nominees typically are confirmed by narrower margins or even fail of confirmation due to Senate vote or withdrawal. The most recent example of the latter is Harriet Miers, who was widely criticized as a mediocre nominee lacking the requisite background to be a Supreme Court justice and risked the possibility of receiving an "unqualified" or, at best, "qualified" rather than "well qualified" ranking from the American Bar Association.[20]

The case of Judge Benjamin Cardozo's nomination is the best evidence of how merit can triumph over other factors, at least on occasion. Cardozo was recommended by law faculty, deans, labor, business, liberals and conservatives, as well as senators. Cardozo had been suggested for appointments in the 1920s but was passed over by previous Republican presidents. Reportedly, Herbert Hoover had several others he preferred over Cardozo and was inclined to reject him due to his being Jewish, a New Yorker, and a Democrat. Hoover, facing a tough re-election campaign that year, bowed to the pressure to appoint Cardozo.[21]

Even when merit does become the major criterion, it is far from alone. As just mentioned, Hoover considered Cardozo meritorious, but he also considered his own re-election prospects and how Cardozo's appointment might help him with certain groups. Indeed, some degree of merit is essential, but merit typically is balanced by other factors.

One problem in using merit is determining what it is and who gets to decide whether someone has merit to be on the Court. The Constitution offers no guidance here. Nowhere in the document is there an explanation of meritorious requirements for potential judicial nominees. A Supreme Court justice need not be a law school graduate. In fact, many of the early justices were not; they studied law as apprentices in law firms. Indeed, the Constitution is silent on who holds the qualifications to serve on the Supreme Court.

By contrast, most other liberal democracies impose some specific requirements on candidates for appointment to their nation's respective highest court.[22] For example, in Spain, an individual must have been a lawyer, judge, or law professor for at least 15 years. In Italy, the required service length is 20 years. In India, a Supreme Court justice must have served as a judge for at least five years, while in Iceland the requirement is three years as a judge or in a government legal office and the candidate must be at least 35 years old.[23]

Despite the absence of specific constitutional requirements, some elements of a nominee's background have acquired a traditional status in assessing merit. One is a legal background. Nearly all Supreme Court nominees have possessed some type of legal background. No individual without a law degree has been nominated since James Byrnes in 1942. Indeed, a law degree from an Ivy League or comparable school has become expected. No nominee since John Paul Stevens in 1975 has graduated from a law school other than Yale, Harvard, Stanford, or Columbia.

Another generally expected background, particularly in recent years, is judicial experience. Sixty nominees were serving as judges at the time of their appointment.[24] Initially, judicial experience was less important. In recent years, its absence has become rare. Since 1968, only four of 21 nominees (William Rehnquist, Lewis Powell, Harriet Miers, and Elena Kagan) have lacked a judicial background.

One explanation for the increased emphasis on judicial experience is the difficulty of challenging the merit of a nominee with such a background. Three of the four more recent nominees without judicial experience were criticized on that point. Nominating an individual without judicial experience offers an opening for opposition to the nominee.

Only rarely have nominees with judicial experience been criticized as lacking merit. One such exception was G. Harrold Carswell, Richard Nixon's nominee in 1970. While he was a federal district judge, Carswell's decisions had been reversed by an appellate court 58 percent of the time, a rate higher than that of any other federal judge.[25] But Carswell's experience is rare. Judicial experience typically has shielded nominees from criticism over merit.

Personal Relationship

Like Washington, some presidents have preferred nominees they know personally. Personal knowledge of a nominee carries certain advantages. A president may feel more capable of assessing whether a nominee as justice would follow a certain ideological path if the president already has experience with the nominee in various settings. Moreover, a nomination can become a reward for personal service rendered.

Personal relationships may be more critical for presidents who have limited legal experience themselves and use criteria other than legal background for determining merit. Harry Truman's four appointments included former Senate colleagues (Harold Burton and Sherman Minton) and members of his administration (Fred Vinson and Tom C. Clark). John F. Kennedy's two appointments both were members of his administration. Arthur Goldberg was secretary of labor and someone Kennedy had worked with over the past year. Byron White was associate attorney general, but he had no judicial experience and had served in the Justice Department for only little over a year. White was not unqualified to serve on the Court; he had been a Rhodes Scholar and was a graduate of Yale Law School. But Kennedy passed over more senior administration officials, prominent legal scholars, and federal appellate judges to pick White. It was not insignificant that White had been a friend of the Kennedys for some time and had served as the Western states coordinator for the 1960 Kennedy presidential campaign.[26]

Lyndon Johnson's three nominees not only were individuals Johnson knew well, but two of them (Abe Fortas and Homer Thornberry) were longtime friends. Abe Fortas, who was nominated twice by Johnson, aided Johnson in his effort to win the legal battle over the scandal-ridden 1948 US Senate Democratic primary runoff race in Texas that Johnson won by 87 votes.[27] During his presidency, Johnson relied heavily on Fortas as a domestic policy adviser—both before and after Fortas became a Supreme Court justice. He counseled Johnson on policy issues for matters as varied as the Middle East, Vietnam, student protests, and crime. He also recommended people for executive branch positions.[28]

Judge Homer Thornberry also had a long personal and professional relationship with Johnson. He had been a mayor of Austin, Texas, before he was elected to Congress in the district where Johnson had previously served in the 1940s. Then, he was appointed as a federal district judge and then appellate judge— both nominations made by Johnson.[29] Thurgood Marshall, Johnson's third nominee, was well known to Johnson because Kennedy had appointed Marshall to the federal appellate court for the Second Circuit and Johnson had placed him in the job of US solicitor general.

Similarly, to replace Sandra Day O'Connor in 2005, George W. Bush chose his White House legal counsel, Harriet Miers, who had been a close associate of Bush for a decade. Miers had no judicial experience, was not a constitutional law scholar, and was not well known in legal circles. But she had worked closely with Bush for several years.

Personal relationships have their drawbacks. One is the implication that the justice would be beholden to the president in terms of decisions and would not maintain a distance between the two branches of government. A more immediate concern, however, is that personal relationships trumped merit. While some nominees who have close connections to presidents, such as Felix Frankfurter, are well qualified for the Court, others are not. Truman's choices, although not unqualified, were not viewed as the best candidates available to Truman. Johnson even admitted that Thornberry would not be "exceptionally outstanding."[30]

Most of the people Johnson considered for the Supreme Court were close to him personally—Cyrus Vance, Clark Clifford, Abe Fortas, and Homer

Thornberry. Johnson placed great significance on personal relationships as a way of gauging suitability. He dismissed a candidate for the Court proposed by his attorney general, saying: "I don't want to appoint Dunaway who I don't know at all."[31]

In some cases, the personal relationship is not with the president but with others close to the president. In those cases, the president trusts others' personal relationships to assess the value of a candidate. This may be more common when a president is not familiar with individuals in legal circles and is willing to rely on those who are.

An example is the selection of Judge John Paul Stevens. President Gerald Ford deferred to his attorney general, Edward Levi, who knew Stevens well from their service on the House Judiciary Committee; also, Levi's residence was in Chicago where Stevens was a federal appellate judge. Ford was willing to accept Levi's judgment based on Levi's personal relationship.[32]

For many presidents, the familiarity with prominent individuals in the legal community has become more difficult, particularly when the president lacks a legal background. This is particularly true as the nation has grown in geographical size and population, making it difficult for presidents to be personally familiar with possible candidates across the country, even if the president was a member of the broader legal community. Yet most recent presidents do not come from legal backgrounds. Of the 17 who have served in the past 100 years, 13 did not possess legal degrees.

Yet, as noted above, some presidents still have relied heavily on personal connections. Two of Lincoln's five appointees were close to him. David Davis had been a longtime friend and ally since Lincoln's 1858 US Senate campaign. Salmon Chase, Lincoln's chief justice nominee, was secretary of the treasury. (Lincoln's other top candidate for the chief justice vacancy was the former postmaster general.) One of President Grover Cleveland's criteria for appointment was that he know the nominee personally. President William McKinley's sole appointment was a friend who had served on the same Congressional committee with him.[33]

Some presidents coupled personal relationships with the need to return political favors. Lyndon Johnson was the classic example with his appointments of Abe Fortas, but he was not alone in that practice. David Davis had been Lincoln's 1860 presidential campaign manager. President Rutherford B. Hayes nominated John M. Harlan, who had helped Hayes in his presidential campaign, including the contentious Republican national convention. Hayes also was well served by Harlan's service on the election commission that reviewed Louisiana's contested electoral votes and awarded them to Hayes.[34]

Ideology

Ideology has been a predominant theme of presidential selection criteria. Presidents are well aware of the opportunity they possess to shape the ideological direction of the Court. Most have sought to use that power. Moreover, the success of their predecessors gives them reason to expect that they, too, will not be disappointed. Although there is a tendency to focus on justices who do not match the ideological tendencies of their appointers, such as Justice David Souter appointed by George H. W. Bush or Byron White by John F. Kennedy, for the most part presidents have succeeded in placing ideologically similar individuals on the bench, at least for most of a justice's career.[35] That is due to the tendency of presidents to seek overtly to "pack" the Court with correspondingly minded nominees.

Admittedly, not all presidents have adhered to ideological compatriots as their appointees. Some have intentionally departed from that practice for political reasons, such as Herbert Hoover bowing to intense pressure to nominate Benjamin Cardozo or Dwight Eisenhower's choice of William Brennan despite Brennan's reputation as a more liberal Democrat.

However, since the days of George Washington, the vast majority of presidents have sought to choose nominees with similar political views. According to Henry Abraham, President John Quincy Adams's criteria included "geographic location, appropriate judicial experience, a scholarly background in constitutional law, and, like Adams who had straddled the fence between political parties, a nominee who would be acceptable to both major political camps in the Senate."[36] Andrew Jackson was similar in his insistence that his nominees agree with him ideologically. All but one of Jackson's nominees was a staunch supporter of Jacksonian ideals. Even the one, John McLean, was not an opponent but successfully courted Jacksonians and non-Jacksonians.[37]

The ideological objectives of presidents have varied depending on the historical era. President Theodore Roosevelt wanted justices who shared his progressive political views, particularly on economic issues, while William Howard Taft, as president, selected nominees based on ideological compatibility with his conservative tendencies. For President Woodrow Wilson, progressive views were paramount, particularly on economic issues.[38]

Ideology was essential in Franklin Roosevelt's nominations, particularly while he worried about Court support for the New Deal. Adherence to the New Deal dominated Roosevelt's thinking because of the Court's repeated rejection of New Deal programs during Roosevelt's first term. Roosevelt's litmus test was so powerful that, as mentioned earlier, he even had concerns that Senate Majority Leader Joseph Robinson was too conservative, even though Robinson had been a vocal proponent of Roosevelt's controversial Court-packing plan. Whether Roosevelt would have moderated his ideological criterion became a moot point when Robinson died suddenly while Roosevelt was in the middle of the selection process.[39]

Of course, the success of an ideologically driven appointment has been questionable from nearly the beginning of the judicial selection process. Thomas Jefferson appointed three justices to the Court with the hope that they would blunt the power of Chief Justice John Marshall.[40] However, all three agreed with Marshall more than they disagreed. More recently, John Paul Stevens, Harry Blackmun, and David Souter were expected to follow the ideologies of their appointing presidents far more than they actually did.[41]

Clearly, those cases are exceptions. They receive attention from scholars and journalists because of their departure from expectations. However, presidents are usually successful in appointing justices who adhere to their ideological views. Most appointees of recent presidents have remained consistent with the ideologies of appointing presidents.[42]

The use of ideology as a criterion is easier for presidents than senators because the selection process occurs behind closed doors and out of the public view. By contrast, the confirmation stage is characterized by public events—committee hearings, debates, and votes—as well as extensive discussion and explanation by individual senators of their reasoning for voting a certain way. Yet the public does not hear the president and aides discussing judicial philosophy, confirmability with certain ideological records, or the political implications of selecting various candidates.

Some presidents are explicit about their use of ideology. They do not necessarily express it as such, but the effect is the same. Richard Nixon made it clear that his nominees "had to be men who shared my legal philosophy of strict construction of the Constitution."[43] Nixon used his 1968 presidential campaign to reinforce that theme and repeated it during his first term.[44]

But most presidents give the impression that their selection process is devoid of concerns about ideology or politics. Indeed, presidents sometimes assert that the Senate is playing politics with the process while they are above such tactics. George W. Bush once claimed that the "American people expect the nomination process to be as free of partisanship as possible, and for senators to rise above tricks and gimmicks designed to thwart nominees."[45]

Party Affiliation

Partisanship is typically a gauge for ideology. Presidents nearly always select fellow partisans. Since 1972, when Republican Richard Nixon appointed southern Democrat Lewis Powell, no president has nominated someone of a different party.

In eras when partisanship crossed ideological lines, party has served less as a surrogate for ideology. Three of Republican William Howard Taft's six nominees were Democrats. Taft favored conservatives whether they were Republicans or Democrats. Richard Nixon's appointment of Powell stemmed from Powell's reputation as a southern conservative Democrat. Of course, it did not hurt that Powell's nomination might help Nixon's re-election efforts, particularly with southern Democratic voters. Lyndon Johnson was willing to consider appointing a Republican, as long as the person agreed with Johnson: "I would like to get the ablest Republican liberal I could that would make it impossible for [Republican senators] to go against."[46]

In the traditional process, party has been an important factor but not an overriding one. That is true not only when ideology does not necessarily match party, but also because appointing an opposition party member suggests the partisan neutrality of the Court. Presidents such as Franklin Roosevelt, Truman, Eisenhower, and Nixon purposely appointed nominees of opposing parties, and Kennedy considered doing so when he included four Republicans on his short list.[47]

Some presidents have sought a partisan balance on the Court. Roosevelt and Truman appointed Republicans to the Court to offset the dominance of the majority of Democrats, particularly those appointed by Roosevelt. In fact, Roosevelt's chief justice appointment went to a Republican, Justice Harlan Fiske Stone. And Eisenhower exhibited similar concerns. In 1956, he appointed William Brennan, an Irish Catholic Democrat from New Jersey. Two years later, for his fifth appointment, Eisenhower considered nominating another Democrat to the Court, former Secretary of War Kenneth Royall. However, his concern was not the reaction of Republicans. Rather, it was the super-majority of Democrats already on the Court. Eisenhower told his attorney general that "I do not want further to overbalance the Court as between the two major parties."[48]

The preferred ideological perspective of a nominee is shaped by the current political environment as well as the balance on the Court. In the 1930s, support for the New Deal was explicit, primarily because Roosevelt wanted to win battles over his New Deal programs. Moreover, his supporters were hostile to a Court they viewed as unwilling to shift to respond to a changing political climate.

By the 1980s and 1990s, the watchword was moderate or centrist. For example, the Reagan administration sought to portray Robert Bork as someone in the mold of Lewis Powell. By doing so, they hoped senators would view Bork as maintaining the current balance of power between liberals and conservatives. Bork's long record as an ideological conservative made that effort difficult.[49]

In a time of national crisis, Supreme Court appointments take on more of a non-partisan, non-ideological tone. Roosevelt nominated Harlan Fiske Stone, a Republican, to be chief justice because he agreed with Felix Frankfurter that when the nation was on the verge of war, "few things would contribute as much to confidence in you as a national and not a partisan President than for you to name a Republican ... as Chief Justice."[50] Similarly, Truman's first nominee, appointed while war still waged in the Pacific, was Senator Harold Burton (R-IN). Through the appointment, Truman wanted to show national unity.[51]

Age

All things being equal, presidents prefer younger Supreme Court nominees to older ones. Richard Nixon kept discussing with his aides the ages of people on his short lists and ultimately nominated one person who was only 47 and another who was just 50.[52] A nominee older than 60 is considered unlikely to remain on the Court for a long time, while one who is younger than 50 is highly desirable due to the expectations of a long tenure and an elongated period of influence that makes a significant mark on the Court.

This dilemma was apparent for Franklin Roosevelt in 1937 as he faced his first appointment. As mentioned earlier, Joseph Robinson, Senate Majority Leader, was a logical choice. In addition to Robinson's conservatism, age worked against him, as he was already 65. Since Robinson died before Roosevelt chose a nominee, the president's dilemma was resolved.[53] Robinson's death may have reinforced the notion that older presidential appointments will not leave much of a legacy for their appointing presidents.

Yet younger nominees are criticized for being too young and too inexperienced to be on the Court. The Reagan administration faced this challenge with the nomination of Douglas Ginsburg in 1987, as did the Bush administration with the Clarence Thomas nomination. Ginsburg was 41 when he was nominated; Thomas was 43. Both had short records as judges; Ginsburg had served only a year as a federal appellate judge while Thomas had been a judge for only a year and a half. To blunt criticism of Ginsburg's age, the Reagan administration researched other nominees who had been confirmed on or before the age of 45, including Chief Justice John Jay (43), Justice William O. Douglas (40), and Justice William Story (32).[54]

As a result, most nominees are in their 50s. That means they are old enough to have sufficient experience to be considered meritorious while young enough to anticipate a long term as a justice, perhaps two or three decades. In considering replacements for two vacancies in 1971, Nixon told his attorney general heading the search what he considered the ideal age, explaining that the nominee "must be . . . fifty, fifty-five, if we put two sixty-one-year-old men on there, it's too many. I'd like to get a guy who can serve the Court twenty years."[55]

Electoral Considerations

Some presidents have used a Supreme Court nomination as an opportunity to gain the support of a particular electoral constituency. Dwight Eisenhower understood the political advantage of nominating an Irish Catholic Democrat from New Jersey in the midst of his 1956 re-election campaign. The move was designed to help keep Eisenhower Democrats who had voted for Ike in 1952 from returning to their party's presidential candidate in 1956.[56]

Woodrow Wilson's task was even more difficult. He faced a united Republican Party in 1916 that, through its fracture in 1912, had helped him win a plurality of the popular vote and the election. By 1916, Progressive candidate Theodore Roosevelt had returned to the Republican Party. However, Wilson knew that Roosevelt's supporters, the core of his Progressive Party bid in 1912, were open to persuasion to vote for Wilson.

Wilson's nomination of Louis Brandeis in the midst of his re-election campaign helped win support for Wilson among those who had backed Roosevelt. Progressive Senator Robert La Follette of Wisconsin considered the appointment "a great public service" and "proof indisputable that when the President sees the light he is not afraid to follow it." Organized labor quickly heaped praise on Wilson. One progressive noted the electoral effect: Amos Pinchot wrote to a progressive journalist that the appointment "will pull a strong oar for Wilson in Wis, Minn, S and N Dakota and other Roosevelt strongholds."[57]

Electoral considerations may have the most potency soon before a re-election battle. Therefore, the timing of a nomination is important in determining its role in an upcoming election. In 1971, as Richard Nixon geared up for a re-election campaign the following year, he faced two appointments. During that period, Secretary of Transportation John Volpe urged him to appoint an Italian American; Volpe said that in conversations he had had with Italian American judges in New York, there was a "unanimous view that a nomination by the President of an outstanding American of Italian ancestry . . . would ensure the President's carrying New York State as well as a number of other states where there were heavy concentrations of Americans of Italian origin."[58]

However, the role of particular Supreme Court nominees in shaping voters' attitudes is difficult to gauge. Eisenhower's recess appointment of William Brennan came during the fall general election campaign. That is a rarity. A presidential appointment during a general election campaign has not occurred since 1956. Only two have occurred in a presidential election year at all (Abe Fortas in

1968 and Merrick Garland in 2016). A nominee selected well before an election is likely to have little impact on the election itself since the nomination is likely to fade in voters' minds as the nominee recedes into the relative anonymity of the Court and other issues come to the fore.

Representation

As mentioned earlier, representation has been an objective of presidential selection since the days of George Washington. That initial representation was geographical as Washington sought a regional balance on the Court. Since Washington's day, representation has broadened into other aspects, particularly demographic. Yet geography, as the first feature of representation, is a good place to start in understanding how the concept of representation has affected presidential selection.

Geography

Since early Supreme Court justices actually rode geographical circuits, geographical diversity was a pragmatic consideration. A justice who hailed from a certain region of the country would ride that circuit and remain closer to home. The justices gathered in the nation's capital only occasionally to hear cases appealed to them. They spent most of their time presiding over federal court trials, a role that only later would be given to lower federal judges.

Appointment by geography was defined as representation by circuit, since circuits were regionally based. Geographical diversity was a paramount consideration over time because circuits expected to be represented on the Court. Presidents took close notice of the regional fit of a nominee. Indeed, Jefferson's two important traits for a potential nominee were ideological solidness as a Republican and geographical correctness.[59] But geographical representation also united the nation since it assured that each region had a stake in the success of the Court. The practice communicated a critical message about the workings of government being inclusive of all rather than just a certain region.

Geography continued to play a role throughout the 19th century as well.[60] Most presidents still worried about what state a potential nominee was from, ruling out those who came from the wrong part of the country to fill a spot allocated to a particular circuit. The demand for representation also affected Senate confirmation. When Grover Cleveland nominated an Illinois native, the chair of the Senate Judiciary Committee, a Vermonter, held up the nomination for two months on the grounds that Cleveland had promised to nominate a Vermonter.[61]

As the number of states grew during the 19th century, the number of circuits also expanded, increasing the geographical breadth of appointments. However, this expansion also meant that presidents were more narrowly restricted in the locations from which they could draw a new justice if he was intended to "represent" a particular circuit. When the new 10th Circuit was created to cover California and Oregon, Lincoln was expected to appoint someone from one of those two states. As a result, he nominated California Supreme Court Chief Justice Stephen Field.[62]

The idea of geographic representation on the Court constrained presidents who sought to appoint well-qualified candidates who came from a state already "represented" on the Court. While considering a chief justice vacancy in 1888, Grover Cleveland passed over an eminent attorney from Kentucky because the state already had a representative on the Court—John M. Harlan.[63]

The connection of a particular justice with a particular circuit faded by the end of the 19th century. Through creation of circuit courts, justices had been freed from circuit-riding. Federal appellate judges carried out roles previously performed by Supreme Court justices. By the time of Theodore Roosevelt's administration, geography was diminishing in significance. Roosevelt nominated two people from the same state, as did Warren Harding.[64] Roosevelt remarked: "I have grown to feel, most emphatically, that the Supreme Court is a matter of too great importance to me to pay heed to where a man comes from."[65] However, geography was important to Herbert Hoover, who wanted to augment the representation from the South and the West. Hoover nominated John J. Parker at least partly because of Parker's southern roots and initially resisted Benjamin Cardozo because his appointment would place three New Yorkers on the Court.[66]

At times, geography was still considered in the 20th century. Franklin Roosevelt wanted a southerner on the Court, and his first two nominations were from Alabama (Hugo Black) and Kentucky (Stanley Reed). And then he sought other candidates who came from less "represented" states or regions, such as the Midwest (Wiley Rutledge and Frank Murphy), the South (James Byrnes), and the West (William O. Douglas).[67]

But as the 20th century proceeded, geography became less important in presidential consideration as a means to achieve regional balance. Two exceptions were Lyndon Johnson and Richard Nixon. However, they considered geography for different reasons.

Johnson was concerned about regional balance. He told Senator James Eastland (D-MS) that when he was looking for a successor for Earl Warren, he considered Warren's seat to be "a California vacancy," as he viewed Tom Clark's seat vacated the previous year as a "Texas vacancy." And Johnson's short list included federal judges from the West, although he ultimately did not select any of them. He also ruled out a judge from Alabama, saying, "I don't think you should have two from Alabama."[68]

Nixon admitted that in filling a seat in 1969 and in 1970 he wanted to appoint a southerner because he felt that the Court's decisions were better received "when each section of the country and every major segment of our people can look to the Court and see there its legal philosophy articulately represented."[69] However, unlike earlier considerations of geography that intended to broaden representation to create greater regional support for the Court, Nixon's primary motive in the year before his re-election campaign was electoral—he hoped to win the votes of southern whites who had supported George Wallace in 1968.

The irrelevance of geography has become more apparent in the past 40 years. For 16 years, two Minnesotans (Warren Burger and Harry Blackmun) sat together on the Court. Within a decade, two Arizonans (Rehnquist and O'Connor) were appointed to the Court. After Elena Kagan's confirmation in 2010, the Court consisted of three justices from New York and two from New Jersey—a majority from a single region. An analysis in 1976 found that more justices have come from New York than any other state.[70] With the addition of three additional justices from New York since that time, the New York dominance has continued. In 2009, a federal appellate judge from Montana reportedly was on Barack Obama's short list, which commentators noted would have provided more geographical diversity for the Court.[71]

Geography was not an issue for Senate confirmation either, with few exceptions. Senator William Langer of North Dakota, who served in the 1940s and 1950s, followed up on a promise to vote against all Supreme Court nominees until one from his home state was nominated. Langer's solitary action emphasizes that one-third of the states have never been represented on the Court.[72] Yet the absence of greater geographical diversity has not been a barrier for confirmation. Even though senators lobby for their own state candidates, regional representation is not a factor in Senate confirmation or rejection of nominees today.

Religion

Another element of diversity for some time was religion. Only Protestants sat on the Court until the appointment of Roger B. Taney, a Catholic, in 1836. After Taney, the Court has included at least one Catholic justice for nearly all of its history. For many years, a tacit Catholic seat existed.

In 1956, Eisenhower did consider Brennan's religion with the thought of restoring the Catholic seat, which had lapsed since Frank Murphy's death in 1949.[73] But by the middle of the 20th century, the Catholic seat disappeared, as representation of Catholicism did not become an issue in presidential selection or Senate confirmation. By the end of the 20th century, three Catholics

(Scalia, Kennedy, and Thomas) sat on the Supreme Court. By 2017, three more Catholics were serving (Roberts, Alito, and Sotomayor), making a majority of the justices Catholic.

A Jewish seat apparently was created in 1916 with the appointment of the first Jew, Louis Brandeis. A Jewish justice has served on the Court since then, with the exception of the period between 1969 and 1993. But the Jewish seat also faded by the end of the 20th century with two Jewish justices (Ginsburg and Breyer) on the bench. By 2017, Elena Kagan became the third on the Court serving simultaneously. The "seat" concept became an issue when Benjamin Cardozo was recommended for the Court in the 1920s and 1930s. Presidents Harding, Coolidge, and Hoover initially passed over Cardozo because they objected to the idea of two Jewish justices.[74]

Religion has lost its place in presidential selection. There has been little call for other religions to be represented, such as the unrepresented minority Christian religions including members of the Seventh-day Adventist Church, Christian Science, or the Church of Jesus Christ of Latter-day Saints, not to mention the non-Christian religions Islam or Hinduism. In 2016, Barack Obama's short list included a Hindu, Sri Srinivasan. Had Obama appointed him, he would have been the first nominee not a Christian or a Jew, as well as the first Asian American. But discussion of Srinivasan's religion was minimal.[75]

Religion has served presidential electoral interests. William McKinley considered religion when appointing Joseph McKenna, a Catholic. McKinley's move was designed to blunt the rumor that McKinley was anti-Catholic.[76] Similarly, Eisenhower's appointment of Brennan in 1956 was designed to assist Eisenhower with the Catholic vote in his re-election bid.

Race/Gender/Ethnicity

Religion has been replaced by other facets of demographic representation, primarily gender, race, and ethnicity. However, gender, race, and ethnicity were not part of the "representativeness" criteria until the 20th century, and particularly the latter half of the 20th century.

African Americans were considered for the Court prior to the appointment of Thurgood Marshall in 1967. John F. Kennedy considered appointing a black federal judge, William Hastie, who was the first African American to be a federal appellate judge.[77] Indeed, Kennedy received letters urging the appointment of a minority nominee. The president of the National Bar Association, the primary African American legal community, wrote Kennedy recommending three candidates—Hastie; William Ming, a prominent African

American attorney and University of Chicago law professor; and Samuel Pierce, a New York attorney who later served in Ronald Reagan's cabinet.[78] One of Kennedy's top aides suggested Hastie as Kennedy's third appointment, which did not occur due to the lack of another vacancy before Kennedy's assassination.[79]

Not until the 1960s and early 1970s did women make it on to presidential short lists. In 1965, Lyndon Johnson and Ramsey Clark discussed appointing a woman to the Court. Clark said he would "love to see a woman on the Supreme Court." But he advised Johnson that he "was afraid it might look gimmicky" for Johnson to appoint a woman.[80] Richard Nixon came close to appointing a woman. A California judge was a likely nominee until she was rated "unqualified" by the American Bar Association.[81]

Gerald Ford specifically urged Attorney General Edward Levi and White House Counsel Philip Buchen to include women on his short list for the Douglas vacancy. The public list included several women, and the president's wife, Betty, publicly expressed her support for Carla Hills, Ford's Secretary of Housing and Urban Development. However, Ford eventually appointed one of Levi's top candidates—John Paul Stevens.[82]

During the 1980 presidential campaign, Ronald Reagan sought to win over the votes of women by promising to appoint a woman to the Supreme Court as "one of the first Supreme Court vacancies in my administration."[83] Reagan's campaign promise was made at a press conference in Los Angeles on October 14, 1980, and came in response to polls showing a gender gap in support for Reagan.[84] Reagan fulfilled his promise in 1981 with the nomination of Sandra Day O'Connor.

Hispanic candidates began to appear on short lists by the 1990s. When Thurgood Marshall retired, George H. W. Bush's administration briefly considered not continuing the concept of an African American seat by appointing a female or a Hispanic nominee. As a result, the short list contained primarily female or Hispanic candidates.[85] Jose Cabranes, a Hispanic federal judge, appeared on short lists in the 1990s, while Miguel Estrada, a Hispanic attorney, was considered a possible choice in the early 2000s. However, that speculation may have contributed to the filibuster of Estrada as an appellate judge and his subsequent withdrawal from the confirmation process. It would be 2009 before a Latina was nominated.[86]

The first Italian American, Antonin Scalia, was nominated in 1986 and ethnicity was an important consideration in Scalia's nomination. The ability of the president to appoint the first Italian American helped elevate Scalia above a candidate initially more favored by the president—Robert Bork.[87] But Scalia's nomination was not the first time the advantage of nominating an Italian American was noted. One White House aide in the Nixon administration urged the president to appoint an Italian American because "the Italians are coming into their own."[88] In 2006, Scalia was joined by a second Italian American, Samuel Alito.

"Firsts" in demographic representation have not necessarily been universally celebrated. Brandeis's nomination met stiff opposition, which carried anti-Semitic overtones.[89] Similarly, in 1968, some opposition to Fortas centered on the fact that, if confirmed, he would be the first Jewish chief justice. B'nai B'rith did not specifically accuse opponents of Fortas with bigotry. However, they did suggest that a Fortas filibuster might bring "the bigots out of the woodwork."[90]

When Sonia Sotomayor was nominated in 2009, some opponents suggested that she was prejudiced, pointing to a remark she had made several years previously that a "wise Latina woman with the richness of her experiences would more often than not reach a better conclusion than a white male who hasn't lived that life."[91] However, some Republicans suggested backing off from the criticism of Sotomayor because it would offend Latino voters, particularly when the Republican Party was attempting to woo them to vote for GOP candidates. The result was muted criticism of Sotomayor by many Republican senators, particularly those with large Hispanic constituencies.[92]

Creating or Losing Vacancies

Presidents cannot appoint Supreme Court justices unless one leaves the Court or the Congress creates a new seat on the Court. The latter has happened rarely. Obviously, the Congress's determination in the Judiciary Act of 1789 to create six justices gave George Washington six automatic appointments. Since then, few presidents have been given new appointment opportunities through expansion of the Court.

During the 1800s, Congress gradually increased the size of the Court to reflect new states, a growing population, expanding judicial demands, and enlargement of the number of judicial circuits. Expansion took place first in 1807 when the Seventh Circuit was created, along with a seventh Supreme Court seat. The next occurred 30 years later when two new circuits and two new Supreme Court seats were created. And then again in 1863, Congress added a 10th seat, giving Abraham Lincoln an opportunity to appoint a new justice.

The practice of expanding or contracting the size of the Court to create or remove potential appointments for partisan purposes began with the Federalists' passage of the Judiciary Act of 1801. After losing the presidential election, the Federalist-controlled Congress reduced the size of the Supreme Court to five members in order to deny the new president, Thomas Jefferson, the opportunity to fill a Supreme Court vacancy if a justice died or resigned. (The Judiciary Act of 1801 was repealed in 1802 and the seat was restored.)[93]

With each increase, the current president gained an opportunity to make appointments. The Jeffersonian Republicans gained more representation on the Court in 1807. The Democrats were able to do the same in 1837.[94]

But the next occasion for Congress to use Court size as a political weapon was the impeachment of President Andrew Johnson in 1868. Congress reduced the size of the Court to eight justices in 1866. The move denied Johnson the opportunity to fill a vacancy, as well as the next vacancy, if it occurred during his presidency. Congress's action was intended to spite Johnson, since he was highly unpopular with the Republican-led Congress, as well as to increase the power of the Republicans already on the Court.[95] Then, in 1869, with Johnson out of office, the Congress enlarged the Court to nine justices, thus giving the new president an unexpected nomination.[96]

Since the late 1860s, Congress has not "played with" the size of the Court to help or hinder a president. However, Congress possesses the power to do so. It came close to doing so in 1937 when Franklin Roosevelt urged Congress to create up to an additional six seats on the Court. The proposal would have offered Roosevelt an opportunity to pack the Court with New Deal supporters. Roosevelt seemed confident of victory since, in the wake of his overwhelming re-election victory in 1936, the president's popularity was high and Democrats held a dominant majority in both houses of Congress. Moreover, the Supreme Court's opposition to the New Deal was broadly unpopular. However, Roosevelt's inability to push his legislation through Congress, even in the most favorable circumstances for a presidential initiative, signaled the difficulty presidents face in using the size of the Court to fiddle with the nomination process.[97]

Encouraging Resignation or Retirement

Only three presidents never had the occasion to make a Supreme Court nomination. Two of these, William Henry Harrison and Zachary Taylor, served only briefly—one month and 16 months, respectively. Jimmy Carter was the only president who served a full four-year term but never appointed a justice.

On the other hand, some presidents have had abundant appointment opportunities. The most fortuitous was William Howard Taft, the only person to serve as both president and chief justice; he was able to make a remarkable six appointments, including a chief justice nomination, during his single four-year term. The average has been two appointments per four-year term.

Some presidents have sought more appointments than they got and were frustrated by their inability to shape the Court. Theodore Roosevelt appointed three justices in seven and a half years. But, disappointed at not having more opportunities, he reportedly joked that Supreme Court justices never resign and seldom die.[98]

Bill Clinton gained an opportunity because a retiring justice wanted to leave when a president of his party took office, particularly after a long period when the opposition party controlled the White House. Byron White, appointed by President John F. Kennedy, retired shortly after Bill Clinton, another Democrat, took office following 12 years of Republican presidents. Others who retired at certain junctures may not have shared partisan affiliation, but they had common ideological approaches with the new president. David Souter and John Paul Stevens both retired during Barack Obama's first two years. Even though both were Republicans and had been appointed by Republican presidents, they had become more independent than their Republican roots would predict.

Beyond the structural approach of increasing the number of seats, Congress can encourage retirement of justices through economic incentives. During most of the 19th century, justices were reluctant to step down from the bench, even in the face of physical and mental deterioration, because no pension was provided for retired justices. Not until 1869 did the justices receive a retirement package once they reached the age of 70 and had served for at least 10 years.[99]

Over time, the pension requirements have loosened, with eligibility as low as age 65 with 15 years of service. Each time the requirements were changed, lower federal judges retired as soon as they were newly eligible, giving presidents an opportunity to fill their slots with judges more amenable to the administration at that time.[100] But the effect on the Supreme Court has been more muted. Since 1954, when eligibility was lowered, only four justices have retired before the age of 70.[101] The average of retiring Supreme Court justices since 1954 has been 77.

Today, Supreme Court justices may be less motivated by economics anyway. Current justices already possess significant financial resources and do not rely as much on pensions. For example, in 2013, the net worth of the nine Supreme Court justices on the Court at that time ranged from $300,000 to $700,000 for Anthony Kennedy to $4 million to $18 million for Ruth Bader Ginsburg. Seven of the nine had a net worth of more than $1 million.[102] The changed financial world for justices is indicated in the book advance of $1.9 million that Justice Sonia Sotomayor received in 2012.[103] Pension benefits may seem less essential in an age of such book deals.

Another tactic has been to encourage retirement or resignation through professional or personal incentives. Two presidents did use other tactics to create vacancies that offered them the ability to make appointments that otherwise would not have happened. In one case, the president used a carrot to lure a justice to resign for a larger prize. The second, however, was more malevolent and involved threats of exposure of a scandal and a tarnishing of the reputation of the Court itself.

The first president was Lyndon Johnson, who, in 1965, heard that Arthur Goldberg was restless as a Supreme Court justice. Johnson used that information to lobby Goldberg to take a position as US Ambassador to the United Nations. With promises that Goldberg could contribute to world peace and harmony among nations, Johnson urged Goldberg to accept the new appointment. Goldberg did so, which allowed Johnson to appoint his old friend Abe Fortas in Goldberg's place.

Two years later, Johnson wanted another Supreme Court appointment. To make that happen, he appointed Ramsey Clark, son of Justice Tom Clark, as US attorney general. Since the federal government is a party in a large proportion of cases that go before the Court, the elder Clark decided to retire from the Court rather than recuse himself in many of the cases the Court took. Clark's resignation allowed Johnson to appoint Thurgood Marshall as the first African American justice.[104]

In May 1969, news reports circulated that Abe Fortas was involved in an ethics scandal. The Nixon administration initiated a criminal investigation. At first, the administration sought to start impeachment proceedings. Instead, they enlisted Earl Warren, then chief justice, to encourage Fortas to resign in order to forestall an investigation that would harm the Court's image. Warren and his colleagues did just that. Fortas resigned and opened up another vacancy for Nixon to fill.[105]

The search for more appointments even affected the chief justice appointment Nixon made in spring 1969. Earl Warren had already announced his retirement as chief justice and Nixon was contemplating a replacement. At that time, White House aide Pat Buchanan urged Nixon to appoint John M. Harlan to the chief justiceship in 1969 because the appointment would be well regarded, but also, because of Harlan's advanced age, Nixon likely would be able to appoint two chief justices in his first term.[106]

Other presidents have tried and failed to get appointments. An effort was made to encourage Thurgood Marshall to retire in order for Carter to have an appointment and deny successor Ronald Reagan the chance to fill the seat during his term. However, Marshall expressed no interest in leaving the Court. Similarly, the Reagan administration sounded out Byron White about becoming FBI director, but White declined.[107]

In 1988, rumors circulated that then-Republican presidential candidate George H. W. Bush was considering Sandra Day O'Connor as a possible vice-presidential running mate. The talk was serious enough that O'Connor issued a statement through the Court Public Information Office stating that she was "not considering any other position in or out of government."[108]

Perhaps this example is more of a stretch, but William Howard Taft seemed to create a future vacancy when he appointed Edward D. White as chief justice. Taft was disconsolate when he appointed White because the job he really wanted was the one he was giving to someone else. White was 65 at the time, thus becoming the oldest chief justice nominee in the Court's history. Indeed, White died in 1921 and Taft became his successor.[109]

Filling a Non-Vacancy?

Presidents do not control when a justice leaves the Court, although occasionally they try. They also do not control how a justice does so. Some justices have conditioned their retirement on the successful confirmation of a successor. That means the justice remains on the Court while the selection and confirmation stages occur and leaves only when that process has successfully concluded. The most recent example is Sandra Day O'Connor, whose retirement was effective on Senate approval of her successor. Her willingness to continue on the Court became critical when Chief Justice William Rehnquist died and George W. Bush named her intended successor to the chief justice vacancy instead. With the withdrawal of Harriet Miers and controversy over Samuel Alito's confirmation, O'Connor remained on the bench for seven months beyond her retirement announcement.

That approach has the advantage of assuring that the Court is at full complement at all times. Yet, at times, that practice by some justices has raised the issue of whether a vacancy even exists. In 1968, Earl Warren tied his retirement as chief justice to the successful conclusion of the confirmation process. Senate Republicans charged that Warren had not really retired because he had worded his announcement in such a way that he could change his mind and stay on if a successor were not confirmed. Indeed, Lyndon Johnson admitted in a telephone conversation with the Senate Judiciary Committee chair that he expected just such a scenario to occur if he failed to get a successor confirmed.[110]

Future Vacancies

Another factor in presidential selection is the expectation of additional vacancies. A vacancy early in a term may mean that a president will have additional chances to shape the Court over a four-year or eight-year term. That expectation rests on an assessment of what justices will do. For example, the Obama administration likely assumed that John Paul Stevens would retire during Obama's term. Stevens was considered among the liberal bloc of the Court and therefore would want a successor appointed by Obama rather than a Republican. Also, Stevens already was nearly 90. And it was more likely that Stevens would retire earlier than later in Obama's term, despite the fact that he had the potential of becoming the longest-serving member of the Court. If Stevens waited until he broke Justice William O. Douglas's record for Court service (36 years and 209 days), he would be retiring in the middle of the 2012 presidential election. That was an unlikely prospect. When David Souter notified the White House that he was planning to retire at the end of the term in 2009, Obama could expect to have two vacancies for the Court during his first term.

The prospect of additional vacancies may influence a president's decision making regarding the choice of an eventual nominee. This was part of the calculation in the Kennedy administration. Kennedy adviser Ted Sorensen urged Kennedy to think about three potential vacancies in his first term.[111] Barack Obama, similarly, may have concluded that he would have another vacancy for Elena Kagan, who was high on the president's short list, if she were not chosen in 2009.

The Selection Process

The process of presidential decision making is the means by which presidents decide whom to nominate for the Senate's confirmation. Since presidents possess individual styles and temperaments, the decision-making process has varied somewhat over time. The level of presidential involvement differs based on the background of the president. Presidents like Nixon, Clinton, and Obama with legal backgrounds take powerful roles in vetting potential nominees. Other presidents are less interested and defer more to their advisers. As George H. W. Bush did not know David Souter, he left the vetting process to aides. He was given two names, from which he chose one.[112] Even with that one, Bush deferred to White House Chief of Staff John Sununu's knowledge of Souter. Dwight Eisenhower made a point of telling others that he was very deliberate in his study of potential nominees, but his chief of staff said Eisenhower "didn't have the background or I suppose the inclination to really dig into the characteristics of Warren's decisions. He wouldn't have made an examination of the record."[113]

Nevertheless, there are standard elements that have characterized most presidents' approach to the process. As discussed earlier, one is involvement of the Senate. No president has given the Senate a formal role in presidential selection. Washington's interpretation of "advice and consent" became precedent for all subsequent presidents.

Another is the creation of lists of potential candidates that presidents work from. These lists are drawn up by the White House staff, particularly the White

House Office of Legal Counsel, or the Department of Justice. At times, they are supplemented by other senators, interest group leaders, and individuals, particularly those the president knows personally. Barack Obama asked his White House counsel, Greg Craig, to create a short list of potential Supreme Court nominees during the presidential transition in December 2008, and Obama added to the list names of people he knew personally. The George W. Bush administration drew up a short list in December 2000, while the Trump administration released one four days after his inauguration in 2017.[114]

Many times, however, there have been no short lists. The presidential choice is obvious, as indicated by the rapidity of decision-making. Three presidents have nominated replacements the same day a vacancy occurred. Others have been almost as rapid, such as Kennedy's two days for one nominee and one day for another.[115]

Still another element is the solicitation of advice from others. These include various individuals within the administration, senators, and others interested in the process and who hold the president's trust. In some cases, former presidents were consulted. For example, James Madison acquiesced to Thomas Jefferson's advice, for the most part, including in matters of judicial selection, although Jefferson was leery of Joseph Story, who turned out to be Madison's most significant Supreme Court appointment.[116]

Presidential Advisers

The most likely source of presidential advice, especially what is actually heeded, will come from those in the administration, particularly White House advisers who interact with the president on a daily basis. John Sununu was instrumental in placing David Souter on George H. W. Bush's short list and then strongly advocating his nomination. As a former New Hampshire governor, Sununu was familiar with Souter, who had once served as a state Supreme Court justice. White House aides John Dean and Dick Moore played important roles in urging Richard Nixon to appoint William Rehnquist, a deputy attorney general whom Nixon initially had dismissed as a possibility.[117]

Aides offer candid analyses to the president of various nominees—either in person or by memorandum. In 1993, Bill Clinton's vetting team, headed by White House Counsel Bernard Nussbaum, told Clinton that Stephen Breyer would be "a safe—if unspectacular—choice" who would "be easy to confirm and unlikely to generate controversy in the process." They concluded that Breyer would "receive a lukewarm reception from women's and civil rights groups, as his views on key questions of constitutional doctrine are not as well known—or likely as progressive—as those of other potential candidates."[118]

However, some presidents ignore their advisers' preferences. Clark Clifford, Theodore Sorensen, and McGeorge Bundy, all close advisers to John F. Kennedy, advocated the nomination of Harvard Law professor Paul Freund in 1962. Clifford considered Freund another Frankfurter and told the president the appointment would be met with "great applause by the bench and bar and editorial writers all over the country."[119] Bundy wrote Kennedy a memo terming Freund a "Brandeis in conviction, but a Cardozo in temperament." He predicted that Freund, among those Kennedy was considering, was "most likely to be a great judge." In addition, wrote Bundy, Freund, who was 54, is "ripe for appointment now," while Sorensen urged Kennedy to "appoint now the highly-respected Freund."[120] But Kennedy ultimately rejected all that advice by passing over Freund, twice.

Lyndon Johnson wanted to appoint his friends to the Court despite concerns raised by his advisers. When Johnson was ready to nominate Abe Fortas as chief justice, he wanted to appoint his old friend Homer Thornberry as Fortas's replacement as associate justice. Clark Clifford warned Johnson that the dual nomination of two Johnson cronies would be potentially damaging to their confirmation processes and suggested that Johnson instead nominate a non-political Republican lawyer who would gain the support of Republicans.[121] Johnson brushed aside the suggestion, nominated his two friends, and saw neither of them win confirmation.

The attorney general often plays a prominent role, depending on the preferences of the president. Dwight D. Eisenhower relied heavily on his attorney general, Herbert Brownell. Eisenhower's chief of staff, Sherman Adams, termed the four justices Eisenhower chose while Brownell was attorney general "a Brownell court."[122]

Similarly, Gerald Ford leaned on his attorney general, Edward Levi, eventually choosing a candidate (John Paul Stevens) who was not on the original list provided by the White House chief of staff, but was high on Levi's list. Levi apparently played a significant role in the decision-making process, even in opposition to Ford's own wife.[123] Betty Ford, along with various women's organizations, including the National Women's Political Caucus and the Professional Women's Clubs, were urging the nomination of a woman. The list forwarded to the president by White House Chief of Staff Dick Cheney included the names of 30 women, most suggested by the National Women's Political Caucus. These included prominent women such as Secretary of Housing and Urban Development Carla Hills; US Appellate Judge Shirley Hufstedler; and US District Judge Cornelia Kennedy.[124] Interestingly, Levi's initial list included no women (although he later added two), and Ford's eventual pick was among the top three suggested by Levi. The attorney general's approach to his role was methodical. He created his own list for Ford's perusal, which included 18 federal judges, lawyers, administration officials, and legal scholars. He then pared his own list down to six, which he prioritized in two groups. Stevens was in the top group.[125]

Other cabinet members can be influential, since presidents may turn to whomever they wish in seeking advice on a Supreme Court nomination. In 1932, Secretary of State Henry Stimson went to the White House to discuss a Supreme Court vacancy with Herbert Hoover. He urged Hoover to avoid seeking to achieve a geographical balance by filling the seat from a southwesterner, but instead to appoint Benjamin Cardozo or Learned Hand, both of whom were from New York.[126]

Senators

Presidents typically have consulted informally with members of the Senate about potential nominees. The administration also interacts with senators on lower-level appointments, because of senatorial courtesy regarding appointments at that level. Without such consultation, the administration risks offending a senator who could put a hold on the nomination that would doom or delay it. The Senate uses a process called "blue slips" in which a federal judicial nominee must be approved by one or both senators from the home state of the nominee. Without that approval, the Judiciary Committee chair typically will not act on the nomination.[127]

Supreme Court nominees are a different story. Opposition from home state senators does not doom a Supreme Court nomination. For example, both senators from New Jersey voted against the confirmation of New Jersey native Samuel Alito in 2006 and even supported a filibuster of his nomination.[128] Since Supreme Court seats are national appointments, senators today do not consider them "plum positions" for their particular state, as is true for lower court nominations.

Nevertheless, senators will lobby for candidates from their own state. Senators from the same state may work together to advance a particular nominee, especially if they are from the same party. The odds they will be listened to are lower if they do not share the president's party affiliation. In 1969, the two North Carolina senators, both Democrats, lobbied for Susie Sharpe, a North Carolina Supreme Court justice to fill a vacancy. They realized their chances of convincing the Nixon administration to appoint her were slim because she was a Democrat and also because she was a woman.[129]

It is expected today that the president consult informally with key senators, particularly those on the Senate Judiciary Committee. However, that practice varies with the personality of the president. Franklin Roosevelt was known for not consulting senators. One senator remarked about one nomination that he had no idea what Roosevelt would do because the "President certainly has not consulted anybody in the Senate about it." Richard Nixon made decisions in private or with a small set of advisers and was loath to involve others beyond that small circle. White House aide Charles Colson blamed the administration's confirmation defeats on the failure to be more inclusive. "I would like to suggest for your consideration that on the next go-around we discuss the nominee in advance with a number of key senators, particularly those on the Judiciary Committee." Colson suggested this consultation not be done to "obtain their concurrence but simply to see if they happen to know anything that might turn [out] to be a real problem."[130]

Some presidents target influential senators, particularly the chair of the Judiciary Committee, for advice. In 1968, Lyndon Johnson called Senator James Eastland (D-MS), then chair of the Judiciary Committee, to tell him "about the problem I have." That was that Earl Warren was retiring and that Johnson was considering naming Abe Fortas as the chief justice. Johnson listed several possibilities to replace Fortas as associate justice. Johnson flattered Eastland by asking him what he should do as president. Johnson asked Eastland: "What would you do if you were me?"[131]

Johnson told Eastland that "I've got to get somebody that would be satisfactory to all of [the senators]. Wouldn't make the Democrats too mad, but would satisfy the Republicans. We've got three or four we're thinking of, and I want to talk to you about it." Johnson told Eastland he was thinking about appointing Homer Thornberry, who had been a Texas congressman but was then a federal judge. "I don't believe the liberal Democrats would get too mad at him . . . and I would not be charged with cronyism."[132]

Johnson shared with Eastland the conflicting advice he was getting from advisers. He told him that Earl Warren wanted Goldberg, while Fortas wanted Thornberry. "Fortas says the Court is badly in need of legislative experience." "Most of the Court's work is trying to figure out what Congress wanted." However, Clark Clifford wanted Cyrus Vance. But Johnson worried that southern Democrats would oppose Goldberg, as would the Republicans.[133]

Clearly, Johnson was flattering Eastland, particularly since Johnson already knew whom he wanted to choose. The call was intended to elicit Eastland's political sense of how these various individuals would fare in the Judiciary Committee and among senators generally. He also hoped that this consultation would mean Eastland would provide political support to the nominee Johnson eventually chose. When presidents seek advice from senators, it may be more to vet names than to seek them. Presidents need information on who can or cannot be confirmed. Johnson was explicit in asking Eastland whether Johnson's choices would be confirmed and whether Eastland, the Judiciary Committee chair, would work to make that happen. "Do you think you can confirm Fortas and Thornberry?" Johnson asked bluntly. Eastland replied that he would ask around.[134]

Other presidents have cast their net for advice more broadly. In 1987, Ronald Reagan sent his chief of staff and attorney general to discuss a list of possible nominees with Senate leaders of both parties.[135] In 2009, Barack Obama consulted with every member of the Senate Judiciary Committee to solicit their views on filling the vacancy.[136]

The inclusion of senators in the process raises risks, however. One is the prospect of leaks. If the White House vets a short list of potential nominees with a wide array of senators, it is possible at least one of them will relay the short list to the press.

Another issue is deciding which senators to include. If the majority party is the president's party, then the president may not need to consult the minority party, particularly if the majority is filibuster-proof. That situation is rare. It is more likely the minority possesses the ability to engage in a filibuster, or at least to cause problems for a nominee. Hence, such consultation may be helpful in smoothing the confirmation process since opposition senators will be less likely to oppose a nominee they have encouraged the president to select.

One example was the nomination of Harriet Miers by President Bush in 2005. Miers had been recommended by Senator Harry Reid (D-NV), the Senate minority leader.[137] Bush must have anticipated that Miers would receive Democratic support (or at least tepid opposition) because of Reid's lack of opposition.

On the other hand, including opposing senators in the consultation process may tie the president's hands. As one aide to Bill Clinton put it: "Consultation does not mean that we need to heed the Senators' preferences, but it does carry one additional risk: if they strongly disapprove of someone, and the President chooses to nominate that person anyway, senatorial ire will be further stirred."[138]

An example of such ire was the chief justice nomination of Abe Fortas in 1968. The Johnson administration, including the president, consulted some southern senators just before announcing the nomination and found strong opposition. One senator said he would oppose Fortas because he considered him a "leftist." He also said that had he known what Fortas would do on the Court as an associate justice he would not have voted for his confirmation three years earlier. Two southern senators even hinted that the nomination would result in a filibuster, which it did. Later, Senator Eastland warned the White House that Fortas could not be confirmed. Despite all their attempts to forestall a Fortas nomination, Johnson went ahead.[139]

Presidents also face the reality that even consulting senators in advance does not mean they will support a nomination once it is public, particularly if they receive pressure from others. In 1968, Senate Minority Leader Everett Dirksen told the White House he would not oppose the Fortas nomination, but he eventually voted against cloture on the filibuster, thus effectively voting against Fortas. Similarly, Senator Richard Russell initially indicated to the White House he would support Fortas, but he subsequently opposed Fortas because the White House did not back a lower court judgeship he supported.[140]

Rarely do presidents use the Senate to generate names. In 1807, Thomas Jefferson faced a vacancy because the Court was expanded when a new judicial circuit was created in Ohio, Kentucky, and Tennessee. Jefferson limited his consideration to candidates from those three states. He also sent letters to all the members of Congress from those three states, soliciting ideas for potential nominees. Interestingly, Jefferson acquiesced, to some extent, to the group's wishes. He rejected the group's first choice, but did appoint the most popular second choice.[141]

Senators constantly provide names for the president. They propose prominent jurists from their own states. Clearly, the honor of being responsible for a Supreme Court justice's appointment is something senators can boast about back home. Senator Warren Rudman (R-NH) played that role in the appointment of David Souter. Similarly, Senator Edward Kennedy (D-MA) helped place Stephen Breyer on the Court.[142]

Kennedy's lobbying for Breyer is indicative of senators' efforts to gain White House notice and support for their favored candidates. In 1993, Kennedy wrote a lengthy letter to Bill Clinton urging the nomination of Breyer. Kennedy assured Clinton that Breyer "easily passes muster on abortion, civil rights, the environment, and other key issues that Democrats care deeply about." Kennedy predicted that Breyer would be the "intellectual equal of Justice Scalia on the Supreme Court." Moreover, Kennedy assured Clinton that Breyer would be confirmed because of his good relations with committee Republicans and that Kennedy himself would do all he could to shepherd Breyer's nomination through the Senate.[143] Clinton did not choose Breyer that year, but Kennedy's predictions and promises were utilized one year later.

Senators on the Judiciary Committee who are likely to be approached by the president may offer two sets of names, depending on who the president is. A president of their party will get the senator's ideal candidates. But if the senator is in opposition to the president, the names will reflect those who are closer to the senator's views but still come from the other party. One Democratic staffer explained that, when a Republican was president, the senator is not going "to march in there and say 'nominate a very liberal justice' because that won't pass the test."[144]

The Candidates

Potential nominees are expected not to be self-promoters who orchestrate their campaigns for the Supreme Court. They are supposed to be like Benjamin Cardozo, who discouraged efforts to promote his candidacy for appointment and forced such efforts to take place without his cooperation or even knowledge.[145] But such modesty is not universal.

At times, candidates for vacancies have lobbied aggressively for their own nominations. The first such case was in 1795 when John Rutledge, who had been an associate justice of the US Supreme Court and was currently chief justice of the South Carolina Supreme Court, wrote a letter to the president expressing his interest in the vacancy caused by Chief Justice John Jay's resignation. In the formal language of the day, Rutledge said he had never solicited a position and that Washington should not consider his letter an application, but he wanted Washington to know that Rutledge would "have no objection to take the place which he [Jay] now holds."[146] Washington immediately nominated Rutledge for a recess appointment.

One person who longed to be on the Supreme Court was William Howard Taft. He hoped Theodore Roosevelt would appoint him to the Court in 1908. Instead, Roosevelt chose Taft to succeed him as president. Nearly 10 years after he had left the White House, Taft wrote that he was afraid his time to serve on the Court had passed because he was already 63. "If the position, which I would rather have than any other in the world, is not to come to me, I have no right to complain, for the Lord has been very good to me."[147] But once a Republican president occupied the White House again (following Taft's successor Woodrow Wilson) and a vacancy occurred, Taft began to lobby indirectly and discreetly for the appointment. Taft communicated his strategy to a lobbyist who spoke with the president and senators to urge Taft's appointment. Taft was nominated and confirmed.[148]

Abraham Lincoln's attorney general, Edward Bates, wrote to Lincoln upon Chief Justice Roger B. Taney's death asking that he be appointed since it would be the "crowning, retiring honor of my life." Bates was not appointed.[149] Former Treasury Secretary Salmon Chase also sought the nomination. Even before Taney had passed away, Chase had hinted to Abraham Lincoln that he wanted to be on the court when he said he "would rather be Chief Justice than hold any other position that could be given."[150] Chase did not lobby Lincoln directly, although he communicated to others his interest in the position. He asked a friend in Washington to "talk as you always do cordially and friendly with the President and those who are near him in places of confidence."[151] He told Senator Charles Sumner (R-MA) that he could "do more for our cause and the country in that place than in any other." Sumner, in turn, wrote three letters to

Lincoln urging Chase's appointment. His lobbying was successful and Lincoln nominated him.[152]

For some candidates, the campaign is waged exclusively by supporters who lobby the president for the nomination. One concerted effort was the campaign to pressure Herbert Hoover to nominate Benjamin Cardozo. Cardozo was well known through the legal community and supporters quickly mobilized once Oliver Wendell Holmes Jr. retired in January 1932. Hoover received letters from academics, attorneys, and leaders of state bars across the nation. Two of the main organizers of this successful campaign were Samuel Seabury, head of the New York State Bar Association, and Senator Robert Wagner (D-NY).[153]

In one case of an organized effort to win a nomination, the instigator of the lobbying effort was the potential nominee's spouse. In March 1993, Martin Ginsburg, a Georgetown University law professor and husband of Ruth Bader Ginsburg, along with Stephen Hess, a former journalist and prominent Brookings Institution fellow, undertook a lobbying campaign to secure a Supreme Court appointment for his wife. The two sent appeals to friends of Ginsburg, particularly from the legal community. Legal academic letter writers for Ginsburg included Gerhard Casper, president of Stanford University; Herma Hill Kay, law school dean at the University of California–Berkeley; and Michael Sovern, president of Columbia University. Another group Ginsburg and Hess recruited was the corps of feminist legal attorneys who had worked with Ginsburg. These included Janet Benshoof, president of the Center for Reproductive Law and Policy, and women's rights attorneys Kathleen Peratis and Susan Penry-Williams. Other prominent Ginsburg supporters not from the legal community also weighed in, including then-Governor Ann Richards of Texas and former Democratic vice-presidential candidate Sargent Shriver.[154] The Ginsburg letters to the White House far exceeded in volume those for any other potential nominee that year.

The effort was an eventual, unheralded success. The letter writers supporting Ginsburg never mentioned the solicitation from Ginsburg and Hess. But one indication of their success was the attachment of Ginsburg's resume, which had been provided by Ginsburg and Hess, to some of those letters sent to the White House. The letter writing campaign succeeded not only because of the volume of letters from prominent academicians but also because the president's own protracted indecision, lasting nearly three months after the announcement of the vacancy, led to the need to act quickly with a "home run" candidate. The letters also helped frame the White House image-making process. One of the letter writers, Kathleen Peratis, termed Ginsburg the "Thurgood Marshall of the women's movement." That language was incorporated in the president's announcement statement when Clinton said that "many admirers of her work say that she is to the women's movement what former Supreme Court Justice Thurgood Marshall was to the movement for the rights of African Americans."[155]

The Ginsburg lobbying effort was not an exception. In fact, prominent attorneys and scholars typically weigh in on nominees. For example, also in 1993, Lloyd N. Cutler, former White House counsel, privately advocated for Stephen Breyer. In a letter to White House Counsel Bernard Nussbaum, Cutler described Breyer has having "most of the qualities you are seeking."[156] Legal scholars, including Arthur N. Miller (Harvard) and Milton Handler (Columbia), also wrote letters to the White House advocating Breyer, who with the help of such advocates, eventually, was appointed.[157]

The Justices

Another group not typically associated with lobbying the president is the membership of the Supreme Court itself, particularly the chief justice. In fact, some chief justices have become informal advisers to presidents, particularly on matters related to the Court. William Howard Taft, as chief justice, readily advised Harding, Coolidge, and Hoover on who should be appointed to the Court.[158] As soon as he became chief justice in 1921, he asked Attorney General Harry Daugherty to include him in the process of judicial nominations, which Daugherty did. Taft's objective was to block possible nominees he disapproved of. As mentioned earlier, while president, Taft, a Republican, was more concerned that a candidate held conservative views and less concerned about party affiliation. Later as chief justice, he continued to be worried about the ideological purity of nominees and felt that Louis Brandeis and possible nominee Learned Hand were liberals bent on destroying the Constitution. He once said that he needed to stay on the Court "in order to prevent the Bolsheviki from getting control."[159]

Taft lobbied Warren G. Harding, providing him with suggestions for nominees and advising him on possible candidates. Taft's efforts led to an offer extended to prominent attorney John W. Davis (although Davis declined) and the eventual appointment of Pierce Butler. Indeed, Taft even strategized with Butler on how to convince the president to nominate him, including whom he should solicit for letters of support.[160]

Taft also sought to discourage the appointment of others he disapproved of. He told Harding that one potential candidate was a "silver tongued orator" and had "an indolent mental tendency." Another candidate was "a politician more than a judge," while another was "a progressive judge," which Taft did not mean as a compliment.[161] The chief justice was so active that reports circulated about his lobbying, a fact that annoyed him.[162]

Taft wanted to have a united court and sought appointments that achieved that end. He did not value dissent and felt the justices had dissented too much prior to his ascension as chief. The ability to affect appointments offered him the opportunity to "pack" the Court with justices who would side with him philosophically and contribute to the united court he coveted.[163]

Taft was not the only chief justice advising presidents on Supreme Court nominations. In 1932, Chief Justice Charles Evans Hughes met with President Herbert Hoover to inform him of a pending vacancy on the Court. Then, Hughes went on to say that a majority of the justices wanted the man who was attorney general at that time to be nominated to the vacancy.[164] Hoover did not nominate him.

Chief Justice Warren Burger also was an activist in attempting to shape the selection of future colleagues. He recommended potential nominees to the Nixon administration. In 1971, he even threatened to resign if Richard Nixon appointed California judge Mildred Lillie, whom Burger considered to be undistinguished.[165] He also played a role in the Ford administration, even before a vacancy occurred. Two days before William O. Douglas retired from the Court, Burger wrote a confidential note to Gerald Ford about a possible vacancy. Burger brought to the attention of the president certain factors he felt were important in the president's consideration of a future nominee. Burger made no specific recommendations, but he pointedly advised the president on confirmability, judicial experience, and age.

Pointing out that the Court had not been operating at full strength for some time due to Douglas's ill health and that the Court's workload was expected to increase in the near future, he urged the president to appoint someone who would be easily confirmed: "It must be a nominee of such known and obvious professional quality, experience, and integrity that valid opposition will not be possible." Additionally, Burger wanted a nominee with "substantial judicial experience" so the individual would have "familiarity with the enormous amount of 'new law'" in recent decades and also would have "insulation from controversy and partisanship by reason of judicial service."[166]

Although he did not mention it specifically, Burger was responding to the fact that the most recent appointments to the Court—Lewis Powell and William Rehnquist—had not had judicial experience prior to their appointment, suggesting that Burger felt they had needed time to get a handle on their share of the Court's docket. He also was referring to two of Nixon's appointments—Clement Haynsworth and G. Harrold Carswell—who had failed to be confirmed, resulting in a year-long period of an eight-justice Court. Burger emphasized that cases had been put off due to that situation and that such delays "hurt the Court and the country." Burger went further in noting that the president need not be concerned about geography because each region of the country was represented, but he did want to remind the president of "the crucial factor of age" since the average age of justices at the time was 65.[167]

The note was remarkable in the sense that there was no indication it had been solicited by the president. Seemingly, Burger had initiated the recommendations on his own. Yet Ford's ultimate selection—a non-controversial, long-serving federal judge—may have been affected by Burger's specific suggestions.

Chief justices have not been the only ones who have sought to intervene in the selection process. Harlan Fiske Stone, while an associate justice, met regularly with Herbert Hoover and took those opportunities to press for the appointment of Benjamin Cardozo. He also had arranged for Hoover to meet Cardozo. Harlan even offered to resign and let Cardozo take his place to allay Hoover's concern about three New Yorkers serving on the Court at the same time.[168]

Another supplicant was Antonin Scalia. Former Obama White House adviser David Axelrod related that Scalia had lobbied him on a Supreme Court vacancy in 2009. According to Axelrod, Scalia told the White House adviser when they were seated together at a White House Correspondents Association dinner that he did not expect President Obama to nominate "someone who shares my orientation," but added, "I hope he sends us Elena Kagan."[169]

One justice claimed to have affected the process more than the outcome. Potter Stewart told a reporter that he had contacted the Nixon administration after the failed Haynsworth and Carswell nominations to urge Nixon in the future to actually meet with potential nominees. Nixon did so with his next nominee, Harry Blackmun.[170]

Even when justices may not be influential in the selection of a nominee, they may play a role in encouraging a potential nominee to accept a presidential nomination. Abe Fortas was a reluctant judicial nominee in 1965. Two associate justices—Hugo Black and William O. Douglas—lobbied Fortas to persuade him to accept a Court nomination.[171]

In one case, the initiative of soliciting judicial input on the nomination process came from the president. As president, William Howard Taft took the unusual step of polling the members of the Court about candidates to fill a chief justice vacancy. The vote was for associate justice Edward Douglass White, whom Taft picked.[172]

Senate Confirmation

On the Senate side, senators over time have wrestled with the issue of what "advice and consent" really means. At first, the Senate's response was that the role was largely pro forma. As mentioned earlier, the first six nominees were confirmed unanimously in 48 hours. Subsequent Washington nominees also received speedy confirmations. In no case did the Senate take more than a week to vote on a nominee after receiving Washington's nomination.[173] As mentioned earlier, only one nominee—John Rutledge—was not confirmed.

At the time of his nomination to chief justice, Rutledge was the chief justice of the South Carolina Supreme Court. Earlier, he had been an associate justice on the US Supreme Court. He was on Washington's original short list for the first chief justice of the United States in 1789 and was disappointed to be passed over in favor of John Jay. Rutledge's initial appointment to the Court had been brief because of the rigors of circuit-riding; he served only two years.[174]

By the beginning of July 1795, Jay had been elected governor of New York and had resigned from the chief justiceship. George Washington immediately made a recess appointment of Rutledge as chief, with the expectation that when the Senate convened again in December, that body would make the appointment permanent. However, Rutledge did not know of Washington's appointment when he made a fiery speech in opposition to the Jay Treaty, a recent agreement with Britain that critics argued was harmful to US interests. The Jay Treaty was barely approved by the Federalist-controlled Senate. Federalist politicians, including perhaps Washington himself, began to have serious doubts about whether Rutledge should be confirmed.

Adding to the political difficulties, rumors abounded about Rutledge's deteriorating mental state. He was accused by Federalists of suffering a mental breakdown due to financial setbacks and the deaths of his wife and mother. Alexander Hamilton urged a senator to vote no if Rutledge "was sottish or his mind is otherwise deranged."[175] His anti–Jay Treaty speech was offered as evidence of his mental instability.

Unlike prior nominations, the Rutledge nomination became enmeshed in a partisan divide. Federalists questioned Rutledge's political views as well as his mental capabilities, while Republicans defended his merits and dismissed the claims of mental instability. The final vote clearly was ideological. All the senators who voted no on Rutledge's confirmation also had voted for the Jay Treaty.[176]

The rejection of Rutledge was a rarity. In the first nearly 40 years of the Court's existence, only two nominees were rejected by the Senate. However, Rutledge's confirmation process was a precursor to subsequent controversial nomination processes. First, the merits of the nominee became less important than political factors. Also, although ideology (or, in this case, a single issue) was not necessarily a sufficient reason to reject a nominee, in this case, Rutledge's mental fitness for the job became perhaps a cover issue that made ideological rejection more palatable.

However, by the mid-1800s, the Senate had become active in blocking nominees. During the next 70 years of the Court's history, 14 nominees were rejected, tabled, or postponed by the Senate.[177] That does not include those who withdrew in the face of likely rejection.

As in the rejection of John Rutledge in 1795, the reasons, typically, were unrelated to judicial issues. Roger B. Taney's nomination as chief justice was debated for nearly three months in the Senate because Taney, as secretary of the treasury, had followed Jackson's order to remove government deposits from the controversial national bank.[178] In 1870, the Senate rejected Ebenezer Hoar, who was the attorney general at the time, because of Hoar's positions on key issues of the day: Andrew Johnson's impeachment (which he opposed), a federal service system (which he favored), and opposition to senators' suggestions for lower court nominees that were based primarily on partisanship.[179]

During most of the 20th century, the approach toward nominees turned 180 degrees from what it had been in the 1800s. The presumption was confirmation. During the first half of the 20th century, rejection of a Supreme Court nominee happened only once. Senators adopted an attitude that presidents appointed Supreme Court justices and the Senate's role as a check was only important in egregious cases. One senator lobbied by the White House told an administration official that "it is the constitutional duty of the President to fill the vacancy."[180] And another, Senator George D. Aiken (R-VT) admitted that he had a policy of never opposing a president's Supreme Court nomination, either Republican or Democrat.[181]

The Role of the Senate Judiciary Committee

When George Washington submitted his first six nominees to the Senate, there was no committee to which the nominees were referred. Nor did the Senate scrutinize the nominees with hearings or even lengthy floor debate. Instead, each nominee was agreed to almost immediately after the president's nomination and without reference to committee or even debate.[182] For the first two decades of the history of the Senate, confirmation was handled by the full Senate. Since nominees were not typically controversial, there was no need for a formal process beyond brief debate and a vote.

In 1811, James Madison nominated Alexander Wolcott, a federal revenue collector who was known for his strong Republican views. However, Wolcott lacked judicial experience and had made many enemies among merchants as he rigorously enforced his revenue collection duties. For the first time, the Senate appointed a three-person ad hoc committee to consider Wolcott's nomination.[183] Ultimately, Wolcott was rejected by a vote of 24 against and only 9 for, the widest margin of any failed nominee. No other nominee has had less than one-third of senators voting affirmatively.[184]

Not until 1816 was a permanent committee—the Judiciary Committee— created to handle judicial issues.[185] However, even the formation of the Judiciary Committee did not initiate a standard procedure for considering Supreme Court nominees. This committee did not become the nearly exclusive vehicle for considering Supreme Court nominations until 1868. More than two-thirds of the nominations during the period 1816–1868 were referred to the Judiciary Committee, which means that many were not. Referral to the committee did not seem to make any difference in the nominee's success rate. It was roughly the same for those who were referred to committee and those who were not.[186]

Even when the Judiciary Committee was determined to be the primary committee for judicial nominations, the Senate still reserved the right to bypass the committee and decide nominations directly from the floor. However, by that point, the committee's role covered nearly all Supreme Court nominations. Since 1868, only seven nominations have not been referred to the Judiciary Committee. Those nominations fell in special categories: a former president, William Howard Taft; a sitting associate justice nominated as chief justice, Edward D. White; a current attorney general, Joseph McKenna; a former secretary of war, Edwin Stanton; a former US senator, George Sutherland; and two current US senators, Edward D. White and James F. Byrnes.[187] In some cases, such as that of Sutherland, confirmation occurred on the same day the Senate received the nomination from the president.[188]

Gradually, even those exceptions were removed. The nomination of Senator Hugo Black in 1937 largely ended the practice of bypassing the committee for a nominee who was then or had been a US senator. The explanation lies in the controversial nature of Black's nomination, which was unexpected by many and widely opposed by the press. Indeed, following Black's confirmation, calls were made by the press and various groups for Black to resign because of the revelation of his past membership in the Ku Klux Klan.[189]

However, the move to greater scrutiny was not universally accepted. Interestingly, when Black was nominated, it was Senator Henry F. Ashurst (D-VA), chairman of the Senate Judiciary Committee, who moved that the nomination be approved without reference to his committee. As Ashurst explained,

> It is an immemorial usage of the Senate that whenever the Executive honors this body by nominating a member thereof that nomination is confirmed without reference to a committee, for the obvious reason that no amount of investigation or consideration by a committee of the Senate could disclose any new fact or shed any new light upon the character, attainments, and ability of the nominee, because if we do not know him after long service with him, no one will ever know him.[190]

However, two senators objected to Ashurst's unanimous consent motion and the nomination did move to the Judiciary Committee. That was the first time in 50 years that the Senate had not automatically moved to a floor vote on the nomination of one of its own members. A subcommittee met only briefly, skipped public hearings, and quickly recommended Black.[191] The treatment of Black, though not the same as that accorded previous former senator nominations, still was preferential, particularly compared to the greater scrutiny given to Felix Frankfurter only two years later.

The new approach still endured one more exception. When Senator James Byrnes (D-SC) was nominated five years later, his nomination was not referred to the Judiciary Committee. The Senate then confirmed Byrnes by unanimous consent.[192]

However, following Byrnes's confirmation in 1941, the Senate has referred all Supreme Court nominations to the Judiciary Committee, regardless of the nominee's Senate status. But the only case of a sitting senator to be nominated was Harold Burton in 1945. Burton's nomination was referred to the Judiciary Committee, suggesting a greater role for the committee and a desire to be more deliberate in the confirmation process. Nevertheless, Burton's nomination was handled with great speed. The Judiciary Committee did not hold a hearing but unanimously recommended Burton's nomination to the full Senate only one day after the nomination had been received from the president.[193]

Since then, the Senate has not addressed the issue of whether to continue its practice since no sitting senator has been nominated. Several senators have appeared on short lists of presidents, such as Senator George Mitchell (D-ME) in 1994; Senator Robert Byrd (D-WV) in 1971; Senator Howard Baker (R-TN), also in 1971; and Senator Orrin Hatch (R-UT) in 1987. Others have been proposed by fellow senators, such as Senator Jon Kyl (R-AZ), 2005, and Senator Jon Cornyn (R-TX), 2005.[194] However, none was nominated, making the question of preferential treatment moot.

The closest case was the nomination of US Appellate Judge Sherman Minton, who had served in the Senate prior to becoming a judge. Minton's nomination was referred to the Judiciary Committee and a hearing was held. Minton's status as a former senator did not prevent the nomination from going through the increasingly routinized process of Judiciary Committee involvement (and not just in a pro forma way) in the confirmation process.[195]

It is unlikely the Senate today would treat one of its own members with the deference members were accorded prior to the late 1940s. The routine of the confirmation process is so well established that any departure would need to be publicly justified and legitimated. Media coverage would be unfavorable. Public opinion would register opposition. The Senate would be perceived as excluding the media, group, and public scrutiny that has come to characterize the process today. Instead of arguing for special consideration, today, senators are more likely to emphasize their unwillingness to give favorable treatment to a colleague.

The Senate Judiciary Committee has attained the preeminent filtering role since the 1940s. However, the internal handling of judicial nominations has varied over time. Generally, judicial nominations have been centered on the full

Judiciary Committee level and not delegated to a subcommittee. In late 1986, incoming Senate Judiciary Committee chair Joe Biden proposed the creation of a new permanent subcommittee to handle judicial nominations.[196] Biden's motives may have been related to his likely presidential bid in 1988, but the institutional change had potential ramifications. Proponents argued that the new subcommittee would highlight the seriousness of judicial nominations. But opponents countered that it would increase delays. Additionally, a small group of senators would have greater power over a nominee's fate, that is, a recommendation by the subcommittee would be difficult to overturn by the full committee. The proposal became enmeshed in partisan wrangling and was shelved.

Senate Confirmation Hearings

After the formation of the Judiciary Committee in 1816, public committee hearings did not exist until well into the 20th century. Even when public hearings were held, they bore little resemblance to today's lengthy sessions. In some cases, they featured only a few witnesses testifying against the nominee. The sessions were perfunctory and ended quickly with a positive recommendation to the full Senate.

Hearings only gradually became a standard feature for every nomination, beginning in 1946 when Fred Vinson was nominated as chief justice.[197] Still, today's type of hearing is of recent vintage. Until 1972, only 14 nominations featured hearings lasting more than one day and only four had hearings that were four days or longer.[198]

Today, only members of the Senate Judiciary Committee question nominees. But there have been times in the past when non-Judiciary Committee members requested opportunities to query a nominee. In 1957, Senator Joseph McCarthy (R-WI) asked Senator James O. Eastland, committee chair, if he could examine William J. Brennan on his views of Congressional hearings about communism.[199] Brennan had spoken publicly against McCarthy's committee hearings on communism, calling them "Salem witch hunts."[200]

That practice is unlikely today because of the territorial nature of the committee regarding nominations, and also because senators on the committee barely have enough time to ask their own questions of the nominee. The testimony of the nominee stretches over several days to allow senators to ask desired questions. If other senators were allowed to do so as well, the hearings would extend weeks rather than days. Senators on the committee would be reluctant to share the public spotlight with other senators. One of the perks of membership on the committee since television coverage commenced in 1981 is the opportunity for each member to acquire several minutes of national live television coverage.

Other senators do testify before the committee. Almost universally such testimony is favorable, usually involves one or both senators from the home state of the nominee, and occurs as a form of introduction of the nominee to the Judiciary Committee. Senators also can testify in opposition. In 1957, McCarthy testified against Brennan on the grounds that Brennan's vote on the Court would be likely "to harm our efforts to fight Communism."[201]

Nominee Testimony

In the early days of the Judiciary Committee, the nominee did not testify. The first Supreme Court nominee to do so was Harlan Fiske Stone in 1925. However, that was not because the Judiciary Committee wanted to hear from Stone; it was because Stone asked the committee to allow him to testify. He wanted to explain a controversy regarding an action when he was attorney general. The first instance of a nominee being requested by the committee to testify was Felix Frankfurter. Even in that instance, Frankfurter's appearance was relatively brief, especially by modern standards; the nominee was questioned for less than 90 minutes.[202] Nor did the committee's treatment of Frankfurter set a precedent. The next nominee, William O. Douglas, made himself available to be questioned, but the committee did not ask him to testify.[203]

Even when those early hearings were scheduled, witnesses testifying for or against a nominee were few. In 1939, for example, no witnesses testified for or against the nomination of Douglas, so the Judiciary Committee went into executive session for a vote.[204] In 1941, a subcommittee held hearings on the nomination of Harlan Fiske Stone as chief justice. However, the subcommittee finished its business in minutes as the chair realized there were no witnesses. No one had asked to testify. Typically, those who sought to testify were opponents. If any individual or group opposed the nomination, they had not bothered to seek time to testify before the subcommittee, even though it had publicly solicited such testimony. The subcommittee then voted quickly to report the confirmation to the full Senate.[205] Stone was confirmed by the Senate six days later, or 15 days after his nomination had been received by the Senate.[206]

Democratic Elements

The presidential selection and Senate confirmation processes retained a largely non-democratic nature throughout their first century and a half. As will be discussed in the next chapter, change occurred through the 20th century. However, for most of its history, the confirmation process involved almost exclusively presidents and senators. The president made decisions based on a small coterie of advisers. Senators were quiescent to presidential preference in the vast majority of nominations. Even during the period of the mid to late 19th century, when rejections reached their peak, most nominees were confirmed. In those cases where confirmation did not occur, the issue primarily was not merit. Rather, it was disagreement with the political views or actions of the nominee (such as John Rutledge, Roger B. Taney, Ebenezer Hoar), scandal connected with the nominee (George Williams), or enemies the nominee had made (Alexander Wolcott). In some cases, it was timing—the nomination came in the last days of a president's term, particularly a less popular president, such as John Tyler (John C. Spencer or Jeremiah Black)—and in others, an opposition Senate was unwilling to confirm an opposing partisan (George Badger).[207]

External players who have become staples of the process in the modern era were rare prior to that. Even when external players were included, they were not ordinary citizens, but political and legal elites. For example, extensive public lobbying for a nominee was demonstrated in the nomination of Samuel Miller in 1862. Lobbyists for Miller included governors, judges, and prominent members of the legal community, but not the general public or interest group representatives. When Abraham Lincoln submitted Miller's name to the Senate, the nominee was confirmed within half an hour.[208] Two notable exceptions were the nominations of Louis Brandeis and John J. Parker, which animated business groups in the former and labor and civil rights groups in the latter. But their involvement was specific to those particular nominees and did not continue in other nomination processes.

Journalists covered the two stages of the process. However, the level of scrutiny was minimal compared to current standards. One problem was that Supreme Court nominations often proceeded from announcement to confirmation vote so quickly that journalists lacked time to investigate. This problem became apparent in the case of Hugo Black when an investigative journalist found evidence of Black's membership in the Ku Klux Klan only after Black had been confirmed just five days after he was nominated by President Roosevelt.[209]

The next chapter describes the changes that began to occur throughout the 20th century and led to active involvement by external players. That shift occurred gradually and was spurred by both societal and institutional developments. While that evolution occurred, the traditional process experienced a dramatic transformation to a more democratic process that was grafted uneasily onto the traditional process.

The Transition toward Democracy

Throughout the South in the 1960s, new billboard signs appeared next to highways. They read "Save Our Republic: Impeach Earl Warren." The signs, along with a national grassroots letter-writing campaign against Warren, represented a new animosity by right-wing Americans toward the US Supreme Court and those who sat on it.[1] Warren, as the leader of the Warren Court, was the embodiment of the social changes that many white southerners, as well as other conservative Americans throughout the nation, vehemently opposed.

The "Impeach Earl Warren" campaign was one indication of the shift occurring in views about the Supreme Court and those who served on it. Not surprisingly, those views began to carry over into the process of selecting the personnel of the Court. For example, in a 1941 Gallup Poll, 19 percent of Americans felt the Court was not conservative enough in its decisions. Forty-three percent felt it was just right or too conservative. By 1968, in another Gallup poll, 51 percent of Americans said they wanted the president to appoint conservatives to the Court; only 30 percent wanted liberals.[2]

The campaign also signaled a change in tactics. Not only would opponents seek to remove Earl Warren, but they also intended to prevent more "Earl Warrens" from sitting on the bench in the first place. That meant seeking to influence the Supreme Court nomination process.

Over the past half-century or so, the traditional process of Supreme Court nominations has undergone a significant transformation as the Court has gained the attention of groups willing to engage in grassroots efforts, media coverage, and public appeals in order to achieve group goals. Moreover, institutional changes have facilitated—indeed, have been accelerated by—those efforts. A modern process has emerged that features players, procedures, and practices that were largely unknown in an earlier era.

To be sure, the modern process looks similar to the traditional process in some ways. Many elements remain: A vacancy occurs, presidents mull the process of filling the vacancy, a nominee emerges and is announced, and the Senate acts to confirm or not. That basic process still exists.

However, the traditional process looks strangely antique compared to the modern one. That traditional process featured the absence of players who now seek to exert influence on a regular basis. These are not just the legal elites of an earlier day—such as prominent attorneys, judges, and law professors—who sought internal influence in presidential and senatorial decision making. They consist of interest groups, the media, and the general public. The traditional process, as emerged from George Washington on, occasionally saw the influence of other players beyond traditional ones and legal elites. Yet their role was limited. It occurred in rare instances and then only briefly.

In the modern process, their role is constant. They appear in each nomination. They carry on most of the same practices in each case. The extent to which they do so varies depending on the political environment in which they are operating, that is, who controls the White House and the Senate, who the nominee is, and how likely their efforts are to affect the outcome. Regardless of those circumstances, they are still present as players seeking to shape public opinion.

This chapter describes elements of the transition from the traditional process to the modern one. In other words, how did the process evolve to include these new, regular players? What changes occurred—institutional and political—that facilitated a new process with a set of new players?

The Role of Interest Groups

One of the most dramatic transitions in the nomination process has been the role of interest groups. Groups have gone from rare participants in the process through most of its history to active advocates for or against confirmation, as well as participants during and even before the presidential selection stage. Why did this shift happen?

The most significant change occurred in the 1960s. As the Court's decisions entered areas that touched on many aspects of society—such as business regulation, consumer protection, environment, racial discrimination—many groups began to perceive the Court as an institution that affected their own interests. As a result, those groups sought to use the Court to further their own policy ends by pursuing litigation.

An early advocate of such a strategy was the National Association for the Advancement of Colored People (NAACP), which sought to undermine racial discrimination laws through a series of cases brought through the federal courts in the 1930s through the 1950s. The success of the NAACP in cases involving the desegregation of elementary, secondary, and higher educational systems suggested that a litigation strategy could achieve group goals more effectively than legislation through Congress or state legislatures.[3] By the 1960s and 1970s, other groups pursed litigation strategies to further policy ends that primarily would have been pursued using Congress, the White House, or the bureaucracy. Civil liberties organizations, particularly, sought to implement changes in laws broadening interpretation of the First Amendment and instituting a legal framework for a right to privacy.[4] Women's organizations like the Women's Rights Project of the ACLU brought cases of sexual discrimination to overturn gender-oriented laws.[5] Groups now engage in a symbiotic interaction with the Court that invites litigation and then leads to policy resolution the group expects to be favorable to their interests.[6]

At first, conservative groups charged the Supreme Court with judicial imperialism, prompting Republican presidential candidates to promise to appoint "strict constructionists" who would not "legislate from the bench." Eventually, conservatives learned to utilize the same strategies to use Court decisions to achieve political ends. With a more sympathetic Supreme Court, conservatives pursued a litigation strategy intended to sway the Court in their direction.[7]

Groups realized that litigation was a fruitless strategy unless the justices reading their amicus briefs and hearing their appeals were inclined to rule in the group's favor. In order to succeed, they needed a Supreme Court disposed to rule on their side. That meant having a majority of justices who agreed with their views.

The means for achieving that predisposed majority was the judicial selection process. By shaping who won confirmation, they could determine the personnel of the Court. Eventually, the groups also began to focus on affecting not only how senators voted, but also whom presidents considered potential nominees.

Legal Groups

The first group to acquire a permanent role in the process was the American Bar Association. The ABA was not considered an "interest group" in the same sense that unions or trade associations would be. They were viewed as the representatives of the legal community who would be able to serve as a resource for the White House and the Senate in judging what was considered the most important criterion for appointment—merit.

Yet the ABA was an outside group, neither executive nor legislative. Therefore, the development of a role for it was the first "official" position given to an entity not specifically designated in the Constitution. The term "official" is perhaps too strong. As became apparent later, the special role of the ABA could be removed by the White House and the Senate.

The role of the ABA was intended to be strictly advisory. The ABA was a resource for the president since the organization's influence occurred mainly in the presidential selection stage when presidents vetted nominees through the organization prior to announcement. For a half-century, the American Bar Association enjoyed that special status in the Supreme Court judicial selection process with the White House. For most of the period between 1953 to 2000, a short list of potential nominees often was vetted by the ABA Standing Committee on Federal Judiciary prior to their selection by the president. This process was intended to help guide the president in the selection process by offering assessments on legal credentials. The ABA's input meant the president could know how the organization would react before a nomination was made.[8]

While the ABA was advising the president, it also performed a separate role for the Senate Judiciary Committee. The ABA also has provided information directly to the Senate Judiciary Committee since 1947 when the chair of the committee at the time first requested its assessments of judicial nominees.[9] From the 1950s on, the ABA has written an extensive report on each nominee and then presented that report in testimony before the Senate Judiciary Committee. The ABA received a special status through most of that period as the first witness in a confirmation hearing following the nominee. The ABA rating was a much-awaited decision by the White House and senators.

The ABA's approach to assessing candidates itself has become controversial. In 1962, the organization decided to incorporate two categories for Supreme Court nominees—qualified and not qualified. For lower court nominations, the ABA had four classifications—not qualified, qualified, well qualified, and exceptionally well qualified. By the early 1970s, there was debate about adding a third category to the Supreme Court nominee evaluation—well qualified. That level would be reserved for those nominees who were nationally recognized leaders. The issue of the third category arose with the nomination of G. Harrold Carswell to the Court in 1970. Carswell was ranked "qualified" by the Standing Committee, which led to reports that the ABA's ranking was only lukewarm, even though it was the higher of the two ratings possible for nominees.[10]

The standards for evaluation have evolved over time and become more transparent. When Edward J. Fox Jr., chairman of the Standing Committee on Federal Judiciary, responded to the request from the Senate Judiciary Committee for an ABA assessment of Earl Warren as a chief justice nominee in 1954, he sent a one-page letter stating that Warren had been scrutinized by the association and that he was well qualified for the position.[11] By 1970, when the ABA evaluated Harry Blackmun, the eight-page review covered Blackmun's professional background and legal opinions and used as sources a series of interviews with fellow judges as well as lawyers who had interacted with Blackmun on the Eighth Circuit Court of Appeals, law school deans and faculty, and the nominee himself. The two potential criticisms of Blackmun were that he lacked a national reputation and that he was known to write more slowly than other federal appellate judges. However, the committee "was reassured in our interview that Judge Blackmun recognizes the need for an Associate Justice of the Supreme Court to work rapidly and deal with an enormous volume of work under great time pressure and we believe that he would be able to meet the challenge."[12]

The ABA evaluation is issued prior to hearings and can impact subsequent debate about the nominee. In the Haynsworth confirmation, the ABA Standing Committee on the Federal Judiciary took an unusual step in re-evaluating the nominee in the wake of allegations of ethical improprieties. The possibility of the ABA changing its evaluation to "not qualified" was viewed as a potentially fatal act for the nominee. Senate Majority Leader Mike Mansfield (D-MT) went so far as to admit a new rating of Haynsworth would significantly affect the Senate vote. Ultimately, the majority of the ABA committee voted to maintain its previous rating of Haynsworth.[13]

Other Groups

The opening for the ABA was not the first time that groups had played a role in the nomination process. For the first nearly 100 years of Supreme Court nominations, interest groups were absent, but in 1881 the National Grange and other farm groups lobbied to block the nomination of Stanley Matthews. They feared that, as a justice, Matthews would side with the railroad interests. Indeed, such interests had lobbied in favor of Matthews's appointment.[14]

Groups would play some role in certain nominations over the first half of the 20th century, albeit this was significantly limited. Labor unions sought to block the nomination of John J. Parker in 1930 in response to previous decisions they considered anti-labor. They were joined by civil rights groups who labeled Parker a segregationist.[15] Left-leaning groups such as the National Lawyers' Guild, the Civil Rights Congress, and the Communist Party opposed the nomination of Tom C. Clark in 1949. They contended that Clark, as US attorney general, had not done enough to protect civil liberties and had been responsible for loyalty investigations that began in the Truman administration as a reaction to the post–World War II anti-communist fervor.[16]

On the rare occasions that group involvement did occur, it typically meant organizing to oppose a particular nominee. Since the presumption of nomination led to a high rate of confirmation success, organizing to support a nominee would have been superfluous. That very presumption of confirmation—coupled with the process that shut out external forces—made group success in influencing a nomination difficult to achieve. Of those attempts to block nominations, groups were successful only in the case of Parker. Generally, groups would not have regular success until the modern period beginning in the late 1960s.

The onset of the change came in the 1950s and it originated from two forces—the anti-communism movement and pro-segregationists. In the wake of the Warren Court decisions on First Amendment areas, groups formed in opposition to the policy changes regarding issues such as school prayer, pornography distribution, and the rights of the accused. These groups organized to oppose the nomination of Abe Fortas as chief justice in 1968.

The battle was joined when liberal groups collaborated to fight the Nixon administration's approach to the Supreme Court. For groups on the left, the Nixon administration signaled a distinct change in their approach to involvement. These groups feared the gains they had made during the Warren Court years would be erased by a new Nixon-appointed Court. The late 1960s and early 1970s saw the mobilization of groups that had not been involved previously in Supreme Court nominations. The American Civil Liberties Union (ACLU), which had been in existence since 1920, took a position on a Supreme Court nominee for the first time in 1972 when it opposed William Rehnquist's nomination for associate justice. In 1987, the organization decided to make involvement a regular feature of nominations when they promised to take a position in opposition to any nominee "whose record demonstrates a judicial philosophy that would fundamentally jeopardize the Supreme Court's critical and unique role in protecting civil liberties in the United States."[17]

By the 1980s, more permanent coalitions began to form to affect judicial selection on an ongoing basis. First, liberal groups formed the Judicial Monitoring Project, which was intended to monitor and help defeat Reagan administration nominees. The coalition, which was sponsored by the Alliance for Justice and consisted of various organizations such as People for the American Way and the Children's Defense Fund, became instrumental in fighting the Bork nomination.[18]

Initially, conservative groups saw no need to form their own competing groups. Between 1969 and 1993, only one Democratic president served in office. And that one, Jimmy Carter, had no Supreme Court appointments. With the presumption of confirmation of nominees (and the success of eight nominations by Republican presidents and only two defeats—Haynsworth and Carswell), conservatives were largely successful in securing confirmation. However, the Bork nomination created a new fear in conservatives that liberals would dominate the confirmation process if conservatives did not counter-organize. After the Bork nomination, conservatives adopted the same permanent coalition-building strategy that liberals had adopted. Conservative legal activists, led by Thomas Jipping, formed the Free Congress Foundation to oppose liberal nominees and support conservative ones.

Groups became involved through avenues of access into the process. One was the request to testify before the Senate Judiciary Committee. The opening of hearings allowed for that opportunity. One means was serving as a witness.

During the 1950s, increasing numbers of groups testified in successive hearings. These included groups opposing nominees who were Catholic and therefore, they claimed, would follow the pope and not the Constitution. Others questioned a nominee's commitment to American values. In the midst of McCarthyism, fear that the nominee was not sufficiently anti-Communist was a concern for some witnesses. Still others worried about whether the nominee would support the *Brown* decision."[19]

Groups began to incorporate grassroots efforts. They began to involve members and supporters in an effort to contact senators and express opposition to a nominee. In 1949, groups organized thousands of letters and telegrams to pour into Senate offices to oppose the confirmation of Attorney General Tom C. Clark as a Supreme Court justice, although the efforts failed miserably as only eight senators voted against confirmation.[20]

The Role of the Media

Another newly significant player was the news media. In one sense, news media organizations were hardly new components of Supreme Court nominations. News media coverage of Supreme Court nominations has occurred since the early days of the process. Indeed, the first rejection of a nominee was facilitated by newspaper coverage. John Rutledge's speech was covered by the press and then read by senators as well as Federalists across the country who objected to its contents. Had the press ignored the speech and it had remained unknown to the senators, perhaps Rutledge would have been confirmed.[21]

Press coverage was limited by institutional constraints such as secrecy and therefore the absence of public events to even cover. But opportunities for press coverage increased as the number of public events was expanded. The press was allowed to cover floor debate, hearings, and votes. Moreover, those events became more newsworthy as nominees began to testify, senators used questioning to address controversial issues, and larger numbers of witnesses participated (including those who opposed the nominee).

A crucial news value of conflict became apparent on a regular basis where it had not been before. If conflict occurred previously, it had been largely private and not public. But the public settings created new drama as Joseph McCarthy grilled William Brennan on communism or southern senators queried nominees on *Brown v. Board of Education*. These hearings began to contain newsworthy conflict rather than perfunctory discussion followed by quick, unanimous votes.

Another change involved journalistic scrutiny. During the 19th century, the news media lacked the resources to scrutinize Supreme Court nominees' lives. During most of the 20th century, the issue may not have been resources as much as it was a culture of keeping governmental leaders' personal lives off the front pages as much as possible. The line between the personal and the public was one that reporters generally observed for various reasons, including the attitude that personal behavior did not affect public roles and that unseemly personal behavior (adultery, occasional drunkenness, attendance at stag parties or strip clubs) was common and socially acceptable as long as the police did not become involved.

Moreover, Supreme Court nominees were less well known personalities. Would the public be interested in the personal life of someone unknown to them? And the effort would likely be unproductive since such investigations rarely turned up scandalous behavior. For example, no Supreme Court justice was even divorced until William O. Douglas in 1953. Until Douglas, Supreme Court justices simply did not make news regarding their personal lives.

In the wake of Watergate, reporters began to emphasize character, which was defined by personal activities. Of course, coverage of such activities also sold newspapers and boosted ratings. The personal lives of political figures such as Gary Hart and Bill Clinton became sensational news.

By the late 1980s, Supreme Court nominees became subject to the same standards, particularly as opposition groups sought to direct journalists into avenues of investigation that would undermine a nominee's chances through embarrassing information. The emphasis on the "background" of Supreme Court nominees was a product of the investigative journalism boom of the 1970s. Other journalists sought to mimic the success of Bob Woodward and Carl Bernstein.

The first to experience such scrutiny was Robert Bork, who saw reports on his youth, family life, and even video rentals. Douglas Ginsburg's confirmation process was scuttled by personal background news stories about smoking marijuana while a Harvard law professor. Those were compounded by reports of his wife, who was a physician, performing abortions. These stories made many in the Republican base uneasy about the nomination, leading to the collapse of support.

When the book *The Brethren* appeared in 1979, the robes were pulled off the justices by this exposé about life within the Court.[22] Indeed, the justices themselves became more interesting as news subjects with the ethical problems of Abe Fortas in 1968 and 1969, as well as the public profile of William O. Douglas's professional writings.[23] Journalists sought to uncover information about Clement Haynsworth's financial dealings, and then applied that same level of financial scrutiny to subsequent nominees. Similarly, G. Harrold Carswell's past racist statements unleashed subsequent searches for past verbal tendencies and political mistakes by other nominees. When the Bork nomination came along, journalists already had experience in researching nominee backgrounds.

Public Opinion

A third leg of the democratic stool was the role of the public. Public opinion was difficult to engage systematically. Were the relatively few letter writers who expressed views about nominees typical of the public generally? Public officials did not know. Since a Supreme Court nomination was a low-profile event, only the most attentive—and the most opinionated—were familiar with what was going on in the nomination process. Prior to the 1960s and 1970s, senators received letters from relatively few constituents regarding nominees.

Until the 1930s, public opinion was difficult to gauge scientifically. Scientific measurement of public opinion did not become a standard feature of public discussion until the rise of polling firms in the 1930s and 1940s. Questions about specific Supreme Court nominees on public opinion survey questionnaires were uncommon until the Bork nomination and after. One reason was the paucity of information ordinary citizens had on Supreme Court nominees. Such information became difficult to obtain when presidential selection and Senate confirmation occurred without much publicity. Even in a more modern era, levels of citizen knowledge can be low. In the case of Ruth Bader Ginsburg's nomination in 1993, 50 percent of Americans said they didn't know anything about her views; and 23 years later, 59 percent said they had heard very little or nothing at all about Merrick Garland's record and qualifications.[24]

Nor was there an expectation that the public would, or should, be a part of the process. In 1930, after the defeat of his nominee, John J. Parker, Herbert Hoover issued a statement condemning the "vigorous nation-wide propaganda from different groups among our citizens." Hoover worried about the effects of public opinion on the nomination process and claimed that "public opinion as a whole cannot function in this manner."[25]

Gradually, the attitude about the public's role began to shift toward concern for representation of the people's will. In a speech in 1949, Senator Homer Ferguson (R-MI) termed a Court appointment "the people's appointment." He added, "The Senate in giving its advice and consent is acting for the people."[26]

The change occurred as confirmation events became public and the press covered these events. In the 1950s, letters from ordinary citizens who were stimulated by press coverage and, likely, various interest groups, appeared in senators' mailboxes. During the confirmation process of William Brennan in late 1956 and early 1957, someone (probably a committee staffer) created a list of unfavorable letters sent to various senators. The list of complaints by the letter writers focused on Brennan's religion. One asked: "How can a Catholic who has taken his oath to the Roman Catholic Church be anything but a traitor to the Constitution of the United States?" Another offered evidence of the "Un-American stand of the Roman Catholic Church."[27]

Institutional Democratization

The period between 1894 and 1968 included only one rejection of a Supreme Court nominee. The Senate's consent could be viewed as nearly automatic. However, even during this period of seeming quiescence, the Senate already was changing its process of providing consent in ways that contributed to the creation of a modern process where Senate approval was not a given.

The change within the Senate can be seen in the Senate Judiciary Committee. Gradually, the committee adopted changes that helped alter the nature of the process. As the Senate Judiciary Committee expanded the deliberation process during the 1940s and 1950s (standardization of hearings, expectation of nominee testimony, and the inclusion of witnesses), the opportunities for democratic input expanded.

Committee Hearings

The most publicized event of the modern process is the Judiciary Committee hearing. After the formation of the Judiciary Committee in 1816, apparently, there were no committee hearings held until 1873. Those held that year were intended to consider the nomination of George Williams in 1873. Williams was accused of participation in a scandal and faced strong opposition within the Senate. His nomination was eventually withdrawn.[28] These hearings seem to have been the first effort by the committee to deliberate on a nominee through hearings, including the testimony of witnesses. However, these hearings were held behind closed doors and were not open to the public.[29]

The first public Senate Judiciary Committee hearing on a Supreme Court nomination was held in 1916 for the confirmation of Louis Brandeis. Brandeis did not testify at these first public hearings, but others did. In fact, 38 witnesses— both pro and con—appeared over 19 days of public hearings; these included the mayor of Cleveland, Ohio, the editor of *Harper's Weekly*, the president of the Dow Jones Company, and representatives from nine state and county bar associations.[30] The opposition to Brandeis centered on ethical conflicts of interest in his legal practice, such as representing a client when he was actually being paid by a third party and switching sides on a case. However, two other issues stoked controversy. Brandeis was known as a social liberal and was considered a radical by establishment figures of the day. The other was Brandeis's status as the first Jew to be nominated for the Court at a time when anti-Semitism was common.[31]

Yet the Brandeis hearings did not set a precedent. There were no hearings for the next six nominees. The Brandeis hearings and the Parker hearings in 1930 were elongated events involving multiple witnesses and extensive questioning by the members of the Senate Judiciary Committee over multiple days.[32] But they were viewed as anomalies rather than as routine.

For 21 years following the Brandeis hearings, the Judiciary Committee varied in its approach to holding confirmation hearings. Ten of the Supreme Court nominations referred to the committee during that period included hearings, while four did not. Three of those four were, again, special cases. One involved Charles Evans Hughes, who already had served as an associate justice and in the 1920s was secretary of state. The other two were the nominations of sitting US senators—Hugo Black in 1937 and Harold H. Burton in 1945.[33]

Interestingly, these early hearings were criticized for potentially violating the rights of nominees. When Earl Warren was accused of various charges in open committee hearings during his confirmation proceedings in 1954, the ACLU's Washington director complained to the Judiciary Committee about some of the testimony. He objected to the airing of "completely unproven charges and allegations." To ameliorate the situation, he suggested a code of procedures for hearings that would be fair to nominees.[34]

Opening the Doors to the Public

Initially, the Senate's consideration of a nominee took place only on the Senate floor. Those sessions were closed to the public. The Senate rule was that all nominations occurred in executive session unless two-thirds of the Senate voted otherwise. In 1925, the Senate suspended that rule and allowed for debate over a Supreme Court nominee in open session. By a vote of 60 to 27, senators agreed to debate the nomination of Attorney General Harlan Fiske Stone in public. Actually, this was their second consideration of Stone. The first had been in executive or closed session and had resulted in the nomination being referred back to the Senate Judiciary Committee.[35]

The move was in response to a concern on the part of some senators that the controversy around Stone's nomination should receive a public airing. Opposition to Stone centered on his support of an indictment against a senator, Burton Wheeler (D-MT), on the charge that Wheeler had been engaged in a conspiracy to defraud the federal government on the sale of oil lands. Wheeler supported an open session.[36] Supporters of Stone did as well. As a result, transparency was viewed by both supporters and opponents of Stone as a means to get their side of the controversy out to the public. And the public responded: News reports of the time indicated that the debate drew a large crowd of spectators in the public galleries.[37]

The opponents of an open session were senators who believed the vote for an open session would set a bad precedent.[38] An executive session allowed for senators to speak more freely about a nominee. Information about a nominee could be debated without harming the reputation of the nominee. An open session would not allow such a debate.

But secrecy was becoming difficult to maintain even in executive sessions. With 96 members, it was difficult to keep them from relating to the press what occurred in a secret session. Reporters covering the Senate were able to get reports on the executive session relatively easily from senators who leaked the proceedings to them. In a debate over whether to go into secret session, according to a report in the *New York Times*, "the charge was made [by a senator] that practically all that had occurred at Saturday's executive session, when the Stone matter was under consideration, had appeared in the newspapers on Sunday." Senators accused each other of leaking accounts of the proceedings to the press and violating the rules of the Senate.[39]

In 1929, the Senate changed its rules to make confirmation debates public unless a majority of senators voted otherwise. The move was controversial. But proponents of change pointed to the perpetual leaks coming out of closed sessions that already undermined secrecy as well as the need for the public's business to be open to the public.[40]

When the Senate began to use the Judiciary Committee, public access to its proceedings did not immediately follow. As mentioned above, hearings were closed until 1916. Even when hearings were opened, the actual decision-making point was closed to the public; when the Judiciary Committee met to discuss and vote on a nominee, it sat in executive or closed session. For example, even though the Senate Judiciary Committee had held open hearings on Harlan Fiske Stone's nomination, the committee closed its doors when an actual debate and vote occurred on the nomination.[41] Unless senators talked, which they often did, the public did not know who had voted which way. When Potter Stewart was approved by the Senate Judiciary Committee in 1959, the procedure occurred in a closed-door session that excluded the press and the public. In that case, the chair of the committee announced the vote afterward.[42] That policy eventually ended as the call for openness gained greater support.

Yet another mark of secrecy fell in the 1960s. Until that decade, most nominees were confirmed without recorded votes. From 1789 to 1967, 61 percent of Senate votes were not recorded votes. They were voice votes that placed no senator on record. However, again in response to a demand for greater transparency, senators began to call for recorded votes. Since 1967, all votes on Supreme Court nominees have been recorded.[43] These votes increase the amount of information the public knows about the process. Citizens now are aware of how the senators from their state voted. Recorded votes also provide information for interest groups who may use them to reward or punish senators. In turn, senators clearly understand that this vote is one that will be well publicized and used to indicate support or opposition to the goals of various groups. It also will be noted by the White House, which may affect relations with the president. No longer could senators simply skip the vote without accountability.

Still another barrier to transparency was broken in 1981 when the first gavel-to-gavel televised Judiciary Committee hearings for a Supreme Court justice occurred with the confirmation process of Sandra Day O'Connor. Broadcast media had covered hearings previously, but not live and gavel to gavel. Snippets had appeared on the nightly news programs. Television would have been privy to some potentially newsworthy moments in the hearings on Thurgood Marshall as the first African American nominee, Abe Fortas's contentious hearings in 1968, Clement Haynsworth's testimony about ethical issues in 1969, and G. Harrold Carswell's questioning on racial views in 1970. There were a couple of exceptions. In 1939, newsreel footage was taken of the Felix Frankfurter confirmation hearings. And CBS News was allowed to film a few minutes of the confirmation hearing of William Brennan in 1957.[44]

The decision to cover O'Connor's hearings came long after the first live televised coverage of Congressional committee hearings several decades earlier. In fact, the first live televised coverage of Congressional hearings occurred in 1948, and live televised committee hearings became standard in the 1950s, the 1960s, and the 1970s with the Kefauver Committee hearings on organized crime, the Army-McCarthy hearings chaired by Senator Joseph McCarthy (R-WI) in 1954, the Senate Foreign Affairs Committee hearings on Vietnam in 1966, the Senate Watergate Hearings in 1973, and the House Judiciary Committee hearings on the impeachment of Richard Nixon in 1974.[45] However, nominee hearings were viewed differently from other types of hearings on issues such as racketeering or Vietnam policy.

Moreover, the Senate itself did not open television to its floor proceedings until 1986. Nor had the House done so until 1978, nearly three years after the Stevens confirmation hearings. For the first time, the creation of cable networks offered the opportunity for continuous live coverage rather than snippets on the nightly news. C-SPAN covered the proceedings gavel to gavel, unlike the regular broadcast networks.[46]

Clearly, there was high public interest in the confirmation of the first female Supreme Court nominee. O'Connor's appointment was big news, and the image of the first female nominee sitting at the witness table was an appealing one to the networks. Given public interest, the opportunity to participate in this historic event could not have been lost on members of the Senate Judiciary Committee.

Even after hearings became public, the Senate Judiciary Committee still held closed votes. Even though the Senate Judiciary Committee had held open hearings on Harlan Fiske Stone's nomination, and even invited him to testify, the committee closed its doors when an actual debate and vote occurred on the nomination.[47] That practice still occurred in the late 1950s. When Potter Stewart was approved by the Senate Judiciary Committee in 1959, the action occurred in a closed-door session that excluded the press and the public. The chair of the committee announced the vote afterward.[48] However, the openness of the 1960s and 1970s changed that policy as well.

The Nominee as Star

Sandra Day O'Connor may have been the most high-profile nominee to testify on her own behalf to that date. However, by 1981, the change had already occurred in an expectation of nominees appearing before the Judiciary Committee. This was another significant change between the two processes, although its evolution was gradual. Interestingly, the two most controversial nominations of the first half of the 20th century (Brandeis in 1916 and Parker in 1930) did not include testimony from the nominee.

The first Supreme Court nominee to testify was Harlan Fiske Stone in 1925. As mentioned above, Stone had asked to appear. His appearance was a success. His four-hour testimony squelched the opposition and he was unanimously recommended by the committee.[49]

Following Stone's precedent, the committee was selective in its willingness to hear from a nominee. John J. Parker also asked to testify when he was nominated in 1930. Parker wanted to blunt charges that he was anti-labor and racist. However, by a vote of 10–6, the committee rejected his request and took only written testimony from him. Parker sent letters and telegrams to the committee after they reported his nomination adversely.[50] Ultimately, Parker was not confirmed by the Senate.

Felix Frankfurter was the first nominee requested by the committee to testify, in 1939. At first, Frankfurter declined. But then, after witnesses criticized his ACLU connections and implied he was a member of the Communist Party, Frankfurter gave brief testimony reaffirming his belief in America. He warned the senators that he was not going to talk about his personal views on issues related to the Court. However, senators did grill him on his associations, including whether he was or had been a Communist Party member. The committee's treatment of Frankfurter did not set a precedent either. The next nominee,

William O. Douglas, made himself available to be questioned, but the committee did not ask him to testify.[51] The committee's interest in hearing from a nominee seemed to hinge on whether there was some controversy about the nominee that the nominee could address. That applied to Stone and Frankfurter.

In 1939, when Stanley Reed, then the solicitor general, was nominated, the committee left open the possibility of Reed testifying. The committee chair offered to call Reed if the members were interested in questioning him. None wanted to do so, even though Reed was sitting at the witness table apparently ready to testify. Similarly, William O. Douglas was present as the Judiciary Committee looked at some endorsement letters, asked no questions of him, and unanimously approved his nomination in a matter of minutes. The next year, Frank Murphy appeared but spoke only briefly before the committee unanimously approved him.[52]

However, by the late 1940s, there was a growing expectation that nominees routinely would appear before the committee and be asked to testify. The assumption of a nominee testifying was becoming more routine, necessitating some justification for not calling the nominee to testify. The issue was raised in 1949 when Sherman Minton, a former US senator from Indiana, was nominated. The Judiciary Committee voted to request that Minton appear personally before the committee when two members of the committee asked that Minton answer questions.[53]

Minton ultimately did not testify. He sent a letter to the committee explaining why he felt he should not appear before the committee. In the letter, Minton said that his "record speaks for itself" and that an appearance would present "a serious question of propriety, particularly when I might be required to express my views on highly controversial and litigious issues affecting the Court."[54] Yet evidence of the growing expectation of nominee testimony was apparent in the effort to recommit Minton's nomination to the Judiciary Committee to compel him to testify in order to be confirmed. However, that effort failed. Minton's status as a former senator may have helped smooth the way for him to be confirmed without testifying. Despite opposition to his refusal to testify as well as the nomination generally, Minton was confirmed by a large margin.[55]

The Judiciary Committee did not call Attorney General Tom Clark when he was nominated to the Court in 1949. No sitting attorney general had been called to testify before. (Harlan Fiske Stone was attorney general when he requested to testify and felt that it was unseemly for an attorney general to be grilled by the Senate Judiciary Committee about his personal character to serve on the Court, although his desire to deal with the implication of scandal overcame that feeling.)[56]

Nevertheless, the Judiciary Committee's failure to call Clark to testify became an issue in his confirmation. One of two senators who voted against Clark's confirmation criticized the committee's failure. He called the committee's decision "an outrage to the American public" because there were "various matters now of public record that should be subject to an open hearing."[57]

The expectation gradually was applied to all subsequent nominees, regardless of who they were. Even sitting justices were not exempt. In the 1950s, the Senate Judiciary Committee called each of the associate justice recess appointments (individuals who were already sitting on the Court) to testify. William Brennan (in 1957) and Potter Stewart (in 1959) appeared before the committee while they were sitting on the Court. (Earl Warren, who was in a recess appointment during his confirmation process, was not asked to testify.) Felix Frankfurter urged Stewart not to testify, even drafting a letter for Stewart to send to the committee explaining his reasoning. But Stewart ultimately rejected Frankfurter's advice in the interest of good public relations.[58]

Even a nominee in a permanent justice appointment is no longer exempt. Abe Fortas was an associate justice when he testified at his confirmation hearings for chief justice, even though he faced the possibility that he would be asked about cases pending before the Court. However, when some members of the Judiciary Committee asked him to appear a second time to discuss allegations of improper behavior in accepting payments from wealthy donors, Fortas declined. In a letter to the committee, he pointed out that already he had set a precedent as a sitting justice appearing before the committee.[59]

While serving as an associate justice, William Rehnquist attempted to avoid the hearings in 1986 when he was nominated as chief justice. Rehnquist claimed it would be inappropriate for a sitting associate justice to testify before the committee. His advisers convinced him that he needed to testify.[60] Rehnquist explained that he would not defend his decisions nor would he signal any positions in future cases. So, he believed a hearing was unnecessary.[61] However, Rehnquist ultimately acceded to the committee's request.

By the mid-1940s, confirmation hearings had become the rule. Harold Burton, nominated by President Harry Truman in 1945, was the last nominee not to have any confirmation hearings. As mentioned above, he was a senator and received the courtesy of a quick confirmation without referral to the Judiciary Committee and only one day after the nomination was received by the Senate.[62]

Treatment of Burton matched that of previous sitting senators who had been nominated. Hugo Black, then a senator from Alabama, was approved by the Senate Judiciary Committee with no hearings and little discussion, despite controversy surrounding Black's former membership in the Ku Klux Klan. Senatorial courtesy was a strong force in pushing through his nomination. Opponents of the nomination sought to question Black and debate his fitness for the Court, but Roosevelt had asked the committee chairman to "get hard-boiled and push the Black matter through the Committee."[63] The six-hour floor debate, which occurred just five days after the presidential nomination, included accusations of Black's KKK membership. However, supportive senators chided opponents for an absence of proof. Black was confirmed overwhelmingly. As discussed earlier, it was only after Black's confirmation vote that a reporter for the *Pittsburgh Post-Gazette* found Black's application for Ku Klux Klan membership, his service card in the KKK, and a listing of the offices he had held in the organization. By that time, the Senate had already acted and Black was a sitting justice.[64] However, the story reinforced the need for more Senate scrutiny.

Since 1946, the Senate Judiciary Committee's role has been routinized. The committee has handled all Supreme Court nominations and that process has included public committee hearings, regardless of who the nominee is. And it has nearly always handled them exclusively. The only exception was in 1954, when a subcommittee held hearings on the chief justice nomination of Earl Warren. Since then, all hearings have been held by the full committee.[65]

Open Mike

Another change during this period was the regular appearance of witnesses. Obviously, no one testified when hearings did not exist. Even in the initial days of hearings, appearances by witnesses were rare. In 1939, for example, no witnesses testified for or against the nomination of William O. Douglas as an associate justice, so the Judiciary Committee went into executive session.[66]

Some witnesses began to be solicited, such as the American Bar Association Standing Committee on the Judiciary chair, as well as the senators from the nominee's state and others who were present to introduce the nominee. The committee may solicit testimony from others who may have some particular knowledge relevant to the committee's deliberations, as is illustrated by committee staff who requested testimony from Anita Hill against Clarence Thomas, which led to both Republicans and Democrats seeking witnesses who could corroborate either Hill's or Thomas's testimony.

Who comes to testify has varied over time. Group representatives and academics have become more frequent witnesses. And as the number of witnesses has grown, elected officials have become a smaller proportion, particularly compared to the 1960s. (See Table 3.)

The total number of witnesses testifying has grown significantly since 1949. (See Figure 1) Also, even though more witnesses testify, that does not mean that they are primarily in opposition to the nominee. A larger number of opposition witnesses testify today than in the 1940s–1960s. But overall, supportive witnesses are more predominant since the 1970s. Controversial nominations,

Table 3 **Witness Backgrounds in Senate Judiciary Committee Hearings – 1949–2010**

	1940s	1950s	1960s	1970s	1980s	1990s	2000s
Academic	6%	3%	2%	13%	28%	13%	30%
Bar Association	0	10	8	6	6	21	8
Judge	0	4	2	2	1	2	8
Interest Group Representative	50	14	30	29	27	27	17
Elected Official	17	31	40	34	11	22	9
Administration Official	0	3	6	2	1	1	2
Participant in Case	6	3	0	0	0	0	2
Private Individual	22	14	10	4	17	8	15
Other	0	17	3	10	8	6	9
Totals	**101%** **(18)**	**99%*** **(31)**	**101%*** **(61)**	**100%** **(68)**	**99%*** **(223)**	**100%** **(83)**	**100%** **(115)**

*rounding error

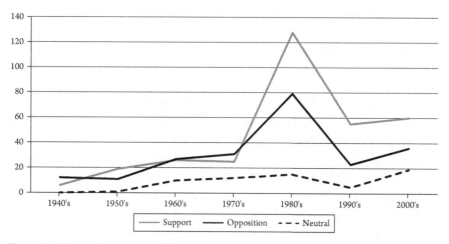

Figure 1 Witness Position over Time

such as the Bork nomination and the Roberts and Alito nominations, attract a larger number of opposition witnesses. But the presence of opposition has spurred support as well from witnesses.

Today, the committee chooses who can participate. When regular hearings were still a novelty, groups could more easily petition to testify. During the Brennan hearings, a group calling itself the National Liberal League from New York City sent a representative to testify that they opposed Brennan "on the same ground that a Catholic in a predominantly Catholic country would oppose the nomination of a Protestant. This is a predominantly Protestant country. In Catholic nations, we believe Protestants are not appointed to the highest court."[67] In the Fortas confirmation hearing in 1965, a single individual spoke against Fortas on her own without any role within an interest group.[68] Today, the number of witnesses demanding a role in the hearings would make such testimony unlikely.

The Questions

When senators became interested in what a nominee's views were on specific issues, questions began to reflect that interest. Questions about a nominee's ideology began to be asked in 1939 with Felix Frankfurter's testimony. Frankfurter was asked about his attitudes towards the American Civil Liberties Union as well as the Communist Party. Senators made specific queries about Frankfurter's ideology, including whether he belonged to the Communist Party. Frankfurter answered emphatically that not only was he not a member, but also that "I have never been qualified to be enrolled, because that does not represent my view of life, nor my view of government."[69]

Southern senators were pressured to ask questions about race during hearings on Supreme Court nominees. One southerner wrote to Senator James Eastland (D-MS) that he was surprised to hear the senator was endorsing Byron White for the Supreme Court and informed Eastland that White was "against us on the race question."[70] Senator John McClellan (D-AR) promised his constituents that he would work to defeat the nomination of Thurgood Marshall.[71] That pressure was reflected in questions of nominees about their views on *Brown v. Board of Education* or the power of the Court to resolve such issues.

Another issue that arose during the 1950s was communism. Senator Joseph McCarthy (R-WI) opposed Brennan because the nominee had spoken out against McCarthy's investigations of communism. McCarthy claimed the American people "have a right to know whether Justice Brennan can be counted on to help or hinder the fight against Communism."[72] John M. Harlan was asked about his membership in the Atlantic Union, an organization dedicated to greater world governance, but viewed by some conservatives as a Communist-related group.[73]

Increasingly, nominees were asked about their views on specific cases. In 1967, Thurgood Marshall was queried about his opinions concerning the recently decided *Miranda* case. Abe Fortas fielded questions about Warren Court cases.[74]

Even at this point, some questions were veering into territory that would become Bork-like. In 1967, Thurgood Marshall was asked by a southern senator: "Are you prejudiced against white people in the South?" Marshall replied that he was not.[75]

The Senate was now more interested in playing its role as a check on the president's appointment process. However, initially, the check was minimal. It consisted of some southern Democratic senators asking questions that seemed more pointed toward satisfying a base of conservative activists than actually stopping a presidential nominee. But some southerners, likely reflecting increasing pressure from constituents, were not content just to ask questions. They also began to vote against a series of nominees they believed would uphold *Brown*. When there were "nay" votes for Supreme Court nominees in the 1950s and 1960s, they came from the southerners. Nine of the 11 votes against Harlan (1955) were southerners, as were all 17 of the votes against Stewart (1959) and all of the 11 against Thurgood Marshall (1967).[76]

Views about the Senate's role in determining the ideology of a nominee were shifting during this period. And intellectual defense was not coming merely from the South. The use of ideology was being defended by scholars, some making the case long before southern senators adopted the practice. In 1930, Felix Frankfurter, then a Harvard law professor, argued that the Senate should consider a nominee's philosophy and not simply his merits when deciding on confirmation. Joseph P. Harris went further and suggested that the Senate should focus on "the social and economic philosophy of persons nominated to the Supreme Court" and that those considerations were more important than merit.[77] Interestingly, in 1959, the future chief justice, William Rehnquist, who wanted to decline to appear before the Judiciary Committee, argued in a law publication that the Senate needed to ask questions about ideology because that is the only way senators can know how nominees interpret phrases such as "due process of law" or "equal protection of the laws."[78]

By the mid-1960s, the role of questioning had changed dramatically from a generation before. Now, all nominees realized that their appearance at a hearing was a necessity, not a choice. Moreover, they could not escape being asked questions about Supreme Court cases, judicial philosophy, communism, racial desegregation, and other current issues of interest beyond the legal community.

Undermining the Presumption of Confirmation

For most of the history of the nomination process, the presumption of confirmation has permeated Senate response to a nominee. The record of confirmation is a testament to that attitude. In 1949, Senator Homer Ferguson (R-MI) expressed this view when, in opposing Tom C. Clark's confirmation, he explained that "no man can find pleasure in standing on the floor of the Senate . . . to oppose the confirmation of any person nominated to the Supreme Court of the United States."[79]

However, the presumption of confirmation slowly began to unravel as senators added more standard elements to the Senate confirmation process rather than adopting them only in cases of controversy. Indeed, Ferguson chastised the Senate Judiciary Committee for not performing its function of holding hearings and inviting the nominee to participate. He drew a distinction between a Cabinet appointment that "should be resolved, if possible, in favor of the President, to whom the appointee will be responsible" and a Supreme Court appointment, which "is not a matter in which the Executive should enjoy primary responsibility."[80] Ferguson sought to shame the Senate into acting more aggressively: He decried the apathy shown toward Supreme Court appointments and charged that this "apathy which I am protesting is a reflection upon each and every one of us."[81]

One measure of this transformation was the approach to the use of the filibuster. Filibusters had been tools for blocking policy bills but were rarely used for nominations and never for a Supreme Court nominee. (A vote on cloture was not allowed on presidential nominations, including judicial nominations, until 1949.)[82] That is, until 1968 when Lyndon Johnson chose Fortas as Earl Warren's successor as chief justice. With only six months remaining in Johnson's term and the strong prospect of a Republican winning the White House in the November elections, Republicans employed the filibuster as a means to avoid a confirmation vote on Fortas. With a significant Democratic majority, even despite strong southern Democratic opposition, such a vote, had it occurred, likely would have confirmed Fortas. However, the filibuster and the subsequent failed cloture vote, led to Fortas's withdrawal as a nominee and the end of Johnson's ability to appoint a new chief justice.

Facilitating Democratic Involvement

How did democratic forces—groups, the media, and the public—become involved with and gain influence over the Supreme Court nomination process?

One reason is the democratization of the process within the institution. That democratization did not occur in a vacuum. It was part of the larger democratic trends of openness. These trends were fed by technology changes, such as broadcast media and the development of public opinion survey research. None of these were applied specifically to the nomination process. Indeed, their connection to the process came later than it did for others. But the Senate undertook two important changes that increased democratization—transparency and access.

Transparency

The Senate gradually moved toward greater transparency in its proceedings. It opened up floor debates so that journalists could see and report on the debates and votes on confirmations. Then the Senate Judiciary Committee instituted public hearings: first sporadically and then, by the early 1950s, regularly. When the first female Supreme Court nominee was announced in 1981, the hearings were televised live, which set the precedent for all subsequent hearings.

Not only did hearings open up, but so did the committee's deliberations and votes. No longer would the Judiciary Committee go into executive session to discuss a nomination and cast votes. Those actions were now open to press and group view, and therefore public examination.

These changes forced Senate accountability. It allowed groups, the press, and constituents to observe senators' statements and actions. Senators not only were unable to hide, but they were now expected to play roles scripted by the White House, the groups, the party, or their party bases. These included not just votes, but, as will be seen shortly, for Senate Judiciary Committee members, lines of questioning and public statements in hearings. And for senators generally, groups expected senators to become vocal advocates of the groups' positions through the confirmation process.

Offering Access Points

Not only did the Senate make itself more transparent, but it also provided greater opportunities for external players to play specific roles. The most important development was the use of time. Time offered the best opportunity for access for external players. When confirmations occurred in days, if not hours, there was no time for external players to participate.

When the Senate slowed down the process to a window of two to three months, as is typical today, then it provided groups with the time to conduct research, lobby individual senators, mobilize grass roots, and use the media to shape public opinion. As will be discussed in subsequent chapters, groups use that time to build coalitions, launch public relations campaigns, and solicit grassroots reaction to influence senators. Time is essential to carry out these new functions in Supreme Court nominations.

The issue of time also applies to presidential selection. When presidents made decisions the same day a vacancy occurred or within a few days, then external players had no time to influence presidential decision making. Presidents today may take a month or two to decide on a Supreme Court nominee. That time is not unusual in the history of Supreme Court nominations. Presidents have elongated the presidential selection stage over many months. Lyndon Johnson took three and a half months to make a nomination; Franklin Roosevelt, six months; and Theodore Roosevelt, eight.[83] From the 1950s on, some of that time was devoted to the process of ABA evaluation of potential nominees. But most simply reflected the ability of the president to be casual in filling a vacancy without news outlets continually requesting short lists and updates on the process. The difference with the delays of the past is that those presidents did not face intense interest group pressure, media scrutiny of the process and the potential nominees, or public opinion polls. The time delay would have been related to the lesser imperative of speed in the decision making at that time rather than providing the opportunity for groups to lobby the president.

That does not mean lobbying campaigns did not exist, but those campaigns were far more internal than external and were composed of elites rather than involving the public. Presidents were hearing from advisers, senators, and justices far more than from the media, groups, and the public.

As will be discussed in the next chapter, the time presidents take for decision making today offers an access point for groups—either in private or in public or both—to seek to influence the president's choice. The transitions in presidential selection have allowed that opening for group involvement. Groups are not the only beneficiaries. The media have the time to research various candidates, opine on the possibilities, and increase public interest in the ultimate announcement of a choice.

External Player Motivations

Yet none of these changes necessarily would have been important to external players without the motivation to participate. That motivation likely was propelled by the higher visibility of the process. But the motivation also originated from the perception that what the Court did affected these players. Therefore, who was on the Court mattered in terms of influencing what the Court did.

To demonstrate, those groups and individuals opposed to school desegregation viewed the Court as an important component in policymaking regarding an issue of great importance to them. If nominees like John M. Harlan, Potter Stewart, or Thurgood Marshall served on the Court, the racial desegregation emphasis of the Court would continue. The anti-communist movement believed the same, fearing that nominees like John M. Harlan and William Brennan posed threats to their cause. So, did the right-wing groups who opposed Abe Fortas due to his involvement in socially liberal decisions they opposed.

All of that occurred prior to the late 1960s and early 1970s when external player involvement boomed during the nominations of Fortas, Haynsworth, Carswell, and Rehnquist, and prior to the 1987 Bork nomination that placed the issue of a changed nomination process into the public debate. But these motivations did set the scene for the modern Supreme Court process.

The public's involvement came through group and media efforts to portray Supreme Court decisions in stark political terms and to view the personnel selection process as critical to the lives of ordinary Americans. Without those political terms, it would be more difficult for average citizens to become interested in what the Court does or who serves on it, as was true through the 19th century and most of the 20th. Without these efforts to make the selection process meaningful, the public would not consider Supreme Court nominations relevant to their lives.

The following three chapters describe the modern process. First the presidential selection process in the era of democratization. This is a process more limited in public view, but one that still has been shaped by groups, the media, and the public. Next is the confirmation stage. The third chapter of this trio addresses how presidents seek to manage nominations in the modern era.

Presidential Selection

When presidents respond to retirement letters from justices, they always express "deep regret" at the receipt of such a letter. Yet the regret must be mixed with elation over the prospect of doing what most presidents long to do during a term—fill a vacancy on the US Supreme Court. They know that the opportunity is a unique chance to shape the judicial branch.

Presidents know they have the power to influence another branch of government and to have an impact that could last a long time. Bill Clinton declared at the beginning of one nomination process that "there are few decisions a president makes which are more weighty, more significant, and have greater impact on more Americans than an appointment to the Supreme Court."[1] Barack Obama used nearly the same words when he announced the appointment of Elena Kagan: "Of the many responsibilities accorded to the President by our Constitution, few are more weighty or consequential than that of appointing a Supreme Court justice."[2] As a new president announcing a new chief justice appointment, Richard Nixon commented that "the most important nomination that a President of the United States makes during his term of office is that of Chief Justice of the United States."[3]

Presidents know a transformative appointment that would change the course of the Court's policy direction would solidify the president's place in history.[4] Franklin Roosevelt has been widely viewed as the most successful president in shaping the Court through his multiple appointments of New Deal advocates who institutionalized the Court's new approach to federal economic power. Other presidents also have made transformative appointments that affected the Court's decision making. Richard Nixon's appointments created a court that moderated the Warren Court. He was helped in that effort by appointments made by a trio of conservative presidents: Ronald Reagan, George H. W. Bush, and George W. Bush. Clearly, the number of appointments a president can make (Roosevelt had 9; Nixon, 4; and Reagan/Bush/Bush collectively, 8) as well as the environment for the appointment of "leaders" on the Court matters in the capability of the president to make transformative appointments.

The potential of long-term impact is one reason presidents prefer younger nominees who can serve for many years following the end of the president's term. Franklin Roosevelt appointed William O. Douglas at the age of 40. Douglas served for 36 years, the longest to date in the Court's history. George H. W. Bush's appointment of Clarence Thomas was intended to influence the Court for years to come. By 2017, Thomas had served on the Court for more than 26 years, but was only 69.

In 1986, Antonin Scalia benefited from Ronald Reagan's desire for a young nominee. Robert Bork, who was the president's top candidate, already was 59, was overweight, and chainsmoked. Scalia, on the other hand, was only 50 and smoked less. Attorney General Ed Meese admitted that the president "had to think about age and health."[5] (Ironically, Bork lived almost as long as Scalia, dying only three years and two months before him.)

Of course, the record of success at setting such policy direction is mixed. Initially, David Souter lived up to the Bush administration's expectations when he voted consistently with the conservative bloc in the early 1990s, including Kennedy, O'Connor, and Scalia.[6] But over time, Souter deviated from that group and disappointed his conservative supporters.

Nevertheless, presidents crave the ability to shape the Supreme Court through appointments. Lyndon Johnson was desperate to make an appointment in the waning days of his term. After Abe Fortas withdrew, Johnson considered making a chief justice nomination one month before the presidential election. Fortas advised him to drop the idea because no one Johnson nominated would be confirmed.[7]

The President's Environment

A successful Supreme Court nomination, like any other initiative of a president, is an indication of the president's effectiveness in influencing Congress to carry out the president's will. Presidents do not seek failure in Supreme Court nominees. At times, they have taunted the Senate. In the wake of the defeat of Robert Bork, Ronald Reagan at one point said that he would nominate a Supreme Court candidate the Senate would dislike as much as Bork. And Richard Nixon used the defeats of Clement Haynsworth and G. Harrold Carswell to show that he was seeking to place a southerner on the bench, but liberal senators were standing in the way. In 2016, it is unlikely that the Obama administration really believed that the Senate would confirm Merrick Garland, particularly after Republicans nearly en masse asserted their unwillingness to even consider the nomination. Therefore, Garland's failed confirmation became a Democratic electoral rallying cry.

For the most, however, presidents expect to succeed in filling a Supreme Court vacancy. They nearly always see confirmation as the goal and work toward that end. They know that the ability of the president to influence the direction of the Court, as presidents typically wish to do, requires success in winning confirmation, not failure.

However, presidents do not make Supreme Court nominations in a vacuum. The environment in which a president serves impacts his or her ability to achieve success. That environment consists of several factors presidents need to consider when making appointments—presidential popularity at the time of the process, the status of the president's agenda, timing, and the power of the opposition in the Senate.

Presidential Popularity

When presidents enter a process with high popularity ratings, they are more likely to possess greater flexibility in achieving confirmation success. More popular presidents generally are more successful in setting Congressional agendas.[8] In nomination processes, a president who already enjoys popularity has more political capital to expend on a nomination than a president who is unpopular. The amount of political leverage the president has with the Senate, and the nation generally, can be important in the determination of the president's appointee.

For example, when Lyndon Johnson was seeking to gain confirmation of Abe Fortas in 1968, his approval ratings were low. Only 35 percent of Americans approved of the job he was doing. With such low popularity, Johnson had little leverage to use to win over senators. Similarly, Bill Clinton's approval rating was 37 percent in June 1993, just as he announced Ruth Bader Ginsburg's nomination. Clinton chose a "safe" nominee because he lacked much sway with the Senate.

However, Ronald Reagan reached a high in public approval in May 1986, just a month before announcing two nominees, including one for chief justice. Reagan's slide began when the Iran-Contra scandal was revealed, which did not occur until after Reagan's nominees had been confirmed.[9]

The Status of the President's Agenda

Another aspect of the president's environment is the status of the president's policy agenda. Presidents typically have other agenda items that a Supreme Court nomination intrudes on. This is particularly true for a president faced with making a nomination in the first few months of his or her presidency. The president may not want to let a Supreme Court battle deflect Congressional, group, and public attention away from the main policy agenda items.

For instance, in 1993, but also particularly in 1994, Bill Clinton was in the midst of a debate over health care reform. A contentious Supreme Court nomination would detract from the president's signature policy proposal. The president wanted safe choices who would be confirmable. Initially, Clinton wanted to appoint Bruce Babbitt, and the chair of the Senate Judiciary Committee reassured Clinton that Babbitt could be confirmed. However, western Republican senators opposed Babbitt, including ranking Judiciary Committee member Orrin Hatch. Clinton worried that, although Babbitt could be confirmed, the fight during the hearings would negatively impact the 1994 midterm campaign as well as weaken Clinton for the 1996 campaign.[10]

Clinton opted instead for a safe choice, Stephen Breyer, who was not opposed by Hatch and therefore would engender almost no opposition. Clinton's choice would not require the president to expend political capital on a Supreme Court nominee. Indeed, Breyer was passed by the Senate Judiciary Committee with a unanimous vote and received only nine "no" votes on the Senate floor.[11] The Clinton administration could continue to place its emphasis on the president's other agenda items.

Timing

A president's success seems correlated with the timing of the vacancy in the president's term. Presidential success in achieving legislative objectives is correlated with timing within a presidential term. Not surprisingly, lame-duck presidents typically are less successful in working their will with Congress.[12]

This also applies to Supreme Court nominations. Additionally, the potential or actual short-term nature of a president's power (either near the end of a first or second term) means opponents can become bolder. In the past 100 years, only one nomination (of eight) made in the first year after the election of a new president has failed (Haynsworth in 1969). Conversely, in the same time period, of 12 nominations made in the last two years of a president's term, four have failed.

Another issue is a president late in the second term and not running for re-election. Prior to ratification of the Twentieth Amendment, four months passed between the presidential election and the inauguration of a new president. When Supreme Court vacancies occurred during that period, presidents sought to fill them, even though the president's term was nearly over and presidential influence was at a low ebb. However, the confirmation rate was only 50 percent, well below the overall presidential success rate.[13] Now, the gap between election and inauguration has been reduced to two and a half months. Since the passage of the Twentieth Amendment, no vacancy has occurred during that period.

Today, the lame-duck status applies to any president who cannot run for re-election due to term limits. The label is particularly applicable to a president in the last year of a second term. Late-term nominations, even before the Twentieth Amendment, were less successful than nominations at other time periods. Sixty percent of nominations occurring within the last six months of a president's term have failed.[14]

When Lyndon Johnson made a nomination in June 1968, five months before the presidential election to choose his successor, the White House knew that Johnson would face criticism for filling the vacancy. To prepare for negative reaction to even the idea of an appointment, White House aides looked into previous situations in the 20th century where presidential election year vacancies had occurred, and the result. They found that all such nominees had been confirmed during the election year except William Brennan, who was confirmed following the election.[15]

The fact that it was a chief justice vacancy bolstered Johnson's case that the nomination should be filled. An associate justice vacancy probably would have created stronger opposition to the idea of a lame-duck president filling the spot, although confirmation may have been likely due to Democratic control of the Senate. Had the Republicans been in control, it is unlikely a Johnson nominee would have been considered. That exact situation occurred in 2016 when Barack Obama nominated a successor to Antonin Scalia while Obama was in his last year as president and Republicans held a majority in the Senate, with that same result.

Presidents may be able to predict the imminent retirement of a justice by their actions. Often in the year before actually retiring, a justice will give signals of intending to leave by hiring fewer law clerks for the next term. This is because a retired justice will need a smaller contingent of clerks than an active one. More recently, most justices have left the Court through planned retirements, giving the president notice of their intent. Some justices, such as Warren Burger, Lewis Powell, Thurgood Marshall, and Sandra Day O'Connor, announced their retirements at the end of the term in late June or early July. (William Brennan announced in mid-July, but did so for medical reasons and not due to a planned retirement at that time.) Another example is a justice in declining health. For example, William O. Douglas struggled physically to remain on the Court throughout 1975. The Ford administration could predict that a Douglas retirement announcement was imminent.[16]

Obviously, deaths of justices are different situations since they are not planned. Understandably, the death of a justice midterm will leave a hole at the Court for several months at the earliest, as occurred with the deaths of John M. Harlan II and Hugo Black in the fall of 1971, which caused vacancies for three and a half months during the term, as well as Antonin Scalia's death in February 2016, nearly five months before the end of the Court's term. William Rehnquist's passing in late August could have led to a vacancy in the chief's position had George W. Bush not nominated someone who was already being vetted by the Senate for the O'Connor vacancy (John Roberts) and had the Senate not acted quickly on Roberts's nomination to fill the chief justice chair before the October term start date.

However, this timing of judicial vacancies left a small window for presidential selection and, ultimately, Senate confirmation. Since the Senate goes into recess in August, no action would occur on the part of the Senate until September at the earliest. That narrow time frame meant that the Court could well meet without a ninth justice. That occurred in 1987 when a new justice (Anthony Kennedy) was not confirmed until February 1988.

Byron White, Harry Blackmun, David Souter, and John Paul Stevens announced retirements in the spring, which allowed for six or seven months to pass before the beginning of the Court's new term on the first Monday in October. The earlier retirement announcement date in those cases provided presidents with time to elongate the presidential selection process through the spring and still give the Senate time for confirmation before the August recess. In fact, the Clinton vetting team drew up just such a timing strategy in 1993 after White's retirement announcement in March. The schedule expected a presidential nominee announcement by April 15, committee hearings in early June, a committee vote by the end of June, and a Senate vote by early July.[17] (None of this took into consideration President Clinton's own highly deliberative decision making as well as his sensitivity to making a non-controversial appointment.)

The Senate Opposition

Traditionally, presidents have been forced to adjust their preferences based on the composition of the Senate. The most advantageous situation for a president is a filibuster-proof Senate majority. It offers the president the opportunity to satisfy the constituency with a bold choice without having to worry about blockage by the minority. That occurred in 2009 when Democrats (supported by two independents) held 60 seats. Such a prospect is rare: the previous incidence of such one-party dominance was 1966.

Even a majority that is not filibuster-proof means a president will face a likely positive confirmation vote. First, the president's allies will control the committee's activities and deliberations, as well as the majority of its votes. And those allies will control the full Senate's agenda, as well, guaranteeing that a vote will occur, and at a time most conducive to victory.

However, opposition control has been a more likely scenario for presidents in recent years. As a result, presidents cannot expect to choose a constituency candidate and obtain confirmation. They must compromise with the opposition majority. This is not a new situation. Herbert Hoover faced this quandary in 1932 when an opposition-controlled Senate convinced him to appoint a progressive rather than a conservative as he had been able to do two years earlier.[18]

But what is new about control of the Senate is the prospect of a filibuster. When presidents and a majority of senators share party affiliation, it is rarely in a filibuster-proof situation. In those cases, the president must consider whether the opposition party would undertake a filibuster of a nominee. Since several filibusters of Supreme Court nominees have occurred in the past 50 years (and even more for lower-level court appointments), presidents must assess whether they can hold together most of their own party and possibly win over minority party members. The latter possibility has become more remote as partisanship has intensified. While only three Republicans opposed Ruth Bader Ginsburg in 1993 and nine opposed Stephen Breyer the following year, both appointed by a Democratic president, that unity had disappeared by 2006 and beyond: Samuel Alito's confirmation vote garnered only four Democratic votes (he was appointed by a Republican president), while only nine Republicans voted for Sotomayor and five for Kagan (a Democratic president's appointees). The question of how likely a minority party member would be to defect from a party-backed filibuster is yet to be answered.

President Clinton weighed the prospect of a filibuster of a Supreme Court nominee in 1994 when Republicans had waged successful party-backed filibusters on Democratic initiatives. The Clinton White House was concerned about the need for obtaining a supermajority to get a nominee confirmed. Appointment of a confirmable nominee such as Ginsburg in 1993 and Breyer in 1994 assured that there would be limited opposition and no filibuster.[19]

Influences on Presidential Selection

The Influence of the Party

Campaign rhetoric, particularly directed at the partisan base, suggests that presidents, even as candidates, understand the importance of the Supreme Court to their partisan bases. The struggle over control of the Supreme Court has become a partisan battle cry in the modern era. Party bases play a role in the nomination process today.

It is not the case that party was not considered previously. Party influence occurred prior to the 1960s. The Eisenhower administration, for example, conducted a "political clearance" of Supreme Court nominees with the Republican National Committee.[20] However, that clearance was with the chair of the Republican National Committee and not with the partisan base. Moreover, the average American would have been unaware that such a "clearance" even occurred.

Today, who sits on the Supreme Court matters to the partisan base. In the Alito nomination, three-fourths of Americans agreed that who serves as the next Supreme Court justice was at least *somewhat* important to them personally, while nearly half said it was very important. Among more ideological Americans, who are more likely to be strong partisans, the salience was even higher. Two-thirds of conservative Republicans and 62 percent of liberal Democrats felt that who was on the Supreme Court was *very* important to them personally. Ten years later, those percentages had increased to 57 percent of Americans saying that the Supreme Court choice was "very important" to them. And the strong partisans also increased as well: 68 percent for conservative Republicans and 67 percent for liberal Democrats.[21]

Americans view Supreme Court battles through partisan lenses. Shortly after Antonin Scalia's death in February 2016, 82 percent of Democrats supported Barack Obama's nominating a successor, while only 29 percent of Republicans agreed that he should. After Merrick Garland was nominated by Barack Obama in March 2016, public opinion on whether the Senate should even vote on Garland split along party lines again, with 65 percent of Republicans believing the Senate should wait for a new president and 75 percent of Democrats favoring a vote on Garland during that year.[22]

Partisan attitudes are not limited to one nominee, but to nominees generally. Democrats and Republicans divide on whether a nominee should be confirmed, depending on the partisanship of the president who is nominating. While Democrats heavily favored the confirmation of Elena Kagan (76 percent), only 36 percent of Republicans did so. The numbers were nearly the same for Sonia Sotomayor a year earlier. Conversely, when the nominating president was a Republican, only one-quarter of liberal Democrats agreed that the Senate should confirm John Roberts, while 76 percent of Republicans wanted him confirmed.[23]

Moreover, partisan differences on confirmation are growing. The gap between Democrats and Republicans on the confirmation of Merrick Garland was larger than it was for Elena Kagan or Sonia Sotomayor.[24] That means increasing use of partisanship in assessing whether a nominee should be confirmed.

The differing perceptions of the Supreme Court nomination process by partisans are similar to the divide on the Supreme Court itself. Republicans are more likely to disapprove of the Court, to have an unfavorable view of Chief Justice John Roberts, and generally view the Court as too liberal.[25] The partisan gap in views about the Supreme Court are growing. By 2015, only one-third of Republicans viewed the Court favorably, compared with 62 percent of Democrats.[26]

These partisan bases are expressing themselves not only by increasing interest and concern in the outcome of nomination processes but also through party platforms. In 1980, the Republican Party platform called for the "appointment of judges at all levels of the judiciary who respect traditional family values and the sanctity of innocent life." That line was repeated in subsequent Republican platforms. In 2008, the Democratic Party platform urged the appointment of judges "who understand that the Constitution protects not only the powerful, but also the disadvantaged and the powerless." The 2016 version promised to "appoint judges who defend the constitutional principles of liberty and equality for all, and will protect a woman's right to safe and legal abortion."[27]

Presidential candidates understand the increasing interest in the Supreme Court on the part of the base of activists within their party. Supreme Court judicial selection has become a theme in some campaigns in the era of the modern judicial selection process. Candidates have used Supreme Court justices as political targets and have promised change in direction through the appointment power. In 1964, Senator Barry Goldwater warned that Lyndon Johnson's re-election would lead to "more capricious people" being appointed as justices, while he would appoint justices "who will support the Constitution, not scoff at it."[28] Twenty years later, former Vice President Walter Mondale similarly charged that Ronald Reagan would choose poorly by following the guidance of Moral Majority leader Reverend Jerry Falwell: "If you pull their lever, you'll be handing over the Supreme Court to Jerry Falwell, who wants to run the most private questions of your life."[29] In 2000, Vice President Al Gore mentioned his potential role as nominator in a speech, saying that "there are going to be three, maybe four . . . maybe even five justices of the Supreme Court appointed by the next president."[30]

Presidential candidates have offered promises that Supreme Court nominees would satisfy issue concerns of their bases, particularly on abortion. In 2000, Democratic nominee Al Gore, responding to the influence of pro-choice groups in the Democratic Party, said his nominees would probably be pro-choice.[31] When 2016 Republican nominee Donald Trump was asked by Fox News host Bill O'Reilly if he would "protect the sanctity of life," Trump responded that "the biggest way you can protect it is through the Supreme Court and putting people on the court."[32]

During the 2016 presidential primary season, Trump took the unusual step of releasing a list of possible Supreme Court nominees. The presumed purpose was to reassure conservatives in the party base that Trump shared their concern about a Republican president appointing a conservative nominee. Trump added that he would choose from that list and promised Republicans: "I'm not appointing a liberal judge."[33]

To clarify the type of nominee they prefer or oppose, presidential candidates have used current justices as examples of who they would or would not appoint. In 2008, GOP presidential nominee John McCain promised that John Roberts and Samuel Alito "would serve as the models for my own nominees."[34] Barack Obama pointed to Clarence Thomas as someone he would not have nominated.[35]

The Court is featured in convention speeches and even television ads. In 2016, both Democratic presidential nominee Hillary Clinton and Republican presidential nominee Donald Trump referred to Supreme Court nominations in their convention acceptance speeches, with Trump promising to appoint justices "who will uphold our laws and our Constitution" and Clinton vowing to "appoint Supreme Court justices who will get money out of politics and expand voting rights, not restrict them."[36] In 2004, Democratic presidential candidate John Kerry used the Court in a television ad claiming that his opponent, George W. Bush, "will appoint anti-choice, anti-privacy justices. But you can stop him. Help elect John Kerry."[37]

Reporters' questions in presidential debates now regularly include Supreme Court nominations. In 1976, both presidential candidates were asked about their possible Supreme Court appointments. While Ford pointed to his appointment of John Paul Stevens the previous year as a model for future judicial candidates, Carter discussed reform of the process to place more emphasis on merit.[38] In 1988, a reporter on the debate press panel asked George H. W. Bush if he had "a kind of conservative ideological litmus test" for appointing Supreme Court justices.[39] Twelve years later, George W. Bush was asked whether a voter should "assume that all judicial appointments you make to the Supreme Court or any other court . . . will also be pro-life." Bush answered that he did not have a litmus test but only that he would appoint people who would "strictly interpret the Constitution and not use the bench to write social policy." The question for Gore was less pointed and only asked "what kind of appointments should they expect from you?" Gore answered he would not use a litmus test but would appoint people who would "have a philosophy that I think would have it quite likely they would uphold *Roe v. Wade*."[40] Again, in 2004, both candidates were asked whom they would choose to fill a Court vacancy. Bush talked about not appointing someone who would legislate from the bench. John Kerry, however, explicitly mentioned specific issues that would affect his selection—women's rights, abortion, and equal pay.[41]

Even justices have helped make nominations a presidential campaign topic. In 1988, Harry Blackmun mentioned the presidential election in a speech to federal judges when he said the election would be "a very significant one" and the "court could become very conservative into the 21st century."[42] In two 2016 press interviews, Ruth Bader Ginsburg called Republican presidential candidate Donald Trump a "faker" and criticized him for not releasing his tax returns and complained that "the press was very gentle with him on that."[43] To another reporter, she said: "I can't imagine what the country would be—with Donald Trump as our president." She said her late husband, Martin, would have told her that "now it's time for us to move to New Zealand." Ginsburg specifically mentioned the effect of a Trump presidency on the selection of justices who could remain on the Court for many years, when she stated: "For the country, it could be four years. For the court, it could be—I don't even want to contemplate that." After extensive criticism, Ginsburg later issued a statement admitting her remarks were ill-advised, she regretted them, and that "judges should avoid commenting on a candidate for public office."[44]

Blackmun also used an opinion to discuss future Supreme Court nominations in an election year. In a separate opinion in *Planned Parenthood v. Casey* in 1992, he noted that "I cannot remain on this Court forever, and when I do step down, the confirmation process for my successor well may focus on the issue before us today." In response, Antonin Scalia wrote that Blackmun's discussion of abortion and the confirmation process means that justices were really simply imposing their values and that the result will be confirmation hearings that "deteriorate into question-and-answer sessions in which Senators go through a list of their constituents' most favored and most disfavored alleged constitutional rights, and see the nominee's commitment to support or oppose them."[45]

The demands of the party base bump up against the expectations of merit. On one hand, presidents are not supposed to use litmus tests in order to maintain the independence of the judiciary. On the other hand, the base expects just such litmus tests in gauging whether to support a candidate's bid for the nomination as well as his or her campaign during the general election. In 2008, Barack Obama sought to split the difference by explaining that there shouldn't be "a strict litmus test."[46]

The use of code words such as "strict constructionist," "won't legislate from the bench," and won't "allow personal opinion to determine their decisions" have become Republican mantras In 2008, John McCain said that "I certainly would not impose a litmus test," but also said that "someone who supported *Roe v. Wade*" would not meet his qualifications for appointment.[47] Democrats are more explicit in relating that they will use a specific litmus test of support for *Roe v. Wade* and, as John Kerry and Hillary Clinton suggested, other issues such as equal pay, voting rights, and campaign finance.

Commitments made to partisan bases prior to election make it difficult for presidents to reach across the aisle and appoint an opposing partisan today as Franklin Roosevelt, Harry Truman, Dwight Eisenhower, and Richard Nixon were able to do previously. In 1993, Bill Clinton considered nominating Amalya Kearse, an African American female federal US appellate judge. But Democrats objected to Kearse, a Republican, particularly since a Democratic president had not been able to appoint a justice for 25 years. The party activists argued that it was time for a Democratic Supreme Court nominee to join the Court. In 2005, Republican activists opposed the nomination of Harriet Miers, at least partly due to their questioning of whether she was a true conservative. Conservative critics pointed out that she had donated to Democratic presidential candidate Al Gore's campaign in 1988.[48]

The best opportunity for a president to reach across the aisle recently was in 2016 when Barack Obama faced a vacancy as well as a Republican-majority Senate promising not to hold confirmation hearings in a presidential election year. One Republican senator suggested that Obama nominate a Republican senator who would be a consensus choice. Obama did consider appointing Nevada Governor Brian Sandoval, a Republican, who was praised and likely encouraged by Senator Harry Reid (D-NV). However, Sandoval declined to be considered.[49]

But the reaction to such a consensus nomination by Democrats was negative. Then-Democratic presidential candidate Hillary Clinton urged Obama to appoint a "true progressive." One liberal activist group leader said that the appointment of a consensus candidate would be "downright absurd" and would lead the group to oppose the nomination.[50] Liberal Democrats felt betrayed by the prospect of the president nominating a moderate Republican even when he faced a Republican-controlled Senate.

The intensity of partisan interest in the Supreme Court nomination constrains presidential selections. Clearly, when a presidential candidate releases a list of potential nominees and promises to choose one of them, that constraint has reached a new high. However, presidents who have not done that as candidates still must satisfy partisan bases by repeating the campaign themes of appointing certain types of justices once elected president. Moreover, the president needs the party organization and the activists within it to provide the grassroots support for shaping public opinion and affecting Senate confirmation, as will be discussed in greater length in a later chapter.

The Influence of Groups

While the partisan bases are active during campaign years, the groups that represent the ideological extremes of both parties are involved in the nomination processes in and out of election years. Those groups seek influence not just in the Senate confirmation stage but also in presidential selection. They also constrain a modern era president's ability to decide whom to select as a nominee and how to do so.

If such groups, particularly constituent groups, have White House access, they offer names to the White House and seek to be consulted on short lists. In 2009, for example, a half dozen groups asked to meet with White House staff to advocate certain individuals as potential nominees and express their views on those the press said the White House was considering.[51]

If they do not have White House access and are in opposition, their interaction with the White House will be indirect, primarily through the media. From their outsider status, they may signal to a president which nominees they would fight vigorously and which might elicit only tepid opposition. In 1993, a conservative group leader warned the Clinton administration about what would happen if certain types of candidate were nominated in the wake of liberal groups' opposition to Robert Bork and Clarence Thomas: "If Clinton nominates an ideologue, it's payback time."[52]

While presidents may expect opposition groups to make certain demands of the administration in terms of a nominee, they have come to realize that even constituent groups may well go public also. Such groups are seeking to pressure the White House to respond to their demands by exerting public pressure as well as private lobbying. In 1993, NOW president Eleanor Smeal publicly demanded that Clinton appoint a woman to the Court.[53]

That advice can become more pointed and be intended to put the president in a box. If he acquiesces to the groups' demands, then he looks like a puppet for the groups' interests. On the other hand, if he does not follow what the group wants, he may engender the groups' hostility or at least inaction in supporting the nominee. Presidents may be ill-served by both their supporters and their opponents.

Moreover, groups and the White House may have conflicting objectives in the process. The president wants confirmation success. However, the reputations of the groups that are exerting the pressure are not at stake like the president's. Win or lose, these groups will be able to use the nomination process to gain publicity, support, increased membership, and status as either instrumental in gaining a Court seat for a favored candidate or fighting the good fight to prevent an un-favored nominee from securing confirmation. A moderate candidate who does not animate their group one way or the other fails to achieve that purpose.

Constituent groups seek to influence by favoring a particular nominee or type of nominee or by discouraging White House consideration of potential candidates who do not meet the group's favor. In 1994, Hispanic and Asian groups lobbied Bill Clinton to nominate Jose Cabranes, who was a federal district court judge, with the specific intent of urging the president to appoint a justice who would "be a source of great pride to the entire community of people of all races in this nation."[54]

But other groups lobby to discourage the president from a particular nomination. Several groups opposed Stephen Breyer and urged Clinton not to appoint him when he first appeared on the short list in 1993. The chair of the National Association for the Self-Employed told Clinton the group concluded "Breyer's decisions on the Court of Appeals indicate that he is strongly against enforcement of the antitrust laws and small business. Placing such an individual on the Supreme Court would not be in the country's best interest."[55] A representative of the Automotive Service Association wrote to Clinton that Breyer was opposed to small business and had a judicial philosophy "about how the economy should work which closely mirrors that favored by Justice Scalia."[56]

Since groups represent particular narrow interests, they concentrate on that particular agenda in attempting to influence presidential decision making. Pro-choice groups were unhappy with Ruth Bader Ginsburg because she found fault with the reasoning, although not the outcome, of *Roe v. Wade*. They lobbied against Ginsburg because of a recent lecture she had given that questioned the breadth of the Court's 1973 decision.[57]

New York Times columnist and former Supreme Court correspondent Anthony Lewis wondered about the effect of such demands by groups for complete agreement with the group's position on a particular issue. Lewis asked: "What kind of Supreme Court would we have if a president allowed interest groups to veto possible nominees on such narrow grounds? It would be a court of people with their minds irrevocably made up: a court of lobbyists, not judges."[58]

Groups' involvement at this stage may impact the extent of their role in the confirmation process. This is true both in the process and in the outcome. There was a time when groups would accept a presidential nominee and support the president's choice. However, those days are gone. A significant turning point was the Souter nomination. When George H. W. Bush took only five days to make a decision to appoint David Souter, conservative groups were not pleased. Souter was not on their short list of potential conservative judges. They knew little about him. One group leader called Souter's nomination "something of a 'thud' for conservatives."[59] Conservatives were unwilling to perform the same supportive role when George W. Bush made a similar choice of a virtually unknown candidate (Harriet Miers) and received immediate criticism from conservative groups.

Presidents no longer can make decisions within a matter of a few days since groups expect an open process that allows them to publicly vet candidates, whether they are supportive or in the opposition, and to do so privately if they are constituent groups supporting the administration. They expect to play a role in the presidential selection process and their willingness to provide presidential support may hinge on that expectation.

Indeed, one reason groups can be influential is the element of time. When presidents decide quickly and the Senate acts in a matter of days, as was true for most of the nominations in the traditional process, there is little time for groups, particularly those in opposition, to mobilize in response to a nomination. In the presidential selection process, time allows groups to perform the functions of suggesting nominees, vetting prospects, and lobbying the White House in behalf of (or in opposition to) certain candidates.

The White House is keenly aware that the more time the president spends in the decision-making process, the more likely it is that groups will seek to influence the president's selection decision through both internal and external means. After David Souter's nomination was decided in less than 72 hours, a senior George H. W. Bush administration official explained that the speed of selection was intended to maintain White House control of the process: "The President saw immediately that he needed to move quickly. Otherwise, the interest groups were going to take control of the debate, narrow his options, and make confirmation more difficult."[60]

Presidents today, typically, decide in more elongated fashion rather than seeking to truncate the process as George H. W. Bush did. Instead of seeking to avoid a group role, they are more likely to use it to determine confirmability. When short lists of potential nominees are circulated internally to constituent groups and externally to other groups, those in the opposition can potentially provide the administration with a gauge of how a nominee might fare in the nomination process. Clearly, time is a factor in group involvement in presidential selection, and one that presidents themselves provide.

The Role of the Media

The retirement or death of a Supreme Court justice is always breaking news on cable news networks and circulates through websites and social media with rapid speed. At that point, the White House faces a press corps anxious for information about not only who is on the short list but also when a decision will be made. A publicly announced vacancy on the Supreme Court means a months-long news story for the president, including not only short lists, interviews, and an announcement, but also a lengthy Senate confirmation process. The president plays a major role in the first stage of that process, as well as an important secondary one in the confirmation stage.

There are times, even in an age of media saturation of some news events, when the White House still can conduct some if not all of the presidential selection process in secret. That occurs when a justice offers advance notice to the White House that a retirement is pending. Due to Warren Burger's secret announcement to the White House that he was resigning in 1986, the whole process of selecting a successor, and a successor to the successor, was conducted outside public scrutiny. A similar case arose for Bill Clinton when Harry Blackmun made an informal comment to Clinton, who was the incoming president, that Blackmun might retire in the coming months.[61]

More recently, the Obama administration was tipped off early in 2009 that David Souter was retiring. In late February or early March, Souter asked a former clerk to inform the White House that he planned to leave the Court. Souter also wanted to work with the White House on when the best time was for him to announce his retirement.[62] According to Greg Craig, White House counsel, administration officials were concerned about other appointments getting under way first: "We told Justice Souter's intermediary that we would like to delay the announcement until April/May because we were hopeful we would get as many other judges confirmed as possible during these early months and we were concerned that if everybody knew there was going to be a Supreme Court nomination during the summer, it might put a freeze on the Judiciary Committee."[63] Since Souter did not announce until April 30, the White House had several weeks to consider a replacement before external players were informed.

The luxury of such notice is the ability to conduct an initial search without press or group involvement. Lists can be circulated internally, vetting can be done secretly, and initial interviews can be conducted privately. There is no pressure from the White House press corps concerning the timetable for decision making or the release of short lists.

Typically, the president cannot avoid public scrutiny of the process. Reporters want short lists so they can undertake some research on those potential nominees. Also, they need to be able to report other players' reactions to that list. This is particularly true for interest groups, who often are willing to express opinions and even approach reporters themselves to acquire press coverage for their reactions.

Press attention to the process does mean the administration can use the media for its own purposes. One means is to leak short lists in order to glean reactions from groups, individuals, and senators. When Bruce Babbitt was publicly considered by Bill Clinton in 1993, environmental groups reacted negatively because they wanted Babbitt to stay in his job as head of the Interior Department.[64]

The release of the name of a federal appellate judge in Little Rock as a potential Supreme Court nominee in 1971 prompted Winthrop Rockefeller, Arkansas governor at that time, to communicate to the White House that the judge was "an avid redneck segregationist." Also that year, when Senator Robert Byrd (D-WV) was discussed as a possible nominee, Republican senators signaled their near unanimous opposition to Byrd on the grounds of "economic populism" as well as his lack of legal experience.[65]

Others can use the media as well, particularly senators. Early in the selection process, the president does communicate with some key senators, such as senior members of the Senate Judiciary Committee and party leaders, to get their views on potential nominees, but the vast majority of senators are not accorded such treatment. Yet they may still seek to influence the process. In the traditional process, they might do so through a letter to the president. But in the modern process, they also may attempt to influence the presidential process by utilizing press coverage to publicly advise the president on what type of nominee would or would not make it through confirmation.

Indeed, in 2016, Republican senators went a major step further by recommending to the president, through the press, that he not make any nomination at all. Senator Mitch McConnell (R-KY) urged Barack Obama to forgo a selection process and simply allow the next president to choose the nominee. Other Republican senators did the same, even refusing to meet with any nominee in a courtesy call.[66]

Opposition senators are more common users of the public route because they typically lack access to the president. They may use the press to suggest names. For example, in 2016, Senator Lindsey Graham (R-SC) urged Obama to nominate Senator Orrin Hatch (R-UT) for the vacancy caused by the unexpected death of Justice Scalia. (Hatch quickly dismissed the suggestion, saying that "I'm not sure I would want to be appointed and to have all the Democrats praying that I'd die real soon after.")[67]

Or they may make public statements opposing a particular potential nominee. In 1987, Senator Byrd publicly warned the Reagan administration that a Bork nomination would run into trouble in the Senate. However, the White House nominated Bork the next day and Byrd's warning became prescient.[68] Similarly, in 1993, Senator Hatch appeared on television talk shows signaling his opposition to the possible appointment of Interior Secretary Bruce Babbitt. Hatch charged that Babbitt was too much a politician to serve on the Court. President Clinton initially was strongly considering Babbitt but ultimately did not appoint him.[69]

The means for announcing the nominee also has been altered in the modern era. No longer does this occur through a press release or even just the formal nomination document sent to the Senate. The release of the name is accompanied by a ceremony featuring invited guests drawn from senators, administration officials, and constituent interest group representatives. The announcement is televised live. As will be discussed in a later chapter, presidents do not want to miss the opportunity to shape first impressions of the nominee.

Handling Pressures

Modern presidents have taken one of two approaches to Supreme Court selection.[70] One is the constituency approach, which seeks to satisfy the party base and associated interest groups. This approach results in a nominee who meets the litmus tests imposed by party leaders, party activists, and issue leaders. This type of nominee may fit Bruce Ackerman's category of a "leader" nominee who has identified himself or herself with intellectual views on questions of constitutional law. In contrast to the "solid professional" who has worked as a technician in various aspects of law as a prominent official in the American Bar Association, an attorney general or solicitor general, or an appellate judge.[71]

Interest groups supportive of the White House, as well as party activists, favor this type of appointment because the prospects are high that the desired goal of policy direction will be met by the new justice. Several presidents have taken the constituency approach, at least for some of their nominees. Richard Nixon adopted this approach when he nominated Clement Haynsworth and G. Harrold Carswell, both of whom matched Nixon's desire to satisfy conservative Republicans and southern Democrats. Ronald Reagan's nominations of William Rehnquist, Antonin Scalia, Robert Bork, and Douglas Ginsburg also fit in this category.

Groups suggest such candidates to the White House—both privately and publicly—as "dream" candidates for the group's interests. During recent Republican administrations, conservative groups have pressed for candidates who have solid conservative records on the federal bench that the groups like. During Democratic administrations, popular candidates among liberal groups have included judges, politicians, or academics who were viewed as intellectual counterweights to conservatives.

The second avenue for selection of a nominee is the consensual approach. Presidents seeking consensus and easy confirmation will choose a nominee who will receive broad-based bipartisan support because they lack a controversial record or easy appeal to a particular ideological base. George H. W. Bush's choice of David Souter was an example, someone who had a scant record on issues important to party bases or constituent groups. Another was Clinton's pick of Stephen Breyer, who had previously served as chief counsel on the Senate Judiciary Committee and was well regarded by senators in both parties. Breyer had developed a favorable rapport with Senate Republicans. Indeed, Breyer had been confirmed as a federal appellate judge when Senate Republicans, slated to take over the majority, easily could have blocked his confirmation vote.

Constituency does not necessarily mean a close vote margin, nor does consensus necessarily equate to near unanimity. Scalia's nomination sailed through the Senate partly because opponents' ire had already been spent over William Rehnquist's successful chief justice confirmation process. Additionally, Scalia's role as the first Italian American on the Court dampened the efforts of opponents to scuttle the nomination because they did not want to upset Italian Americans in their states who saw Scalia as an ethnic symbol. Senators noted Scalia's Italian roots and mentioned their own connection with Italian Americans.[72] Conversely, Sonia Sotomayor was a consensus choice in 2009. Yet she still received 31 opposition votes because the time of bipartisan support had disappeared.

Deciding which approach to use typically depends on the political factors facing the president. A popular president may attempt the constituency approach because there is sufficient political capital and a ripe political environment to push through a potentially controversial nominee. Indeed, in such a situation, constituent groups and party bases anticipate that the president will use the opportunity to make an appointment that satisfies them.

Yet even with those advantages, presidents may still make consensual rather than constituency choices. When Bill Clinton nominated Stephen Breyer, his poll numbers were not high but Democrats did control the Senate. Similarly, Barack Obama was criticized for not being bolder given his advantages of relatively high public approval and the fact Democrats controlled 60 seats—a filibuster-proof majority—in the Senate. Sotomayor was considered a consensual choice because her first judicial appointment was made by President George H. W. Bush and her confirmation as an appellate judge in 1998 had been approved by 25 Republicans.[73]

In both cases, Clinton and Obama may have viewed Supreme Court confirmation processes as potential diversions from their legislative agendas. Also, in both cases, the primary legislative initiative was health care reform. In Clinton's case, the memories of the Bork and Thomas nominations, featuring elongated processes that weakened their respective nominators, were still fresh.

On the other hand, presidents still must deal with the pressure to acquiesce to those who want a philosophical debate. That view was epitomized by a Republican strategist when Harriet Miers was nominated; he wrote that "a good, heated debate over striking 'under God' from the pledge, the merits of governments taking property from individual A to give to individual B, the validity of basing court decisions on foreign law, and, of course, abortion on demand is not something we should shy away from."[74]

Vetting the Candidates

At one time, vetting was a process of determining whether a potential nominee had a significantly distinguished background, possessed some judicial experience (although the lack of it was not a detriment), and was well regarded in the legal community. Particularly as the pool began to include primarily federal judges, the vetting process included previous opinions. Several presidents, such as Truman, Kennedy, and Johnson, believed they already knew their nominees well enough. Moreover, scrutiny to uncover past problems for the nominee was unlikely. The Hugo Black case discussed earlier was an anomaly in terms of media investigation of a nominee. The media would not investigate, nor were groups organized to conduct research and gain publicity for such examinations of a nominee.

In the modern process, vetting has become a more complicated process. It is essential to avoid problems that could arise during the confirmation process. Unlike in the traditional process, groups and journalists will scour candidate backgrounds for past mistakes. Opponents will publicize the nominee's problems and undercut the chances for confirmation with doubts about the candidate's suitability due to his or her background.

That explains the lengths to which vetting goes today to handle potential problems before they become public. Information about prospective nominees collected by the administration now includes financial background, personal relationships, previous writings and speeches, and past professional and personal activities. The expansion of the process has come from the necessity to avoid surprises.

Confirmation stage surprises have doomed nominees. One example was the financial arrangement featuring private donors paying for a stipend for Abe Fortas to teach classes at American University, news of which emerged during Fortas's confirmation process for chief justice in 1968 and helped mobilize opposition to the nomination.[75] In other cases, the surprise could have scuttled a nomination. In 1971, the Nixon administration did little to vet William Rehnquist. Had they done so, they might have discovered the claim of Rehnquist's involvement in the discouragement of African American voters in the 1968 election in Phoenix, Arizona. The issue was raised in his 1971 confirmation hearing, but since Rehnquist denied the accusation it did not become a factor in confirmation that year.[76]

Vetting begins with the creation of files on potential nominees. White House aides do not assume they know enough about a nominee from personal acquaintance or because of the person's extensive public service. The administration wants to know everything possible about potential candidates on the public record first. Names on presidential short lists are accompanied by files that include background information, writings, texts of speeches, opinions, and other information. According to Greg Craig, White House counsel in the Obama administration, his office examined articles written, speeches delivered, and quotes published in newspaper stories, along with opinions rendered, in the case of a judge.[77]

These files may include past controversies involving the candidate, statements made by others (particularly opposition senators) about the nominee during previous confirmation processes (likely a federal appellate judgeship), possible controversial writings or opinions, and positions on critical issues that may arise as the confirmation proceedings unfold. The file also may offer confirmability assessments. All of this information is intended to shorten the list to include only candidates who can be considered seriously by the president.

For example, the short list the White House Counsel's Office created for the Warren Burger retirement in 1986 included a file on Robert Bork. The information included biographical data such as his birthdate, educational background, military service, health status, religion, and party affiliation. The file also described Bork's position on critical issues such as federalism, separation of powers, and economics. It also offered a confirmability analysis including the statement that "liberals respect Bork's intellectual force" and that he was considered a leading thinker. The file also suggested that Bork was "more likely to be confirmed by even a Democratic Senate because he is 'much older and less radical than some of the other alternatives'" and that he was considered to be "about as liberal a nominee as the Democrats believe they will get from President Reagan." But the report also concluded that "some of these factors . . . could suggest he would not be the most aggressive conservative who could be named to the Supreme Court."[78]

The next year, a similar file was created for Douglas Ginsburg. He was described to the president as "young, extremely intelligent and able" and "generally perceived as a judge in the mold of Justice Scalia and Judge Bork." The potential controversies involving Ginsburg that the administration should consider included a short-lived row with Congressman John Dingell when the Justice Department destroyed papers regarding a proposed sale of Conrail, and possible emphasis in the confirmation hearings on Justice Department policies while Ginsburg was an assistant attorney general. The president learned that Ginsburg was praised by both Senators John Kerry (D-MA) and Edward Kennedy (D-MA) during his confirmation hearings as possessing "the highest possible degree of qualifications," and was "willing to consider views which he has not himself held."[79]

Vetting Practices

The first administration to implement extensive vetting procedures for Supreme Court nominees was the Nixon White House. In the process of handling the two nominations that were occurring in 1971, and in the wake of the two failed confirmations of 1969 and 1970 related to inadequate vetting, a White House aide suggested that White House staff meet with possible nominees for extended interviews lasting potentially several hours rather than relying on casual conversations or FBI investigations. These interviews were intended to consist of "questioning and probing into every facet of his professional life, personal life, trips, businesses, etc."[80]

The Nixon administration implemented this plan. Two White House aides met at least two potential nominees—one for four and a half hours and the other for nine hours. They delivered lengthy reports to John D. Ehrlichman, White House counsel and head of the vetting team, and Attorney General John Mitchell. These reports detailed biographies, judicial philosophy, health, hobbies, travel, club memberships, potential financial issues, religious affiliation, and the nominee's assessment of potential group support and opposition.[81]

The aides began by asking questions from a questionnaire that has been duplicated by subsequent administrations to determine potential problems with a nominee during the confirmation process. The vetting team wanted to know the nominee's positions on issues such as civil rights, right of privacy, First Amendment, federalism, and other topics. But the questionnaire dealt primarily with personal issues, including how much the nominee was worth and how that money was acquired and whether there were any financial or ethical conflicts of interest. Questions included the nominee's relationships with immediate family, any embarrassing family connections, any extramarital affairs, abortions, or illegitimate children. Also asked were questions of whether the nominee or any family member had ever undergone psychiatric analysis, whether the nominee gambled and how often, what the nominee's religious views were (and had been in the past), and how much the nominee drank.[82]

Subsequent administrations have adopted the interview and questionnaire approach to vet potential nominees. The Reagan administration developed a form with a list of 31 personal questions such as these: Have you ever been audited by the IRS? Have you ever taken any actions or not taken any actions that could be construed, even mistakenly, as racist or sexist? Have you ever owned property that contained restrictive covenants prohibiting resale to individuals on the basis of their race, religion, or national origin? Have you ever been associated with a political party other than the two major parties? Can you think of anyone who has any reason or is likely to oppose your confirmation? Is there anything in your personal life that could embarrass you, your family, or the president? The last question was asked twice in differing forms.[83]

The interviews conducted through the questionnaire also explore domestic issues that might become controversial, as well as medical conditions that could undermine the case for the nominee. In 1993, Bill Clinton was told by a doctor that Richard Arnold's cancer could be an obstacle to his service on the Supreme

Court, and, in 2009, the Obama administration considered Sotomayor's dia-
betes and asked doctors how that condition would affect her service on the
Court.[84]

Even these practices are not foolproof. The nominee may not be forthcoming
about past problems that might dissuade the president from extending a nomination. G. Harrold Carswell never mentioned that he had made racist statements
in speeches. And Douglas Ginsburg did not reveal his marijuana smoking while
a Harvard law professor.

The forms are accompanied by independent staff investigation. In 1987, a
member of the Reagan judicial nominee confirmation team raised questions
about Anthony Kennedy's lobbying experience. He suggested the vetters find
out whether Kennedy had paid for golf trips or vacations for legislators, paid a
campaign contribution in cash, or hired legislators as lobbyists after they had
left the legislature.[85] Similarly, the Clinton White House prepared a report on
Stephen Breyer's activities as chief counsel of the Senate Judiciary Committee,
reviewing his role in each of the major legislative issues facing the committee
during his tenure.[86]

The objective of vetting is to become aware of problems before others do and,
if the nominee is selected, create responses to them that will defuse the issue.
According to Greg Craig, Obama's White House counsel during the Sotomayor
nomination process, all nominees have something that can be used by opponents. The goal is not to find the candidate who cannot be challenged by adver-
saries. Rather, it is to assess how much the particular candidate's problems will
affect confirmability, that is, lose votes in the Senate.[87]

The staff probe does not replace the Federal Bureau of Investigation's own
research. The FBI's role began by the 1950s, perhaps in the wake of the anti-
communism campaigns of the late 1940s and early 1950s. During the 1950s,
John M. Harlan II, William Brennan, and Potter Stewart went through an FBI
security clearance requested by the administration.[88] The chairman of the Senate
Judiciary Committee requested the FBI to conduct an investigation of Earl
Warren after he was nominated for chief justice.[89]

Yet even FBI investigations were not so thorough at first. In 1970, the FBI
investigation of G. Harrold Carswell did not uncover the fact that Carswell was
a known homosexual in the Tallahassee area where he lived. Had that been
disclosed to Nixon at the time, it is doubtful that Carswell would have been
nominated.[90]

The FBI conducts background investigations before a presidential announcement or immediately after. The FBI interviewed Anthony Kennedy for 10 hours
and reviewed prior confirmation questionnaires as well as financial disclosure
forms. They also looked into his law practice and lobbying. After his nomination
but prior to his confirmation, the FBI completed a full-field investigation.[91]

At first, the vetting was sporadic. The Nixon administration vetted Mildred Lillie and Herschel Friday, two potential nominees Nixon wanted to nominate to fill the vacancies left by John M. Harlan II and Hugo Black in the fall of 1971. However, they did little vetting of William Rehnquist who actually became the nominee.

Today, such investigations are routine. White House staff complete the questionnaires as they conduct interviews of potential nominees to screen out potential problems. These interviews also may examine a candidate's views on various issues that could become controversial. Often, the candidate's weakness may be fatal. For example, White House Counsel John Dean discovered that one potential nominee in 1971 had little background in constitutional law and had almost no views on legal issues of the day. The potential nominee told Dean: "John, you're going to have to tell me what to say when I'm asked about these things." Dean's report gave Nixon pause, and eventually, the candidate was not nominated.[92] Bill Clinton wanted to appoint Richard Arnold, a federal appellate judge in Little Rock who had befriended Clinton years before. However, Arnold's health problems eventually dissuaded Clinton.[93]

The interview process today includes presidential interviews of those at the very top of the president's short list. Interviewing, however, is not a recent phenomenon. Potter Stewart was interviewed by President Dwight Eisenhower in 1959 for about two hours.[94] But such interviews were the exception rather than the rule. John F. Kennedy and Lyndon Johnson already knew their nominees personally, which made interviews unnecessary.

However, the cronyism charge, which accompanied nominees like Abe Fortas and Homer Thornberry whom the president knew personally, signaled to presidents that close relationships would be accorded great scrutiny and could doom a nominee. That consideration affected Bill Clinton's consideration of Richard Arnold.[95] It did not deter George W. Bush in naming Harriet Miers. But the raising of the issue and her eventual withdrawal underscored the importance of avoiding the accusation of cronyism in Supreme Court appointments.

Still, the practice of presidential interviews came gradually. Richard Nixon did not interview Clement Haynsworth or G. Harrold Carswell prior to their nominations. He did interview Harry Blackmun, but he had only a phone conversation with Lewis Powell and never spoke with William Rehnquist at all.[96] Bill Clinton interviewed Stephen Breyer and Ruth Bader Ginsburg in 1993 before choosing Ginsburg that year. President Donald Trump interviewed three federal appellate judges—William Pryor, Neil Gorsuch, and Thomas Hardiman—in January 2017 before choosing Gorsuch a few days later.[97]

The substance of the interview varies as well. Potter Stewart said that Eisenhower did not ask him about his opinions on cases that might come before the Court. Instead the president was sizing him up, asking him questions about his wife, his college years, and his war record.[98] Similarly, Clinton was doing the same with Breyer and Ginsburg in 1993. The interview with Breyer did not go well. Breyer was recovering from surgery due to a bicycle accident. Nevertheless, Clinton was not impressed with him, which encouraged the president to keep looking.[99]

Indeed, presidents and their staffs must be careful what they ask nominees today. The Senate Judiciary Committee questionnaire that nominees complete in preparation for the hearings specifically inquires whether the nominee was asked questions by administration officials, including the president, before being nominated, and what kinds of questions were asked that might commit the nominee as justice. Therefore, the president and aides cannot ask litmus test questions such as how a candidate would rule in a certain case without the potential that the nominee will reveal the fact that such questions were asked.

In 1987, the White House Counsel's Office gave President Reagan a set of talking points for his interview with Anthony Kennedy. They included specific questions Reagan should pose to Kennedy. Reagan was told to ask Kennedy "if there was anything in your background that might create problems for you if you were nominated to the Supreme Court" and whether there was "any reason why you might not want to go through a confirmation process at this time." Specifically missing from the list was any mention of specific issues, such as abortion, or of Kennedy's views on any cases. Perhaps worried that Reagan would go too far in the interview, the White House counsel "recommended that you do not offer the nomination to Judge Kennedy at this time, since the preliminary background checking being done by the Federal Bureau of Investigation will not be finished until tomorrow morning."[100]

Similarly, the White House Counsel's Office prepped Bill Clinton for his interview with Stephen Breyer in 1993 by telling him what questions he should and should not ask and what to expect from Breyer in response. Suggested questions for Breyer included these: "What guides your overall constitutional philosophy? How do you define the scope of liberty in the Constitution? Why have you devoted your career to the dry subject of economic regulation?"[101] What Clinton actually asked was between Clinton and Breyer, but whatever was asked of Breyer, he was able to answer that he had not been asked for commitments.

The Vetting Team

In an earlier day, the vetting was done by one or two individuals. Herbert Brownell, Eisenhower's first attorney general, simply maintained a file of prospective nominees and passed his recommendations on to Eisenhower.[102] When the first Court vacancy occurred in the Kennedy administration in 1962, the president asked Ted Sorensen to draw up a short list of 19 potential nominees through consultation with others. Sorensen provided basic information such as age, party affiliation, and current position.[103] But Sorensen also handicapped the possible nominees. He urged the president to make his first appointment to the court one that would be "hailed by all for his judicial mien—not known primarily as a politician—not subject to confirmation delays because of controversial associations."[104]

As mentioned above, the Nixon administration began to devote more resources to the vetting task than previous administrations had. They set up a team of individuals, primarily from various departments in the White House and headed by White House Counsel John Ehrlichman. The team handled the various facets of selecting a nominee as well as confirmation. These included preparing a Congressional relations plan to handle interactions with members of Congress, a press announcement plan, the cultivation of group support, and interviews with potential nominees.[105]

The Clinton administration prepared a confidential memo outlining how to vet potential nominees. The process included recruiting an outside team to read each of the nominee's legal opinions, as well as each en banc opinion the candidate joined, along with every published writing and oral statement such as Congressional testimony at a previous confirmation hearing. This team was to provide a report on hot button issues such as abortion, death penalty, gay rights, and obscenity. It also should provide a description of the potential areas of controversy for a nominee, how the candidate's thinking had evolved over time, and what the candidate's position seemed to be on these issues.

The outside team was assembled under the direction of James Hamilton, a Washington attorney. The team consisted of 75 lawyers who read 3,000 opinions and over 5,000 writings of potential nominees.[106] This group offered the Clinton White House external assessments of potential nominees' records. The conclusions of these attorneys about Ginsburg and Breyer were based on analyses of their written opinions and off-the-bench writings.[107] The team also was responsible for creating a vote analysis to determine whether the nominee, if a federal judge, was consistently voting with appointees from previous Democratic administrations or had a pattern of voting with conservatives.[108]

Even with vetting teams, the nominating decision still rests with the president. Presidents potentially receive large quantities of information and rely on vetting teams to head off problems that may occur during the confirmation process, but the president is still responsible for making an ultimate selection. How presidents do that varies. Richard Nixon kept his decision making exclusive, largely including only his attorney general and close friend, John Mitchell, and, to some extent, John Ehrlichman. Similarly, George H. W. Bush's decision making included a small group of advisers.[109] Yet, Clinton's was broad-based.

Selection Criteria

In the modern process, presidents still must announce merit as their main criterion for selection—both before and after a nominee announcement. Shortly after the death of Antonin Scalia in February 2016, Barack Obama promised that his nominee would be "indisputably qualified" to sit on the Supreme Court.[110] That statement is not dissimilar to earlier presidents' insistence that they were most interested in a candidate's merit. In a letter to his brother, who had criticized his pending appointment of Earl Warren, Dwight Eisenhower replied: "I get a bit weary of having the word 'political' used with respect to such decisions. These appointments get my long and earnest study, and I am not trying to please anybody politically."[111]

In speaking to the general public, presidents also must avoid the implication that they made their decision based on ideology, particularly the use of a specific litmus test such as abortion. In 1990, President George H. W. Bush said that in choosing David Souter, his selection process "was not geared simply to one legal issue; it is not appropriate in choosing a Supreme Court Justice to use any 'litmus test.'"[112]

To the extent that ideology is discussed, the nominee must be able to be portrayed as centrist and holding bipartisan appeal. The Reagan administration sought to portray Robert Bork as someone in the mold of Lewis Powell to suggest that Bork would maintain the current balance of power between liberals and conservatives. Bork's long record as an ideological conservative made that effort difficult.[113] More successfully, the White House's announcement of Ruth Bader Ginsburg repeated her role as a centrist. In announcing Ginsburg's nomination, Bill Clinton called her a consensus-builder, a healer, and a moderate.[114] The White House's image-making efforts on Ginsburg stuck with the press. Newspaper editorials praised Ginsburg and emphasized her centrism. The *Rocky Mountain News* (Denver) titled its editorial "Ginsburg: Signs of a Centrist." The *Houston Chronicle* said she had "essentially moderate views," while the *Miami Herald* opined that "her judicial career reveals an innate centrism."[115] The White House wanted a confirmation that would not be a battle. The reaction from the press corresponded to that aim. Press reports termed Ginsburg "safe." One editorial said "it is hard to get excited about President Clinton's choice of Ruth Bader Ginsburg." Another concluded that "the president has really displeased no group."[116]

The need for centrist appeal is particularly acute when the opposition controls the Senate. However, even when the president's party controls the Senate, the centrist image is important in avoiding the potential of a filibuster or at least obstructionism that necessitates the expenditure of additional political capital by the president. The importance of the symbol of bipartisanship is so important that Barack Obama even used it in 2009 when nominating Sonia Sotomayor, even though he did have a filibuster-proof Senate. Obama made a point of noting that Sotomayor had been appointed a district judge by George H. W. Bush and urged the Senate to act "in a bipartisan fashion" to confirm her quickly.[117]

At the same time, the president wants to signal to constituent groups that the nomination satisfies their interests. Richard Nixon did so by stressing the "strict constructionist" nature of the appointee's views. Similarly, in announcing his nominees, George W. Bush said that Samuel Alito "has a deep understanding of the proper role of judges in our society" and that John Roberts "will strictly apply the Constitution and laws, and not legislate from the bench."[118]

One new criterion for the modern era is the emphasis on a nominee who understands Americans generally. One example is the search for non-judges as potential nominees. Two recent presidents—Clinton and Obama—have attempted to appoint politicians without judicial experience. Clinton reached out to New York Governor Mario Cuomo, Senate Majority Leader George Mitchell, and Secretary of Interior Bruce Babbitt. The first two declined and Clinton received negative reaction from Republicans on Babbitt.[119] Clinton found that gaining confirmation of a politician was problematic. Opposition was voiced for a politician such as Bruce Babbitt, Mario Cuomo, or George Mitchell; a non-national figure without previous political experience was a safer bet for confirmation.[120]

Barack Obama also started with such a goal. According to Greg Craig, White House counsel, Obama "did not want to necessarily draw on the ordinary pool of candidates that had always produced Supreme Court justices, you know, right off the circuit courts. He was very much in favor of having a nominee who had real life experience in terms of something other than being a judge."[121] Obama did succeed in appointing a non-judge, Elena Kagan. Although not a judge, Kagan's background was almost exclusively legal as a law school professor and dean and solicitor general. However, had Obama selected one of the politicians he was considering, such as Janet Napolitano, at that time secretary of homeland security, or Jennifer Granholm, governor of Michigan, confirmation may have been more difficult.

Even without the non-judge background, presidents have sought nominees they could describe as having connections with the American people. Bill Clinton mentioned that Ginsburg had the "heart and spirit, the talent and discipline, the knowledge, common sense, and wisdom to translate the hopes of the American people . . . into an enduring body of constitutional law."[122] Similarly, Barack Obama explained that Sotomayor was his choice because she had more than intellect; she also had a "practical understanding of how the law works in the everyday lives of the American people."[123]

The inability to portray a potential nominee as understanding of the concerns of ordinary people may be detrimental to a candidate's chance of being nominated. The perception that Stephen Breyer was not empathetic enough may have been one reason Clinton moved away from appointing him in 1993. The outside reviewers of Breyer's file wrote a memorandum to the head of the team, Jim Hamilton, which concluded that Breyer's writings are "the workings of a mind that struggles so hard to analyze every problem he is considering within a framework bounded by economic theory or rules of logic that the result seems devoid of emotion and even—though this surely stretches the point too far—humanity."[124]

Conclusion

Presidential selection is the more closed and insular stage of the Supreme Court nomination process. Of the two stages, one might assume this stage would be immune from outside pressure. For most of the history of the nomination process, that was the case. Presidents made decisions about nominations in the midst of lobbying by elites. But external players performed only limited roles.

Presidential selection in the modern process is affected by various forces that can shape confirmation. Those forces are more potent than they were in the 19th century or early 20th century because presidential success generally is tied more closely to them. External players affect the president's success today much more so than in that period. Not just elites are interested in the process, but so are millions of party activists and members of interest groups seeking to influence the process to achieve their goals. The White House cannot ignore them; indeed, the president needs them to carry the process through confirmation.

The vetting process no longer is an insular exercise. Groups have found avenues of access to the president—either directly or indirectly. Media coverage keeps an interested public clued in on presidential selection. Nor is it, typically, a quick process that can be accomplished in a matter of days. The risk of group and party rejection of the nominee is too high for that.

The selection process has been altered by the inclusion of external players. Presidents must consider how groups, their own party bases, the media, and public opinion will respond to the nominee. The administration cannot skimp on the vetting process since group and media scrutiny will fill in the gaps missed by the White House.

The more public part of the process is the Senate confirmation stage. In that stage, the effects of the changes characteristic of the modern process are even more apparent. That is the topic of the next chapter.

The Changing Role of the Senate

Introduction

On April 11, 1962, Senator James O. Eastland, chair of the Senate Judiciary Committee, called to order the committee to initiate hearings on the nomination of Byron White to the US Supreme Court. Eastland announced that the blue slips of the two senators from White's home state, Colorado, had been returned (meaning they approved of White's confirmation) and then told the committee he had letters from the American Bar Association and the Colorado Bar Association regarding the nomination and their desire to send representatives to testify. Then, Eastland turned to the audience and asked, "First, does anyone present here desire to oppose this nomination." There was silence.[1]

Such a scene would be unimaginable today. If White were nominated in the present climate, his confirmation would be opposed by a number of interest groups, perhaps on both the right and the left. Moreover, it is likely that a significant number of opposition party senators would vote against confirmation, as has occurred with most of the recent nominees to the Court.

Nor was White's confirmation hearing unusual. When Arthur Goldberg testified before the Senate Judiciary Committee in his own October 1962 confirmation hearing, Senator Everett Dirksen, the Senate minority leader, used his interaction with the nominee to ask no questions. However, he did praise Goldberg as "one of the ablest lawyers in the country," "impeccably fair at all times," and someone who could because of "his competence, his ability, and his fairness completely dissociate himself and render an impartial judgment as a Justice of the Supreme Court."[2] And Senator Barry Goldwater (R-AZ), a possible Republican presidential nominee in 1964, wrote to Kennedy to tell him that "your choice of Goldberg is an excellent one."[3]

The modern Senate confirmation process does not look like that. This chapter describes what it does look like—far more partisan, far more contentious, and far more democratic than the elite-driven processes of the past. This chapter explains how democratization has shaped the Senate's handling of Supreme Court nominations today.

The Constitution states that the president appoints with the "advice and consent" of the Senate. As discussed earlier, what it does not say is how that occurs. Nor does it specify that the Senate must act on a nominee at all. Is the Senate required to hold hearings, debate, and vote on a nominee?

This issue arose in 2016 when the Senate failed to act on the nomination of Merrick Garland to succeed Antonin Scalia. Partisanship defined the contours of the debate: Democrats argued that the Senate had an obligation to act while Republicans claimed it did not.

The Senate has failed to act on a nominee before, but, short of an actual withdrawal of a candidate, such inaction had not occurred before Garland since the 19th century. That one exception was the nomination of John M. Harlan II. The nomination occurred in November 1954 and a special session of the Senate held after the election declined to act on the nomination. Dwight Eisenhower re-nominated Harlan for the next session of Congress and he was confirmed.[4]

The Garland case suggests that the Senate's "advice and consent" can include not deliberating at all. The president has no leverage to force the Senate to act. Barack Obama attempted to use public opinion to pressure senators to act, but public opinion was split—again along party lines. The party base of Senate Republicans approved of no action by the Senate.[5]

Presidents can use recess appointments to fill positions on the Supreme Court, particularly when the Senate does not act. Dwight Eisenhower did that in the 1950s. He appointed Earl Warren, William Brennan, and Potter Stewart to recess appointments. In each case, confirmation came later.

Recess appointments bring their own sets of problems, however. A major one is the possibility of an acting associate justice considering his or her opinions in light of a pending confirmation hearing. The *Washington Post* editorialized on the Judiciary Committee's delay in acting on the nomination of Potter Stewart in 1959. The newspaper called the current situation "unhealthy" because Stewart's decisions were under scrutiny by the Senate, which could, according to the *Post*, "sharp-shoot at any opinions he may write instead of considering only his previous record and qualifications."[6]

But the Supreme Court itself has made such recess appointments more difficult to carry out since it has agreed that the Senate has power over determining when the Senate is and is not in recess.[7] (In order to avoid recess appointments, the Senate has adopted the process of rarely adjourning.) As a result, Barack Obama was not able to use a recess appointment in the Garland case in the way that Dwight Eisenhower or earlier presidents were.

With rare exceptions, Senate deliberation does mean acting on a nomination. But what the Senate does in the modern era is still strongly connected to which party controls the White House and the Senate. The prospect of defeat at the hands of an opposition Senate was less common through most of the history of the US Congress than it is today. Presidents today are far more likely to face an opposition party–controlled Senate and the prospect of defeat of a nominee. Of the presidents since 1969, all but one (Carter) have experienced some period of opposition party control. Of those, five (Nixon, Ford, Reagan, Bush I, and Obama) made Supreme Court appointments during that period of split party control.

The effects of opposition party control are more significant today than they were 50 years ago. Two political scientists writing in 1972 noted that "groups normally not associated with the President's party are unlikely to be influential in opposing the nomination unless they can provide substantial evidence demonstrating either the candidate's complete lack of qualifications or his adherence to views unacceptable to either political party."[8] That is no longer the case.

Today, the opposition can be influential, if not in blocking a nomination, at least in mobilizing opposition and making a confirmation costly for the administration to wage. The partisanship of the caucuses has divided the Senate in a way that makes broad consensus in the confirmation process more difficult to achieve. Both parties have determined to make confirmation a partisan exercise.

In 2001, most of the current Democratic senators met to create a unified strategy on Bush administration nominees. They heard two Democratic legal scholars—Cass Sunstein of the University of Chicago and Laurence Tribe of Harvard—lecture them on the importance of blocking Bush administration nominees because conservatives were planning to pack the courts. (The advice was not new. Even before the Bork nomination, Tribe had urged senators to be more aggressive in questioning nominees about their ideology.)[9] In response, Democratic leaders urged senators to be unified by not offering quick endorsements of Bush administration nominees.[10] One Republican staffer argued that the Democrats "used Larry Tribe's [book] *God Save This Honorable Court* as their blueprint, and they followed it to a T."[11]

Similarly, Republicans have coalesced around a position opposing Democratic nominees. While nearly all Republican senators voted for Ruth Bader Ginsburg in 1993 and Stephen Breyer in 1994, only a handful voted for Sonia Sotomayor in 2009 or Elena Kagan in 2010.[12] The Senate Republican Caucus largely united in its approach to a Democratic president's Supreme Court nominees. In 2016, the caucus agreed not to act on Merrick Garland's nomination and remained united through that session of Congress.[13]

Senate Deliberation

The Senate's deliberation today is fraught with partisan conflict, coupled with pressures from groups, the media, and the party base. Throughout the process, these players are seeking to affect senators' actions and ultimate votes. The steps in this stage are undertaken by senators with the roles of external players in mind.

The first stage of the Senate's deliberative process in the modern era is the custom of courtesy calls. The White House schedules visits with senators who want to meet with the nominee. Typically, at some point in the weeks prior to hearings, the nominee visits the offices of the majority of senators, representing both parties. Senate party leaders, as well as senior Judiciary Committee members tend to be scheduled first. Even some House members, particularly those on the House Judiciary Committee, are scheduled.

These courtesy calls may be in private with only the nominee and the senator present, although it is more likely the senator will invite staff from the White House as well as the senator's own aides to participate. The home state senator who recommended the nominee, or at least supports the nominee's confirmation, often accompanies the nominee on some of the courtesy calls.

The senator may use the opportunity to ask difficult questions of the nominee, particularly if the senator is likely to oppose, or to prepare the nominee for the hearings, particularly if the senator is a supporter. For example, Senator Joe Biden, chair of the Senate Judiciary Committee at the time, told then-nominee Anthony Kennedy in their courtesy call meeting that he should prepare to discuss the Fifth, Ninth, and Fourteenth Amendments to the Constitution, as well as gender discrimination, equal protection, the right of privacy, the role of Congress, and the one house legislative veto case that the Court had decided four years earlier.[14]

While courtesy calls initially included the members of the Judiciary Committee, they have expanded to include any senator who wishes to meet the nominee. Indeed, for senators not on the Judiciary Committee, this will be the only opportunity to interact with the nominee. Robert Bork made 48 courtesy calls. But Samuel Alito made more than 80 such calls, while Elena Kagan did 89.[15]

Courtesy calls are not just meet-and-greet occasions. They serve important interests of the senator, particularly with media. Courtesy calls allow senators to get some publicity with the newest celebrity in town—a Supreme Court nominee. The press covers the nominee as he or she enters or leaves a senator's office. In addition, the senator may speak to the press afterward about the nominee. Reporters may even be invited in to the office to provide images of the two talking. One senator asked that his courtesy call with Samuel Alito take place on the Capitol steps so the news media could see them looking over at the Supreme Court building while they spoke.[16]

Senators issue press releases and write op-eds regarding their visits with the nominee. For example, Senator Jeff Merkley (D-OR) issued a press statement saying he was the 50th senator to meet with Garland. On the day of Senator Orrin

Hatch's (R-UT) courtesy call with Garland, an op-ed appeared in a local newspaper by Hatch explaining that although he had met Garland, he would not be urging the Senate to take action. The op-ed was intended to reassure Republican constituents that Hatch was not defecting from the united Republican rejection of action on the nomination.[17]

The Judiciary Committee and the Senate

In the modern era, the most prominent and influential aspect of Senate deliberation is the work of the Judiciary Committee. As discussed earlier, the committee has gradually acquired that role. It now jealously guards it, since the visibility of the Judiciary Committee's actions is much higher today than it was 50 years ago.

The Senate does not use the Judiciary Committee as a means for rejecting a nomination, as it does the Judiciary and other committees as a resting place for most of the bills that are introduced in Congress. But the Judiciary Committee does play a role in influencing the final Senate vote. The committee's recommendation is a strong predictor of full Senate confirmation.

In its early years, the committee merely reported the nomination without making any statement about the nominee. However, by 1870, it began to offer a recommendation along with its report. Over 140 years, the committee has favorably recommended in 75 cases. All but six were confirmed. The committee's unfavorable recommendation similarly was predictive of difficulty with the full Senate. Of the seven forwarded to the Senate with an unfavorable recommendation, only two were subsequently confirmed.[18]

Pre-Hearing Preparation

The Senate Judiciary Committee has acquired a critical role in vetting a nominee, and undertaking the task of scrutinizing that the Senate feels compelled to do in the modern era. That vetting process commences as soon as the president announces a nominee. The Judiciary Committee begins collecting information about the nominee's background and views immediately. The Senate Judiciary Committee undertakes an FBI background check of each nominee. When this process began is unknown, although it was undertaken as early as 1954 when Senator William Langer (R-ND), Senate Judiciary Committee chair, requested the US attorney general to conduct an FBI background report of the nominee.[19] The results of the background check are made available to the chair and ranking member of the committee and some of their staff, but these are not widely circulated among the committee members and staff.[20]

Senators' staff, particularly the staff of the chair and the ranking member on the committee, also begin the process of collecting information about the nominee. Committee staff members research public information about the nominee, including opinions, writings, speeches, official actions, and other data. Some of this is done immediately after the president's announcement in order to give the senator something to say to the press about the nominee.

The chair also sends the nominee a lengthy questionnaire the committee has prepared in order to obtain information that may not be publicly available or that the committee may miss otherwise. The questions explore past employment, organizational memberships, and financial activities. In addition, nominees are expected to locate texts of their speeches and transcripts of statements and writings and make these available.[21] In response to the questionnaire he received, David Souter asked the Harvard College Library to send him a copy of a thesis he wrote while an undergraduate at Harvard 30 years earlier.[22] These questionnaires can be more than 200 pages long.[23] The nominees dedicate significant amounts of time to collecting relevant data and then responding to the queries.

But full completion of the questionnaire is expected by the nominee. Failure to take the questionnaire seriously can be considered an insult to the Senate. In 2005, Harriet Miers treated the questionnaire lightly, answering questions inadequately and offending senators.[24]

The questionnaire is developed by the Judiciary Committee chair, but it consists largely of the same questions time after time regardless of who the chair is or which party is in control. Occasionally, some more ideologically loaded questions are inserted by a chair of one party and removed by another. One question inserted by Strom Thurmond (R-SC), while he chaired the committee, asked about the nominee's views on judicial activism, but Patrick Leahy (D-VT) removed it when he became chair.[25]

Nor is the single questionnaire the end of the written correspondence with the nominee by members of the committee. The Senate Judiciary Committee may create supplemental questionnaires. In the case of Robert Bork, the committee developed a set of questions specifically related to Bork's background, such as whether he had considering recusing himself from any cases while a federal appellate judge and what the circumstances were of each instance, how much time he consulted while teaching and how much he charged for such consulting as well as the most significant consulting cases he had.[26]

In addition, senators pose individual questions to the nominees. These can be members of the Judiciary Committee or any other senator. These questions may follow up on the questionnaire or address other issues that the senators believe are relevant to their decision making regarding the nominee. They also may come to the nominee at any time before or after the hearings. They can concern cases the nominee has been involved with in the past, activities mentioned in the answers to the questionnaire, and positions on various issues. They also may relate to potentially controversial aspects of the nominee's background. These have included membership in various groups. For example, Ruth Bader Ginsburg answered questions about membership in a country club that had changed its by-laws to exclude a black judge.[27]

But they also may consist of questions about the nominee's personal views. Senator Robert Byrd (D-WV) asked Clarence Thomas whether he considered a line-item veto constitutional, and if so, "please cite the authority under which you conclude that." He also asked that Thomas respond to him within four days.[28]

Or they may seek background information to discern the nominee's views. Senator Howard Metzenbaum used his courtesy call with David Souter to glean information about Souter's charitable giving. In response, Souter sent Metzenbaum a list of the 24 organizations Souter had donated to in the previous 18 months, although not the amounts of the donations. The list contained no political or controversial organizations, but did show that, in addition to his own alma mater, his professional associations, and various museums, Souter gave to the United Way, his church's hurricane relief fund, the Shaker Village, and the Appalachian Mountain Club. Similarly, Senator Carl Levin (D-MI) asked Souter in a letter "which two U.S. presidents and Supreme Court justices of the last fifty years do you most admire and why?"[29]

The Senate Judiciary Committee also probes into the selection stage itself by posing questions to the White House. The Committee asks the White House to release to them all communications between the nominee and the White House or the Justice Department relating to the nominee's "views on any case, issue, or subject that could come before the United States Supreme Court." In addition, they wish to have documents that put any questions to the nominee in relation to his or her consideration for the Court.[30]

The questionnaire, and the multitude of questions that may precede from its contents, suggest a Senate that is attempting to take the "advice and consent" role much more seriously than in the traditional process. Even when the Senate was not a rubber stamp of presidential will in the 19th century, it did not undertake this level of scrutiny of a nominee. The questionnaire is a sign that in a more transparent process than occurred previously, the Senate wants to be viewed by the public as meticulous in the performance of its duty. Even if it ultimately confirms nominees, it still seeks a public image of due diligence in the process.

That image reinforces the press angle that the Senate is doing its duty. In an age of ideology, it allows the Senate to direct press attention to activity that appears to be examining the nominee's qualifications for serving rather than senators merely supporting or opposing on partisan or ideological grounds. Additionally, that kind of activity reinforces the message to opposition groups (particularly from opposition senators) that senators in opposition are working to determine the past actions and decisions that will undermine the administration's case for the nominee.

The Hearings

Not only has the process become more deliberate, but it also has become more public. As discussed earlier, the Senate Judiciary Committee gradually moved toward greater transparency in its proceedings, particularly in the hearings it holds on Supreme Court nominations. During the transition period when hearings occurred some of the time but had not become routine, some senators were wary of them. When a senator suggested that Hugo Black's nomination be tabled and referred back to the Senate Judiciary Committee for public hearings, another senator strongly opposed the proposal. Denouncing the idea of public hearings, he explained that "hearings are for the information of the committee, not for the purpose of public amusement; not to have a legislative rodeo so that everybody may come in and have a good time."[31]

Such sentiments, even if shared privately by senators, would not be expressed today. The expectations of groups, the media, and the public are that hearings are open to the public and will be televised live, and that these players, particularly groups, will have roles to play in the process. The hearings are the premier public event of the confirmation process. They constitute the showdown between the Senate and the nominee, and, by extension, the president.

Senators know this, but they also know the White House and the nominee understand this as well. They are aware that the nominee is sitting through extensive mock questioning sessions, termed "murder boards," that have been arranged by the White House or the Justice Department to prepare him or her for the sessions with Judiciary Committee members. In 2010, Elena Kagan participated in mock hearings with approximately 20 people asking her questions that she might anticipate from senators. John Roberts reportedly endured a dozen such sessions in preparation for his chief justice hearings in 2005.[32]

Senators know the nominee is provided with briefing materials on a range of topics likely to be raised by senators, including potential answers to senators' questions. They are aware that nominees typically spend many hours poring over those materials to help them prepare answers for questions on a variety of topics and cases. And that confirmation consultants—both within and outside the administration—are being called in to assist in confirmation preparation.

One such consultant for Republican administrations was Tom Korologos, who primarily advised nominees for executive branch appointments, but he also assisted in Supreme Court nominations. Senators know that nominees receive advice from people like Korologos on how to act in front of the committee.

Korologos even devised a set of commandments for nominees that included advice such as, "Model yourself after a bridegroom at a wedding. Be on time, stay out of the way, and keep your mouth shut." Korologos also suggested, "Between your nomination and confirmation, give no speeches, write no letters, make no public appearances," and "follow the 80–20 rule. If the senators are talking 80 percent of the time and you're talking 20, you're winning. If it's 50–50, you're losing."[33]

Senators and nominees have found ways to ask and answer questions in front of cameras. Since groups, the media, and the public are watching, it is not a surprise that questions have become more contentious. Interestingly, according to Dion Farganis and Justin Wedeking, the nature of the answers nominees provide has not changed post-Bork. They found that since the 1950s, when their study begins, Supreme Court nominees have been just as forthcoming recently as they were in the past. They do find that answers to specific types of questions have changed. The nominee's candor has diminished as the questions have moved toward civil liberties and civil rights. These include questions on controversial issues such as abortion, same-sex marriage, and affirmative action.[34] Those types of question, however, are the ones that are of greatest interest to most external players. To groups, such questions indicate whether the nominee supports or opposes the groups' positions.

Senators' attempts to discover nominee's views on issues are fraught with difficulty. One is the interpretation of the question and the answer. John Paul Stevens once described his ability to redefine answers. He said that at his confirmation hearings in 1975, "practically everyone asked me if I believed in judicial restraint, and I always said 'I did—and I do.'" Yet, Stevens explained, "I'm not sure it means the same thing to me as it does to others."[35]

Nominees have little interest in speaking beyond what is essential to get confirmed. They do not want to appear craven in answering questions that would satisfy senators' (and groups') demands at the moment while appearing to commit themselves to specific positions while on the Court. Any willingness to express views about current and future issues robs them of the perception of impartiality in deciding future cases.

Ruth Bader Ginsburg articulated this dilemma in 1993 when she explained to the Judiciary Committee in her opening statement specifically what she would and would not answer. She said it would be improper for her to "preview in this legislative chamber how I would cast my vote on questions the Supreme Court may be called upon to decide. Were I to rehearse here what I would say and how I would reason on such questions, I would act injudiciously." Ginsburg went on to say that "a judge sworn to decide impartially can offer no forecasts, no hints, for that would show not only disregard for the specifics of the particular case, it would display disdain for the entire judicial process."[36]

Ginsburg was willing to address those issues she had discussed in previous writings, such as abortion. But she was unwilling to move beyond those previous statements to predict how she would rule in particular cases or even to take positions on issues she had not spoken or written about previously. Her articulation of the lines she had drawn in testifying was called the "Ginsburg Rule." However, Ginsburg was not the first nominee to set boundaries on what he or she would say. Since the beginning of regularized hearings, nominees have declined to answer questions on the grounds that they may be predetermining their votes on cases.

The change in approach to questioning has had dramatic consequences. Where senators at one point were reticent to ask such questions, now they do so regularly. And through the repetition of the question (sometimes across multiple senators) and the willingness to vote on whether questions are answered, it appears that senators today expect the nominee to answer the question. It may not be enough for the senator to ask (and to do so aggressively); the senator is expected to solicit an answer from the nominee.

This practice has spurred a debate over whether such questions are appropriate. Scholars and commenters have urged the Senate not to ask specific questions about what a nominee would do once on the Court. Ronald Rotunda argues that while asking an executive branch appointee about policy views makes sense because they do make policy, a judge is different because his or her job is to apply legal principles.[37] Former White House Counsel Lloyd Cutler stressed that "the mystery of its future actions" is critical to the Court's role. If a nominee commits his or her vote to the president or the Senate "we will no longer trust them as our ultimate authority on the Constitution's meaning."[38]

Nevertheless, senators continue to probe in a variety of ways with limited success. A nominee's avoidance of explicit answers extends to personal written correspondence by the nominee with individual senators. Senator Carl Levin (D-MI) asked David Souter in written correspondence whether he believed that marital status affected an individual's privacy rights. Souter responded that since the issue "will probably come before the Supreme Court in the near future," he would decline to answer the question.[39]

Senators act frustrated with the lack of candor on the part of nominees, although it is difficult to believe they are surprised. They have even threatened not to vote for confirmation on that basis alone. Senator Arlen Specter (R-PA) suggested that rejection of a nominee simply based on lack of responsiveness to senators' questions may be the "only way to establish the appropriate balance that will allow the Senate to perform its constitutional duty to advise and consent."[40] However, it is likely that for most senators the avoidance of questions is part of the theatre. And the senator's expression of frustration is particularly for the benefit of groups and party activists who expect as much from an opposing senator.

The willingness on the part of senators to even ask questions is fairly new. Prior to the 1980s, questions emanated primarily from opposing party senators. (One notable exception was the questioning by southern Democrats of Kennedy and Johnson appointees in the 1960s.) Since the 1980s, there has been a partisan balance in the questioning. Half the questioning comes from senators of the president's party. [41] The hearings have increased in length due to the expanding number of questions from members of the committee. While committee hearings in the 1950s and 1960s consisted of fewer than 100 questions, the Roberts, Alito, Sotomayor, and Kagan hearings included up to 700 senatorial questions.[42]

Why do senators of the president's party ask questions if they intend to support the nominee, which they nearly always do? According to a Republican Judiciary Committee staffer, there are two types of question the nominee's supporters ask. One is the softball question that gives nominees "an opportunity to shine" by discussing personal experiences, their areas of knowledge, or their general views. Another is the "rehab" question that allows that nominee to recover from a potentially damaging exchange with an opposition senator. An example is when a senator rephrases a negative question from an opposition senator in a more favorable light for the nominee and then asks the nominee to answer that question. Senator Lindsey Graham (R-SC) did that in 2006 with Samuel Alito when he gave Alito the opportunity to explain that he was not a racist, as Graham believed Democratic senators had implied in their questioning.[43]

These types of question allow the nominee some respite from the aggressive questioning of opponents. The White House even preps senators on how to help "rehabilitate" a nominee if he or she stumbles on a question and needs to be rescued by a friendlier interlocutor.[44] Supportive senators, with the aid of the White House, provide cover for the nominee. Such support is critical when the public is watching because the supporters' tactics may offer a mixed view of the nominee to the public rather than the critical view that would be provided if questioning was handed over to the opponents.

Supporters go to great lengths to offer softball questions on behalf of the nominee. While asking about a terrorist incident on Christmas Day the previous year, Graham, the rare Republican supporter of Elena Kagan, asked where she was that day. At first, Kagan did not understand what he meant. But then Graham persisted and she answered that "like all Jews, I was probably at a Chinese restaurant." Graham asked, "You were with your family on Christmas Day at a Chinese restaurant?" She responded, "Yes, sir." Graham replied: "Ok. That's great. That's what Hanukkah and Christmas is all about."[45]

The questions, particularly from supporters, can be nearly irrelevant to the process at hand. Senator Herbert Kohl (D-WI) asked Ruth Bader Ginsburg what she thought were the "major problems and challenges that face our society." He also asked her what books she had on her shelf and which types of books she liked more—fiction or non-fiction.[46] Samuel Alito was asked these questions by Republican senators:

> "Judge Alito, you know the salary that a Federal judge makes, is that right? Do you think you can live on that?"
>
> "Did you enjoy your time in the ROTC and in the Army afterward?"
>
> "I heard a report yesterday that the ROTC building on the Princeton campus was actually firebombed at about the same time that American servicemen of college age were fighting in Vietnam? Is that accurate? Was anybody injured?"[47]

While Sonia Sotomayor got these from Democrats:

> "First, am I correct you share my love for America's pastime?"
>
> "What was the one case in 'Perry Mason' that Burger won?"
>
> "What would you like history to say about you when all is said and done?"[48]

The Filibuster

One of the most significant changes in the Senate's deliberative process is the use or threat of use of the filibuster. Filibusters in Supreme Court confirmations were unheard of prior to 1968. Today, filibusters are now real potential tools an opposition can attempt to use to defeat a nominee.

Historically, the filibuster is known as a tool for blocking policy bills. The purposes of filibustering vary, but the use of filibuster for that purpose has dramatically increased in the past half century.[49] The filibuster was unknown in the first 40 years of the Senate's history. Its use became more common in the late 1800s but still was not a tactic used for judicial nominations. It was not until 1917 that the Senate felt the problem of filibustering was acute enough to institute a cloture rule. Between 1917 and 1970, cloture was successfully invoked on only eight occasions.[50]

In the midst of the Congressional reforms of the 1970s, the required vote for cloture was lowered from 67 to 60 senators, although changes to the rules still required a two-thirds vote.[51] The current 60 vote requirement dates only to 1975.[52] Yet that change has not reduced the number of filibusters. Indeed, filibusters have increased.[53]

The filibuster of Abe Fortas in 1968 began the use of the filibuster as a minority weapon in Supreme Court nominations. Republicans and southern Democrats lacked the votes to block Fortas's confirmation. But supporters of Fortas's nomination also lacked the votes to invoke cloture and end the filibuster. A combination of Republicans and southern Democrats combined to defeat cloture and continue the Republicans' filibuster, leading to Fortas's withdrawal.[54]

The debate over the use of the filibuster hinged on whether it was appropriate to filibuster a Supreme Court nomination. A group of legal scholars and administrators and prominent attorneys organized to express opposition to the use of the filibuster. Their joint statement decried the use of the filibuster arguing that "its use to frustrate a judicial appointment creates a dangerous precedent with important implications for the very structure of our government."[55]

Many Democratic senators, not from the South, were unhappy with the use of this new tactic but realized that it could be a double-edged sword. Three other filibusters have been attempted since the Fortas vote in 1968, all by Democrats. The first occurred against William Rehnquist in 1971. A cloture vote to limit debate failed, but the Senate ended debate anyway and confirmed Rehnquist that same day.[56] A similar attempt in 1986, when Rehnquist was nominated for chief justice, was thwarted. This time, nominee supporters mustered a two-thirds majority for a successful cloture vote. Again, in 2006, a filibuster was attempted, this time against Samuel Alito. The filibuster was a half-hearted affair started by Senator John Kerry (D-MA) while he was in Europe. It never achieved much support and three-fourths of senators supported a cloture vote to cut off debate and proceed with a vote on confirmation. Even 19 Democratic senators supported cloture, particularly those from states where Republicans might use a vote on a filibuster motion against them in the next election.[57]

The filibuster is a tool used when the White House and the Senate majority are in the same hands. The reality of divided government through the 1970s made the filibuster largely unnecessary. With the subsequent election of Richard Nixon in 1968, Senate Democrats could use a majority to block Nixon nominees, which they did in two cases.[58] The filibuster was not necessary in other periods of divided control—1987, 1990, 1991, and 2016—because the opposition could employ its majority status to block nominations.

Nevertheless, the use of the filibuster in the Fortas confirmation battle now became part of the culture. Filibusters of Supreme Court nominations were not off the table as an option for a disgruntled minority, as has been indicated by its occasional use. Moreover, filibusters have become common at lower levels of judicial selection. An increase in filibusters for lower court judicial nominations prompted widespread concerns that the Senate was bogging down consideration of judicial appointments. According to Richard S. Beth and Betsy Palmer, filibusters and cloture votes became increasingly common following the Fortas nomination. Cloture on judicial nominations was invoked five times between 1967 and 1992, but 18 times from 1993 to 2008. In one case, the appellate court nomination of Miguel Estrada in 2003, the Senate went through seven cloture votes before Estrada eventually withdrew.[59] Ten of President George W. Bush's nominees for federal appellate judgeships were withdrawn after failed cloture votes.[60] Both parties have employed the filibuster to block lower court judicial nominees over the past 25 years.

In 2005, Senate Majority Leader Bill Frist proposed what became known as the "nuclear" option. His proposal would have changed the rules to decrease the number of necessary votes to invoke cloture with each succeeding cloture vote until only a simple majority was necessary. Frist's proposal was never voted on by the Senate, but it did raise the question of whether the majority would seek to limit the power of the minority to filibuster nominations, including those for Supreme Court justices.[61]

There are other variants of the nuclear option, but all are similar in the intended result of changing the rules of the Senate without requiring a two-thirds vote of the body. That would mean a simple majority would alter the rules and damage the ability of the minority to block that change. Filibusters would be more difficult for a minority to sustain.

Whether the nuclear option is consistent with Senate tradition or a deviation has been a matter of academic debate. To stave off Frist's use of the nuclear option, a group of 14 Democratic and Republican senators, commonly known as the "Gang of 14," agreed to step in and prevent a filibuster or the nuclear option if either was employed against judicial nominees. Their mutual agreement was to block filibusters of judicial nominations except under extraordinary circumstances. Exactly what those circumstances might be varied from senator to senator, although some interpreted those circumstances as not including ideology.[62]

During the Obama administration, the Gang of 14 broke down through retirement or electoral defeat. Those who remained in the Senate were willing to invoke "extraordinary circumstances." For example, three Republican senators who upheld a filibuster of an Obama judicial nominee for an appellate position justified their positions on the grounds that the nominee was an ideologue.[63]

In 2013, the Democrats enacted a rule that would require a simple majority of 51 senators rather than a cloture vote–majority of 60 to approve judicial and executive nominations. However, Supreme Court nominations were purposely excluded from the new rule, which would still allow filibusters to take place on those nominations. But when the Republicans regained the Senate majority in 2015, they considered expanding the simple majority rule to include Supreme Court nominees as well.[64]

Democratic Pressures on the Senate

The Senate's institutional deliberation today has changed due to external pressures that have come from players not involved in the traditional process. Those pressures are similar to the ones placed on the White House. They include the influence of party, groups, and the media. Moreover, the public also plays a role in this process due to the higher level of transparency in the Senate confirmation stage. We will take each of these forces in turn.

Party

When the Senate confirmation process was less public—no televised Judiciary Committee hearings (or no hearings at all), limited Senate debate, and a quick resolution—the reaction from the party base was muted. Without encouragement from groups and information from the media, most had little idea what was going on in the process. Like the White House, senators today are subject to external pressures from the party bases who become an attentive public seeking senatorial support for their positions. A senator's party base can place pressure on senators to vote with the rest of the party on Supreme Court nominations. Since confirmation votes are high-profile votes, and they are important to party activists who interpret them in ideological terms, senators today cannot easily avoid the consequences of voting against the party as they might have in the 1950s.

In 1968, the two senators from Mississippi were worried that Mississippi's governor, who was a strong critic of the Warren Court, would run against one of them in the Democratic primary. Indeed, the governor reportedly already had privately threatened to do that. Also in 1968, a White House aide warned one of the aides responsible for the Fortas nomination that both senators "are liable to run scared, and will show this by their actions on the Fortas nomination."[65] And a senator from North Carolina related that "his state Democratic party had started telling him he could not participate in the local [party] rallies . . . unless he stated to them that he would not support Fortas."[66]

The problem has become more acute today. The number of senators willing to defect from the rest of their party on a nominee has dwindled as party pressures have enhanced. In 2006, only one Republican voted against Samuel Alito—Lincoln Chafee (R-RI). Chafee expected that Olympia Snowe (R-ME) would vote against Alito as well. However, Snowe explained to Chafee that she would be voting for Alito because the state Republican Party was fielding a challenger to Snowe in the Republican primary. Snowe worried that she would have to spend too much of her campaign war chest fending off an intraparty challenge, and that challenge would encourage a stronger candidate in the general election.[67] The vote on Alito, Snowe was saying, was one of the few votes Snowe would cast that Republicans in her state would pay close attention to.

Even in swing states where a senator's vote margin in a general election typically is thin, the party constituency remains a potent force in shaping approaches to nominations. For example, in 2016, some Republican senators from swing states met with Merrick Garland in courtesy calls, but they did not deviate from the party line on not holding hearings or a vote on the nominee in 2016.[68]

More than votes may be at stake. Senators increasingly are expected to cast a vote for ideological reasons to satisfy a party base that demands such a rationale. Public statements by senators that conform to partisan expectations are more likely to ward off potential challengers in primary elections and secure party base support back home.

Ideology as an explanation for a vote once was considered a rarity. Indeed, there was a sense on the part of some senators that the checking power was only to be used in extreme circumstances anyway. One senator said: "I will support that nominee [the president proposes] unless something develops that shows him to be a real scoundrel."[69] In such cases, ideology did not matter.

Over time, ideological rhetoric has become more common, more acceptable, and even more expected. Occasional rhetoric that a candidate is radical or out of the mainstream did not begin with Robert Bork. When Felix Frankfurter was nominated in 1939, one member of Congress concluded that "he could not conceive of a worse appointment" and that the president "might as well have appointed Earl Browder."[70] At that time, Browder was the head of the Communist Party in the United States.

It was not liberals who first raised ideology as a justification for opposition. Conservatives and southern Democrats led the way publicly by their use of ideology as a gauge for opposing Supreme Court nominees in the 1950s and 1960s, including John M. Harlan II, Potter Stewart, Thurgood Marshall, and Abe Fortas. These senators queried nominees on ties to Communists and their views on racial desegregation, law and order, and social liberalism.

By the late 1960s and early 1970s, however, liberal Democrats had turned the tables and spearheaded ideological opposition, particularly to G. Harrold Carswell and William Rehnquist in the Nixon administration and, in the 1980s, Rehnquist again (as chief justice nominee). Now, ideological expressions are nearly expected of senators by party activists and interest groups. Activists want senators to support or oppose nominees for the same reasons they do. Granted, even prior to the open expression of ideology as a factor, senators were more likely to vote for a nominee who agreed with their policy positions than one who did not.[71] Yet those were not commonly expressed as the reasons for a vote.

But an actual defense of such behavior is characteristic of the modern era. Senator Arlen Specter (R-PA) articulated a changed Senate view of ideology when, in an op-ed, he explained that while he did not believe that a nominee should discuss particular pending cases, that doesn't mean the nominee, who at some time has expressed opinions on issues, should not "state some of these positions, in order to give us an idea of who they are."[72]

That approach conforms to what the party base anticipates from senators of their party today. It is what partisan donors, activists, and even rank-and-file partisans want to hear from home state senators of their party. And failure to provide it may be fatal to re-election prospects in primary elections.

Groups

Immediately after Barack Obama nominated Judge Merrick Garland to the Supreme Court on March 16, 2016, groups began mobilizing to affect the outcome of the confirmation fight. Groups on the right decried the prospect that an Obama appointee might replace the conservative icon Antonin Scalia and undo Scalia's nearly 30-year record of conservative votes on high-profile issues. Groups on the left viewed this vacancy as an opportunity to tip the balance of the Court solidly to the left with a five-justice liberal bloc.

While large coalitions of groups have formed at times to block nominees, the divide has become more stark. In the Garland case, groups on the left and the right were united in their coalition efforts in the sense that both viewed the appointment as potentially seismic. One liberal group leader described "an incredibly diverse and deep coalition of organizations that have left their institutional egos at the door and have come together for the purpose of advancing a unified goal."[73]

However, more was at stake than a nomination—the existence or at least status of the groups on either side. Even if groups lose the battle, they can still win if they see an increase in donations as well as new members. They also can become viewed as players in judicial selection generally, which will enhance their leverage with administrations as vetters of future nominees, as well as with senators who fear the power of the groups. In addition, they gain media coverage, which feeds the perception of power.

In an era of democratization, and the media tools to implement it, groups can utilize a Supreme Court nomination to actively engage their bases in the cause. Through encouragement to donate money, send emails, make phone calls, write and circulate social media posts, and directly lobby senators as well as the media, groups can channel their members' energies toward the groups' goals. Such efforts, even when dedicated to a losing cause, can signal the groups' value to members and gain continued material support for the groups' goals.

It is easy for the general public, particularly people living in swing states, to perceive a Supreme Court nomination as a battle between competing interest groups. Groups are the most vocal in the press. They are the ones mobilizing the grass roots to weigh in on the nominee with their senators. And they are the ones running advertisements either pro or con.

The Legal Community as Interest Group

One group that does none of those things but nevertheless is highly influential in the Senate confirmation process is the American Bar Association. Its involvement is, in a sense, a throwback to the past of the elite legal community performing the most important outsider role in the process. However, it is how the ABA's rating is used by other external players that matters in their role in the confirmation process.

Even in a political body such as the US Senate, merit has been an important public criterion in decision making. Nominees who are considered well qualified historically have been more difficult for opponents to vote against. Conversely, less-qualified candidates have been open to senatorial opposition on that basis alone. The ABA rating has become the most important gauge of merit and has impacted how senators react to nominees. As Epstein and Segal concluded, since 1953, nominees considered "very qualified" by the ABA have received significantly larger vote margins than those who are only moderately qualified or those who are considered unqualified to serve on the Supreme Court.[74]

The ABA categorization can empower or weaken opponents. However, since 1991, the ABA has given its highest rating to all nominees, reducing the effectiveness of the "merit" argument for senators. Opponents of a nominee with a rating of "well qualified" needed to resort to other measures such as judicial temperament and philosophy or insensitivity.

What the ABA says is powerful because senators typically do not want to be viewed as voting for a nominee perceived as being undeserving of a Supreme Court seat. One exception was Senator Roman Hruska (R-NE), who became famous for an offhand remark he made during the Carswell nomination that mediocre people deserve representation on the Court: "Even if he were mediocre," Hruska explained, "there are a lot of mediocre judges and people and lawyers, and they are entitled to a little representation, aren't they? We can't have all Brandeises, Frankfurters, and Cardozos."[75] However, more senators are like Senator Thomas Eagleton (D-MO), who distanced himself from Carswell because he considered him "a jurist of the most pedestrian and distressingly mediocre talents and with a remarkable proclivity for being reversed by higher courts."[76]

Others can use the ABA as cover to support or oppose a nominee, or to urge others to do the same. In opposing Carswell in 1970, Eagleton quoted prominent legal scholars who urged Senate rejection.[77] In 2016, the ABA rating of "well qualified" for Merrick Garland spurred the White House to, once again, urge the Senate to act on Garland's nomination.[78]

Groups also incorporate the ABA's rating if it corresponds with their position. When the ABA rated Clarence Thomas as "qualified" rather than "well qualified," opposition groups pointed to the rating as a sign of Thomas's mediocrity and unfitness for the job. The head of People for the American Way described the rating as "a direct contradiction of President Bush's assertion that Clarence Thomas is the best man for the job. His peers in the legal community regard him as anything but." And the president of the Women's Legal Defense Fund called Thomas the wrong man for the job.[79]

However, the ABA's role today is controversial, and when Republican presidents have been in office it has been limited to the confirmation stage. Some presidents, like Richard Nixon, Ronald Reagan, and George W. Bush, have concluded the ABA was biased in its assessment of nominees. Scholars have found some basis for these claims.[80] Ronald Reagan changed the process to include the ABA only in the period between the announcement and the formal nomination to the Senate. George H. W. Bush continued that narrower role. Bill Clinton restored the ABA's previous status as a factor in pre-selection. The formal review of the actual nominee still occurred following presidential announcement. The George W. Bush administration declined to grant the ABA a special status in the presidential selection process—either before or after the nominee announcement. The Obama administration, however, reinstated the ABA's pre-nomination role.[81]

The contrast between Democratic and Republican administrations suggests that the ABA's role is now viewed as politicized. The ABA committee is expected to "not take into account the nominee's philosophy, political affiliation, or ideology."[82] The review by the Standing Committee on the Judiciary is designed to focus on the professional competence, integrity, and temperament of the nominee.[83] However, divisions over some nominations have led to questions over those standards. While there was some discrepancy in the Thomas nomination with the majority of the ABA committee supporting a "qualified" rating and two favoring "not qualified," the greater controversy came in the Bork nomination where four of the committee voted "not qualified" while the majority believed the nominee to be "well qualified." And in 2016, the ABA president stepped into the controversy over whether Garland's nomination should be considered by the Senate in an election year by urging the Senate to act on Garland's nomination "with all deliberate speed."[84]

Other legal groups beyond the American Bar Association also weigh in on nominees. These include national legal organizations such as the National Association of Black Lawyers and the Hispanic National Bar Association, as well as state and local bar associations. Additionally, various ad hoc legal groups form in order to influence the nomination. These include groups of lawyers or judges or law clerks. In 1968, a group called the Lawyers Committee on Supreme Court Nominations, which claimed to include seven former presidents of the American Bar Association and 20 law school deans, formed to express its opposition to the filibuster of Abe Fortas's confirmation.[85] Even individual lawyers feel the need to express support or opposition, particularly those from the nominee's state. These are likely the products of orchestrated efforts by lawyers within a state and/or friends and associates of the nominee.

Political Groups

Many more groups involved in Senate confirmations today are not "legal" groups. These include various professional associations, trade associations, and labor organizations. Most are established groups while some are ad hoc organizations formed specifically to support or oppose the nominee. Even churches have become involved. In 1991, the United Church of Christ General Synod voted to oppose Clarence Thomas's confirmation. In 1987, the National Council of Churches opposed Robert Bork and even submitted a letter to the Senate Judiciary Committee regarding his nomination.[86]

Support or opposition by these groups tends to hinge on the same kinds of rhetoric that dominate group action regarding legislation or executive branch appointments. The Urban Coalition Action Council considered G. Harrold Carswell's nomination "offensive to the basic concept of equal justice" and the National Education Association called Carswell's ascension to the Court "a gratuitous insult to black Americans."[87] The American Association of University Women opposed Clarence Thomas because they considered him "hostile to the economic survival of working women" and to the rights of individuals. They specifically mentioned that while chair of the Equal Employment Opportunity Commission (EEOC), Thomas had "failed to investigate over 13,000 age discrimination cases, many involving pension claims by older women." The National Women's Political Caucus also noted Thomas's refusal "to enforce laws to protect women and the elderly" and his "insensitivity to the human needs of others."[88]

When a nominee is announced, groups mobilize into action immediately. Press releases state support or opposition. Research reports are generated quickly. Groups issue statements urging confirmation or rejection if a nominee is already well known, as was true with Robert Bork or John Roberts.

But when the individual is less well known and the group still needs to conduct research on the nominee, the watchword is scrutiny. For instance, the chair of Youth for Democratic Action wrote to Senator Orrin Hatch (R-UT), at that time the ranking member of the Judiciary Committee, to urge him to probe David Souter's commitment to youth-related issues such as "reproductive freedom and education-related rights" and provided him with specific questions they wanted Hatch to pose.[89]

For the better-known nominee possibilities, groups already have prepared research on those individuals before any announcement. Some even weighed in on those names when the administration was considering them, that is, as soon as they appeared on a short list. For some nominees, the preparation is long-standing. Robert Bork's name was on short lists for several nominations before 1987. Groups already had prepared for the possibility of a Bork nomination. That is why they could coordinate with Senator Edward Kennedy (D-MA) for rapid response in the eventuality of a Bork nomination, which led to Kennedy's famous Senate floor speech within hours of Bork's being named. Kennedy was able to discuss Bork positions and offer concrete objections to Bork during the same 24-hour news cycle that carried the announcement by the White House of Bork's nomination.[90]

A few major groups produce research reports that offer their take on the nominee's background and qualifications. For example, the Alliance for Justice's report on Merrick Garland concluded after an exhaustive review of his record as a federal appellate judge that he was "highly qualified to serve on the Supreme Court." But the NAACP's report on Clarence Thomas charged that he lacked judicial temperament because he had made intemperate public remarks about the Equal Employment Opportunity Commission staff, insulted his predecessor at the EEOC, and unfairly criticized civil rights leaders and groups.[91]

Sometimes the group will express caution about the justice rather than outright support or opposition. The People for the American Way concluded in its report on David Souter that their review "has led to serious concerns about whether the nominee has the clear and demonstrated commitment to basic constitutional values which the Senate and the American people expect from a Justice of the Supreme Court." The group urged the Judiciary Committee to "thoroughly probe these issues."[92]

Initial opposition on substantive grounds is particularly difficult when presidents appoint less-known individuals, such as Douglas Ginsburg, David Souter, or Harriet Miers. Yet it is that "unknown" quality that is attractive to presidents who face opposition party–controlled Senates. Douglas Ginsburg, David Souter, and Clarence Thomas lacked extensive records, particularly in comparison to Robert Bork. They had only served for two months to 18 months as federal judges and had written little outside limited-scope judicial opinions or administrative decisions. Indeed, Douglas Ginsburg's non-record was particularly appealing to the Reagan administration. The summary the president saw about Ginsburg described him as not having "a pool of writings on the issues that proved to be controversial during Judge Bork's confirmation. . . . Nor are any of the opinions he has authored to date likely to generate significant opposition." The president was informed that the lack of a substantial record might worry conservatives, but "much of his support within the Administration likely comes from people who have worked with him and are reassured by his private statements on the appropriate role of judges etc."[93]

If the confirmation seems a foregone conclusion, then the group may attempt to use the report to urge the nominee, as justice, in a certain direction. In the case of Ruth Bader Ginsburg, the Alliance for Justice concluded with neither support nor opposition but an admonition to her that the measure of what she has said in the past "will be whether she uses her authority to shield the disenfranchised and those most in need of the Court's protection."[94] How much these efforts to advise the nominee are successful is questionable. Groups may not be powerful in influencing justices, but they could be more powerful in shaping senators' positions. In one case, interest group pressure flipped a senator who had even suggested the nominee to the president. In 2005, Senator Harry Reid reportedly recommended John Roberts to George W. Bush as an associate justice nominee who would be acceptable to Democrats. However, after Democratic interest groups opposed Roberts, Reid ultimately voted against him.[95]

Grassroots Pressure

Lobbying by groups in the modern era goes well beyond interest group representatives meeting with senators to urge confirmation or rejection of a nominee, although that does occur. Group strategies are more complex today. Groups use "outside" strategies to influence confirmation, just as they would for some other kind of lobbying campaign regarding a piece of legislation.

One tactic is to urge group members to visit with senators, either in Washington or in state offices, and then report back to the organization each senator's position on the nomination. After the Bork nomination, the NAACP circulated a form asking its members who visit senators to find out what types of constituent response the senator was receiving, how much was supportive or opposing, and what materials might be helpful to persuade the senator on the nomination.[96]

At one point, the grassroots pressure came from letters and phone calls. In the 1990 David Souter confirmation process, the National Abortion Rights Action League used a postcard campaign to apply grassroots pressure to senators.[97] By the mid 1990s, faxes and emails became new means for reaching senators. Today, the ease of these methods means that the volume of communication has increased dramatically. Senate staff are inundated as people register their opinions on a Supreme Court nominee. The effort to sift through that correspondence is much more time-consuming than it was 30 years ago.[98] As one Republican Judiciary Committee staffer put it, "An action alert goes by email to [a group's] 100,000 members and, suddenly, you're getting in a couple of weeks a thousand emails or postcards saying the same thing. Or a radio talk show host will talk about the nominee in a particular way and, suddenly, you've got 500 of his listeners calling you in the next 24 hours repeating a phrase that he said."[99]

In the modern era, senators today receive enormous amounts of mail on Supreme Court nominations, particularly a high-profile one. Most of this mail is generated by interest groups. In the Fortas confirmation process, approximately 50,000 pieces of mail concerning the nomination appeared in the offices of senators. One California senator received over 7,000 letters regarding the Fortas nomination.[100] During the Haynsworth nomination process in 1969, one senator admitted that during his time in the Senate "few issues have generated more pressure on my office than has the confirmation of Judge Haynsworth."[101] The role of interest groups in the anti-Fortas effort is indicated in one senator's report on his mail. A senator from North Dakota admitted that his mail was 20 to 1 against Fortas and that most of the mail related to Fortas's opinion in the pornography case and therefore the need to uphold morality.[102]

In the midst of the Bork confirmation process, the White House surveyed Republican Senate offices to assess the mail they were receiving. Most reported strong support for Bork, 2, 3, or 4 to 1 in favor. But these were from solid Republican states like Nebraska, Iowa, and Oklahoma. Republican senators from swing states were reporting that their mail was mixed or even negative. Communications to the senator from Vermont were 3 to 1 against Bork, while for Rhode Island the trend was 4 to 1 against and for California 6 to 1 against.[103] A senator who opposed such public sentiment did so at his or her own peril.

Another method for some groups is the rally. In 1990, the National Organization for Women held a "Stop Souter" rally. The group advertised the rally as a time to stop Souter or "women will die."[104] By 2016, the single national rally had been replaced by local rallies across the nation supporting Merrick Garland by calling on senators to act on his nomination. MoveOn.org organized rallies in Texas, Ohio, Pennsylvania, and Wisconsin with demonstrators gaining media attention holding signs outside senators' local offices.[105] Such rallies get senatorial notice because they occur directly outside a senator's local office, but also they are designed for media attention to highlight the group's views on the nominee and shape public opinion.

Senators note this public pressure. After the Fortas nomination, Senator Russell Long (D-LA) admitted to a White House aide that he felt pressure to oppose Fortas because that was a popular position to take in Louisiana. Senator Herman Talmadge (D-GA) said that "all his telephone calls, telegrams, and letters are against confirmation of Fortas and Thornberry."[106] Senator Richard Russell (D-GA) wrote to Lyndon Johnson to inform him of his impending vote against Fortas. Although Russell recognized Fortas's "great legal ability" as well as Johnson's "profound interest in the nomination," he said, "The people of my State, including the bench and bar, are overwhelmingly opposed to the nomination. Out of more than a thousand letters that I have received, at least 99% of them urge me to vote against Justice Fortas. For a time, I rode out this flood of protests without making any categorical public statement on the nomination. . . . Due to all of the circumstances, I felt in duty bound to tell you frankly and in all candor of the conclusions to which I have been driven in this case."[107]

Another method is the paid media campaign. The first such campaign was the anti-Bork campaign in 1987 when a series of television ads featured actor Gregory Peck warning of the danger to civil liberties if Robert Bork ascended to the Supreme Court. However, today's efforts dwarf such campaigns. In 2016, the Judicial Crisis Network spent $4.5 million on television ads providing support for swing Republicans who were up for re-election and had opposed Senate action on Merrick Garland. At the same time, the Senate Majority PAC, End Citizens United, Majority Forward, and Planned Parenthood spent at least $1.4 million on ads attacking those same Republicans.[108]

Creating Momentum

When the president announces a new nominee, groups swing into action to create a sense of momentum toward or away from eventual confirmation. This is accomplished with early statements by opinion leaders intended to convince the public, the media, and other groups that the nomination is headed toward confirmation or is in serious trouble. The steady stream of position announcements creates a sense of momentum. For example, in the Carswell nomination in 1970, within the first two weeks of the announcement, the NAACP, the president of the AFL-CIO, and the president of NOW had announced opposition to the nominee.[109]

However, group expectations and senatorial practices now collide on the issue of early endorsements. Groups expect senators to take early positions support-ing the group's position to assist the momentum regarding the nominee. This is particularly true for members of the Judiciary Committee, who already have familiarized themselves with records of various potential nominees prepared by their own staff as well as friendly interest groups. Moreover, groups know that their endorsements—one way or the other—carry weight with other senators.

However, group expectation conflicts with a tendency on the part of senators to wait to make a decision on a nominee. A hasty position makes the senator appear to be unwilling to examine the record and hear the evidence before mak-ing a decision. Many senators still share the opinion of Senator Philip Hart (D-MI), who once told *New York Times* reporter Fred Graham that the "one thing that I've learned around here is not to come out for a Supreme Court candidate too early."[110]

But groups now expect senators to express their views on a nominee earlier rather than later, particularly to assist in the battle over the nominee. They hope that early support will create a momentum of inevitability of confirmation or, in the case of opposition, will freeze the movement toward support by offering models of opposition. The fiery speech that Senator Edward Kennedy (D-MA) delivered against Robert Bork the day Bork was nominated set a precedent of quick response to a nominee by a Senate leader.

The compromise may be for a senator to issue a statement that suggests which way the senator is likely to go, and therefore satisfy groups, without making a firm commitment early on. One example was the response of Senator Patrick Leahy (D-VT) the day Samuel Alito was announced as George W. Bush's pick in 2005. Leahy did not promise to vote against Alito, but he did accuse Alito of being someone who would divide the country because his appointment was a reward to "one faction of his party."[111]

Early announcements can help other senators make decisions more quickly than they might have otherwise. Groups know that senators look to each other for cover. Kennedy's immediate opposition to Bork in 1987 offered cover for other Democratic senators either to wait to decide or to express opposition. Similarly, after Fortas had been named, Senator John Stennis (D-MS) asked the White House what Senator Richard Russell (D-GA) thought of the Fortas nom-ination. An aide to Lyndon Johnson urged Johnson to call Stennis and tell him that Russell was supportive of the nomination.[112] A North Carolina senator said he would not vote for confirmation of Fortas partly because the more senior senator from his state (who was on the Judiciary Committee) had taken a strong stand against confirmation. That made him vulnerable within his state and, in explaining his position to the White House, he said "he knew the President would not want him to allow himself to be destroyed."[113]

Due to their reputations as Senate leaders, certain senators have significant clout that other senators respect and often follow. Kennedy performed that role for liberal senators in the Bork confirmation battle. Another case was the position of Senator John J. Williams (R-DE), a well-known advocate of Senate ethics. When Williams announced his opposition to Clement Haynsworth in 1969, another senator predicted that another 11 or 12 votes would turn against Haynsworth due to the Williams's position.[114]

Other senators, however, may try to convince their colleagues unsuccessfully. In 1994, Senator Richard Lugar (R-IN) wrote a "dear colleague" letter to other Republican senators explaining his opposition to Stephen Breyer's confirmation and urging them to vote similarly. However, Lugar was joined in opposition to Breyer by only eight other senators.[115]

Groups and the Hearings

Groups seek to influence not only early announcements but also the content of the hearings. One means to do so is to provide senators with the types of question they want addressed. They typically do this privately but also may do so publicly. For example, during the Stevens nomination process in 1975, the National Women's Political Caucus urged the Senate Judiciary Committee to ask questions of Stevens to elicit his views about sex discrimination. The group's statement urged senators to use their questioning "to ascertain whether the nominee has a proper commitment to the constitutional protection of all Americans."[116]

The questions the groups want senators to ask are designed to place the nominee on the record regarding the issues of importance to the group. Planned Parenthood announced its opposition to David Souter with the explanation that the nominee "has failed to give the American people what they deserve to know." According to the group, the "American people have a right to know whether Mr. Souter supports the rights of all Americans to control their reproductive lives."[117] While David Souter was testifying before the Judiciary Committee, the Society of American Law Teachers issued a statement specifically requesting that senators "judge all nominees to the Supreme Court according to whether they have demonstrated a commitment to equal justice and empathy for the experience of discrete and insular minorities." And that, since the "record cries out for an in-depth inquiry," the committee should ask about Souter's "understanding of the complexity of race and gender discrimination," "his views on discrimination against lesbians and gays," and "issues of separation of church and state," among others.[118]

Groups also go further and provide senators with drafts of specific questions they want the senator to ask at the hearing.[119] They are more likely to approach supportive senators privately with submitted questions to ask the nominee, but the public approach may reinforce the pressure placed on the senator to ask the group's questions. Senators know groups will be watching closely what senators do.

In addition, groups vie for the opportunity to testify regarding a nominee. The witnesses in Senate confirmation hearings are primarily group representatives who are using the witness table to support or oppose a nominee. Groups petition the chair of the Judiciary Committee to be allowed to testify, and do so based on their claim that their perspective is critical to the decision-making process of senators. For example, the director of government affairs for the Eagle Forum requested permission from the Judiciary Committee chair to testify in opposition to Ruth Bader Ginsburg because the group represented 80,000 women who opposed Ginsburg's positions and it is "very important that the Judiciary Committee allow full consideration of all her views so that Americans, no matter what their political views, will know her record."[120]

The decision of who gets to testify and when is made by the chair of the Judiciary Committee, in consultation with the ranking member. Witnesses include a balance of supporters and opponents since the witness list is negotiated by the majority and the minority. However, even with a balance of witnesses, the timing of their testimony is determined by the majority. In the case of the Bork hearings, anti-Bork witnesses were allowed to testify first, while pro-Bork witnesses appeared late on the hearing schedule, particularly after the news cameras had left.[121]

Group Strategy on Influencing Senators

Groups seek to affect nominations even when the odds are against them. This is true for opposition groups facing a Senate majority inclined to support a nominee. But in those cases, the groups are seeking to identify their allies. Groups also may use a senator's vote against them in the future, particularly if the nominee as a justice turns out to be hostile to the group's positions.

Groups pressure senators to prove that the senators support the groups' interests. In 2006, liberal groups urged Democratic senators to filibuster Samuel Alito's nomination, even if only to place Democrats on record as supporting the groups' positions. The People for the American Way sent an email to its supporters claiming that Senator John Kerry's filibuster effort was "heeding your calls to do everything possible to defeat it [Alito's confirmation]."[122]

During the Bork confirmation process, one Democratic senator confessed to the White House that he "may have no political alternative (in light of interest group pressure in Arizona) other than to oppose Bork."[123] The connection be-tween groups and senators' re-election efforts has become more explicit in the minds of senators. Senators are aware that not fulfilling groups' expectations about votes, including votes on the high-profile Supreme Court nominations, may lead to opposition or at least tepid support during difficult re-election cam-paigns. As an example, Bill Bradley (D-NJ) was one of only nine senators to vote against Souter. He not only voted against Souter but also penned an op-ed in the *Washington Post* declaring his opposition to Souter on a single issue—abortion.[124] Bradley also was facing a tough re-election battle that he narrowly won.

In a sense, for a senator, a "no" vote is the safest vote. The "no" vote is not likely to be remembered if a justice exceeds expectations. But a "yes" vote makes the senator partially responsible for a justice who votes contrary to the positions of certain groups, and senator's constituent groups. In retrospect, senators have expressed regret for their votes on certain nominees such as Antonin Scalia (Democrats) or John Roberts (Republicans). Joe Biden (D-DE) admitted seven years after the Scalia nomination that the "vote I most regret casting out of all the ones I ever cast was voting for [Scalia]—because he was so effective."[125] Groups also oppose a nominee in the face of slim odds of success because they hope to affect the nominee's behavior once on the Court. Paul Weyrich of the Free Congress Foundation admitted to a Republican sena-tor that he had opposed Sandra Day O'Connor to pressure her to move to the right and prove as a justice that charges against her by conservatives were unjustified.[126] As mentioned earlier, whether such a tactic actually works is debatable.

The Media

A poll of public knowledge of Supreme Court justices in 2009 found that few Americans know who is on the Supreme Court. The best-known justice is Clarence Thomas, who was identified by 14 percent of Americans.[127] Thomas also is a justice who rarely makes news. He almost never asks questions in oral arguments. He promoted an autobiography, *My Grandfather's Son*, in 2007, but largely stays out of the public eye.[128] Yet he is the best-known justice. Thomas's notoriety stems from his confirmation process.

Media Scrutiny

Clarence Thomas's personal life was the object of intense scrutiny in the media during his confirmation process. Opponents of the nomination sought to blunt the image of Thomas as a potential respected Supreme Court justice through emphasis on his personal relationship with women, particularly Anita Hill.

For the news media, the emphasis on personal aspects was helpful in attracting readers and viewers. The story angle avoided complex legal discussion that sometimes characterizes Supreme Court confirmation stories and offered news content that appealed to a wide audience. The second round of the Clarence Thomas confirmation hearings, which featured Thomas, Hill, and others discussing Thomas's sexual talk and actions, was accorded saturation news coverage by news organizations.

The live televised coverage of the Thomas hearings led the Senate Judiciary Committee to change its procedures on considering such information about a nominee. Since 1993, the Judiciary Committee has held an executive or closed session for each nominee to discuss issues arising from the background check.[129] That practice arose after the Thomas hearings and has a resemblance to the Senate's executive session debate prior to 1929, although much more limited in scope. However, these sessions may occur even when there are no issues to discuss. In 2005, the Senate Judiciary Committee went into executive session to consider items related to the background check on John Roberts, but came out of the session only 30 minutes later.[130] The press keeps track of the length of the session to guess whether any issues arose. One committee staffer explained that it is a really important thing when members can say, "I saw that you had this drunk driving arrest or I saw that you tried marijuana in college. . . ."[131] However, chairs of the Judiciary Committee have made such sessions routine in order to avoid speculation about them.

Media scrutiny has become a prominent feature of the nomination process in the modern era. Bork and Thomas were not the only nominees affected by such coverage. The Clement Haynsworth nomination was undone by reports of his ethical dealings, including failure to recuse himself in a case involving a business in which he had a financial interest. When G. Harrold Carswell became the next nominee, journalists looked for similar problems. For example, *New York Times* reporter Fred Graham investigated Carswell's home purchases to undercover potential ethical irregularities similar to those that had doomed Haynsworth's nomination. Graham examined public records of Carswell's property sales and found that rather than becoming wealthy from unethical deals, Carswell had become increasingly indebted by living beyond his means. While living on a $42,500 annual government salary, Carswell carried a nearly $300,000 debt to maintain an affluent lifestyle he could not afford. Indeed, the nominee was selling off property to maintain his lifestyle.[132] All this personal information collected by a reporter would have been unheard of 20 years previously.

For investigative reporting on nominees, journalists rely on leaks from those with insider information on the nominees. The White House document to the Senate Judiciary Committee describing William Rehnquist's financial status when he was nominated to be an associate justice in 1971, which included the balance of his checking and savings accounts, his mutual fund accounts, and mortgages, was leaked to Fred Graham, Court reporter for the *New York Times*.[133] In 1991, Anita Hill's testimony of sexual harassment against Clarence Thomas was leaked to National Public Radio reporter Nina Totenberg. An investigation of that leak was inconclusive, but it led to an effort to plug such committee leaks to avoid embarrassing situations like the Thomas–Anita Hill case. The Senate expanded a rule on leaks to include committees.[134]

Hearings as Theatre

Since television coverage of Senate Judiciary Committee hearings began in 1981, senators' approach to the hearings has undergone a dramatic transformation. Prior to television, senators might forgo attending the hearings of a Supreme Court nominee, particularly an uncontroversial one. In preparation for the hearings on Charles E. Whittaker in 1957, the chair of the Judiciary Committee polled the 14 other members of the committee to determine who would actually attend the hearings. Two replied they would not attend. Two years later he did the same with the Potter Stewart hearings, and three members said they would not be in attendance. That would be an unthinkable response today.[135]

One effect of television's presence is the nature of questioning. While most senators on the Judiciary Committee in the pre-television era declined to ask questions in most confirmation hearings, today senators do not pass up that opportunity for national television coverage. Since 1990, every senator on the committee has had an exchange with a nominee.[136] The number of comments by senators and nominees—and the relative volume of the two—has mushroomed since the 1980s. The average number of comments made by nominees in confirmation hearings increased from 210 to 770 in the post-1981 period compared with the period between 1939 and 1981. But senators' comments increased from 294 to 1,009.[137] In addition to the opening statements made by each senator, which are speeches, the questions senators ask nominees often sound like speeches as well. The allure of speaking live on national television is too much for any senator to pass up. One senator explained about the Senate Judiciary Committee that "if we didn't have television, a lot of them wouldn't be giving those speeches."[138]

Nominees view televised hearings differently from the way they considered hearings prior to television coverage. Today, the public has been invited to watch the exchange, and nominees are well aware that they are testifying not just before a group of senators but also to the public at large. David Souter made this point while testifying when he was asked to make a statement he felt would jeopardize his impartiality as a Supreme Court justice: "Can you imagine the pressure that would be on a judge who had stated an opinion, or seemed to have given a commitment in these circumstances to the Senate of the United States, and for all practical purposes to the American people?"[139]

The presence of television affects how nominees respond in the sessions. They know, as senators know they know, that their answers are expected to operate on two simultaneous levels. One is the intellectual level. They should be able to answer senators' questions about precedents. They should be familiar with constitutional law and approaches to judging.

But the other level is emotional. That level is primarily for the attentive public. That public is not interested in legal specifics. Instead, television viewers will judge a nominee based on whether he or she can speak to them about those issues that matter to them. One former White House aide explained the difference in discussing Robert Bork's murder board preparation. "[Bork's answers] weren't playing to the political mind. Maybe they were brilliant scholarly . . . discussions of various issues of original intent and their impact." The aide felt guilty that he had not "paid closer attention and realized that [Bork's] answers weren't washing."[140]

The effects of such presentations may be important in shaping public opinion about the nominee. For example, during the Thomas nomination, African Americans became more supportive of Thomas, particularly as race became an increasingly significant issue. However, women became somewhat less supportive after the Hill accusations emerged.[141] In the Fortas nomination, as information emerged about Fortas's potential ethics problems, as well as his opinion in a pornography case, public opinion became increasingly negative. Even supporters of the nomination admitted most of their mail was negative. In response, they pulled back as vocal advocates of the nomination.[142]

The Public

As David Souter pointed out, the Senate confirmation process now involves a player that was nearly absent for the vast majority of nominations prior to the modern era. The general public's attitudes about nominees and whether they should serve on the Court are now part of the general discussion. Interest groups claim to speak for the public. Senators make note of it. Presidents want a justice who connects with the public. And, as Souter demonstrated, so do nominees.

With the increased use of polling, public opinion surveys about Supreme Court nominees have proliferated. The first significant use was during the Fortas confirmation struggle when a public conflict on the nomination involved groups and the media—precursors of public involvement. A poll taken in August 1968, six weeks after the announcement, found that 45 percent of Americans believed Abe Fortas should be confirmed. One-quarter felt he should not be confirmed, while 30 percent said they were not sure. The poll found that opposition to Fortas was strongest among George Wallace supporters in the upcoming presidential election (44 percent opposed) and weakest among Hubert Humphrey supporters (59 percent support).[143]

It did not help Fortas that the Supreme Court itself was not popular. Only 35 percent of Americans in a Harris survey rated the Court as "good to excellent." Fifty-eight percent considered the Court "only fair to poor."[144] As a justice, Fortas was associated in the public mind with the Court and its poor reputation.

Public opinion does not actually equate to public knowledge, which should give one pause in hearing claims of representing public opinion about confirmation of a nominee. When Americans are asked whether a nominee should be confirmed, they may be making such judgments based on very little information about the nominee. That does not stop people from expressing an opinion about a nominee. For example, a poll taken on the Haynsworth nomination found that 53 percent of the public opposed the nominee. However, only one-third said they had actually followed news of the nomination.[145] After the Bork nomination had been discussed in the media for 10 weeks, 66 percent of Americans said they could not say whether Bork should be confirmed or not.[146] These levels of public knowledge undercut various claims of groups, senators, or others that their particular position reflects public opinion.

The public generally expresses only moderate interest in most Supreme Court confirmations. The notable exception was the nomination of Clarence Thomas. The Thomas nomination received widespread media coverage and led to increased public knowledge of the nominee. That, in turn, activated citizens who typically were uninterested and disconnected from Supreme Court confirmations. As a result of the Thomas hearings, a larger percentage of Americans than usual expressed opinions on whether the nominee should be confirmed. The Thomas nomination particularly activated groups that are typically less interested in Supreme Court confirmations, such as women, the less educated, and the less informed.[147]

At the same time, there has been an attentive public for a long time, well before the Bork nomination. One indication is the letters that senators receive concerning a nomination. Most of this correspondence from the public seems to be negative.

Letter writers in the Warren confirmation asked Senator William Langer, chair of the Senate Judiciary Committee, to vote against Warren because he was not enough of a Republican or he was too much of a politician.[148] John M. Harlan II was accused by letter writers of supporting "one world government." One letter writer noted that Harlan was a Rhodes Scholar and "Cecil Rhodes set up these scholarships with the avowed purpose of winning over their recipients to a belief in reunion of the United States with the British Empire, which he hoped would eventually be expanded into a world government."[149] Does it matter that the public plays a role in the process? Does the public's role affect the outcome of confirmation processes, particularly the votes of senators? Some evidence suggests such influence.

Constituent reaction to a nominee may affect questioning. Senator Karl Hruska (R-NE) told then-nominee Arthur Goldberg that he had received letters regarding Goldberg's nomination. Hruska admitted that "some of these letters which I have received I am sure are perhaps not necessarily based on facts as they exist, but they do reflect the thinking and the concept that their writers have as to the situation at hand."[150] Hruska raised issues from the letters, particularly Goldberg's lack of judicial experience and his legal work for the Steelworkers Union, suggesting an anti-business bias by Goldberg.[151]

During the Clarence Thomas confirmation process, senators with sizable African American populations among their constituents, and who were facing re-election in the next year, were more likely to vote for confirmation; those who were not facing re-election the next year were more inclined to oppose Thomas. According to L. Marvin Overby and Robert D. Brown, that finding suggests that the public's role was more significant when senators were facing an imminent re-election campaign, but the role of African American interest groups (which were generally in opposition to Thomas's confirmation) was more powerful with senators who were not facing the voters soon.[152]

This finding suggests that the public may be perceived as having an impact on senators, who then vote strategically to satisfy public opinion. However, since only one-third of senators face re-election the year of or the year after a confirmation vote, that influence is limited. Moreover, the Thomas nomination was highly unusual as confirmation processes go. The sexual harassment allegations of Anita Hill engendered widespread national debate on Thomas as well as the general issue of workplace treatment of women. Two rounds of hearings were held, rather than just one, with the second focused on lurid information about the personal relationship between Thomas and Hill. The newsworthiness of sexual harassment charges involving a Supreme Court nominee increased news coverage. As a result, extensive news media coverage also enlarged the extent of public exposure to (and familiarity with) the Thomas hearings.

Rarely do Judiciary Committee hearings reach that level of public recognition. Without that amount of news saturation, the general public (as opposed to an attentive one) will be less aware and less likely to link a senator's vote to the confirmation outcome. Under those circumstances, it becomes more difficult for an average voter to reward or punish a senator who is facing re-election primarily based on a confirmation vote.

However, the higher profile of Supreme Court nomination processes since the 1980s has raised public interest to levels generally unknown prior to that. Some political scientists have viewed that development as positive because it "raises the prospect of a genuine contribution by ordinary citizens to the makeup of the Supreme Court."[153] But high-profile confirmations raise the stakes for senators. In the case of the Thomas confirmation process, several senators who voted for Thomas, particularly Democrats, faced angry women who perceived the senators as ignoring the problems of sexual harassment by supporting Thomas. That year, Alan Dixon of Illinois and Wyche Fowler of Georgia were defeated after criticism of their pro-Thomas vote. Dixon was defeated in a Democratic primary after his Thomas vote and by a woman, Carol Moseley-Braun, who campaigned on the issue.[154]

Does a vote on a Supreme Court nominee help or hurt a senator's re-election prospects? Senator George D. Aiken (R-VT) once publicly wondered about that question. He admitted that his vote on Haynsworth in 1969 might hurt him, or perhaps not: "Something else may come along and everyone will forget how you voted on Haynsworth. The trouble is, you can never be sure."[155] In 1987, every southern Democrat voted against Robert Bork's confirmation. Tom Korologos explained that the charge against Bork that he would overturn civil rights laws "scared them to death. That was something they didn't need politically in their own bailiwick."[156]

Today, the greater danger for senators who vote against the nominee of a president of their own party is likely within the primary rather than the general election. Primaries are held earlier than general elections and therefore closer to the time of a Supreme Court confirmation vote. In the case of Dixon, his losing election took place only five months after his vote for Clarence Thomas's confirmation. Such intraparty opposition votes have become increasingly uncommon. Few senators have opposed a nominee of a president of their party since 1991 when two Republicans opposed Clarence Thomas's confirmation.

Nor can senators hide from public scrutiny of their position. The Senate's process of voting has evolved over time. Over half of Supreme Court nomination votes historically have been by voice vote or unanimous consent. However, most of those occurred in the early 20th century. Since 1967, the Senate has held a roll-call vote on each nomination.[157]

The move to roll-call votes corresponds to the expectations of interest groups and the media that the votes be transparent. Senators in the early 20th century and even into the early 1960s could be anonymous when Supreme Court nomination votes were taken. Now, they cannot. At one time, senators were willing to "take a walk" on votes in order to avoid having to cast a vote one way or the other. If pressure from groups and the lobbying by the White House were headed in opposite directions, they might not vote at all. In 1967, 20 senators did not vote on the Marshall confirmation. In 1968, 12 senators skipped the vote on cloture. Some did so in arrangement with the White House so they would not have to vote against the president.[158]

Groups now expect recorded votes to make clear that a senator supported or opposed their position on a nominee. Senators have obliged with recorded votes to satisfy their desires, and, in turn, to prove they have reflected constituents' positions. In fact, rather than hide behind voice votes, senators in the modern era publicize their positions on Supreme Court nominees because they want to receive credit with constituents for that vote. Senator John McClellan (D-AR) admitted to a White House aide that "he wants to make a record of his opposition [to Fortas] for local purposes."[159]

One problem for many swing state senators is that a Senate confirmation is a "yes" or "no" vote. In almost all cases in the past 50 years, a senator's vote must be cast one way or another. The few exceptions prove the rule. The 2016 case of Merrick Garland is one example where the Senate did not even hold hearings or investigate the nominee, much less vote. Beyond that, the two withdrawals—Douglas Ginsburg and Harriet Miers—and the failure to invoke cloture in the case of Abe Fortas were the only situations in which the Senate avoided a confirmation vote in the modern era. The problem for these senators is that there is no third way—some compromise position that might satisfy, at least partly, opposing sides. And there are plenty of groups who expect senators to adopt their position and will be very dissatisfied if the senator does not do so. One Judiciary Committee staffer explained that, for groups, the nominee's position is reduced to "is he pro me or anti me?"[160]

Democracy and the Senate Confirmation Process

Is the contemporary process better than the previous traditional one where elites dominated and no public debate ensued? Jeffrey Tulis argues that the Bork nomination was a successful confirmation process, not a failed one. He is not referring to the outcome itself but to the process that involved a serious public discussion of constitutional issues.[161]

This is a question that is not likely to be resolved since it is more normative than empirical. However, some conclusions can be reached about the Senate confirmation process in the modern era. These conclusions concern the power of public discourse and public will in today's processes.

Public discourse is a feature of the modern era, perhaps a hallowed feature. The participants in the Senate confirmation process expect transparency and public involvement in a way that did not characterize nominations previously. This stage of the nomination process now revolves around events that are highly open—the publicly released nominee questionnaire, confirmation hearings, public deliberations and votes, as well as individual senators' publicly stated rationales for votes.

What public discourse constitutes, however, may not be as intellectual as is claimed by advocates of the new rhetoric of Senate confirmations. As discussed above, the public's role means there is now more emphasis on a nominee's personal life, not just the professional one. To the extent that the public is assessing nominees, merit is not the strongest component. Rather, due to the emphases of groups and the media, the most salient element is likely to be ideology and the ability of the nominee to connect publicly.

As for public involvement, there is no doubt that party activists, group representatives and members, journalists, and the general public at large all perform roles that were limited or non-existent in the traditional process. Moreover, there is a general acceptance of such roles. A senator who publicly neglected the views of the party base or dismissed group lobbying might not last long. Senators today are expected to respond to these pressures rather than adopt some Burkean approach to nominations that characterized an earlier period when elites ruled.

One question is whether this engagement by the public, and the Senate's response, actually has improved the nomination's outcome as a reflection of the public will. When so many in the public are unaware, or incapable, of making assessments about qualifications, even after exposure to televised hearings, it is questionable whether claims of public will are connected to actual public will. Or is public will even knowable in this setting? Therefore, the claims of public opinion by groups should be viewed cautiously.

The next chapter remains at the Senate confirmation stage but focuses on how democratization has affected the intersection of the executive and the Senate in this part of the process. How do presidents attempt to manage nominations in an era of democratization? How do they seek to get their nominees confirmed in a process that is influenced by external players such as groups, media, and the public?

Presidential Management

In the fall of 1987, when opposition to Robert Bork's Supreme Court nomination mounted and confirmation was in jeopardy, some in the White House were caught off guard. Bork's handler in the process, White House adviser Tom Korologos, later admitted having assumed that Bork's nomination process would be routine.[1] Korologos and some others had believed they had plenty of votes for Bork's confirmation based on how senators had voted in the past on controversial Reagan judicial nominees.[2]

Some supporters also were surprised by the extent of the organized opposition. Suzanne Garment, a Bork supporter, wrote that "there had never been anything remotely resembling the scale of the national media campaign that was launched against Bork. Nor was there ever anything like the degree to which constituency interest groups were organized to put sustained pressure on individual senators."[3]

Bork himself seemed to be shell-shocked by the confirmation battle. In a statement to the press when Senate rejection was increasingly likely, Bork warned that the process he had endured "should not and, indeed, must not be permitted to occur again."[4] And Ronald Reagan admitted in a letter to a friend that "maybe we were overconfident."[5]

Robert Bork's reaction to his own confirmation process, along with that of some in the White House and among his supporters, is a gauge of the difference between the traditional process and the modern era of Supreme Court nominations. Bork and the Reagan administration seemed unaware that things had changed. The changes already had been occurring for some time, as this book has demonstrated to this point; they did not begin with the Bork nomination. The Bork nomination process did not initiate that change; rather, it largely confirmed it.

This chapter focuses on how presidents seek to manage confirmation battles in this new democratic era. As the chapter on the traditional process described, presidents announced nominees and then, in times of controversy, lobbied the Senate for their confirmation. The focal point was the Senate and inside lobbying, if necessary, achieved a successful outcome.

As will be seen in this chapter, the task of the White House in achieving con-firmation is now much more complex and encompasses a wide array of players beyond the Senate. These players—groups, media, and the public—are indirect decision makers in presidential success in the Supreme Court nomination pro-cess. The battle for confirmation has become a democratic one.

The Public Campaign for Confirmation

As the Bork confirmation process progressed in 1987, some Reagan administra-tion officials realized what had changed. They proposed a major public relations campaign to support Bork (and Bork's subsequent replacement if Bork was not confirmed) that included mobilizing groups to hold rallies and other events in behalf of Bork, launching a print and television ad campaign in major media markets, and integrating the party into the effort, particularly by encouraging Republican caucuses in state legislatures to pass resolutions supporting the pres-ident. Op-eds would be solicited by Bork supporters and placed in newspapers around the country. The president, too, would play a direct role. The president would tape messages for supportive groups.

Coordination for this effort would be centered in a conservative group "war room" that would provide the strategy for phone calls, ads, mailings, and press operations. The White House would strategize with that group. Moreover, the effort would be highly partisan. State Republican Party officials were to be con-tacted to issue statements in favor of Bork. Republican elected officials would be expected to voice support. Rank-and-file Republicans would be asked to partici-pate in contacting senators to lobby them and give the impression of widespread support.[6] The whole purpose was to "heat up the environment" in favor of Bork.[7]

The Reagan administration did not launch this wholesale campaign in the Bork nomination, but the lesson learned by them and subsequent administrations was that a public relations campaign is necessary to win confirmation. Indeed, the elements of this proposed game plan have become standard features of admin-istration efforts to win confirmation for a nominee. The Reagan administration did use it for Douglas Ginsburg and Anthony Kennedy. The public campaign for them involved extensive grassroots-oriented activity to mobilize supporters. These included mailing "sample" press releases to activists and local elected offi-cials, identifying activists willing to do media events in targeted states, involving the party committees in planning, organizing resolutions from supportive groups, sending talking points to thousands of activists, and other tactics.[8]

Supreme Court nominations today are political campaigns. They have all the trappings of electoral campaigns—image-making, polling, mobilizing grassroots supporters, and even paid media. Nor are these campaigns limited

to the Supreme Court. They also characterize some appellate court nominations, particularly for those nominees who may in the future be considered for
the Supreme Court. In 1989, Associate White House Counsel Lee Liberman's
office drew up a plan outlining the administration's role in confirming Clarence
Thomas to the District of Columbia Circuit Court. In the memo, Liberman
wrote, "We are beginning a campaign." He identified the candidate as well as
the need to identify the opposition, to identify and mobilize supporters, to understand the issues to emphasize or avoid, to define the campaign message, and
then to "effectively communicate that message via the media and SJC [Senate
Judiciary Committee] members."[9]

Like a major public campaign for a legislative initiative, presidential administrations devote significant resources to the task of managing a Supreme Court
nomination. For example, the Reagan administration held 26 staff strategy meetings on the Bork nomination. It organized two moot sessions or murder boards
for Bork.[10] The Reagan administration assigned four lawyers full time from the
White House Counsel's Office preparing for the confirmation hearings.[11]

The public effort centered on the Office of Public Affairs. Public relations
officials at the White House had a minimal role in Supreme Court nominations
prior to the modern era. During the Bork confirmation process, however, the
Office of Public Affairs had a full-time person devoted to that alone.[12] The office
was responsible for producing advocacy materials for the Bork nomination, conducting research, and supporting the White House staff and surrogates speaking for the nominee.[13] The White House Media Relations Office later reported
that it had prepared and distributed three sets of materials on Bork in July and
September to 2,500 editorial writers and columnists as well as to 800 spokesmen
for the administration who could use it to speak in behalf of the administration
and the nominee. It also wrote 12 op-eds and numerous letters to the editor to
be used by Bork supporters, drafted floor speeches for senators supporting Bork,
and sent materials on Bork to pro-Bork interest groups.[14]

The Reagan administration was not the first to create a campaign plan for
confirmation. In early 1969, when Richard Nixon faced the announcement of a
chief justice to succeed Earl Warren, Special Assistant to the President Dwight
Chapin outlined a "game plan for the new chief justice" that included the des-
ignation of a confirmation team head, Republican National Committee efforts
to cultivate favorable public reaction, involvement of cabinet members, administration outreach to editors of influential newspapers, a background briefing
for television reporters, and a personal call from the president to CBS News
anchor Walter Cronkite. Two years later, when the administration faced two more
vacancies, White House aide Bud Krogh drafted a lengthy memo outlining procedures for White House management of the presidential selection process. He
suggested the creation of a confirmation committee, kept secret from the public,

that would determine the strategy for confirmation and prepare the nominee for confirmation hearings, produce witnesses to testify, and obtain public approval of the nominee through a public relations plan.[15] By the time of the Lewis Powell and William Rehnquist nominations in 1971, the Nixon administration was the most organized in its approach to the presidential selection process and White House management of the Senate confirmation process of any administration up to that time. Yet the administration had good cause to be. It had failed in securing two nominations in a row. That had not occurred since the presidency of Grover Cleveland.

The presence of a plan was essential because, as described earlier, the approach of the Senate toward nominees had changed since 1965 when Abe Fortas was confirmed within two weeks of nomination in a voice vote.[16] No longer could the White House presume rapid confirmation of a nominee. The Haynsworth and Carswell nominations, preceded by the contentious Fortas battle, had emboldened opponents. The White House needed a blueprint for an extended, and possibly contentious, confirmation battle.

The Political Environment

There are common elements to presidential management of modern Supreme Court nomination processes such as the announcement, coordination with groups, crafting the image of a nominee, and so on. However, no universal campaign plan exists for presidents seeking nominee confirmation because any plan must take into consideration the unique elements of a particular nomination. The nomination of Ruth Bader Ginsburg in 1993, for example, was very different from the nomination of Abe Fortas in 1968. Even the same administration cannot use exactly the same strategy. The nomination process to fill the seat of David Souter in 2009 was conducted differently from the one Barack Obama faced seven years later to replace Antonin Scalia.

The differences relate to the particular political environment each president faces when making a nomination. Since variation in the political environment impacts presidential success, that environment is a factor in how presidents approach the confirmation process. The elements of that environment discussed below include the timing of the vacancy, ideology and partisanship, and the existing balance on the Court.

Timing

A critical aspect of the political environment in the modern era is the issue of timing. The timing of a nomination affects how it will unfold. Except in the relatively rare case of a death, timing is controlled by the justice who is retiring since he or she generally chooses the year, the month, and the day to announce a departure. The Senate also has power to affect the timing of the confirmation process by determining when to schedule hearings, debate, and votes. Presidents, however, typically, are more affected by timing than influence it.

Occasionally, retirement may occur due to medical conditions beyond the justice's control. Certainly, William O. Douglas did not choose to retire in the fall of 1975, particularly when Gerald Ford, who, as a member of the House of Representatives, had initiated impeachment proceedings against Douglas, was the president. However, most justices who retire have some luxury in choosing when that will occur.

Most of these justices appeared to have timed their retirement to provide the most opportune conditions for the incumbent president to confirm a nominee matching the president's (and the retiring justice's) preferences. Since 1968, all five of the justices who retired within the first two years of a new president's term (Potter Stewart, Byron White, Harry Blackmun, David Souter, and John Paul Stevens) were more ideologically compatible with the current incumbent than his predecessor. In another case (Sandra Day O'Connor), the justice left at the beginning of the president's second term, but similarly in the administration of a fellow partisan. By comparison, there has been only one case (Thurgood Marshall) when a justice retired without stating a specific medical need to do so during the term of a president with whom the justice did not share party affiliation. Even then, Marshall died 18 months after his retirement, suggesting that an anticipated medical need may have been a factor in that case as well.

Presidents do not control retirement timing, but justices who offer such an opportunity to a new president are assisting a president to gain confirmation at the most advantageous time in a presidential term. Senators may be more inclined to bow to the president's popularity, while a nomination later in a presidential term may occur when presidential power is waning and opposition for senators is less risky.

Another element of timing is a presidential election campaign. Earl Warren's retirement in 1968, discussed previously, was the last time a member of the Court retired during a presidential election year. That effort failed, and no justice has repeated the effort to retire during such a year. In the modern era, it is highly unlikely that a justice would retire in a presidential election year since he or she would be aware of the potential chaos of a fight over whether a justice should even be replaced by a president who could be or will be a former president in less than a year.

It is unlikely today that a president could fill a vacancy created in the middle of a presidential election year. The experience of Barack Obama attempting to fill the vacant seat of Antonin Scalia in 2016 is evidence of this difficulty. This is particularly true if the president is not eligible for re-election. However, it might even be true when a president is a candidate for re-election.

Even before the Garland nomination, there was an unwritten rule that the Senate Judiciary Committee would not act on lower court nominees after June of a presidential election year. Sometimes called the Thurmond Rule after Senator Strom Thurmond (R-SC) who served as Judiciary Committee Chair and followed the rule during his tenure by failing to act on nominees of an opposing party administration, the rule has been adopted and abandoned by both parties, depending on political expediency.[17]

That rule has even been specifically applied to Supreme Court nominations. In June 1992, Joe Biden, chair of the Senate Judiciary Committee at that time, warned George H. W. Bush, who was running for re-election, not to nominate a replacement before the November election if one of the sitting justices retired. He publicly threatened not to hold hearings on a nominee if a nomination was made by Bush.[18] The rule, using Biden as a precedent, was invoked by Republicans in 2016 to justify not acting on the nomination of Merrick Garland.

Even before the Thurmond Rule became entrenched, debate ensued about whether the Senate should act on a nominee in the last year of a presidential term. Some opponents of the Bork nomination argued that President Reagan was a lame-duck president a year and a half before leaving office, therefore he should not have attempted to use his power to nominate someone who would further his social agenda.[19]

Timing also applies to the Senate, particularly the place of nominations on the Senate calendar. Since it is now a common practice for retiring justices to announce a retirement near or at the end of the Supreme Court's term to provide sufficient time for consideration of a replacement, the Senate's summer schedule affects the confirmation process. An announcement in July, shortly after the term ends, may accelerate the process because it means that the president and the Senate must act by late September if the Court is to be at full strength by the beginning of the term on the first Monday in October.

However, a late June or early July announcement of a retirement may not be achievable in this era of Supreme Court nominations when presidents may take weeks to select a nominee and the Senate requires at least a couple of months before it votes, even in less controversial nominations. As a result, justices increasingly are announcing retirements in the spring to provide sufficient time for the president and the Senate to act prior to the beginning of the next term. Such a time frame can be too luxurious. In 1993, Justice Byron White announced his retirement in March in order to provide a six-month window for the president and the Senate. But Bill Clinton took three months of that period before he named a candidate, leading to criticism that he had left too little time for the Senate to do its job.

The Senate's traditional calendar can impact when a confirmation process even occurs. Congress recesses in August. Members go home to meet with constituents or take vacations. Also, in election years, Congress seeks to adjourn no later than the end of September to provide members with at least four weeks of campaigning before the November election. A nomination occurring close to that adjournment point may not be acted upon. The combination of the August recess and the late September adjournment creates a small window for Senate consideration of a nominee, including courtesy calls, collection of materials, background checks, preparation for Senate hearings, holding of the hearings, committee deliberation and vote, and then full Senate debate and vote, particularly in an election year.

Calendar was a potential issue in 1968 when Congress planned to adjourn by early August of that year to allow members to return home to wage re-election campaigns. However, the administration faced the possibility that a filibuster would occur and a cloture vote would fail. The result would be a dead nomination for the session. Nor would Johnson, with only two weeks left in his presidency the next January and a president-elect in place, be able to resurrect the nomination. Thus, Johnson faced the prospect of defeat unless 67 votes were obtained to block the filibuster.

Another option was for Congress not to adjourn. A White House aide urged Johnson to slow down the passage of appropriations bills in the House, which would require the Congress to reconvene in September to pass those bills. Such a move would delay a vote on the nomination until the fall and give the White House more time to obtain the 67 votes necessary to invoke cloture.[20]

Timing is used by both supporters and opponents. The White House seeks a rapid pace and a relatively quick confirmation vote. The need for a ninth justice to sit on the Court by the beginning of the next term on the first Monday in October becomes an argument by supporters, particularly the White House, for the need to act speedily.

However, opponents also use time to their advantage. They seek delay considering a nominee, in the name of full deliberation, because more time offers greater opportunities to build opposition, uncover something damaging about a nominee, and undermine the initial public enthusiasm from the announcement. One aide to Lyndon Johnson admitted that, for opponents, "delay was their great weapon."[21]

The time a nomination occurs affects how an administration approaches the nomination. Again, presidents rarely influence the decision of when a vacancy occurs, but they are affected by that choice. Timing also can affect who the president nominates since the president may be able to take more risks in a first year than in subsequent years of his or her term. The timing of Senate action also is an element outside the president's control. A president can have more influence over a majority of his own party than over the opposition. However, a president can expect that the time the Senate devotes to deliberation will be used by opponents to block confirmation. And if the Senate is in opposition hands, delay of action will be a reality.

Ideology and Partisanship

As discussed previously, ideology is a prime concern for presidents today. Added to their concern, however, is that senators now are more likely to vote for a nominee who is close to them ideologically than one who is not.[22] That aids a president when the majority of the Senate (particularly a filibuster-proof majority) is of the president's party and therefore more compatible with the president's ideology, as well as the nominee's. But it makes confirmation far more difficult when that is not the case.

Indeed, confirmation is significantly affected by partisan control of the Senate. Confirmation is likely even in a situation where the opposition controls the Senate. The Senate has confirmed 92 percent of Supreme Court nominees when the White House and the Senate are in the same party's hands and only 59 percent when they are not.[23] Even when the president's party has a slender majority, confirmation is more likely.[24]

However, a narrower majority in the Senate creates problems and opportunities for a president. If the president's party barely commands a majority in the Senate, then the president must hold on to all or nearly all fellow partisans to achieve a simple majority. Since moderates in the president's party may defect, the challenge is to hold those senators while persuading some opposition members to cross over and support the nominee. Moreover, a filibuster attempt by the minority party may be successful due to the inability of the majority to carry out a successful cloture vote. On the other hand, a narrow opposition majority means the president must win over fewer votes in order to win confirmation.

Even in cases where a majority is fairly substantial, presidents still may be able to pick off enough opposition party senators to achieve confirmation. George H. W. Bush achieved this with the nomination of Clarence Thomas. Although the Senate was 57–43 Democratic, the White House was able to win over 11 Democrats, while losing two Republicans.

In cases of opposition control, whether narrow or large margins, the president must expend more resources and alter strategies to win confirmation in such situations. When presidents fail to nominate a consensus candidate or adopt a strategy of persuasion of the opposing party, defeat is more likely to result. Lyndon Johnson, Richard Nixon, and Ronald Reagan all dug in their heels on nominees, despite warnings from senators that confirmation would be problematic.

The situation of the need for presidential compromise has become more common in modern Supreme Court nominations because divided government has become a more common feature of US politics in recent years. One example of the stark difference in partisan control is the case of Robert Bork. Had Bork been nominated in 1986, rather than 1987, the general consensus is that he would have been confirmed because of Republican control of the Senate. Similarly, in 2016, Merrick Garland at least would have received a hearing, if not an actual vote, had Democrats maintained control in the 2014 elections.

In the past, the conventional wisdom for presidents faced by a majority of opposition-party senators was that Supreme Court nominees would be successful if the president consulted with the opposition party. That was evidenced in the cooperation between Bill Clinton and Senator Orrin Hatch (R-UT) in 1993 and 1994 when Clinton consulted with Hatch during the presidential selection stage and then received Hatch's support when Ginsburg and Breyer subsequently were announced as nominees. In a note to Hatch following the unanimous Judiciary Committee vote on Breyer, Clinton penned a personal addition saying "thanks so much" and then, two weeks later, acknowledged Hatch for his contribution to the Ginsburg process and for "providing me with insightful and candid advice throughout the selection process" that expressed his reliance on Hatch to fend off Republican opposition and prevent a potential filibuster of the nominee.[25]

However, that cooperation strategy with the opposition party has frayed. The demands of the party activist base, fostered by media, places those who cooperate with the opposition president in electoral jeopardy. Independent, well-funded political action committees, such as the Club for Growth or FreedomWorks on the right and PrioritiesUSA on the left, can offer primary opponents the resources to threaten or even defeat senators who collaborate with the opposition.

Orrin Hatch is a classic case of this transformation. While Hatch cooperated with Clinton in the 1990s, he opposed both of Barack Obama's nominees in 2009 and 2010. He said that Sotomayor's views were "too much at odds with the principles about the judiciary in which I deeply believe."[26] But a significant difference between the two points was that most Republicans voted for Ginsburg and Breyer in the 1990s, while Hatch would have stood out among Republicans in 2009 and 2010 had he voted for Sotomayor and Kagan. Moreover, Hatch faced a primary election in 2012 with an opponent who was funded by FreedomWorks.[27]

In the modern nomination process, the simple solution for a president would be to nominate a centrist—a candidate whose views would be closer to a majority of the Senate, assuming the Senate is not so polarized that such a tactic is fruitless. Then, that candidate could draw over moderates from the opposition party. However, that ideological middle has shrunk to the point that crossovers are becoming rarer.

Additionally, a nominee who is centrist enough to garner crossover support may be unacceptable to the party base. George W. Bush faced that dilemma when he nominated Harriet Miers, his White House legal counsel, in 2005. Miers was suggested by Senator Harry Reid but was opposed by conservative bloggers and commentators, the very base of support Bush needed in a confirmation battle. The base offered only tepid support or even outright opposition, which made the path to confirmation difficult for Miers. In contrast to Miers, Samuel Alito was a well-regarded judge whom the base could support. Bill Clinton and Barack Obama experienced the same base angst when Clinton considered Amalya Kearse, a Republican, and Obama actually nominated Merrick Garland, a moderate Democrat.

Ideological Balance on the Court

Another factor in the political environment, particularly relating to ideology, is the ideological position on the Court of the departing justice. When balance is maintained on the Court by replacing one justice with another of similar bent, at least a status quo is preserved. Precedents are not likely to fail. This is especially true when the departing justice did not provide a swing vote on the Court.

If the balance is not shifting in one direction or the other, then the Senate's response to a well-qualified, but ideological nominee may be acquiescence. The response to Antonin Scalia's appointment in 1986 may be an example. Scalia was confirmed unanimously even though many Democratic senators such as Edward Kennedy (D-MA) and Howard Metzenbaum (D-OH) strongly opposed his ideological views. But since Scalia was replacing Chief Justice Warren Burger, who was considered a strong conservative, the ideological balance on the bench would be left unchanged. Similarly, some Republicans were reticent to oppose vigorously the nomination of Elena Kagan because she was replacing a similar liberal.

The fight over Antonin Scalia's replacement in 2017 was similar. Republicans viewed Garland's appointment as a teutonic shift in the Court's ideological balance towards the left and blocked the nomination. However, the same angst did not apply to Democrats. Although they would have liked to shift the balance in their direction, Democrats knew that Trump's nominee would not dramatically alter the balance of the Court. Therefore, the danger of a new ideological imbalance was muted.

Image-Making Strategies

The battle for a nominee in the modern era is a battle over image. In the traditional process, the image within the Senate typically was the only important consideration. Only rarely did the battle extend beyond the confines of the Senate and involve groups or the public. Today, it is that very public image that predicts the success of presidential management.

Frank Donatelli, who worked on Supreme Court nominations in the Reagan administration, early in the Bork nomination described the stakes to another Reagan official: "The Bork nomination is as much a battle of public perceptions as it is a congressional nomination fight." He explained that public opinion would help define the issues in the confirmation process and predicted the influence of outside groups and that they "might even be decisive in the final outcome."[28]

That is why administrations keep close tabs on how the public is reacting to a nominee and the nomination process generally. They want to know whether the general public supports confirmation, as well as what demographic groups within the public are prime targets for administration attention in the public re-lations campaign. In the midst of the second round of hearings on the Thomas nomination, White House Counsel C. Boyden Gray received a memo from poll-ster Robert Teeter summarizing what national polls were saying about the cred-ibility of Clarence Thomas versus Anita Hill as well as the nature of support for Thomas's confirmation among various demographic groups such as blacks and women.[29]

What matters in image-making is a multi-faceted concept. It does include the image of the nominee but is not limited to that image. Indeed, there are three elements in image-making presidential selection—the process, the presidency, and the nominee.

The image of the process needs to be perceived as one that is legitimate in nature. A quick process that suggests a lack of presidential deliberation may taint the outcome; critics will point to a certain hastiness in vetting. For example, in 1991, George H. W. Bush announced Clarence Thomas's nomination only three days after Thurgood Marshall's announced retirement. Bush called Thomas the "best person for this position" even though the president had taken little time to deliberate on the process.[30]

Barack Obama faced this dilemma in the spring of 2016 when he was deciding whom to nominate to replace Justice Antonin Scalia. A quick announcement within days of Scalia's death would have placed the Senate in more of a quandary over whether to act. The Republican majority's reasoning of delaying until the election of a new president would be more suspect given that the election was nine months away and the inauguration of a new president 11 months in the future. The White House could argue that such a time period was a long one to hobble the Court with eight justices, particularly since the president had moved quickly to fill the vacancy. On the other hand, acting too quickly would signal that the president was not deliberative enough in the selection process. Even though the Obama administration already had a potential short list of nominees from the two previous processes in 2009 and 2010 that had resulted in vetting of a number of candidates beyond Sotomayor and Kagan, the president could not be seen as hastening the process for political purposes.

The president's image is at stake as well. A Supreme Court nomination is one of the most high-profile acts a president engages in. Like a major presidential policy initiative, a nomination garners extensive press attention and immediately pits the will of the president against that of the Senate. A loss is an indication of presidential weakness vis-à-vis Congress. Too many losses can undermine a president's influence over Congress and reduce the president's ability to get things done.

That explains the anxiety presidents feel over the outcome of the process. Lyndon Johnson became testy with his staff when he did not get precise reports on senatorial leanings. He demanded that his staff provide him with an accurate count of senators on whether they would support cloture and end the filibuster by Senator Robert Griffin (R-MI). A top aide wrote to the confirmation team staff: "Do not show ANYBODY in IF columns unless it is absolutely, positively all you can get. . . . Prez wants no if, and, or buts on this one!"[31]

A positive outcome in a presidential nomination, on the other hand, carries the potential of enhancing the president's image. That was an explicit goal of the Clinton administration. The White House counsel staff suggested to the White House Chief of Staff that the administration use the confirmation process "as a vehicle to put the President and his staff in the best possible light." Indeed, the White House sought to turn the press strategy into an opportunity for the White House to "elicit praise for the President for the nomination."[32]

A quick and easy confirmation is particularly beneficial, while a lengthy and controversial one can be costly to a president's image. In the former case, not only does the president bask in a high-profile achievement, but he did not need to expend much political capital to accomplish it. However, presidents who expend substantive amounts of resources on securing confirmation of controversial Supreme Court nominees are less successful in aspects of their legislative agendas.[33]

The Image of the Nominee

Earlier, the nominee's public image was not of much concern to presidents, except to give the impression that the choice was a meritorious one. Presidential announcements typically dwelled on the background of the nominee. When John F. Kennedy nominated Byron White in 1962, the White House press release announcing the appointment simply listed White's biographical information— first in law school, Phi Beta Kappa, Rhodes Scholar, law clerk to the chief justice, and deputy attorney general. Plus, the announcement came on a Friday, a day when a story may be buried over the weekend.[34]

Over 50 years later, when Donald Trump nominated Judge Neil Gorsuch in January 2017, the announcement went well the beyond background facts that characterized announcements in the pre-modern era. Trump asserted that "Judge Gorsuch has outstanding legal skills, a brilliant mind, tremendous discipline, and bipartisan support." Gorsuch, according to Trump, was "among the finest and most brilliant" jurists. He considered Gorsuch's qualifications to be "beyond dispute" and "a man our country really needs and needs badly." The press release accompanying the announcement emphasized Gorsuch's part-time jobs as a young man, his hobbies, and his affinity for the West.[35]

Clearly, today, a simple description of merit is not enough. The nominee must be touted as possessing additional traits—compassion, judicial restraint, moderation, bipartisan support, and so on. The public must believe that the individual deserves to be on the Court, in terms of both merit and the service he or she will perform. Even beyond that, the nominee must be someone the public feels represents them. One Reagan administration official argued that a Supreme Court nominee must be shown to be "in agreement with the overwhelming majority of the public."[36]

The nominee must have an appeal beyond party, as befits a Supreme Court justice, but also will attract the support of a broad section of the American public. That imperative becomes more difficult in a highly partisan environment where opposing partisans who support the nominee risk criticism and ostracism from their own partisans. The Reagan administration knew they needed to get support from moderate Democrats in order to win public support for the Bork nomination.[37] They reached out to those in the legal community who would be considered moderate or even liberal who would speak in Bork's behalf. However, there was intense pressure on pro-Bork supporters within the legal community not to publicly support Bork. One law school dean initially gave strongly favorable reaction to the Bork nomination in the press and the White House added him to a list of spokespersons for Bork. But a month later, he was described by the White House as "more ambivalent on the subject" and the White House worried that encouraging the press to speak to him would backfire.[38]

One aspect of image-making of the nominee is to blunt the opposition claim that he or she is too radical to serve on the Court. Nominees must avoid the charge of extremism, that is, holding views that are considered outside mainstream legal values. To blunt the charge that Robert Bork was extreme, the administration sought to prove that Bork's views were within the mainstream of legal thought. Bork's briefing books included discussion of his opinions as well as reference to other prominent justices, such as Lewis Powell, Potter Stewart, and Felix Frankfurter, or current legal scholars, such as Alexander Bickel, Alan

Dershowitz, and Laurence Tribe, who had shared similar views on a particular topic. They also included mention of groups and Supreme Court justices who had agreed with Bork, such as the NAACP Legal Defense Fund that had sided with Bork's position in nine of 10 important civil rights briefs, and Justice William Brennan, who had taken Bork's position in 17 of the 19 cases that came to the Supreme Court. Moreover, Bork was reminded in the briefing books that he had "voted against groups with whom he might be in political sympathy."[39]

The administration also seeks to avoid the label of judicial activist. This has become an issue since the Warren Court, when justices were accused of seeking to set policy and override the will of political institutions such as Congress or state legislatures with decisions in areas such as desegregation, busing, obscenity, the rights of the accused, and reapportionment. During his 1968 chief justice confirmation process, Abe Fortas, as a member of the Warren Court, was accused by conservative Republicans and southern Democrats as a liberal judicial activist. In response, the White House issued a report detailing Fortas's judicial restraint approach in his opinions as an associate justice.[40] In 2016, Merrick Garland used his remarks at the announcement of his nomination to promise that he would "put aside his personal views or preferences, and follow the law."[41]

To connect with ordinary Americans, nominees also must come across as human and, in some ways, average, rather than as distant intellectuals. Administrations emphasize a nominee's human traits. In 2016, Barack Obama mentioned that Merrick Garland had sold shoes to support himself in college, and that Garland even had to sell his baseball card collection to pay tuition. Six years earlier, in announcing Elena Kagan, Obama mentioned that she was a Mets fan and that while she served as a law clerk for Thurgood Marshall, the justice had called her "Shorty."[42] News media coverage in the same vein is encouraged. For example, when Ruth Bader Ginsburg was nominated in 1993, the New York Times discussed her summer camp experiences in the Adirondacks, her role as a high school baton twirler, and her marriage to prominent attorney and law professor Martin Ginsburg.[43]

The image-making strategy features well-publicized testimonials. For an individual who, in nearly all cases in modern nominations, is unknown to the general public, such testimonials offer an opportunity to set the image in the public mind, particularly before the opposition does so. For David Souter, the George H. W. Bush administration gathered and circulated comments that Souter supporters had made in the press. These comments from fellow judges and attorneys addressed Souter's judicial capabilities and temperament ("impeccably fair," "a judge's judge," and "fiercely independent"). Others that focused on his personality ("a warm, friendly person," "very gentlemanly," "loves to tell stories") were elicited from former colleagues, former classmates, and even a former girlfriend.[44]

The President's Theme/The Nominee's Story

When Richard Nixon announced the nomination of Harry Blackmun in April 1970, he wanted his new nominee to be viewed as a "strict constructionist." Blackmun was to be portrayed as "a man who has the same philosophy on the Constitution as Haynsworth and Carswell." He directed White House Counsel Bob Haldeman to make sure to "take this on as a project of the highest urgency, discuss it with the Congressional group, the PR group, John Mitchell, etc. so that we get the right set on it at the earliest possible time."[45]

The theme of "strict constructionist" was a favorite of Nixon's. He had used it in the 1968 presidential campaign and he wanted to continue it into his administration. It was a fulfillment of a campaign promise. Nor did he want it to be forgotten by the time of his nomination of Blackmun after failed efforts to place a strict constructionist on the Court with Haynsworth or Carswell.

Interestingly, Nixon's first appointment was one devoid of the theme that would characterize most of his subsequent appointments. In announcing Warren Burger as his pick for chief justice, Nixon said that Burger, a federal appellate judge for 13 years, was widely praised as well qualified. Yet, Nixon made only a passing reference to Burger's legal philosophy.[46]

However, Nixon's theme was set by the fall of 1969 and continued on throughout his Supreme Court appointments. When announcing the nominations of Lewis Powell and William Rehnquist in October 1971, Nixon talked about Supreme Court decisions weakening law enforcement, the importance of a justice being a constitutionalist, and his pledge to nominate conservative justices.[47]

The concept of a theme for Supreme Court nominations has become the norm in the modern era. Presidents are expected to articulate a common thread for their appointments that addresses a felt need in American life. For Nixon, it was the importance of interpreting the Constitution through a certain lens.

For Bill Clinton, it was appointing someone who understood the real world—a politician—who would have a "big heart" in approaching the dispensing of justice. His thematic emphasis of a politician and someone with a "big heart" led to disappointment when Ruth Bader Ginsburg was nominated. In response to Clinton's expected appointment of a politician, the *Baltimore Sun* editorialized that [the administration] "would have preferred a justice with some background in the hurly-burly of politics."[48]

The idea of a theme originated with the beginning of the modern era. In 1968, a White House aide proposed to Lyndon Johnson that a theme be developed for the confirmations of Abe Fortas and Homer Thornberry. He suggested the theme be that "here are two highly qualified, able men who are being subjected to a vicious, inflammatory, political attack which has nothing to do with their qualifications." He argued that the administration needed to "hammer it daily" rather than respond to individual charges against the nominees. Their opposition, the aide continued, was getting significant publicity and the administration needed to respond with a presidential press conference, a daily speech, and a "hard-hitting" press release by a supportive senator; cabinet and sub-cabinet officials needed to generate newspaper coverage and editorial support in their home states; and state Democratic Party organizations should encourage letters to the editor.[49] Johnson did not take that advice. Nor was that theme one that would have helped Fortas since it is negative in tone rather than positive. But the idea of using a theme has been adopted by most subsequent presidents.

The president's theme needs to be established during the presidential selection stage, reinforced with the announcement, and then maintained throughout the image-making campaign. In the case of Sonia Sotomayor, the theme was the judge's rise from a working-class Puerto Rican family in a South Bronx neighborhood to the Supreme Court of the United States and how such a background epitomized the American dream. The emphasis of the Obama White House on Sotomayor's mother at the East Room announcement visually and verbally reinforced that theme.[50]

During the Scalia confirmation process, Reagan used one of his weekly radio addresses to describe the plight of "a 15-year-old Italian immigrant who spoke not a word of English. Little did he imagine that his son, Antonin Scalia, would be appointed to the highest court in the land, there to uphold and protect our Constitution, the guardian of all our freedoms. Just one of many stories that shows us that every time we swear in a new citizen, America is rededicating herself to the cause of human liberty."[51]

The president's theme is more powerful when it is combined with a prominent story associated with the nominee. That story helps create an image of the nominee's connection with and sensitivity to American values. It becomes a backstory that demonstrates the quintessential nature of the nominee's background. He or she becomes a symbol of the American dream. For the Clinton administration, Ruth Bader Ginsburg could not serve the same role as O'Connor because the first woman was already on the Supreme Court. Instead, Ginsburg was portrayed as an advocate for women's rights. When appointing her, Clinton called her the "Thurgood Marshall" of women's rights, a label made more poignant by Marshall's death earlier that year. It also reinforced the president's theme that Ginsburg had a "big heart" as an advocate of women.

The nominee's story today becomes even more personal than that of a legal advocate. The story often revolves around the nominee's gender, race, or ethnicity. At root, the story communicates to the public that the nominee is "one of us" rather than a distant figure who is unfeeling and lacks concern about the effects of the law on common people.

For Sonia Sotomayor, being the first Latina justice was not enough of a story. When nominating her, Obama recounted her South Bronx housing project childhood, her parents' immigration from Puerto Rico, the judge's working-class roots, and her efforts to gain an education and graduate at the top of her class from Princeton. Obama said that Sotomayor had "faced down barriers, overcome the odds, lived out the American Dream that brought her parents here so long ago."[52]

Ronald Reagan chose Antonin Scalia over Robert Bork at least partly because Reagan was impressed with Scalia's story—the son of an Italian immigrant. Reagan understood that such a story also would be compelling to the public.[53] In 1986, after nominating Scalia, Reagan pointed out that Scalia "is the first Italian-American in history to be named to the Supreme Court." Reagan did more than that: He placed the Scalia nomination squarely within the conception of the American dream.[54]

For George H. W. Bush's nomination of Clarence Thomas, the story was called the Pin Point Strategy. That was the effort to accentuate Thomas's story—the poor boy raised by his grandfather in the small town of Pin Point, Georgia—as evidence of the virtue of Thomas's elevation to the Court as symbol of American, and particularly black American, achievement in the face of overwhelming odds. Just before the confirmation hearings for Thomas, Bush delivered a radio address about his nominee. He praised Thomas's life story as "a story of opportunity." Thomas, Bush explained, grew up poor in a small Georgia town, Pin Point, but was raised by "stern and loving grandparents" who educated him in parochial schools that led to his graduation from Yale Law School. Bush urged Americans who watched the television coverage of the hearings to "think of the values Clarence Thomas embodies: hard work, service, dedication, education." Bush said he was "proud that we have entrusted this son of America with the task of keeping our heart healthy and whole; and proud of this man, who embodies the promise of equality and opportunity in America."[55] The Pin Point strategy was an attempt to capitalize on Thomas's personal roots in order to portray him as a "son of America" who would bring those values to his Supreme Court appointment.

The "story" has significant advantages in image-making. It avoids ideological labels that would narrow the candidate's appeal and invite controversy. Any American can relate to the nominee's "story." Nor is it based on the content of a nominee's educational or professional background. The decisions the nominee has made, the positions he or she has taken, are subsumed in the emphasis on the personal and not the political.

The story becomes the angle for news stories. The goal of the White House is to shape the tone of news coverage and therefore the public perceptions of the nominee. The Reagan administration's emphasis on Scalia's Italian roots did filter into media coverage. Not only did news stories reference Scalia's Italian heritage, but they also used sources heralding the nomination on ethnic grounds. For example, the *New York Times* coverage included statements by Italian American politicians supporting the nomination.[56]

Such stories humanize the nominee and provide real-world connections for nominees who otherwise would be viewed as elitist. The educational background of nominees is mentioned, but not emphasized. Ivy League degrees do not draw Americans toward the nominees. The story does.

The "story" also places opponents in a quandary. They appear to be in the undesirable position of opposing an embodiment of American dreams. Then there is the problem of opposing specific constituent groups (Hispanics, Italians, African Americans, etc.) who are supportive of the success of their particular representative.

Some nominees simply do not fit the "American dream" model. The "story" doesn't work. Stephen Breyer was one of those cases. Breyer was worth over $8 million, due to his family inheritance as well as his wife's wealth. Moreover, he emanated an elitist personal demeanor that even friends acknowledged could be off-putting. Nevertheless, the White House sought to spin a populist image for Breyer. Clinton said Breyer had a devotion to "real people." When nominated, Breyer told the press that he would "make the average person's ordinary life better." While testifying before the Senate Judiciary Committee, Breyer sought to downplay his elite background by discussing that, as a youth, he had dug ditches, made salads at a summer camp, and was a delivery boy.[57]

Countering Opposition Image-Making

The image of the nominee is set within the first days of the confirmation process, but administration officials are not the only ones seeking to shape that image. The opposition to the nominee seeks to paint a portrait of the nominee as well—in their case, an unfavorable one that will taint the nominee throughout the confirmation process. The classic example of that approach was the effort by Senator Edward Kennedy to derail the Bork nomination.

The 24-hour news cycle driven by cable news, talk radio, blogs, and social media demands quick action by opponents. They must enter the news cycle immediately in order to affect first impressions. As example, immediately following the nomination of Neil Gorsuch, NARAL Pro-Choice America issued a statement calling Gorsuch an "existential threat to legal abortion."[58]

Typically, within days of an announcement, groups already have launched pro and con advertising campaigns. Web advertising has facilitated such rapid-response campaigns since it can be both quick and inexpensive. In the case of

Sonia Sotomayor, a supportive group was out within 24 hours with a video of clips by Obama laying out the traits of his desired nominee and then photos and a narrative demonstrating how Sotomayor fit the president's requirements. At the same time, another group included quotes from Sotomayor about her "wise Latina" remark and insinuating that she would undermine, not enhance, equal justice under the law.[59]

Groups are not the only ones using the media to shape nominee images. The Senate Judiciary Committee majority staff issued a response to a White House briefing paper on Robert Bork. The response was drafted by several constitutional law professors and attorneys and was intended to blunt the administration's image of Bork. The committee report contended that Bork was a judicial activist, was not similar jurisprudentially to the retiring justice Lewis Powell, and did not respect precedent. The report criticized the administration's selectivity in culling Bork's record.[60] The White House drafted a statement seeking to undermine the committee report by declaring that it contained factual inaccuracies grossly distorted the evidence, and ignored Bork's tenure as a federal appellate judge.[61]

Rather than allow opposition image-making to gain credibility, the administration engages in public debate with opponents. In the case of Carswell, opponents argued that the Florida appellate judge lacked the requisite qualifications to be a Supreme Court justice. The Nixon administration initiated a publicity campaign to stress that Carswell had more judicial experience than recent nominees and three times the judicial experience of the Kennedy-Johnson nominees. The president wanted that point to be emphasized in press releases, administration statements, and lobbying with undecided senators.[62] For Haynsworth, the opposition asserted that the nominee's ethical issues were comparable to those of Abe Fortas, who had resigned under an ethical cloud earlier that year, and therefore Haynsworth did not belong on the Court. The White House countered with an explanation of the differences between the two situations.[63]

For confirmation success, it is imperative for the White House to counter the image portrayed by opponents. If media coverage rests with the opponents' claim, then the public image becomes the opponents' creation rather than the administration's. Two Reagan administration aides bluntly put the case to their superiors: "It is important for us to get the facts to the editors, reporters, and columnists to counteract the distortions of special interest groups."[64]

At times, countering opponents on the merits of the nominee includes maligning the merits of those opponents. At the explicit direction of the president, the Nixon administration planted stories about Senator Birch Bayh (D-IN) failing the bar exam as a young attorney.[65] During the Bork nomination, stories circulated about Senator Edward Kennedy (D-MA) cheating on an exam while a Harvard student and Senator Joe Biden (D-DE) plagiarizing an essay during law school.[66] The White House effort was gaining so much traction that groups in opposition to Bork worried that the news emphasis would turn to Biden rather than Bork. One group representative sought to redirect the attention back to Bork by arguing that "the issue must be Bork's record, not Biden's."[67]

The White House struggles with determining the most effective strategy of countering negative images. A White House aide in the Johnson administration reported that "the South is being flooded with literature portraying Abe [Fortas] as pro-Communist. This apparently has influenced Senator Hollings [D-SC] to harden his position [in opposition]. If this is in fact the case, we may wish to consider a counter move to determine whether such would be desirable or would merely draw more attention to the non-existent issue."[68] The Reagan administration considered a major paid media drive to support the Bork nomination in its waning days. One idea was a spot narrated by Charlton Heston with the theme that Bork had been smeared by special interest groups despite the fact that Bork was well qualified to serve on the Court.[69]

Countering the counter-image efforts requires monitoring opposition efforts. The White House tracks opposition to the nominee—statements by interest groups, announcements of vote intention by senators, news stories on the process, and editorials regarding the nomination—in order to craft responses via press statements. The George W. Bush administration had a war room constantly monitoring news stories, interest group websites, and blogs.[70] The Reagan administration labeled editorials, columns, letters to the editor, and news stories on the basis of whether they were favorable or unfavorable.[71] The day after the nomination of Fortas and Thornberry, the White House Press Secretary reported on the press response, which he labeled "very good." "The *Times* and *Post* accounts will have considerable influence on the magazines this weekend." And he noted that the nominations got "excellent commentaries from Sevareid and Reynolds on television last night." Moreover, the filibuster announcement "is resulting in the 'politics' label being attached to the Republicans."[72] In 1969, Richard Nixon responded to a news story about Clement Haynsworth's ethics problems and the possibility that Haynsworth opponents would link the ethics issue to Justice Abe Fortas, who had resigned earlier that year. Nixon asked White House aide John Ehrlichman, "Is this problem a serious one from a PR standpoint? And are [White House Counselor Bryce] Harlow and Attorney General [John] Mitchell on top of it?"[73]

Countering the opposition also necessitates a range of outlets for response. These occur through statements from the administration as well as op-eds from others. The White House drafts op-eds that refute the opposition's press statements, speeches, or op-eds and then puts them out under the name of an administration official or supporter who appears to be independent of the White House.[74]

Tactics for Image-Making

Image-making does not happen automatically. Indeed, as will be discussed below, the administration's desired image is countered by opponents who seek to slow momentum for confirmation and offer a contrasting portrayal of the nominee. The administration must establish the image on the first public notice of the nominee and then use several continuing tactics to reinforce it.

The Announcement

The first impression of the new nominee on the part of the public comes with the announcement. And the White House has an advantage in setting that first impression. The White House holds the element of surprise over the opposition. It has time to craft the initial announcement and to anticipate reactions to attacks on the nominee from opponents. Opponents are expected to respond immediately, and this may be difficult if the nominee is a surprise candidate who is unknown to most of the legal community, such as David Souter or Harriet Miers.

At one time, presidents often simply announced nominees by sending the name to the Senate or issuing a press release; today presidents have imbued the announcement with ceremony that is intended to attract immediate media attention. Now, the announcement is a major event, typically in the Rose Garden or the East Room of the White House, complete with extensive scripting. The president's remarks must be written and approved, the nominee's remarks must be vetted. Interest group representatives are notified in advance and invited to attend, along with Judiciary Committee members, Congressional leaders, and legal community members.

Indeed, the announcement offers the administration a precious opportunity to set those impressions before others do. Two Reagan administration aides expressed this when they wrote that "through interviews, editorials, and dissemination of facts, perhaps we can set a few minds before the national media has a chance to make their pitch."[75] But the first opportunity is the announcement.

Reinforcing themes through the announcement helps set news story angles and affects the initial impression of the nominee with the public. These impressions are critical because nominees rarely have any public image prior to the nomination. According to Greg Craig, White House counsel in the Obama administration, "you never get a second chance to make a first impression, and that is very, very true in the Supreme Court nomination process."[76]

The nominee's standing in the legal community almost never leads to widespread public knowledge. Few nominees in history could have registered more than single digits in public opinion polls prior to their nomination. In nearly all cases, particularly with modern nominations, public knowledge comes for the first time with the announcement.

As mentioned above, the announcement humanizes the nominee to set first impressions that make the nominee attractive to Americans watching on television or reading news reports. Sometimes those efforts can turn out even better than planned. When George W. Bush announced the nomination of John Roberts as an associate justice in 2005, Roberts's son, Jack, broke free from his parents and wandered around in the front of the room. After a few minutes, he began to mimic Spiderman as he shot webs from his hands. Finally, his mother scooped him up and took him to another room. But one Republican political strategist noted that after Jack Roberts's performance, "I knew the little guy had just made it all but impossible for Democrats to cast Judge John G. Roberts as 'another Robert Bork.'"[77]

Reinforcing the verbal announcement comes through a flood of documents for press coverage—the text of the president's speech, a biography of the nominee, and supporting statements. In the case of Ruth Bader Ginsburg, the accompanying documents included the biography of the nominee, a fact sheet about her, a list of cases she had argued before the Supreme Court as an advocate, and copies of eight letters of support from prominent legal academics and attorneys.

The White House also arranges for instantaneous reaction from supporters. That means the feedback that reporters hear is supportive of a presumption of confirmation. Following the defeat of two of his nominees and before naming a third, Richard Nixon sought the commitment of Republican senators, governors, members of the House, and some Democrats to speak out in favor of the new nominee as soon as the announcement was made. The White House staff wrote 17 speeches for senators, a film clip was readied for distribution to select television stations in the South, and Republican National Committee officials were prepared to issue statements endorsing the president's new nominee.[78]

Interestingly, when the announcement was a less public affair without the image-making components, the sending of the formal letter of nomination to the Senate was the news event. Today, the two events are separated—with the formal nomination often coming several days after the public announcement ceremony. In fact, the latter seems a formality. It was so much of a formality that the Reagan administration had not even sent Douglas Ginsburg's name formally to the Senate when Ginsburg withdrew a week after his announcement following allegations that he had smoked marijuana with students while a law professor at Harvard.[79]

Courtesy Calls

The announcement is hardly the end of the image-making effort. Rather, it is just the beginning of a quickly ratcheted-up internal campaign that includes setting up courtesy calls, working with the nominee to fill out forms, preparing the nominee for the hearings, coordinating with the Senate Judiciary Committee on hearing schedules and witnesses, and surveying and lobbying senators individually and in groups. But the announcement also is the commencement of an extensive public relations campaign involving media and interest groups and the eventual shaping of public opinion.

Within a day or two of the announcement, news of the nominee continues with the courtesy calls paid on senators. The White House arranges courtesy calls and then prepares the nominee for them. The nominee is briefed on background information about the senator, what issues they may discuss, what kinds of questions have been asked by this senator before in courtesy calls, and how to make a personal connection with the senator. According to a George W. Bush administration staffer, Alito was encouraged to mention that he had Senator Jim Bunning's (R-KY) baseball cards: "It sounds ridiculous, but . . . it helps a lot if the senators like you."[80]

When Harriet Miers performed poorly in the courtesy calls she conducted in 2005, more preparation was accorded nominees to assure that they were ready for the experience. Greg Craig, White House counsel at the time, explained that "special care was taken with Judge Sotomayor to make sure she was going to be able to deal with these one-on-one meetings and conversations that were sometimes over an hour and had no limitations. They could ask her about anything they wanted to talk about."[81]

A White House staffer also accompanies the nominee. He or she may be in the meeting, along with Senate staff, unless the senator asks to see the nominee alone. This handler keeps notes of the meeting and then reports back to the confirmation team on what was said, such as the issues discussed and the reaction of the senator to the nominee.[82] A handler for David Souter recorded 13 items that had been brought up in one day's courtesy calls and urged that these issues be included in Souter's background briefing book.[83]

Courtesy calls are opportunities for the nominee to show respect to members of Congress, particularly the Senate. They provide signals to the administration about how individual senators might approach the confirmation hearings. That information helps the confirmation team prepare the nominee in the "murder boards."[84]

They also may allow the administration to determine how the nominee would react to a Senate Judiciary Committee hearing question. Raising these issues in private first offers the opportunity to head off a potential problem before it surfaces at a live televised confirmation hearing. For example, the handler accompanying Robert Bork reported that in a meeting with Arlen Specter, Bork was asked his views on medical malpractice. He replied that he had not thought about it. The handler worried that such an answer would not play well on television and that Bork needed to be coached on another answer.[85]

But courtesy calls also contribute to administration image-making. They show the nominee with prominent senators and maintain positive news coverage of the nominee beyond the initial announcement. Rarely is the news from courtesy calls bad. But one such example was the Harriet Miers courtesy call on Senator Arlen Specter (R-PA). Miers said something about *Griswold v. Connecticut* (1965) and the right of privacy that Specter interpreted as support but Miers contended was not. The he said–she said controversy became a major news story and undermined Miers's nomination.[86]

The Public Role of the Nominee

Unlike candidates for other positions, nominees avoid speaking to the press to avoid the appearance of impropriety in publicizing and promoting their own confirmation. The White House does not hold press conferences or schedule interviews since such activities would be viewed as crossing the line of ethics. That limitation means the nominee cannot be a self-advocate.

That does not mean that journalists do not try anyway. When Breyer was nominated in 1994, the Clinton White House got interview requests from National Public Radio, CBS, *Newsweek*, and even Breyer's high school newspaper. The interview requests sometimes specify non-judicial areas, but they are simply seeking to capitalize on the nominee's new notoriety. For example, a local Massachusetts newspaper and *Bicycling* magazine wanted to talk to Breyer about his bicycle commute to work and views about cycling, while NPR sought to discuss exclusively environmental issues. For others, the interview itself is not "on the record." Joan Biskupic of the *Washington Post* asked for a background interview for a newspaper profile of Breyer.[87]

Understanding that the nominee rarely talks to the press, some reporters seek time with family members, such as the nominee's spouse or children, or friends. The requests suggest that the press interest is celebrity-oriented. *USA Today* wanted not so much an interview with Breyer as the opportunity to take photographs of him with his family or prepping for his hearings.[88] The White House often cooperates because these types of stories humanize the nominee while avoiding any controversy from nominee statements.

Supporter Speeches and Media Appearances

The nominee's unavailability means others perform public roles in the process in support of the nominee. The most prized advocate is the president. Those responsible for media relations for the nominee seek presidential time in the promotion of the nominee. This means using the president to lobby wavering senators but also to mention the nominee in speeches, press conferences, and interviews since such media events will maintain nominee news as well as reinforce the messages of the nomination.

The White House also uses other surrogates for the nominee. Many of these surrogates are administration officials, particularly senior White House staff and members of the president's cabinet. During the Bork confirmation process, the Reagan White House coordinated the travel schedules of senior administration officials with media interviews to use such encounters to push for Bork's confirmation.[89] Surrogates are provided with talking points about the nominee. For David Souter, the talking points emphasized that Souter "has a conservative judicial philosophy" and that he "sticks close to the law" and "does not invent new concepts or stretch established ones to the breaking point."[90]

Administration officials and other surrogates also appear on talk shows in behalf of the nominee. The Reagan administration targeted local radio talk shows because of the shows' constant need for content and guests. The administration provided talk show hosts with materials supportive of Bork as well as guests from the administration who would promote Bork. The Media Relations office of the White House became a booking agent for administration officials to make the talk show circuit.[91]

Interacting with the press to emphasize the case for the nominee in the news takes up considerable time of administration officials. Two and a half months into the Bork confirmation process, an aide in the Reagan administration compiled a list of the activities of White House Chief of Staff Howard Baker alone in helping win Bork's confirmation. The report showed that Baker had given 25 press interviews, delivered nine speeches, met with four newspaper editorial boards, and personally lobbied 10 senators.[92] In the week after the Douglas Ginsburg nomination announcement in the fall of 1987, administration officials were interviewed on 56 local television news programs and 15 radio talk shows.[93]

Feeding the Press

Even more persuasive to the media and the public may be those outside the administration who are publicly advocating the nominee. One of the early tasks of the administration is to identify media spokespersons—prominent individuals who support the nominee and can reinforce the White House message without explicit association with the administration. During the Breyer confirmation process, the White House Counsel's Office used friends of Breyer to make phone calls to the press and offer press statements in behalf of the nominee.[94] The Reagan administration collected lists of attorneys who could appear on local talk shows. Within two weeks of the announcement of the nomination, the

Reagan administration had created a list of 13 academics, think tank heads, or group representatives whose names could be offered to the press as Bork advocates available for interviews and statements concerning the nominee.[95]

The administration seeks to place op-eds supporting a nomination with local newspapers, convince newspaper columnists to write favorably, and encourage editorial boards to issue positive editorials. In the Johnson administration, the Department of Justice wrote draft editorials to give to an editorial writer. They also talked with Otis Chandler, publisher at that time of the *Los Angeles Times*, about supporting the Fortas nomination. Chandler promised to editorialize strongly against a filibuster, if there was one.[96]

Op-eds may be published under the name of a supporter, who appears as an independent voice supporting the nominee.[97] But the White House also creates op-ed kits for supporters that include background information on the nominee, suggestions for op-ed themes, and instructions about how to send an op-ed. Those targeted are former colleagues of the nominee. For example, the Reagan administration planned to contact former students and fellow professors of Douglas Ginsburg with such kits before Ginsburg withdrew.[98]

Administrations also seek to influence press coverage by interacting with reporters to challenge information that the administration considers inaccurate in reporting. The objective is to encourage the press to provide the White House side of events. In the Thomas nomination, a White House media relations aide contacted *New York Times* columnist Tom Wicker and told him that his column was factually inaccurate in claiming that George H. W. Bush authorized Republican attacks against Anita Hill. The aide concluded that "at the very least, I think he'll check with Marlin [Fitzwater, White House press secretary] or me before writing next time."[99] Similarly, the Nixon administration complained about a news piece by CBS News reporter Dan Rather. Charles Colson reported that Rather did not "correct" the story, but the administration's "point was made" and that "this may tend to keep Rather honest for a while."[100] Nixon even demanded "equal time" from NBC when he saw a television news story with negative comments from opponents of Clement Haynsworth. Nixon was reminded that "equal time" did not apply to news stories.[101]

Senatorial Speeches

The administration also wants to get its message out through avenues other than the White House. One such additional venue is a floor speech. Prior to the modern era, senators' speeches were heard by those who were on the floor of the Senate or in the gallery, but not elsewhere. They were printed in the *Congressional Record*, which average citizens never read. Today, speeches are watched on C-SPAN. Sometimes excerpts are shown on cable news networks as well. They also can be seen via YouTube. Videos of speeches are more broadly accessible, allowing wider dissemination of the administration's message. Moreover, Senate staff distribute press releases and texts of speeches through various means including news media and social media.

To guarantee that the White House message is heard and to ease the burden on Senate staff, the White House writes floor speeches for senators supportive of the nomination. Clearly, such a practice assures that senators cover the points the administration wants said about nominees and the nomination process. The Johnson White House wrote speeches on Fortas and Thornberry for at least three supportive senators. These speeches covered specific points the administration wanted to make as well as rebuttals of attacks on the nominee by opponents. The Justice Department wrote a floor speech for a senator that defended a decision by Thornberry that had been criticized by a Republican senator.[102] The Johnson administration even drafted a dialogue among four senators, all of whom supported the Fortas nomination. They were supposed to use the information provided to reinforce each other's points favoring confirmation.[103] The Nixon administration wrote floor speeches, as did the White House in the Bork nomination. The Reagan administration wrote 19 of them with varying themes such as the unfairness of the process, the distortions of the opposition, the need for a Court exercising judicial restraint, and so on.[104]

The Hearings

Harvard Law Professor Felix Frankfurter received no preparation from the White House before testifying at his confirmation hearings in 1939. Even though Frankfurter had had a long career as a Harvard law professor rather than as a media celebrity, such preparation was unnecessary. The hearings were not televised live. Relatively few people saw Frankfurter testify.

However, Frankfurter's experience is not one shared by modern nominees. Today, the public glare of confirmation hearings requires an image-making strategy that molds the nominee into an appealing individual who charms senators and exudes everyday ordinariness, but he or she must also demonstrate having the merit essential for consideration for the Court. Yet the effort to cultivate such an image contrasts starkly with the lives of most federal judges or legal scholars. Occupations such as theirs often attract more reserved individuals who are unaccustomed to serving as public relations tools. This can be particularly problematic during courtesy calls and the hearings themselves. Robert Bork, particularly, gave the impression of a distant intellectual. One White House aide explained that Bork "didn't schmooze. He never came in there and humanized himself."[105] Similarly, Samuel Alito's style was reclusive. He commented to one senator during his whirlwind tour of courtesy calls that "this is more human beings than I see in a month."[106]

Since the most public part of the confirmation process is the hearing held by the Judiciary Committee, particularly the days when the nominee testifies, image-making centers on this event that millions of Americans will watch on live television. How the nominee performs in the hearing may affect the outcome of the confirmation process. The Bork nomination is the model of a performance that failed to win over public support. Instead, the image of Robert Bork as an aloof, unfeeling academic was more likely reinforced rather than punctured by his testimony. Following the disastrous Bork hearings, a Reagan Justice Department official explained to his boss that "how Doug [Ginsburg] presents himself during the hearings must govern all else."[107]

As a result of the prominence and significance of the hearings, the administration devotes extensive resources to preparing the nominee for senator questions and appropriate answers. That preparation is both legal and political. No nominee possesses deep knowledge of the multitude of areas of the law. Even federal appellate judges who handle a variety of legal cases endure exhaustive briefings and preparatory sessions to acquaint them with various aspects of the law.

The administration, particularly the Justice Department, prepares briefing books for nominees containing summaries of key cases as well as synopses on the current status of law for a wide variety of topics that may be the subject of questions by the Judiciary Committee members. These include, for instance, such areas as environmental law, native American law, the Fourth Amendment, anti-trust, and intellectual property.

Preparation includes a review of the nominee's own record of decisions and actions he or she has taken in the past, not only as a refresher for the nominee but also to help uncover potential topics that may be raised by senators in the hearings. In the past 50 years, with the exceptions of Sandra Day O'Connor in 1981 and Elena Kagan in 2010, nominees have been federal appellate court judges who have participated in or written opinions on potentially controversial issues. Those opinions are the subject of Justice Department analyses, as are speeches, statements, and writings by the nominee.

Briefing books also contain references to the questions Judiciary Committee members have asked previous nominees in areas such as the First Amendment, civil rights, federalism, and equal protection. To acquaint themselves with the particular interests of each senator, nominees become familiar with issues raised previously, as well as with which senators addressed which topics in their questioning. In Ruth Bader Ginsburg's preparation, the briefing books she used included a section of previous questions categorized by individual senator as well as the specific questions that senator had posed to recent nominees. Ginsburg read that Senator Strom Thurmond (R-SC) had asked Anthony Kennedy "whether the Supreme Court should be covered by the Judicial Conduct and Disability Act; whether there should be a mandatory retirement age for judges," and that Senator Howell Heflin (D-AL) had queried Robert Bork about "where in the Constitution is a general right of privacy?"[108]

The team then went further and constructed likely questions, by senator, that Ginsburg might expect. These were based on "intelligence," that is, getting information from the Senate on what is likely to be asked. The team predicted that Senator Ted Kennedy (D-MA) would inquire about Ginsburg's experiences as a discrimination victim, as well as her views on affirmative action, privacy and abortion, civil rights, the free exercise clause, and free speech. They also expected that Thurmond would ask about the death penalty, gay rights, the ACLU, the Second Amendment, habeas corpus reform, and obscenity.[109]

Some senators disclose what they will ask a nominee, which helps the White House with preparation for that exchange. Senator Larry Pressler (R-SD) wrote to Ruth Bader Ginsburg prior to the confirmation and enclosed the draft questions he planned to ask concerning Indian jurisdiction law. He told Ginsburg he was doing so that she "might have an opportunity to prepare for what I hope to be an enlightening dialogue on a subject of very deep concern to my constituents."[110] Senator Orrin Hatch (R-UT) sent Stephen Breyer a letter in advance of the hearing suggesting that he read a particular law review article on the Ninth Amendment.[111] Similarly, Senator Arlen Specter (R-PA) wrote to John Roberts and Samuel Alito listing the questions he would ask.[112]

Additionally, the confirmation team specifically asks Senate staff about their bosses' anticipated questions. These include both supportive senators and those in the opposition. The Clinton White House knew that Senator Patrick Leahy (D-VT) would ask about the establishment clause and pose general questions about Breyer's judicial philosophy while Senator Orrin Hatch (R-UT) planned to ask about the Ninth Amendment; they also knew that Hatch was concerned that Breyer not answer questions about cases likely to come before the Court.[113]

Some senators do not provide much advance information about questions—only general topics. In Breyer's case, he knew in advance that Senator Charles Grassley (R-IA) would ask about the legislative veto and how Breyer would treat legislative history, and that Senator Arlen Specter (R-PA) wanted to know Breyer's views on the role of judicial activism as it related to specific cases such as *Director, Office of Workers' Comp. v. Greenwich* (which had just been decided the previous term) and *Rust v. Sullivan*. But all Breyer knew about Senator Herb Kohl (D-WI) was that he would ask open-ended questions about the role of judges or that Senator Alan Simpson (R-WY) would talk about home schooling.[114]

The information the White House gleans, coupled with what senators actually signal to the nominees directly or indirectly, demonstrates that the exchanges between senators and nominees are not really spontaneous. Senators are not inclined to surprise nominees and potentially embarrass them in front of a live national television audience. Nominees know what senators will ask and senators know they know.

Given these sources of information, the confirmation team can predict "with almost total accuracy" what will come up.[115] Armed with this information, the confirmation team prepares a set of likely questions senators will ask the nominee and organizes it by senator. The public image is that the nominee is hearing a question for the first time. In reality, in most cases, when the nominee faces a particular senator, he or she can anticipate the types of questions and the topical interests of the senator, if not the actual specific questions.

Additionally, the nominee is briefed by experts on various topics, particularly academics who specialize in these areas of the law. The Ginsburg team had experts brief her on anti-trust, criminal law, First Amendment, federalism, privacy, and other topics.[116] Briefers are typically lawyers or law professors who are ideologically compatible with the nominee. Briefers for Stephen Breyer included Kathleen Sullivan, Stanford Law School; Cass Sunstein, University of Chicago Law School; Charles J. Ogletree Jr., Harvard Law School; and Robert Pitofsky, Arnold & Porter law firm.[117]

Preparation is not simply focused on familiarizing the nominee with legal information. It also has a political component: how to handle the questions in a way that furthers the objectives of the confirmation campaign. That may include how best not to answer a question without appearing obstinate. Reagan administration aides prepared a section in a briefing book on how previous successful nominees had evaded answering senators' questions. The material gave nominees examples of previous nominees refusing to answer questions about their own prior judicial opinions, potential cases before the Court, and judicial philosophy. In addition, the material included statements by senators justifying a nominee's not answering a question.[118]

Of course, this training is not what senators prefer, at least publicly. Indeed, the reticence to express opinions and the tendency to provide vague answers leads to public displays of frustration by senators. One senator suggested that the Senate should hold a hearing within a few days of a nomination announcement so the nominee cannot be trained in handling Senate Judiciary Committee members' questions.[119]

This preparation precedes the "murder boards," the set of mock hearings where staff members pose as specific Judiciary Committee members and grill the nominee with questions the administration expects will be asked. For the John Roberts and Samuel Alito nominations, the George W. Bush administration held four sessions a week for four weeks to prepare the nominee for confirmation hearings.[120] For Ginsburg's preparation, White House aide John Podesta played Senator Patrick Leahy, White House attorney Joel Klein was Senator Orrin Hatch, and James Hamilton, an attorney who led the nomination vetting, became Senator Strom Thurmond.[121] Every committee member is represented in the mock hearing to help the nominee experience interacting with that senator. These sessions are filmed so the nominee and his or her handlers can assess how the nominee performs on camera.

These mock senators try to make the preparation hearings worse than those the nominee actually will experience. For Bork's hearing, his handlers sought to pose difficult questions. These included probing questions on Bork's past positions and decisions, such as whether his opinion in a sexual harassment case showed he felt sexual harassment was legal, whether he agreed that the Constitution allowed the sterilizing of repeat felons, and whether he really believed consenting adults did not have the right to buy contraceptives. Bork was asked why he belonged to an all-male club for nine years and had resigned only after it became an issue in another judge's confirmation process. He also dealt with questions concerning why he did not pay automobile taxes in Connecticut for 14 years and whether he had a problem with alcohol.[122]

Most Supreme Court nominees today are not novices at the process; they have experienced confirmation hearings before when confirmed to other positions, such as lower-level court vacancies or administration positions. Sonia Sotomayor had endured two confirmation hearings—one for district court judge and the other for appellate court judge—before her Supreme Court hearings in 2009. Nevertheless, nominees still may experience what one veteran confirmation handler called "nominitus." He explained that nominees "get sweaty palms, their hair falls out in extreme cases, and they can't sleep nights."[123]

Preparation for the hearings goes beyond the nominee to the supportive witnesses as well. The confirmation team may prepare other witnesses who will be testifying in behalf of the nominee. In the case of Bork, the White House Counsel's Office worked with over 50 witnesses to brief them on the hearings and help prepare them for possible questions from senators.[124]

The administration also targets opposition witnesses. They conduct opposition research on those witnesses to gather information that can be used against them. They want to know what will be said by these witnesses and then seek to develop a strategy of response either through pro-nominee witnesses' rebuttal statements or probing questions from senators supportive of the nominee.[125]

The struggle for the White House in preparing nominees for hearings is to encourage the nominee to portray himself or herself in the most positive light while downplaying those aspects of the nominee's past that are problematic. One of George W. Bush's administration staffers admitted that they don't "put words in the mouth of the nominee" because "the nominee is the nominee and they're going to say what they think." However, they seek to help the person understand the consequences of saying something a certain way: "Well, if you say that, this is going to be the follow up question. How do you handle that?"[126] White House aides tried to persuade Ruth Bader Ginsburg to avoid any mention of ACLU positions on areas such as legalizing prostitution, decriminalizing marijuana, eliminating the death penalty, and decriminalizing pornography for minors because, as one confirmation team member put it, "she has an instinct for defending some rather extreme liberal views on these questions."[127]

Robert Bork was even urged by some senators to shave his beard before he testified. As former White House aide Tom Korologos explained, his beard "gave him sort of an eccentric appearance and that lent credence to the idea that his views were eccentric as well." But Korologos urged him not to shave the beard: "Yesterday there was a photo in the paper of you with your beard. Tomorrow the hearings begin and you want to appear without your beard? This is the ultimate confirmation conversion and proves that you are not holding to your principles?"[128]

Even after all of these efforts to prepare a nominee, the confirmation team still may worry about how a nominee will actually perform. One of Robert Bork's handlers admitted that he had arranged for a senator to ask Bork a crime question to "get the devil off all that other stuff. So Bork said, 'I don't know anything about crime, it's not been my bag.' I almost kicked him!"[129]

Ruth Bader Ginsburg's main handler privately expressed concern that Ginsburg would be unable to answer a senator's questions and address larger issues, but instead had a tendency to nitpick on a particular aspect of the question's premise. Even worse, he feared Ginsburg's style would be off-putting: Her "technique—her failure to make eye contact, her halting speech, her 'laconic' nature . . . is not helpful."[130]

Senators and the Administration

The modern nomination process still includes the presidents who select nominees and the senators who decide whether to grant confirmation or not. Indeed, presidents need to manage relations with senators to achieve the goal of support and eventual confirmation. But in the modern era, that relationship now integrates indirect communication tools and external pressure to achieve that goal.

One important step in securing Senate support is involving senators in the selection process. One White House aide suggested to a presidential counselor that "if some of [the senators] feel more involved in the process of selection, they can become implicitly obligated to support us."[131] Inclusion at this stage not only relates to senators' desire to be influential; it also addresses their need to be "in the know." Senators, particularly leaders, want to know important information before everyone else.

Advance notification of the nominee is a sign of respect. When Douglas Ginsburg was announced, 12 senators met with the White House chief of staff and Ginsburg thirty minutes before the announcement. The White House chief of staff also called the chair of the Senate Judiciary Committee and the Senate majority leaders. Then members of the legislative staff contacted an additional 14 senators, as well as 12 members of the House Judiciary Committee.[132]

Exclusion can be costly to an administration. Excluded senators can be so offended by the lack of notice that they are willing to "punish" the administration for its slight. In 1968, Senator John McClellan of Arkansas complained to the White House that he was not consulted, even though he was the second-ranking senator on the Judiciary Committee. Therefore, he was in no rush "to make known my views" and even supported having "real long hearings."[133] In the wake of the Carswell debacle, White House aide Chuck Colson concluded that the negative vote of one Republican member of the Judiciary Committee could have been avoided "had we discussed the nomination with him a few days in advance."[134]

Particular attention must be paid to members of the Judiciary Committee, particularly those in senior positions and who are ideologically compatible. These members can be influential in signaling to others who are not on the committee. As one Republican Judiciary Committee staffer put it, the "peer to peer network, so to speak, is very powerful here."[135] One White House aide in the Nixon administration urged the Attorney General to consult with a liberal Republican on the Judiciary Committee about potential nominees so that the senator, in turn, would influence other liberal Republican senators to support the administration's nominee.[136]

The administration, like opposing groups, would prefer these senators to announce their support early in order to influence others and create momentum. One Reagan administration confirmation team member compared the Supreme Court nomination process to the presidential primary process, in the sense that early primary states have the greatest impact on the rest of the race. Similarly, he wrote, "the balance of power will be held by Senators from a dozen key states. Some of these Senators, Specter, Heflin, DeConcini, will influence Senators in other states. In addition to our national activities, we must make sure that our message is targeted to reach voters and Senators in these twelve key states."[137] The Reagan administration thought they could win over key Democrats and gain the support of other swing Democrats.[138]

The administration then develops state action plans to influence public opinion in those states and therefore win the vote of senators from those states.

These include coordinating with groups conducting their own advocacy campaigns via paid media, news coverage, opinion pieces, and grassroots pressure. They also feature utilizing networks of party activists.

That does not mean direct lobbying is not used in modern Supreme Court nominations. Presidents do personal lobbying of senators as well. Lyndon Johnson called senior Democratic senators to urge them to support his nominees—Fortas and Thornberry.[139] Ronald Reagan placed calls to senators who already had announced pro-Bork vote intentions to thank them for their support.[140] The cabinet also may be instrumental in lobbying: The Johnson White House assigned the secretary of agriculture to five senators, the secretary of defense to three, and the secretary of state to one.[141]

Merit is an important part of the argument the administration makes to senators. To stress this point, Lyndon Johnson told a senior Democratic senator that Abe Fortas was "one of the great lawyers of this country."[142] To reinforce merit, administrations distribute various documents to senators in order to favorably dispose them toward the nominee. These include background materials such as biographical records, writings by the nominee, selected news clippings, and favorable editorial reaction to the nomination. Senators on the Judiciary Committee receive a White House–prepared briefing book that includes material for senators scrutinizing the nominees' record, such as an analysis of the nominee's writings, speeches, and opinions as well as statements by others about the nominee.

The Clinton White House prepared a chart showing how many times Ruth Bader Ginsburg had agreed or disagreed with her fellow judges on the US Circuit Court of Appeals in order to prove that Ginsburg would be a moderate justice. The chart disclosed that she had voted with Robert Bork 96 percent of the time and Antonin Scalia 97 percent of the time. Since most cases were consensual, the administration then broke down those with dissents. Even there, Ginsburg agreed with Bork two-thirds of the time and Scalia 75 percent.[143]

The Reagan administration prepared a 75-page briefing book on Robert Bork that was distributed to senators as well as the press. They also put together another book (over 200 pages in length), which responded to the charges against Bork by opponents.[144] Similarly, the Bush administration gave the Senate Judiciary Committee Minority Staff a set of briefing materials with biographical material on Clarence Thomas, Thomas's accomplishments at the Equal Employment Opportunity Commission, and sections covering Thomas's record on controversial issues like abortion and civil rights. The Johnson administration was more selective in its distribution of information. It gave certain opinions of Homer Thornberry to "skeptical liberals" in the Senate while other opinions, particularly relating to law enforcement, were targeted to southern senators.[145]

Yet merit is not the only appeal. Hardball politics also comes in handy. Senators know that the White House can be a powerful opponent to someone who is not a team player. Indeed, the White House holds the power to punish senators who do not cooperate with the administration, and that power can be exercised in numerous ways. Senators can worry about what might happen to them if they cross the president. In 1968, Senator Robert Byrd (D-WV) informed the White House he would strongly oppose the Fortas nomination. Then, after reflection, he told a White House aide that the president "has been a good friend of mine" and that he (Byrd) should not have taken such a belligerent attitude toward Fortas. Therefore, he would still vote against Fortas, but not join in formal opposition to Johnson's nominee.[146]

Carrots may be attractive as well. These may come in the form of material incentives. A Johnson administration aide discussing the possibility of building a new postal facility in Shreveport, Louisiana, suggested that the postmaster general "consider bargaining with [Louisiana Senator Russell Long] on this [new postal] facility in an effort to secure his vote [on the Fortas nomination]."[147]

Such bargaining is not out of the question. Since Supreme Court nominations do not operate in a vacuum, the White House is simultaneously interacting with senators on other matters. Supreme Court confirmation votes may become part of the carrot-and-stick strategy of wooing senators.

Indeed, Supreme Court nominations are part of a larger set of interactions with senators that might affect how they vote on a nomination. In 1968, the Johnson White House was on the verge of rejecting a proposed judicial nomination pushed by Senator Wayne Morse (D-OR), a strong defender of the Fortas nomination. The special assistant to the president handling the Fortas nomination urged the White House chief of staff to "go slow on any suggestion about opposing Morse's man. The Senator is one of the few tough, stand up fighters we have on the Fortas-Thornberry confirmations."[148]

At the same time, favors to key senators might be instrumental in securing votes. A Nixon White House aide suggested that when lobbying a key undecided Republican senator to vote for G. Harrold Carswell, the president should "bring up his interest in nominating a Judge to the Sixth Circuit Court of Appeals. Justice says that the judge is too old and very poorly qualified. Yet Cook has mentioned this enough times that a promise to give him the judgeship, if he brings this up, might secure his vote for Carswell."[149]

Similarly, in 1968, Senator Richard Russell (D-GA) had urged the White House to appoint Alexander Lawrence, Russell's favored candidate for a federal district judge vacancy in Georgia. The president had promised to make the nomination, but Ramsey Clark, at that time serving as attorney general, opposed the nomination. Johnson deferred to Clark, as he usually did in cases of federal district judge nominations. However, Russell became miffed at the slight. He wrote a letter to Johnson telling him that the delay in the nomination would now make it appear that he was supporting Fortas and Thornberry, as he had promised Johnson he would do, out of fear that the White House would not appoint Lawrence otherwise. Therefore, he released himself from any promise to support Johnson's nominees.[150]

Facing his own need to gain Russell's support for Fortas and Thornberry, as well as Russell's possible coalition with other southern Democrats opposing the nominations, Johnson promised Russell he would appoint Russell's district judge choice. He wrote a letter to Russell blaming the district judge appointment delay on the American Bar Association and promising Russell that he would send the name as soon as the ABA clearance arrived. In the letter, Johnson sought to downplay any quid pro quo. "I am sure that you will vote for or against the nominations of Justice Fortas and Judge Thornberry as your conscience dictates," Johnson said to Russell. "I am frankly surprised and deeply disappointed that a contrary inference would be suggested."[151]

The quid pro quo between the administration and a senator may not be limited to judicial nominations. It may cover other areas of interest for the senator. In 1970, Senator Winston Prouty (R-VT) faced a tough re-election campaign as Richard Nixon was lobbying for votes for Carswell. In a meeting with Nixon at the White House, Prouty agreed to vote for confirmation if his vote was necessary. In turn, Nixon promised to provide professional help for Prouty's re-election campaign and to look into the possibility of removing trade quotas on heating oil, an important issue for Prouty's Vermont constituents.[152]

The Senate can be divided into three groups—the supporters, the opponents, and the undecideds. The White House interacts the most with the first group and their staff.[153] They coordinate confirmation strategy. They also may collaborate with the Senate party leadership as to when certain supportive senators will announce their endorsement and speak out in behalf of a nominee.[154]

The White House also writes questions for friendly Senate Judiciary Committee members and prepares rebuttal material friendly senators can use when opposition senators attack the nominee in the hearings.[155] For example, the George H. W. Bush administration prepared questions for friendly senators that would provide an opportunity for Clarence Thomas to explain in a supportive context his past controversial positions in areas such as natural law, privacy, and affirmative action. The proffered questions include a script where senators not only could preface the questions with statements about liberals and critics, but also provide follow-up comments to conclude their questioning. At the end of a question about the "inalienable rights" clause of the Declaration of Independence, defending Thomas's views of natural law, the senator was expected to say: "Let me just say that criticizing Judge Thomas for believing in the Declaration of Independence is one of the more absurd and extreme actions that I have yet witnessed his opponents take."[156]

Since the process takes two or more months, the administration needs to reinforce its Senate supporters. To do this, a Johnson administration aide suggested that the White House shore up their supporters by calling them and thanking them for their support and asking for their suggestions about the confirmation.[157] The White House sometimes worries about the loyalty of even core supporters. In the case of the Bork nomination, the Reagan administration feared that Senator Strom Thurmond (R-SC), who was an influential member on the Judiciary Committee, was still interested in his own suggestion for a nominee, Judge William Wilkins from South Carolina, and hoped Wilkins would be the replacement if Bork was not confirmed.[158]

Another interaction with supportive senators is White House signaling of the salience of the nomination to the administration. Supportive senators worry that they may expend their own political capital in offering support for a nominee, particularly a controversial one, and then find themselves abandoned by the White House. Senators don't want to go "high-profile" on a nominee the president is not willing to work for personally.

Presidents communicate support by the extent of their attention to the confirmation process while it is occurring. Every president faces several major problems simultaneous to a Supreme Court nomination. Therefore, senators do not expect a president to devote complete time and attention to one facet of the job. However, they do want the president to clarify the level of importance of the nomination relative to other matters.

The message of high salience is transmitted when the president frequently mentions the nominee in speeches. Moreover, such mentions need to include strong statements of personal interest in the outcome of the nomination process. Additionally, lobbying signals salience, particularly when that lobbying is done personally by the president. When Clement Haynsworth's confirmation was in doubt due to growing opposition, one Republican senator communicated to Nixon that senators "would be more inclined to come out strong for Judge Haynsworth if we could be sure the Administration has decided to stick with him."[159]

Also, there are those senators who are supportive, but who, during the course of the confirmation process, could cause trouble for the White House. These are senators who may ask challenging questions rather than the softball ones the president's party members are expected to ask. During the Breyer nomination, one White House staffer suggested to the White House chief of staff that "someone should talk with [Howard] Metzenbaum [D-OH], for example—so that the confirmation hearings can be as pleasant as possible."[160] Indeed, the White House did work through Senator Edward Kennedy's office to blunt Metzenbaum's criticism of Breyer.[161]

Senators in opposition are not the objects of lobbying by the White House since such an effort is likely to be useless. However, they are of interest to the White House since what they do potentially affects the image of the nominee and eventual confirmation success. For example, the confirmation team for Ginsburg sought intelligence from a few Republicans in order to understand how other Republicans were reacting to the confirmation.[162]

Obviously, the most important group in terms of lobbying is the set of senators who are undecided, but persuadable. This group may be a dozen or so senators who provide the balance of power in the confirmation process. Identifying these individuals and determining the best strategy to woo them is key to the lobbying process.

The White House applies grassroots pressure—local individuals in the state who are willing to lobby the senator. These may include prominent attorneys, law professors, law school deans, members of the state legislature, local government officials, law enforcement groups, and prominent activists. For Thornberry, the Johnson White House recruited the dean of the University of Mississippi School of Law to write to the two Mississippi senators, both of whom were swing senators on the Thornberry nomination. The dean did not urge them explicitly to vote for Thornberry, but he did write that Thornberry has "solid scholarly achievement in the field of law" and that he had "considerable experience in a judicial capacity."[163]

The White House explores who would be most effective in reaching a particular senator. A Johnson White House aide characterized one senator as "a loner and not really close to anyone. Probably the one that could do the most good would be [Virginia] Governor [Mills] Godwin."[164] An aide in the Johnson administration told the president that a Texas supporter of Johnson "is very close to Harry McDermitt, Senator [John] McClellan's son-in-law. He called McDermitt on Homer Thornberry's behalf. . . . McDermitt reacted favorably and asked Frank to send him a letter setting out what Frank told him in the conversation. McDermitt said he would be happy to use that letter as a basis for talking to his father-in-law."[165]

The White House also relies on grassroots pressure through party networks that will provide support in a particular state. The Reagan White House wrote letters to GOP state party chairs soliciting their involvement in supporting the Supreme Court nominee. The White House wanted local Republicans to issue a press statement supporting the nominee, write their senators and seek their vote for the nominee, work with the party's central committee in organizing pro-nominee public events, write an opinion piece or letter to the editor, and attend a senator's town meeting and ask favorable questions about the nominee.[166]

In the Bork confirmation process, the Reagan administration pressured retired Justice Lewis Powell to endorse Bork. The president directly called Powell
to ask for his support after previous calls from the ranking Republican on the
Senate Judiciary Committee and the vice president had failed in obtaining
Powell's endorsement. The White House even sought Chief Justice William
Rehnquist's assistance in swaying Powell. Powell refused to join the pro-Bork
campaign.[167]

Throughout the confirmation process, the White House is coordinating with
others who are using external strategies to apply pressure to the senator. The
confirmation team organizes endorsement letters from organizations and individuals to be sent to members of the Judiciary Committee. For the Ginsburg
nomination, the confirmation team solicited letters from Ginsburg's former colleagues and students, as well as heads of particular organizations including the
NOW Legal Defense and Education Fund, the Fund for the Feminist Majority,
and the Women's Bar Association of DC.[168] The Johnson White House worked
with a fellow judge of Homer Thornberry to "line up some of the Fifth Circuit
Judges to (1) contact their respective Senators in behalf of Homer Thornberry
and (2) send a letter to Senate Judiciary endorsing Homer."[169]

The White House leans on donors to lobby senators. The Johnson administration recruited the president of a local insurance company and the principal
financial supporter of one Democratic senator, who reportedly "almost solely
financed" the senator's last re-election campaign. The donor talked the senator
into supporting Fortas and Thornberry, if his vote was necessary for confirmation. They also discovered that the longshoreman union was a major financial
supporter to a senator's last campaign and urged the president of the union to
lobby the senator to support the president's nominee.[170]

The White House also recruits prominent individuals outside the legal
community to lobby for them. To gain support for Fortas, the Johnson administration solicited members of the National Alliance of Businessmen to
contact the senators they knew to vote for confirmation. These included the
president of Eastern Airlines, the president of Burlington, and the chairman
of the board of McDonnell Douglas. The president of the Hotel Corporation
of America promised to contact seven senators he knew to urge their support of the president's nominations, while Coca-Cola executives worked with
Senator Harry Byrd (D-VA), a swing senator whose vote, they assured the
White House, would be for confirmation.[171] The Nixon administration identified supporters in a host of states, particularly those with swing senators. These
included prominent businessmen, bankers, and attorneys in these states who
were willing to contact their senators and exert pressure on them.[172]

The Nixon administration also orchestrated a letter-writing campaign involving heads of groups such as the Young Americans for Freedom, the American

Farm Bureau, and the National Chamber of Commerce; corporate leaders including the president of Georgia-Pacific and the chairman of Stouffer Foods; and prominent individuals such as conservative women's leader Phyllis Schlafly and nationally syndicated radio commentator Paul Harvey.[173]

The administration's goal is to acquire senators' assurances of their votes for confirmation. Since senators are sensitive about their independence from the administration, the confirmation team must be careful not to engage in tactics that portray senators or the US Senate generally in a negative way. During the Bork nomination, the White House Counsel's Office objected to a proposed op-ed that labeled Democratic senators opposing Bork as "hypocrites" and highlighted the senators' past statements in opposition to using ideology as a factor in a judicial nomination. The counsel suggested the White House continue to take the high road because it seemed to be working for them.[174]

More pointedly, President Reagan disparaged the opponents of Robert Bork by referring to the opposition to Bork as a "lynch mob assault." The term offended Senator John Warner (R-VA), who mentioned Reagan's comment in his floor speech explaining his vote against Bork and termed it "unbecoming the office of the Presidency." Warner's opposition was a surprise to the administration since he was typically a loyal administration supporter.[175] And in the case of the Souter nomination, George H. W. Bush toned down references to Souter in a speech to a judiciary conference under way during Souter's confirmation hearings because he did not want "to do anything that will work against him."[176]

The confirmation team frequently is surveying senators, particularly swing ones, to determine their vote inclinations. This occurs early in the confirmation process to gauge initial reaction and then throughout the process. In 1968, on the day Johnson announced his nomination of Abe Fortas as chief justice, the Johnson White House surveyed 29 senators to determine their level of support. They found that only two Republicans were opposed, although subsequent surveys found increasing opposition among conservative Republicans and southern Democrats.[177] Twenty years later, the White House sought to assess early response to Anthony Kennedy's nomination and developed a report for the White House chief of staff that listed key senators' reactions. According to the report, Senator Arlen Specter (R-PA) reacted that "Kennedy looks good" and hoped "we get this done expeditiously." Senator Thad Cochran (R-MS) said he had hoped for a southerner [to replace Virginian Lewis Powell], but would support Kennedy. Senator Alan Cranston (D-CA) replied that he did not know enough about Kennedy and was reserving judgment.[178]

The Role of Groups

As discussed previously, the role of groups has been one of the most important differences between the traditional process and today's nominations. The question for the White House is whether those groups can be enlisted in the administration's cause. Groups are not automatic supporters of a nominee, as George W. Bush discovered when he nominated Harriet Miers. The White House must cultivate group support.

The beginning of that cultivation comes during the process of presidential selection, as discussed earlier. Giving groups buy-in, similar to the access given senators, may neutralize opposition and even build support. This is particularly true if a favored candidate, such as Samuel Alito or John Roberts for conservatives or Sonia Sotomayor for Hispanics, actually gets the nomination.

On the other hand, exclusion has its costs. Groups are likely to be disappointed by the outcome of the selection process if they feel they have not been adequately included and believe the nominee may not be faithful to the groups' interests. The most famous example was the case of David Souter, where conservative groups were excluded from the presidential selection process and were upset not only because they had not played a major role in the process but also because of their uncertainty about whether the nominee was conservative enough.

The White House must appeal to the group's particular interests because the group must justify its endorsement or opposition based on its mission. The George H. W. Bush administration obtained the endorsement for David Souter of the International Narcotic Enforcement Officers Association; this group called Souter "a tough, anti-crime judge who has demonstrated a deep concern in society's battle against drug traffickers, and drunk driving."[179] On the other hand, the National Rifle Association opposed Merrick Garland on the basis of "a basic analysis of Merrick Garland's judicial record" showing, in the group's view, that Garland "does not respect our fundamental, individual right to keep and bear arms for self-defense."[180]

Narrow groups can be difficult for the White House because of the need to satisfy single-issue interests. Indeed, such groups will provide or withdraw support primarily, if not solely, based on whether their particular narrow interest has been satisfied. During the 1990s selection processes, Bill Clinton was buffeted by groups who sought singular interests. Women's rights groups privately opposed Ginsburg because she had questioned the approach of the Court in *Roe v. Wade*. Also, they publicly opposed Judge Richard Arnold because he had not sided with them on some abortion cases. Mexican American groups opposed a

Puerto Rican candidate Clinton also was considering. And civil rights groups wanted Solicitor General Drew Days to be appointed, but conservative groups opposed Days over his stand on a child pornography case.[181]

Other presidents also have faced unhappy constituent groups who offer criticism more than endorsement. In 2016, Democracy for America, a liberal group, criticized Barack Obama for not appointing an African American woman to the Court. The National Organization for Women issued a statement also criticizing Obama for not appointing an African American woman and for appointing someone with no record on women's rights. They chastised the president for following "so-called political experts" who determined that "the best choice for the highest court in the nation was a cipher—a real nowhere man." And Demand Progress's leader proclaimed: "President Obama missed the opportunity to solidify his legacy by appointing a true progressive to the Supreme Court."[182]

Indeed, presidents face a quandary between confirmability and satisfying group interests. Without a specific record to reassure them, groups can become tepid in their endorsements and not offer the grassroots support the White House sorely needs. The Douglas Ginsburg nomination was an example. Ginsburg had little public record, particularly compared to Robert Bork. Pro-life groups who were reassured by Bork's public record in opposition to *Roe v. Wade* were not reassured by Ginsburg. One group used their newsletter to term Ginsburg the "mystery man" and described anti-abortion groups as mixed in their response to him because he had no record on the issue.[183]

The groups the White House interacts with consist of a relatively small coalition whose function is to plot strategy with the administration. To drive the Kennedy confirmation process beginning in the fall of 1987, representatives of 17 groups met with four administration officials on November 17 in the White House. These groups included the Heritage Foundation, the American Conservative Union, Concerned Women for America, the Free Congress Foundation, Eagle Forum, and others.[184] Similarly, ten days after the announcement of Clarence Thomas's nomination, 17 group leaders were invited to a meeting in the Roosevelt Room in the White House to discuss strategy. They included expected conservative groups such as the Heritage Foundation, the Family Research Council, and the Free Congress Foundation. But others were not necessarily known conservative activists. Representatives were from businesses including Hallmark Cards and Maxima Corporation and trade associations like the Associated General Contractors of America, the US Chamber of Commerce, the National Federation of Independent Businesses, and the Trade Association Legislative Council.[185]

That smaller coalition may represent a larger one that unites with the White House in offering endorsements and mobilizing grassroots support, but does not necessarily participate in strategy. The White House team identifies a broad array of supportive groups who can offer endorsements of the nominee. For example, the list for Stephen Breyer included Hispanics, environmentalists, consumer advocates, women, liberal academics, law enforcement, and legal groups.[186] Similarly, the Bush administration sought support for Clarence Thomas from senior citizens, Hispanics, and women. They identified possible members of a pro-Thomas coalition from groups as diverse as the Older Women's League, the US Hispanic Chamber of Commerce, and the International Chiefs of Police.

The groups vary widely—law enforcement, religious, demographic, issuebased, trade association, union, and others. Trade groups who endorsed Clarence Thomas included the National Association of Truck Stop Operators, the US Chamber of Commerce, and the Associated General Contractors.[187] Similarly, the Reagan White House identified specific groups and then assessed their willingness to support the nominee. They reached out to groups representing Asian Americans, Eastern Europeans, Polish Americans, Hispanics, Jews, African Americans, Christian organizations, pro-life, women, and veterans.[188]

The administration then woos them, soliciting nominee support by sending them information on the nominee relevant to their interests. Also, administration representatives (particularly from the White House or the Department of Justice) meet with them to answer questions and handle group concerns. The Reagan administration sent representatives to meet with the groups, invited representatives from the group to briefings on the nominee, and mailed them information about the nominee (biographies and talking points).[189]

Groups understand their own power in the confirmation process. They are keenly aware that the White House needs them to shape public opinion and even lobby senators. They are even willing to give the White House unsolicited advice on the management of the nomination. In 2005, conservative interest groups advised the White House to end the courtesy calls by Harriet Miers because the groups felt she was doing more harm than good to her own nomination prospects.[190]

Like senators, group interest in Supreme Court nominations is not simply based on principle. Groups also may engage in a quid pro quo with the administration to gain support for other issues important to them. One religious group leader meeting with the White House Office of Legal Counsel on the Bork nomination explained what he was doing to assist the administration in stimulating grassroots efforts. At the same time, he thanked the White House legal counsel for assistance on an anti-pornography bill important to the group.[191] Similarly, Eastern Airlines executives supported the Fortas nomination because they felt that Fortas would be good for business but also because they were concerned that other legislation they were interested in would be "tied up in a filibuster."[192]

For some groups, long-term relations with the White House are important criteria in assessing levels of group support. Groups that interact with the White House on various matters and not just Supreme Court nominations may want to demonstrate their support for the nominee to assure continuing administration goodwill. During the first two months of the Bork confirmation process, the White House surveyed groups about the extent of their past and current activities on behalf of the Bork nomination. Groups quickly reported back to the White House on the activities they had undertaken on behalf of Bork, in order to reassure the White House of continued support. The American Conservative Union, the Family Research Council, and the Concerned Women for America reported they had sent out a mailing to all their members. The Eagle Forum wrote articles on the nomination and had plans to contact senators. The American Coalition for Life already had visited 80 senators and contacted 4,000 grassroots activities, while the Christian Action Council had sent information in their newsletter.[193]

Despite White House pressure, some groups, particularly business organizations, do not want to take public positions; yet they do want to be helpful to the White House to maintain overall good relations. In the Bork nomination, business groups such as the Association of General Contractors, the Business Roundtable, the US Chamber of Commerce, and the National Association of Manufacturers took "neutral" positions but used their newsletters or publications to offer "education" about the nominee. Additionally, individual leaders in the organizations took positions in favor of the nominee.[194] In the Thomas nomination, the National Federation of Independent Business sought to avoid offending the White House when it indicated to administration officials it would endorse Thomas "if absolutely necessary."[195]

Supreme Court nominations are one piece of a broader interaction between constituent groups and the administration. Indeed, support for the nominee is often simply support for the administration, not the nominee. Evidence of this comes from some groups' initial response to a nominee, particularly one they did not suggest. In the Thomas nomination, the National Right to Life Committee issued a press release admitting that Clarence Thomas had "not taken a position on *Roe v. Wade* as far as we know." However, they were pleased with the nomination because George H. W. Bush had promised to appoint a nominee who would "not legislate from the federal bench."[196] The organization was trusting the president based on what the Bush administration had promised rather than any specific record of the nominee.

The president also becomes the focus for opposition groups, particularly when they have little or no information about the nominee's views on their particular issue interests. In those cases, the group may not oppose the nominee so much as they do the president making the nomination. In 2016, the National Rifle Association issued a quick statement of strong opposition to Merrick Garland because "President Obama has nothing but contempt for the Second Amendment and law-abiding gun owners" and since he already had nominated two justices the group opposed, the NRA concluded that "there is absolutely no reason to think he has changed his approach this time."[197]

Already established groups are not the only group participants in the nomination process. The White House may use groups left over from presidential campaigns. Lawyers for Nixon targeted key senators and used its members to lobby for nominee G. Harrold Carswell.[198] The Obama administration used Organizing for America, the offshoot of the Obama presidential campaign, which urged its activists to support the effort to get Merrick Garland a Senate hearing.[199]

Or the administration can seek to form ad hoc committees to organize grassroots involvement supporting the White House. The George H. W. Bush administration formed a "Women for Judge Thomas" group to garner support for Thomas among women. The Bush administration also encouraged the creation of a "Citizens Committee to Confirm Clarence Thomas" to blunt liberal group efforts by preventing "Judge Thomas from being subjected to attacks from the special interest groups that helped hijack the Bork nomination."[200]

One curious phenomenon of group role today is involvement by groups even when confirmation is generally a foregone conclusion. In most confirmation processes since 1987, the president's party has controlled a majority of the Senate. In fact, in 2009, the majority was filibuster proof. Yet opposition groups still participated in issuing research reports, testifying against the nominee, feeding questions to senators, and engaging in other activities. Why?

The fact is that opposition groups lose nothing by actively opposing a nominee. However, they may lose by doing nothing. They may sacrifice prestige if they are moribund while a nominee opposed by their members or supporters slides toward confirmation. This is particularly true if they are dormant while other similar groups are active. Groups also forsake the opportunity to raise donations and solicit new members on the basis of the real threat of an undesirable nominee making policy on the Court or an opposition president achieving his or her objectives without significant efforts at opposition.

Groups use Supreme Court nominations to achieve organizational goals. Nominations are perfect opportunities for publicity and activation of grassroots networks. Without some immediate cause—a nominee who threatens the group's interests or the mobilization of opposing groups seeking to defeat a desired nominee—the group finds it more difficult to justify its own relevance.

Additionally, groups may be able to force the president to use political capital that would be spent on other issues opposed by the group. One conservative group leader during the Clinton administration explained that "at the very least, even if our side can't defeat a nominee in a particular instance, we would force Clinton to expend enormous political capital by mobilizing activists at the grassroots level. This is the issue that energizes conservatives more than any other."[201]

Summary

In a previous era, presidents could transmit a nomination to the Senate and expect that within a few days or weeks, the nominee would be confirmed and take a seat on the Supreme Court. Even when opposition occurred, the administration's lobbying efforts were primarily internal and involved elites, not external players such as the media, interest groups, or the public.

Those days are long gone. The Senate will not act within a few days or weeks. It may take several months to deliberate on the nominee. During that time, extensive scrutiny of the nominee and the presidential selection process will occur. Interest groups will issue reports, journalists will investigate the nominee's background, editorials will examine and comment on the nominee's past statements and decisions, public opinion polls will register the public's attitudes about the nominee and confirmation, and senators will face pressure from constituents and groups to take certain positions. The confirmation process will be neither quick nor painless for the White House.

Moreover, presidents can expect immediate negative public response from some quarters. Opposition groups already have created short lists of potential nominees, complete with dossiers describing particular views of importance to the group. They will mobilize within minutes of a nomination. The particular nominee does not really matter. The machinery for opposition is already in place and the opposition campaign will occur regardless. Since the president opposes the group's policy agenda and the group has been working against the president since Inauguration Day (or before), the Supreme Court nomination is merely the latest iteration of the ongoing battle.

Those opposition groups will be seeking to counter the image of the nominee crafted by the administration. They will point to controversial past opinions and votes, perceived negative associations, and personal background aspects that reflect poorly on the nominee. This ranges from Sonia Sotomayor's "wise Latina" remark to Clarence Thomas's relationship with Anita Hill.

Hence, effective White House management of the nomination process is essential for a successful confirmation process. Without it, a nomination may well fail. The counter image the opposition draws of the nominee would prevail in the public's mind. And senators likely would be pressured only in one direction since one side would apply well-organized pressure while the other would occur only randomly. Supportive groups might still operate, but they would do so without the leadership of the White House, which is a powerful force in effecting the administration's initiatives.

Interestingly, administrations learn from their own processes, as well as those of other administrations. In 1993, a Clinton aide wrote a final report on the confirmation process for Ruth Bader Ginsburg, detailing the stages of the process as well as the actions the White House needs to take at each stage. These include making courtesy calls, facilitating Senate requests for information on the nominee, filling out the Senate questionnaire, preparing materials for the nominee to review prior to the hearings, briefing the nominee through law professors as well as mock hearings or "murder boards," interacting with the media, organizing witnesses, acquiring office space, and so on.[202] The report would have been highly useful for the Breyer nomination, and potentially helpful for the Obama administration.

Not only do reports transcend administrations but so do individuals with knowledge of the process. Ron Klain, who had been extensively involved in the Clinton nominations, wrote a memo to Barack Obama at the commencement of the Sotomayor process explaining the process and the issues involved.[203] On the Republican side, even before a vacancy occurred, George W. Bush administration officials met with those who had been involved in the Souter and Thomas nominations to understand how the previous Bush administration had handled those nominations.[204]

The description above of the Supreme Court nomination process is not dissimilar to that applied to presidential initiatives generally. Presidents must undertake public relations campaigns to gain public support for policy initiatives, particularly controversial ones. George W. Bush traveled the country supporting US military action against Iraq in the wake of 9/11. Similarly, Barack Obama spent months selling health care reform to the American public.

What is different in this era, however, is the application of those management techniques to a process that, throughout most of its history, formally was devoid of them. Supreme Court nominations, like the war in Iraq or Obamacare, require extensive organization, planning, strategizing, and implementation. The degree of attention to such effort is not like those for a major presidential initiative like Obamacare. However, the fact that such effort is necessary is an indication of the transition to the modern era from a traditional process to one that is far more transparent and democratic.

Conclusion

With the inclusion of democratic elements—groups, party activists, the news media, and the public generally—Supreme Court nominations have moved toward a democratic process that occurs more transparently and more messily than it did before the modern era. Rather than a relatively quiet nomination followed by a sleepy confirmation process, which characterized most of the processes over the greater part of the 20th century, Supreme Court nominations today are loud and noisy and conflictual. They are dominated by media and group campaigns that portray the Court and its members as heavily political and, in the rhetoric of the opposition, threats to the good of the nation.

Stephen Breyer was the last nominee to earn near unanimous approval from the Senate, winning confirmation by a vote of 87–9 in 1994.[1] One conservative legal group leader admitted that Breyer's image was that of a restrained judge and "that's about all any senator can ask for, of any party."[2] Is such a response possible today?

On the day of the confirmation vote of Ruth Bader Ginsburg on August 3, 1993, Bill Clinton exclaimed that "too often in the recent past, judicial nominations have prompted a partisan brawl, generating more heat than light. Today we put aside partisanship, and the national interest won out."[3] But the partisanship avoidance was short-lived. It commenced again for the next process in 2005. In the meantime, it was manifested in numerous appellate judgeship confirmation processes that have bogged down over partisanship. That was a process that applied to both the Clinton and Bush presidencies before another Supreme Court nomination occurred in 2005.[4]

The absence of conflict in these two nominations may be due to a general revulsion at the process that occurred in two immediately succeeding processes—the Robert Bork and Clarence Thomas nominations in 1987 and 1991, respectively. The Bork confirmation process was dominated by a wide-scale opposition campaign based on ideological grounds. Groups engaged in tactics such as broad coalition building and paid media campaigns that had not been seen before. The Thomas nomination began on ideological grounds but ended up concentrating on personal traits and relationships. Both prompted introspection about the direction of the Supreme Court nomination process.

In retrospect, the Ginsburg and Breyer nominations were aberrations, throwbacks to an earlier era. Partisan conflict was restored in 2005 and has continued since. There is no evidence it will decline in the near future. If anything, the furor over the Garland nomination in 2016 suggests it may only increase.

The state of the process has been bemoaned for some time, even by the participants themselves. The justices have lamented the process. During his hearings, Clarence Thomas called the second round of hearings focusing on Anita Hill's accusations a "travesty" and a "high-tech lynching."[5]

However, concern about the process goes beyond the justice's own confirmation experiences. Antonin Scalia once told a group of law students that the nation now has a "controversial, bitter confirmation process" because the objective is to "put on the Court somebody who will rewrite the Constitution that you like." Scalia also noted that 20 years after his unanimous nomination that "I couldn't get 60 votes today."[6] Ruth Bader Ginsburg told another group of law students that she wished "we could wave a magic wand and go back to the days when the process was bipartisan."[7] And early in 2016, John Roberts told a group that "the process is not functioning very well" and worried about the image of the Court emanating from partisan confirmation processes:

> When you have a sharply political, divisive hearing process, it increases the danger that whoever comes out of it will be viewed in those terms. If the Democrats and Republicans have been fighting so fiercely about whether you're going to be confirmed, it's natural for some member of the public to think, well, you must be identified in a particular way as a result of that process. . . . We don't work as Democrats or Republicans and I think it's a very unfortunate impression the public might get from the confirmation process.[8]

Presidents as well have been critical of the changed process. After Abe Fortas asked Lyndon Johnson to withdraw his nomination, Johnson mourned the evolution of confirmation into a process that had been "swept by emotionalism, partisanship, and prejudice that compel great care to avoid injury to our Constitutional system."[9] Near the end of the highly contentious Bork nomination, Ronald Reagan opined that "it is time to remove the special interests from the judicial selection process. It is time to stop those who are determined to politicize the judiciary." And when he nominated Douglas Ginsburg he referred to "the campaign of pressure politics that has so recently chilled the judicial selection process." He also called on the Senate to join him in "defending the integrity and independence of the American system of justice."[10]

In 2016, Barack Obama continued that theme as he asked Republicans to put aside partisanship to give a fair hearing to Merrick Garland. Obama argued that the Supreme Court nomination process should be different from other political processes because "our Supreme Court really is unique. It's supposed to be above politics." He also urged the Senate to act because if they did not "it will indicate a process for nominating and confirming judges that is beyond repair. It will mean everything is subject to the most partisan of politics—everything."

As just seen, at first presidents complained privately about the deterioration of the process into partisanship. Then, that complaint became more public. But in 2016, Barack Obama placed the predicted consequences of the partisanship of the process in the starkest terms.

> It will provoke an endless cycle of more tit-for-tat, and make it increasingly impossible for any President, Democrat or Republican, to carry out their constitutional function. The reputation of the Supreme Court will inevitably suffer. Faith in our justice system will inevitably suffer. Our democracy will ultimately suffer, as well.[11]

Twelve years ago I suggested that the Supreme Court nomination process had become like an election and that perhaps we should go ahead and hold nonpartisan elections since we already conducted electoral-like campaigns for the Supreme Court. The idea was not intended to lead to constitutional reform. Rather, that suggestion was made to point out that our judicial selection process for the highest court in the land had been transformed into a process unlike the Framers' vision or the method incorporated for most of the nation's history.

Since then, the process has not become less political, less public, less of a campaign-style effort. The opposite is true: It has become more embroiled in partisan politics. Since then, each nomination has seen significant opposition from the minority party and, in one case, a filibuster attempt. It also has been characterized by an unwillingness by the Senate to even address a nomination by the president.

The intent of this book has been to demonstrate the evolution of the traditional process into the one Lyndon Johnson, Ronald Reagan, and Barack Obama complained about. However, this last chapter turns from the past and the present to the future. What, if anything, should be done about this transformation and the nature of the current process?

What Is to Be Done?

One school of thought says nothing should be done. The process has always been political, is now political, and will yet be political. It is the nature of the process when political actors—presidents and senators—are involved. Not much change is really necessary. Indeed, if anything, the change that has already occurred is a good thing. The public debate is healthy. The process is not an insider game with the public left out. The involvement of groups, the news media, and party activists has offered a vehicle through which the public can become involved. Since the Court affects the public, why should not the public have a role in who sits on that Court?

However, failure to act is not debate, as occurred with Merrick Garland in 2016. Nor is emphasis on the personal and salacious, as has been true for several nominees. Nor is a filibuster since it prevents a decision from even occurring, as took place with Abe Fortas in 1968 and was intended to do so with Samuel Alito in 2006. Nor is the theatre of the confirmation hearings where, for public consumption, senators ask questions that are not answered and not intended to be.

The current process places emphases on areas that would not constitute significant policy debate. Is it a good thing for the justices' private lives to become the focus of public attention? Does the incessant questioning to catch the nominee in some verbal gaffe serve a useful purpose? Should opinions of a judge become reduced to slogans for television advertisements?

But what could be done to improve the Supreme Court nomination process? Two broad categories of reform are possible. One is constitutional and the other is institutional, including reform undertaken by the Court itself.

Constitutional Reform

Some, including myself, have suggested constitutional reform to limit the terms of justices.[12] One recommendation is an 18-year term, which would be long enough for a justice to become effective on the Court but would not be a life-term appointment. The implementation of this proposal would be staggered so that a vacancy would occur regularly every two years.

How would this proposal affect the Supreme Court nomination process? The regular nature of the occurrence of nominations would reduce pressure on each confirmation process. All participants would know when the next vacancy would occur. (In the case of an unexpected death or retirement, the successor would fill the remainder of the term and, perhaps depending on the length of the remainder of the term, could be eligible for his or her own full 18-year term.)

Under the current system, presidents, senators, and groups cannot predict when another vacancy will take place. Therefore, they do not know how important this particular vacancy may be in setting the Court's judicial tone for the near future. The level of political intensity is related to that level of uncertainty.

Another element of this proposal would be the reduction of pressure on each nominee because he or she would have a defined term rather than the prospect of serving for two or three decades. Currently, part of the argument for or against a prospective nominee is the expected longevity on the Court. Presidents seek younger nominees, while opposition senators and groups become frightened at the prospect of a decades-long term for a nominee. Such a practice would become largely unnecessary since even a younger nominee would still serve no more than an 18-year term.

In lieu of term limits, another constitutional reform would be imposition of a retirement age. Most nations with life-term appointments compel justices to retire at a certain age. However, scholarly opinion is divided on whether such a retirement age would help or hurt the Court.[13] The retirement age would have to be high enough to reflect lifestyle change that has led to longer working lives for most Americans. A retirement age of 65 or even 70 is unrealistic. But one set at 75, the retirement age for Canada's justices, might fit the balance between avoiding mental deterioration while still utilizing the talents of mentally alert justices.[14]

Mandatory retirement also would remove, to some extent, the ability of justices to time their retirements for political ends. Clearly, there remains that possibility since a justice could retire at an opportune moment prior to retirement age. But a set retirement age would provide some predictability to the occurrence of Supreme Court nominations. As with term limits, that predictability might reduce the tension of not knowing when another vacancy will arise. (A by-product, however, might be the selection of younger nominees since presidents would seek a potential justice who could serve a lengthy term before mandatory retirement.)

Other constitutional reforms move beyond the frequency of vacancies to areas such as the level of support in the Senate. One proposal might necessitate a supermajority for confirmation—60 votes. That proposal would have the effect of encouraging presidents to nominate individuals with broad-based, bipartisan support in the Senate. But the high hurdle also might lead to more rejection of nominees.[15] The real question is how much of a problem there is. Since 1968, only two of the 17 successful nominees have received less than 60 votes. Moreover, the 60-vote requirement may already exist informally. Unless the Senate changes its rules to avoid filibusters of Supreme Court nominees, the prospect of filibuster is real, requiring presidents to consider filibuster-proof nominees.

Still another issue relates to who appoints. Appointment of judges by other judges has been suggested.[16] Supreme Court nominations could be the task of an ad hoc group of federal judges selected for that task with Senate confirmation following. A variation would be the inclusion of the president. The judicial committee offers the president a short list of, say, five names that the president could choose from. Senate confirmation would remain the same. Such changes would reduce the politics of the selection process. Presidents could not name friends or cronies. Interest groups may well have a more limited role in presidential selection since they have more limited interaction with judges than they do with presidents and senators.

Institutional Reform

Constitutional reform is always problematic, however. The hurdle for passing and ratifying a change in the Constitution has made such occurrences infrequent. Indeed, the reforms discussed above would be nearly impossible to achieve given the constitutional requirements coupled with the overall lack of public interest in advocating such change. However, other reforms can be accomplished more readily. These are within the purview of the president, the Senate, and the Court itself.

The President

The Constitution places no restrictions on the president's selection process. Those checks that occur do so within the confirmation process and are imposed by the Senate. However, it is possible for the executive to self-impose checks through tradition. One of those would be a formal request for the American Bar Association and other state and local bar associations to provide names from which the president would choose. In 1971, a Nixon administration aide suggested that the White House ask bar associations to recommend individuals for the Supreme Court. He recommended that when a vacancy occurs, the ABA identify the "100 best-qualified individuals in the country," and that such a list be supplemented by state bar associations providing names of five individuals from each state who should be considered.[17]

Another formal reform that could be reinforced by tradition is Senate consultation. Barack Obama solicited the views of all members of the Senate Judiciary Committee and, overall, undertook an effort to cooperate with the Senate in facilitating judicial selection.[18] All presidents should institute that practice. Of course, the White House would face the possibility of leaks. The reality is that the more individuals there are involved in the process, the greater is the likelihood of one or more participants currying favor with the press by revealing the content of the discussions. Nevertheless, the tradition may increase cooperation between the president and the Senate.

A more specific proposal is to create bipartisan Senate commissions that would recommend nominees to the president.[19] This proposal would increase the likelihood of confirmation because bipartisan agreement would be reached even prior to the presidential nomination. However, this proposal would have another effect—granting an enlarged role for the Senate in the presidential selection process. Presidents may be wary of a proposal that potentially binds them to consider a particular list drawn up by the Senate.

The Senate

The Senate Judiciary Committee today uses a variety of methods to assess nominees. The most controversial is the use of hearings. From the beginning of nominee testimony, nominees have sought to downplay the importance of their testimony. Felix Frankfurter told the committee in 1939 that they should make its judgment based on his extensive writings prior to his nomination.[20]

One suggestion is to forgo hearings altogether, or at least nominee testimony, as Benjamin Wittes has urged.[21] Paul Freund favored that move in the wake of the Bork nomination when he argued that there are better ways to educate the public about the work of the Court or even to understand the nominee's approach to judging than the spectacle of the hearings.[22] David A. Strauss and Cass R. Sunstein also suggest that the record, rather than testimony, become the principal factor in individual decision making.[23]

The discussion in this book should demonstrate that the hearings have a certain theatrical component to them, and they serve important purposes for some players. But that is different from saying that they illuminate constitutional issues and help the citizen to participate in that debate—not to mention, aiding that person in assessing whether a nominee has sufficient merit to warrant a place on the Court.

Another suggestion is to conduct most deliberations of the Senate Judiciary Committee in closed session; only the opening statements by senators and the nominee would be open to the press and the public.[24] However, it would be nearly impossible for the Senate to close most of its interaction with the nominee without being accused by the news media of undue secrecy and exclusion. As long as a potentially newsworthy session exists, the news media will clamor to be there.

Even if the Senate Judiciary Committee sessions remained open, the committee could be more disciplined in the types of questions its members ask. Still another proposal, then, is the establishment of certain committee rules that would offer guidelines to senators in the nature of questioning. Questions asking about a nominee's personal life, views about future cases, or specific issue positions not already articulated by the nominee might be ruled out of order by the committee. Paul Freund argues that a set of such rules might place at least informal limits on the role of interest groups.[25]

Concern over how nominees are treated before the Senate was addressed by the Brookings Institution in 2001 through the Presidential Appointee Initiative. The initiative, which was endorsed by 354 former presidential appointees, proposed a "Nominee's Bill of Rights." The list of rights include the right to have personal matters about a nominee discussed in a committee's executive session, the right to see and respond to opposition points privately before they are discussed in a public forum, and the right to a "timely review and action on their nominations in the Senate, with a confirmation decision normally occurring within 45 days of Senate receipt of a nomination."[26] The initiative is directed much more at executive appointees, but it also has relevance to judicial nominees, particularly lower federal court judicial candidates.

Setting a limit on the amount of time the Senate could consider a nominee would be another change intended to rein in the process from partisan abuse. Confirmation processes are much longer than they were before the modern era. Such a change in the Senate rules or perhaps in statute would compel the Senate to act in a timely manner. Michael Gerhardt and Richard Painter have suggested that the Senate impose a time limit to reach a decision of no more than 90 days after the Senate receives the president's nomination, pending the nominee's cooperation with the committee.[27]

The suggestion is not a new one. In the wake of the Clarence Thomas nomination, George H. W. Bush sought an agreement with Senate leadership that a vote would occur within six weeks after a nomination was sent to the Senate. The first subsequent nomination came close to that pattern. Ruth Bader Ginsburg was nominated on June 14 and confirmed on August 4. However, the six week (or thereabouts) suggestion was not used for the next nominee, Stephen Breyer, who was nominated on May 13, 1994, but not confirmed until July 29. Nor has it been applied to Samuel Alito, Sonia Sotomayor, and Elena Kagan, whose confirmation processes took two to three months.

Another proposal is to limit the filibuster. One possibility is to make a Supreme Court filibuster off limits through a formal rule of the Senate as discussed earlier. However, the rotation of majority control would seem to lead both parties to understand that they would benefit when they were in power. Moreover, such a rule could absolve senators of responsibility from groups for not doing all in their power to block a nominee a group did not like. Yet, such a change would be a major step in eroding individual power.

A less radical proposal is to force senators to return to the old-fashioned filibuster. At one time, a senator who sought to filibuster was required to literally hold the floor. The Hollywood portrayal of Jefferson Smith becoming hoarse on the Senate floor fit the reality of the expectations of the filibuster. Senators talked non-stop in order to block consideration of a bill. Senator Strom Thurmond, then a Democrat but later a Republican from South Carolina, set the record of

24 hours and 18 minutes.[28] Senator Ted Cruz (R-TX) came close, with 21 hours and 19 minutes.[29]

The return of that approach to the filibuster would stop business on the floor during that time period, but it would not allow invisible filibusters. There would be a cost to a filibuster if it actually stopped the Senate business. Indeed, it would force a single senator or a small group of senators to continue until they were exhausted rather than take down a nomination quietly.[30]

The filibuster for Supreme Court nominations has its proponents and critics. Proponents argue that the nature of the appointment is so important that a slow, deliberative approach is required. When arguing in defense of his filibuster of Abe Fortas, Senator Robert Griffin (R-MI) stated: "If ever there is a time when all Senators should be extremely reluctant to shut off debate, it is when the Senate debates a Supreme Court nomination." According to Griffin, mistaken legislation can be corrected, but "when a lifetime appointment to the Supreme Court is confirmed by the Senate, the nominee is not answerable thereafter to the Senate or to the people."[31]

The Senate should take responsibility for reducing the partisanship of the process and finding the balance between excessive partisanship and exclusion of external players. Currently, institutional objectives are being subordinated to the partisan ones, even in the case of Supreme Court nominations. The majority party seems willing to change the rules to achieve its partisan ends without regard to institutional ends. According to Senator Harry Reid, former majority leader, the two parties need to take a step back from this willingness to subvert the institution. "Unless there is some kind of a truce on how this happens, what is going to happen is if you have a Republican president and a Republican Senate, they will just change the rules; or a Democratic president or a Democratic Senate, they'll just change the rules."[32]

The Court

Since current justices are affected by the outcome of Senate confirmations, their involvement in the process would seem logical, particularly since they occasionally have played roles in presidential selection. However, while private lobbying of the White House and the Justice Department, as discussed previously, is outside the public view, public involvement in the confirmation process in the traditional era was a violation of norms of judicial behavior.

Yet justices have done just that in recent confirmation processes. John Paul Stevens expressed support for the confirmation of Robert Bork by stating in a speech that he considered Bork "a very well-qualified candidate and one who will be a very welcome addition to the Court."[33] In 2016, Ruth Bader Ginsburg told a reporter that she thought Merrick Garland was "about as well qualified as any nominate to this court." She called him "super bright and very nice, very easy to deal with." She said he "would be a great colleague."[34]

Justices have commented publicly on the process as well. During the Souter hearings, John Paul Stevens told attendees at an American Bar Association annual meeting that senators should not seek to pin down a nominee on issues. Stevens warned senators that "it's a mistake to assume that this process is going to enable senators . . . to predict how a nominee will vote after he or she comes on the Court."[35]

As the process has become more nakedly partisan, justices who interfere with that process are drawn into the partisan orbit as well. The recommendation for justices is to avoid comment on current processes (as opposed to the process generally when no nomination is under way). More particularly, they should steer clear of expressing a judgment on the confirmation of a nominee. Expression of support interferes in the process, but the lack of expression of support could be perceived as opposition. For example, did Ginsburg's lack of any mention of support for the nomination of Samuel Alito or John Roberts during their confirmation processes mean that she did not want them to be confirmed? A tradition of making no comment would remove current justices from involvement in the process. Their silence would mean nothing, if it were universally applied.

Changes can and should be made to the nomination process, but the root cause of interest group, public, and media involvement will not be addressed by these changes. Interest groups become engaged because a seat on the Supreme Court is the grand prize for groups using the litigation process to make public policy. Liberals have viewed the Court as a means to bypass the difficult legislative process, particularly at the state level. Why pursue 50 state governments, or even a majority of members of Congress and the approval of the White House when five individuals on the Supreme Court can accomplish the same purpose? These efforts have included litigation to shape public policy regarding school busing, abortion, environmental regulation, marriage, and a host of other issues.

As a consequence, conservatives have blamed "liberal activist judges" and Republican presidents like Reagan, the Bushes, and Trump have promised to appoint justices who do not "legislate from the bench." Yet conservatives have employed the same strategies. They have lobbied for decisions against Obamacare, gun regulations, and campaign finance reform legislation, as well as for ones in favor of partial birth abortion bans.[36]

The "Court" strategy has been employed across various types and ideologies of groups because it is the means for effecting relatively quick changes made by a small group of people. And success in placing individuals on the Court can determine success in Court decision making. A recent example is the replacement of Sandra Day O'Connor, who joined the majority in several cases that were switched by her successor, Samuel Alito. The O'Connor-Alito effect is hardly lost on groups watching the Supreme Court. The replacement of a single justice can result in litigation success or defeat. That is why groups now devote so many resources to affecting who is nominated and confirmed.

Only when that Supreme Court seat no longer has the aura of power will today's players in the process move away to more fruitful endeavors. When they perceive that the Court, for the most part, will neither help them nor harm them in political battles, they will return to political institutions as their venues for policy change. In order for groups not to view the nomination process as a prerequisite for litigation strategies, the Court must not satisfy their demands for action. The Court must restrain itself.

One method for self-restraint is to decline to accept a case until the political process has been able to play out further. The classic example is the battle over the right to an abortion. In 1973, the Court short-circuited political debate on whether a woman had a constitutional right to obtain an abortion, and, if so, what limits could be imposed on that right. In 1973, states were dealing with that issue. Some like California and New York were liberalizing laws to allow more choice, particularly earlier in a pregnancy. Others were not changing those laws. Still others were in debate over whether to do so and what policy outcomes should be chosen. The Court wiped away most states' existing abortion laws.

However, the Court's efforts to settle the issue backfired. Over 40 years after *Roe*, the issue remains alive. States increasingly are moving to impose more regulations on abortion.[37] The number of abortions is declining as they become more difficult to obtain. Public opinion is still divided, with the pro-life position gaining support in recent years, particularly among younger voters.[38]

The role of an activist court should not be overstated. It is not the sole reason for the change occurring in the nomination process. Democratic trends in American government generally have propelled these trends in the nomination process as well. However, such efforts by the Court might reduce the tension in the nomination process since groups may devote more resources to other political strategies than attempting to shape the personnel of the Court.

The Future of Nominations

The nomination process has irrevocably changed. It is not possible to return to the elite-driven process that characterized nominations through most of the nation's history. Nor would it be desirable to do so. A quick process that eliminates a substantial check and places individuals on the Court without much vetting is not one the nation should want to incorporate again.

At the same time, there are ways to ameliorate the process to reduce the intensity of partisanship and ideology, as just discussed. Limits can be placed that channel democratic elements in a way that does not cause the consequences predicted by Barack Obama in announcing Merrick Garland's nomination. Institutions should consider such limitations that would reduce the tension that has built up within this process.

We should not forget that the Supreme Court nomination process is the means by which the nation chooses individuals to sit at the highest level of our judicial branch. Without public respect for that body, it can no longer serve as the final arbiter of our governmental system. A court that loses our trust is useless in settling those issues that only it can handle.

Our Supreme Court nomination process should be designed not to undermine that institutional respect. It does not mean that public agreement with decisions or the outcome of nomination processes is essential. Americans may differ on whether a particular nominee belongs on the Court. However, if the process that leads to that outcome is tainted in the public mind, consequences follow for public respect for the nominee, the process, and the Court itself. The Court no longer can perform the functions it is assigned under the Constitution, weakening the third branch of government. Such a result ultimately harms all Americans.

NOTES

Introduction

1. For a discussion of the politicization of the Senate confirmation process of executive appointments and/or lower-level federal appointments, see Stephen Carter, *The Confirmation Mess: Cleaning Up the Federal Appointments Process* (New York: Basic Books, 1995); G. Calvin McKenzie, ed., *Innocent until Nominated: The Breakdown of the Presidential Appointments Process* (Washington, DC: Brookings, 2001); and Nancy Scherer, *Scoring Points: Politicians, Activists, and the Lower Federal Court Appointment Process* (Stanford, CA: Stanford University Press, 2005).

2. Stuart Taylor Jr., "Politics in the Bork Battle," *New York Times*, September 28, 1987, p. A1.

3. See Richard Davis, *Electing Justice: Fixing the Supreme Court Nomination Process* (New York: Oxford University Press, 2005).

4. Theodore B. Olson, "The Senate Confirmation Process: Advise and Consent, or Search and Destroy," *Gauer Distinguished Lecture in Law and Public Policy*, vol. 15 (Washington, DC: National Legal Center for the Public Interest, 2006), p. 13.

5. Quoted in Nina Totenberg, "Robert Bork's Supreme Court Nomination Changed Everything, Maybe Forever," *National Public Radio*, December 19, 2012, at *http://www.npr.org/sections/ itsallpolitics/2012/12/19/167645600/robert-borks-supreme-court-nomination-changed- everything-maybe-forever*. Accessed June 23, 2015.

6. Speech by Senator Joseph Biden on reform of the confirmation process, *Congressional Record*, June 25, 1992, vol. 138, no. 93, p. S8861.

7. Ethan Bronner, *Battle for Justice: How the Bork Nomination Shook America* (New York: Doubleday, 1990), pp. 274–275.

8. "The Roberts' Adoptions: What We Do Know," *Underneath Their Robes*, August 4, 2005, at *http://underneaththeirrobes.blogs.com/main/2005/08/the_roberts_ado.html*. Accessed April 28, 2005.

9. See Timothy M. Phelps and Helen Winternitz, *Capitol Games: The Inside Story of Clarence Thomas, Anita Hill, and a Supreme Court Nomination* (New York: Hyperion, 1992).

10. George L. Watson and John A. Stookey, *Shaping America: The Politics of Supreme Court Appointments* (New York: HarperCollins, 1995), p. 21.

11. See Bronner, *Battle for Justice*; "Sen. Biden Wants Specifics from Souter," *Los Angeles Times*, September 11, 1990, at *http://articles.latimes.com/1990-09-11/news/mn-406_1_supreme- court-nominee*. Accessed June 23, 2015; Huma Khan and Jake Tapper, "Newt Gingrich on Twitter: Sonia Sotomayor 'Racist,' Should Withdraw," *ABCNews*, May 27, 2009, at *http:// abcnews.go.com/Politics/SoniaSotomayor/story?id=7685284*. Accessed June 23, 2015.

12. Elie Mystal, "Robert Bork: The Man Who Borked the SCOTUS Nomination Process," *Above the Law*, December 19, 2012, at *http://abovethelaw.com/2012/12/robert-bork-the- man-who-borked-the-scotus-nomination-process/*. Accessed June 23, 2015.

13. See Lee Epstein and Jeffrey A. Segal, *Advice and Consent: The Politics of Judicial Appointments* (New York: Oxford University Press, 2005).

14. See Dion Farganis and Justin Wedeking, *Supreme Court Confirmation Hearings in the U.S. Senate: Reconsidering the Charade* (Ann Arbor: University of Michigan Press, 2014); Paul M. Collins Jr. and Lori A. Ringhand, *Supreme Court Confirmation Hearings and Constitutional Change* (New York: Cambridge University Press, 2013); and Michael Comiskey, *Seeking Justices: The Judging of Supreme Court Nominees* (Lawrence: University of Kansas Press, 2004).

15. Davis, *Electing Justice: Fixing the Supreme Court Nomination Process*, pp. 170–172. The proposal was connected to a regular election process.

16. See Farganis and Wedeking, *Supreme Court Confirmation Hearings*; and Collins and Ringhand, *Supreme Court Confirmation Hearings*.

17. See Stephen Carter, *The Confirmation Mess: Cleaning Up the Federal Appointments Process* (New York: Basic Books, 1995); and Ronald Rotunda, "The Role of Ideology in Confirming Federal Court Judges," *Georgetown Journal of Legal Ethics*, 15 (2001–2002): 127–141.

18. See Christopher L. Eisgruber, *The Next Justice: Repairing the Supreme Court Appointments Process* (Princeton, NJ: Princeton University Press, 2007).

19. "Senator Barack Obama on Samuel Alito," C-SPAN, January 26, 2006, at *https://www.c-span.org/video/?c4580879/sen-barack-obama-samuel-alito*. Accessed July 26, 2016.

20. "Remarks by the President in Nominating Judge Sonia Sotomayor to the United States Supreme Court," White House Office of the Press Secretary, May 26, 2009, at *https://www.whitehouse.gov/the-press-office/remarks-president-nominating-judge-sonia-sotomayor-united-states-supreme-court*. Accessed January 27, 2016; and "Remarks by the President and Solicitor General Elena Kagan at the Nomination of Solicitor General Elena Kagan to the Supreme Court," White House Office of the Press Secretary, May 10, 2010, at *https://www.whitehouse.gov/the-press-office/remarks-president-and-solicitor-general-elena-kagan-nomination-solicitor-general-el*. Accessed January 27, 2016.

21. Jordan Fabian, "Obama 'Regrets' His Filibuster of Supreme Court Nominee," *The Hill*, February 17, 2016, at *http://thehill.com/homenews/administration/269719-white-house-obama-regrets-his-filibuster-of-supreme-court-nominee*. Accessed July 26, 2016.

22. See Supreme Court Nominations present–1789, United States Senate, at *http://www.senate.gov/pagelayout/reference/nominations/Nominations.htm*. Accessed March 25, 2015.

23. John P. Frank, "The Appointment of Supreme Court Justices: III," *Wisconsin Law Review*, 1941 (1941): 512.

24. The percentage of all nominations that resulted in confirmation of the nominee.

25. Collins and Ringhand, *Supreme Court Confirmation Hearings*, pp. 51–52.

26. James Haw, *John & Edward Rutledge of South Carolina* (Athens: University of Georgia Press, 1997), pp. 255–258.

27. Richard Davis, *Justices and Journalists: The U.S. Supreme Court and the Media* (New York: Cambridge University Press, 2011), pp. 57–68.

28. Joseph P. Harris, *The Advice and Consent of the Senate: A Study of the Confirmation of Appointments by the United States Senate* (Berkeley: University of California Press, 1953), pp. 303–304.

29. Denis Steven Rutkus et al., *Supreme Court Nominations 1789–2005: Actions (including Speed) by the Senate, the Judiciary Committee, and the President* (New York: Nova Science, 2007), Table 1.

30. Joel B. Grossman and Stephen L. Wasby, "The Senate and Supreme Court Nominations: Some Reflections," *Duke Law Journal* 1972 (1972): 557–591.

31. Richard Dubin, "The 1968 Confirmation Hearings of Justice Abe Fortas," *Colonial Lawyer*, 7 (Spring 1977): 10; and Nomination of Judge Robert H. Bork to Be Associate Justice of the Supreme Court of the United States, Hearings before the Committee on the Judiciary, United States Senate, One Hundredth Congress, first session, September 15, 166, 17, 18, 19, 21, 22, 23, 25, 28, 29, and 30, 1987 (Washington, DC: US Government Printing Office, 1989).

32. See Farganis and Wedeking, *Supreme Court Confirmation Hearings*; Collins and Ringhand, *Supreme Court Confirmation Hearings*; Epstein and Segal, *Advice and Consent*; Davis, *Electing Justice*; Michael Comiskey, *Seeking Justices: The Judging of Supreme Court Nominees* (Lawrence: University Press of Kansas, 2004); David Alistair Yalof, *Pursuit of*

Justices: Presidential Politics and the Selection of Supreme Court Nominees (Chicago: University of Chicago Press, 1999).

33. Bronner, *Battle for Justice*; and Jane Mayer and Jill Abramson, *Strange Justice: The Selling of Clarence Thomas* (New York: Plume, 1995).

34. See Paul Simon, *Advice and Consent: Clarence Thomas, Robert Bork, and the Intriguing History of the Supreme Court's Nomination Battles* (Washington, DC: National Press Books, 1992); and Mark Gitenstein, *Matters of Principle: An Insider's Account of America's Rejection of Robert Bork's Nomination to the Supreme Court* (New York: Simon and Schuster, 1992).

35. Nomination of Judge Clarence Thomas to Be Associate Justice of the Supreme Court of the United States, Hearings before the Committee on the Judiciary, United States Senate, One Hundredth and Second Congress, first session, Part 1 (September 10, 11, 12, 13, and 16, 1991), Part 2 (September 17 and 19, 1991), Part 3 (September 20, 1991), Part 4 (October 11, 12, and 13, 1991), at *http://www.gpo.gov/fdsys/search/pagedetails.action?granuleId=&pac kageId=GPO-CHRG-THOMAS*. Accessed April 28, 2015; and Nomination of Judge Robert H. Bork to Be Associate Justice of the Supreme Court of the United States, Hearings before the Committee on the Judiciary, United States Senate, One Hundredth Congress, first session, September 15, 16, 17, 18, 19, 21, 22, 23, 25, 28, 29, and 30, 1987 (Washington, DC: US Government Printing Office, 1989).

36. Rutkus et al., *Supreme Court Nominations 1789–2005*, Table 1.

37. For discussions of the Clarence Thomas nomination process, see Christopher E. Smith, *Critical Judicial Nominations and Political Change: The Impact of Clarence Thomas* (Westport, CT: Praeger, 1993); Phelps and Winternitz, *Capitol Games*; and Mayer and Abramson, *Strange Justice*.

38. E. J. Dionne Jr., "On Once and Future Supreme Court Nominations," *Washington Post*, June 19, 1992, p. A25.

39. Rutkus et al., *Supreme Court Nominations 1789–2005*, Table 1.

40. For a discussion of the changes in confirmation processes in lower-level judicial appointments, see Sarah A. Binder and Forrest Maltzman, *Advice and Dissent: The Struggle to Shape the Federal Judiciary* (Washington, DC: Brookings, 2009).

Constitutional and Early American Political Underpinnings

1. See Henry J. Abraham, *Justices, Presidents, and Senators*, 5th ed. (Lanham, MD: Rowman and Littlefield, 2008).

2. Viscount James Bryce, *The American Commonwealth*, with an Introduction by Gary L. McDowell, 2 vols. (Indianapolis, IN: Liberty Fund, 1995), at *http://oll.libertyfund.org/titles/809#Bryce_0004-01_199*.

3. Charles L. Black Jr., "A Note on Senatorial Consideration of Supreme Court Nominees," *Yale Law Journal*, 79 (1969–1970): 657; and David A. Strauss and Cass R. Sunstein, "The Senate, the Constitution, and the Confirmation Process," *Yale Law Journal*, 101 (May 1992): 1493.

4. Quoted in Joel B. Grossman and Stephen L. Wasby, "The Senate and Supreme Court Nominations: Some Reflections," *Duke Law Journal*, 1972 (August 1972): 558.

5. "President Bush Discusses Judicial Accomplishments and Philosophy," White House news release, October 6, 2008, at *http://georgewbush-whitehouse.archives.gov/news/releases/2008/10/20081006-5.html*. Accessed February 8, 2016.

6. Quoted in Grossman and Wasby, "The Senate and Supreme Court Nominations," 1972: 560.

7. "Goodell Announces Opposition to Nomination of Carswell," Office of Senator Goodell press release, February 5, 1970, Papers of Fred Graham, Box 5, Manuscript Division, Library of Congress.

8. Senator Orrin Hatch, "Protect the Senate's Important 'Advice and Consent' Role," *The Hill*, April 11, 2014, at *http://thehill.com/opinion/op-ed/203226-protect-the-senates-important-advice-and-consent-role*. Accessed July 26, 2016; and Paul Simon, "Advise and Consent: The Senate's Role in the Judicial Nomination Process," *Journal of Civil Rights and Development*, 7 (Fall 1991): 41–47.

9. Quoted in Grossman and Wasby, "The Senate and Supreme Court Nominations," 1972: 560.

10. Abraham, *Justices, Presidents, and Senators*, p. 156.

11. Denis Steven Rutkus et al., *Supreme Court Nominations 1789–2005: Actions (including Speed) by the Senate, the Judiciary Committee, and the President* (New York: Nova Science, 2007), Table 1.

12. Leo Katcher, *Earl Warren: A Political Biography* (New York: McGraw-Hill, 1967), pp. 289–297; and Bill Severn, *Mr. Chief Justice: Earl Warren* (New York: Van Rees Press, 1968), p. 135.

13. John Woolley and Gerhard Peters, "Ronald Reagan: Governor Reagan's News Conference, October 14, 1980." The American Presidency Project at *http://www.presidency.ucsb.edu/ws/index.php?pid=85232.* Accessed January 7, 2016.

14. William E. Leuchtenberg, *The Supreme Court Reborn: The Constitutional Revolution in the Age of Roosevelt* (New York: Oxford University Press, 1995), pp. 145–152.

15. See John W. Dean, *The Rehnquist Choice: The Untold Story of the Nixon Appointment That Redefined the Supreme Court* (New York: Touchstone, 2001).

16. Letter from George Washington to Senate, September 25, 1789, *George Washington Papers, 1741–1799: Series 2 Letterbooks,* at *http://memory.loc.gov/cgi-bin/ampage?collId=mgw2&fileName=gwpage025.db&recNum=96.* Accessed March 15, 2016.

17. "Remarks by the President in Nominating Judge Sonia Sotomayor to the United States Supreme Court," White House Press Release, May 26, 2009, at *https://www.whitehouse.gov/video/President-Obama-Nominates-Sotomayor/#transcript.* Accessed February 17, 2016.

18. For a brief discussion of the constitutional convention's treatment of judicial selection, see Sarah A. Binder and Forrest Maltzman, *Advice and Dissent: The Struggle to Shape the Federal Judiciary* (Washington, DC: Brookings, 2009), pp. 18–26; and Mitchel A. Sollenberger, *Judicial Appointments and Democratic Controls* (Durham, NC: Carolina Academic Press, 2011), pp. 33–37.

19. Marc W. Kruman, *Between Authority and Liberty: State Constitution Making in Revolutionary America* (Chapel Hill: University of North Carolina Press, 1997), pp. 120–122.

20. Ruth Bader Ginsburg, "Confirming Supreme Court Justices: Thoughts on the Second Opinion Rendered by the Senate," *University of Illinois Law Review,* 1988 (1988): 105.

21. James Madison, *Madison Debates,* May 29, 1787, The Avalon Project, Yale Law School, Lillian Goldman Law Library, at *http://avalon.law.yale.edu/18th_century/debates_605.asp.* Accessed February 17, 2015.

22. Ginsburg, "Confirming Supreme Court Justices," 105.

23. Michael Korzi, *Presidential Term Limits in American History: Power, Principles, and Politics* (College Station: Texas A & M University Press, 2011), p. 22.

24. Binder and Maltzman, *Advice and Dissent,* pp. 18–26.

25. Kruman, *Between Authority and Liberty;* Sollenberger, *Judicial Appointments and Democratic Controls,* p. 7.

26. Max Farrand, Records of the Federal Convention, vol. 1, p. 128, at *http://www.memory.loc.gov/ammem/amlaw/lwfr.html.* Accessed January 13, 2016.

27. Farrand, Records of the Federal Convention, vol. 1, pp. 119–120.

28. Farrand, Records of the Federal Convention, vol. 1, p. 120.

29. Farrand, Records of the Federal Convention, vol. 1, pp. 119, 120, 126; and James Madison, *Madison Debates,* June 5, 1787, The Avalon Project, Yale Law School, Lillian Goldman Law Library, at *http://avalon.law.yale.edu/18th_century/debates_605.asp.* Accessed February 17, 2015.

30. Farrand, Records of the Federal Convention, vol. 3, pp. 236–238.

31. Julius Goebel Jr., *History of the Supreme Court of the United States,* vol. 1 (New York: Macmillan, 1971), pp. 206–207.

32. James Madison, *Madison Debates,* June 15, 1787.

33. James Madison, *Madison Debates,* July 18, 1787.

34. Farrand, Records of the Federal Convention, vol. 2, p. 37; James Madison, *Madison Debates,* July 18, 1787; and Binder and Maltzman, *Advice and Dissent,* pp. 21–22.

35. James Madison, *Madison Debates,* July 21, 1787.

36. James Madison, *Madison Debates,* July 21, 1787.

37. Farrand, Records of the Federal Convention, vol. 2, pp. 71–72.

38. James Madison, *Madison Debates,* August 6, 1787.

39. Goebel, *History of the Supreme Court,* vol. 1, pp. 2224–2225.

40. Farrand, *Records of the Federal Convention*, vol. 2, p. 539.
41. James Madison, *Madison Debates*, September 4, 1787.
42. Farrand, *Records of the Federal Convention*, vol. 2, p. 533; and James Madison, *Madison Debates*, September 7, 1787.
43. Jackson Turner Main, *The Anti-Federalists: Critics of the Constitution 1781–1788* (New York: W. W. Norton, 1961), pp. 138–139.
44. Main, *The Anti-Federalists*, pp. 155–158.
45. Quoted in Main, *The Anti-Federalists*, p. 156.
46. Quoted in Joseph P. Harris, *The Advice and Consent of the Senate* (Berkeley: University of California Press, 1953), p. 25.
47. Jonathan Eliot, *Debates in the Several State Conventions on the Adoption of the Federal Constitution as Recommended by the General Convention at Philadelphia*, vol. II (Philadelphia: J. B. Lippincott, 1891), pp. 504–505.
48. Quoted in Harris, *The Advice and Consent of the Senate*, p. 26.
49. Quoted in Harris, *The Advice and Consent of the Senate*, p. 29.
50. David A. Strauss and Cass R. Sunstein, "The Senate, the Constitution, and the Confirmation Process," *Yale Law Journal*, 101 (May 1992): 1520.

The Traditional Process

1. Henry J. Abraham, *Justices, Presidents, and Senators*, 5th ed. (Lanham, MD: Rowman and Littlefield, 2008), pp. 57–58.
2. Ron Chernow, *Washington: A Life* (New York: Penguin, 2010), pp. 591–592.
3. George Washington, *George Washington to Senate, September 25, 1789, Nominations*. Letter. From Library of Congress, *George Washington Papers, 1741–1799: Series 2 Letterbooks*. Source, Collection. *http://memory.loc.gov/cgi-bin/ampage?collId=mgw2&fileName=gwpage025.db& recNum=96*. Accessed March 15, 2016.
4. Joshua Glick, "On the Road: The Supreme Court and the History of Circuit Riding," *Cardozo Law Review*, 24 (2002–2003): 1753–1816; Walter Stahr, *John Jay: Founding Father* (New York: Hambledon and London, 2005), pp. 273–280.
5. Abraham, *Justices, Presidents, and Senators*, p. 61.
6. Abraham, *Justices, Presidents, and Senators*, Appendix C.
7. Abraham, *Justices, Presidents, and Senators*, pp. 66–67.
8. Walter Stahr, *John Jay: Founding Father* (New York: Hambledon and London, 2005), p. 272; and "Letter of John Jay to John Adams, January 2, 1801," in Maeva Marcus et al., eds., *The Documentary History of the Supreme Court of the United States, 1789–1800, volume 1, Part 1: Appointments and Proceedings* (New York: Columbia University Press, 1985), pp. 146–147.
9. For biographical background on Jay, see Stahr, *John Jay: Founding Father*.
10. Stahr, *John Jay: Founding Father*, p. 273.
11. Abraham, *Justices, Presidents, and Senators*, p. 61.
12. Abraham, *Justices, Presidents, and Senators*, pp. 58–64, 65–66, 74, 78–83.
13. William J. Daniels, "The Geographic Factor in Appointments to the United States Supreme Court: 1789–1976," *Western Political Quarterly*, 31 (June 1978): 227.
14. Quoted in Abraham, *Justices, Presidents, and Senators*, p. 64.
15. "Members of the Supreme Court of the United States," Supreme Court of the United States, at *http://www.supremecourt.gov/about/members_text.aspx*. Accessed July 13, 2016.
16. James Haw, *Stormy Patriot: The Life of Samuel Chase* (Baltimore: Maryland Historical Society, 1980), pp. 209–242.
17. See Richard E. Ellis, *The Jefferson Crisis: Courts and Politics in the Young Republic* (New York: W. W. Norton, 1974); and Abraham, *Justices, Presidents, and Senators*, pp. 68–69.
18. Abraham, *Justices, Presidents, and Senators*, pp. 68–69.
19. Stahr, *John Jay: Founding Father*, pp. 271–272.
20. Alex Markels, "Why Miers Withdrew as a Supreme Court Nominee," National Public Radio, October 27, 2005, at *http://www.npr.org/templates/story/story.php?storyId=4976787*. Accessed July 27, 2016; and Charles Babington and Michael A. Fletcher, "Senators Assail Miers' Replies,

Ask for Details," *Washington Post*, October 20, 2005, at *http://www.washingtonpost.com/wp-dyn/content/article/2005/10/19/AR2005101902402.html*. Accessed July 27, 2016; and Stephen Henderson, "ABA Rating Takes on More Heft; Because Harriet Miers Has Little on Record, the Bar Association's Report Could Play a Key Role," *Philadelphia Inquirer*, October 17, 2005, at *http://articles.philly.com/2005-10-17/news/25442907_1_aba-rating-nominees-for-federal-judgeships-low-rating*. Accessed July 27, 2016.

21. Abraham, *Justices, Presidents, and Senators*, pp. 159–161.

22. Lee Epstein, Jack C. Knight, and Olga Svetsova, "Comparing Judicial Selection Systems," *William & Mary Bill of Rights Journal*, 10 (2001): 7–36.

23. Epstein and Segal, *Advice and Consent*, p. 68.

24. Abraham, *Justices, Presidents, and Senators*, p. 49; and Biographies of Current Justices of the Supreme Court, Supreme Court of the United States, at *http://www.supremecourt.gov/about/biographies.aspx*. Accessed July 8, 2016.

25. John W. Dean, *The Rehnquist Choice: The Untold Story of the Nixon Appointment That Redefined the Supreme Court* (New York: Touchstone, 2001), pp. 20–21.

26. Memorandum to the President from Theodore Sorensen, March 29, 1962, "Supreme Court," Papers of John F. Kennedy, Presidential Papers, President's Office Files, at *http://www.jfklibrary.org/Asset-Viewer/Archives/JFKPOF-088a-011.aspx*. Accessed March 21, 2016.

27. Robert A. Caro, *The Years of Lyndon Johnson: Means of Ascent* (New York: Alfred A. Knopf, 1990), pp. 368–384.

28. See Laura Kalman, *Fortas: A Biography* (New Haven, CT: Yale University Press, 1990).

29. Abraham, *Justices, Presidents, and Senators*, p. 226.

30. "LBJ's Nomination of Abe Fortas to the Supreme Court, July 1965 and Chief Justice, 1968," Miller Center, University of Virginia, at *http://millercenter.org/presidentialclassroom/exhibits/lbjs-nomination-of-abe-fortas*. Accessed May 9, 2016.

31. "LBJ's Nomination of Abe Fortas to the Supreme Court, July 1965 and Chief Justice, 1968."

32. Abraham, *Justices, Presidents, and Senators*, p. 258.

33. Abraham, *Justices, Presidents, and Senators*, pp. 121–122.

34. Abraham, *Justices, Presidents, and Senators*, pp. 95–96, 106–107.

35. Epstein and Segal, *Advice and Consent*, pp. 129–133, 135–137.

36. Abraham, *Justices, Presidents, and Senators*, p. 75.

37. Abraham, *Justices, Presidents, and Senators*, pp. 78–83.

38. Abraham, *Justices, Presidents, and Senators*, pp. 123–145.

39. William E. Leuchtenberg, *The Supreme Court Reborn: The Constitutional Revolution in the Age of Roosevelt* (New York: Oxford University Press, 1995), pp. 145–152; and Abraham, *Justices, Presidents, and Senators*, p. 166.

40. Abraham, *Justices, Presidents, and Senators*, pp. 68–70.

41. See Christopher E. Smith, *John Paul Stevens: Defender of Rights in Criminal Justice* (Lanham, MD: Lexington Books, 2015); Linda Greenhouse, *Becoming Justice Blackmun: Harry Blackmun's Supreme Court Journey* (New York: Times Books, 2006); and Tinsley Yarborough, *David Souter: Traditional Republican on the Rehnquist Court* (New York: Oxford University Press, 2005).

42. William M. Landes and Richard A. Posner, "Rational Judicial Behavior: A Statistical Study," *Journal of Legal Analysis*, 1 (Summer 2009): 775–831.

43. The American Presidency Project, "Richard Nixon, Statement about Nominations to the Supreme Court, April 9, 1970," at *http://www.presidency.ucsb.edu/ws/index.php?pid=2456&st=&st1=*. Accessed May 31, 2016.

44. Kevin J. McMahon, *Nixon's Court: His Challenge to Judicial Liberalism and Its Political Consequences* (Chicago: University of Chicago Press, 2011).

45. "President Bush Discusses Judicial Accomplishments and Philosophy," White House news release, October 6, 2008, at *http://georgewbush-whitehouse.archives.gov/news/releases/2008/10/20081006-5.html*. Accessed February 8, 2016.

46. "LBJ's Nomination of Abe Fortas to the Supreme Court, July 1965 and Chief Justice, 1968," Miller Center, University of Virginia, at *http://millercenter.org/presidentialclassroom/exhibits/lbjs-nomination-of-abe-fortas*. Accessed May 9, 2016.

47. Memorandum to the President from Theodore Sorensen, March 29, 1962, "Supreme Court," Papers of John F. Kennedy, Presidential Papers, President's Office Files, at *http://www.jfklibrary.org/ Asset-Viewer/Archives/JFKPOF-088a-011.aspx*. Accessed March 21, 2016.

48. Memorandum from the President to William Rogers, September 17, 1958, DDE Diary Series, Box 36, Dwight D. Eisenhower Library.

49. Abraham, *Justices, Presidents, and Senators*, p. 283.

50. Quoted in Abraham, *Justices, Presidents, and Senators*, p. 183.

51. Abraham, *Justices, Presidents, and Senators*, p. 189.

52. Dean, *The Rehnquist Choice*, pp. 47, 206, and 213.

53. Leuchtenburg, *The Supreme Court Reborn*, pp. 135–154.

54. Memorandum from Peter D. Keisler, Associate Counsel to the President, to Leslye A. Arsht, Special Assistant to the President and Deputy Press Secretary, "Ginsburg Nomination," October 30, 1987, Peter D. Keisler Files, 1984–1987, Series I: Chronological File— September 16, 1987–December 31, 1987, Box 6, Reagan Presidential Library.

55. Dean, *The Rehnquist Choice*, p. 47.

56. Abraham, *Justices, Presidents, and Senators*, pp. 207–208.

57. Melvin I. Urofsky, "Wilson, Brandeis, and the Supreme Court Nomination," *Journal of Supreme Court History*, 28 (July 2003): 145–156.

58. Letter to John N. Mitchell from John A. Volpe, October 13, 1971, White House Special Files, Staff Member Office Files: Charles Colson, Box 110, Nixon Presidential Library.

59. Abraham, *Justices, Presidents, and Senators*, p. 68.

60. For a discussion of the role of geography in appointments, see Daniels, "The Geographic Factor," pp. 226–237.

61. Abraham, *Justices, Presidents, and Senators*, p. 114.

62. Abraham, *Justices, Presidents, and Senators*, pp. 96–97.

63. Abraham, *Justices, Presidents, and Senators*, p. 113.

64. Daniels, "The Geographic Factor," p. 227.

65. Quoted in Abraham, *Justices, Presidents, and Senators*, p. 124.

66. Ira H. Carmen, "The President, Politics, and the Power of Appointment: Hoover's Nomination of Mr. Justice Cardozo," *Virginia Law Review*, 55 (1969): 627.

67. Abraham, *Justices, Presidents, and Senators*, pp. 166–181.

68. "LBJ's Nomination of Abe Fortas to the Supreme Court, July 1965 and Chief Justice, 1968," Miller Center, University of Virginia, at *http://millercenter.org/presidentialclassroom/exhibits/ lbjs-nomination-of-abe-fortas*. Accessed May 9, 2016.

69. The American Presidency Project, "Richard Nixon, Statement about Nominations to the Supreme Court, April 9, 1970," at *http://www.presidency.ucsb.edu/ws/index.php?pid =2456&st=&st1=*. Accessed May 31, 2016.

70. Daniels, "The Geographic Factor."

71. John Schwartz, "Long Shot for High Court Has Reputation for Compassion and Persuasion," *New York Times*, May 5, 2010, at *http://www.nytimes.com/2010/05/06/us/06thomas.html*. Accessed July 14, 2016.

72. Daniels, "The Geographic Factor." The 17 unrepresented states, along with North Dakota, are Vermont, Rhode Island, Delaware, Florida, West Virginia, Arkansas, Oklahoma, South Dakota, Nebraska, Oregon, Montana, Idaho, Nevada, New Mexico, Alaska, and Hawaii.

73. Abraham, *Justices, Presidents, and Senators*, p. 208.

74. Carmen, "The President, Politics, and the Power of Appointment."

75. Julie Zauzmer, "What Would a Hindhu Justice Mean for the Supreme Court," *Washington Post*, March 10, 2016, at *https://www.washingtonpost.com/news/acts-of-faith/wp/2016/03/ 10/what-would-a-hindu-justice-mean-for-the-supreme-court/*. Accessed July 27, 2016.

76. Abraham, *Justices, Presidents, and Senators*, p. 122.

77. Abraham, *Justices, Presidents, and Senators*, pp. 217–218.

78. Letter to Robert E. Lillard, President, National Bar Association, from Lawrence F. O'Brien, Special Assistant to the President, March 31, 1962, White House Central Files, Name File, Byron White, John F. Kennedy Presidential Library; and Letter to Kenneth Hahn, Chairman, Courts Committee Board of Supervisors, from T. J. Reardon Jr., Special Assistant to the President, May 10, 1962, White House Central File, Name File, Byron White, Box 194, John F. Kennedy Presidential Library.

79. Memorandum to the President from Theodore Sorensen, March 29, 1962, "Supreme Court," Papers of John F. Kennedy, Presidential Papers, President's Office Files, at *http://www.jfklibrary.org/Asset-Viewer/Archives/JFKPOF-088a-011.aspx*. Accessed March 21, 2016.

80. "LBJ's Nomination of Abe Fortas to the Supreme Court, July 1965 and Chief Justice, 1968," Miller Center, University of Virginia, at *http://millercenter.org/presidentialclassroom/exhibits/lbjs-nomination-of-abe-fortas*. Accessed May 9, 2016.

81. Dean, *The Rehnquist Choice*, pp. 150–201.

82. Abraham, *Justices, Presidents, and Senators*, p. 258.

83. Quoted in Abraham, *Justices, Presidents, and Senators*, p. 265.

84. Lou Cannon, *Reagan* (New York: Putnam, 1982), pp. 290–291.

85. Abraham, *Justices, Presidents, and Senators*, pp. 295–296.

86. Andrew L. Kaufman, *Cardozo* (Cambridge, MA: Harvard University Press, 1998), pp. 6–8; and Neil A. Lewis, "Was a Hispanic Justice on the Court in the '30s?" *New York Times*, May 26, 2009, at *http://www.nytimes.com/2009/05/27/us/27hispanic.html*. Accessed July 13, 2016).

87. Memorandum from Alan Charles Raul to Peter J. Wallison, "Summary Information Regarding Certain Judges," June 5, 1986, Thomas Griscom Files, Series III: Subject File, Box 3, Reagan Presidential Library.

88. Memorandum from Pat Buchanan to the President, May 26, 1969, President's Office Files, President's Handwriting: May 1969 to August 1969, Nixon Presidential Library.

89. Abraham, *Justices, Presidents, and Senators*, pp. 142–143.

90. Peter Lisagor, "B'nai B'rith Mobilizes against Fortas Foes," *New York Post*, July 3, 1968, Chron. File—7/7/68–7/13/68, Files Pertaining to Abe Fortas & Homer Thornberry, Papers of Lyndon Baines Johnson President, 1963–1969, Lyndon Baines Johnson Library.

91. Charlie Savage, "A Judge's View of Judging Is on the Record," *New York Times*, May 14, 2009, at *http://www.nytimes.com/2009/05/15/us/15judge.html?_r=0*. Accessed June 23, 2016; Andy Barr, "Rush: Sotomayor a 'Reverse Racist,'" *Politico*, May 26, 2009, at *http://www.politico.com/story/2009/05/rush-sotomayor-a-reverse-racist-022983*. Accessed June 23, 2016.

92. Janet Hook, "A GOP Call for Civility on Sotomayor," *Los Angeles Times*, May 30, 2009, p. A13; and Adam Nagourney, "Republicans Weigh Risks of a Supreme Court Battle," *New York Times*, May 26, 2009, at *http://thecaucus.blogs.nytimes.com/2009/05/26/republicans-weigh-risks-of-a-supreme-court-battle/comment-page-9/*. Accessed June 23 2016.

93. Ellis, *The Jefferson Crisis*, pp. 15–50.

94. See Henry J. Abraham, "President Jefferson's Three Appointments to the Supreme Court of the United States: 1804, 1807, and 1807," *Journal of Supreme Court History*, 31 (July 2006): 141–154; Abraham, *Justices, Presidents, and Senators*, pp. 83, 96–97, 99–102; and John V. Orth, "How Many Judges Does It Take to Make a Supreme Court," *Constitutional Commentary*, 19 (2002): 681–692.

95. Abraham, *Justices, Presidents, and Senators*, p. 99.

96. Abraham, *Justices, Presidents, and Senators*, pp. 101–102.

97. See Leuchtenberg, *The Supreme Court Reborn*.

98. Allen E. Ragan, *Chief Justice Taft* (Columbus: Ohio State Archaeological and Historical Society, 1938), p. 97.

99. Artemus Ward, *Deciding to Leave: The Politics of Retirement from the United States Supreme Court* (Albany: SUNY Press, 2003), pp. 69–81.

100. Epstein and Segal, *Advice and Consent*, p. 36.

101. The four are Sherman Minton (1956), Harold Burton (1958), Potter Stewart (1981), and David Souter (2009).

102. Reity O'Brien and Chris Young, Center for Public Integrity, "Supreme Court Justices' Wealth Explored," *Huffington Post*, June 14, 2013, at *http://www.huffingtonpost.com/2013/06/14/supreme-court-justices-wealth_n_3438107.html*. Accessed May 21, 2015.

103. "Sonia Sotomayor Courts Riches from Book Deal," Center for Public Integrity, June 7, 2013, at *http://www.publicintegrity.org/2013/06/07/12787/sonia-sotomayor-courts-riches-book-deal*. Accessed May 21, 2015.

104. Wil Haygood, *Showdown: Thurgood Marshall and the Supreme Court Nomination That Changed America* (New York: Knopf, 2015), pp. 14–16.

105. Dean, *The Rehnquist Choice*, pp. 4–12.

106. Memorandum from Patrick J. Buchanan to the President, May 6, 1969, White House Central Files, Subject Files, FG-51, Box 1, Nixon Presidential Library.

107. Charles L. Zelsen, *Thurgood Marshall: Race, Rights, and the Struggle for a More Perfect Union* (New York: Routledge, 2013), p. 157; and Lawrence Baum, *The Supreme Court*, 11th ed. (Thousand Oaks, CA: CQ Press, 2013), p. 63.

108. "CAMPAIGN '88: Justice Not Running," *Los Angeles Times*, May 27, 1988, at *http://articles.latimes.com/1988-05-27/news/mn-4363_1_o-connor*. Accessed June 20, 2016.

109. Abraham, *Justices, Presidents, and Senators*, pp. 134–135.

110. "LBJ's Nomination of Abe Fortas to the Supreme Court, July 1965 and Chief Justice, 1968," Miller Center, University of Virginia, at *http://millercenter.org/presidentialclassroom/exhibits/lbjs-nomination-of-abe-fortas*. Accessed May 9, 2016.

111. Memorandum to the President from Theodore Sorensen, March 29, 1962, "Supreme Court," Papers of John F. Kennedy, Presidential Papers, President's Office Files, at *http://www.jfklibrary.org/Asset-Viewer/Archives/JFKPOF-088a-011.aspx*. Accessed March 21, 2016.

112. Abraham, *Justices, Presidents, and Senators*, pp. 289–290.

113. Oral History Interview with Sherman Adams, #4, June 19, 1970, Columbia University Oral History Project, Dwight D. Eisenhower Library.

114. Author telephone interview with Greg Craig, July 6, 7, 2015; anonymous interview with Bush administration official, August 7, 2015.

115. Denis Steven Rutkus et al., *Supreme Court Nominations 1789–2005: Actions (including Speed) by the Senate, the Judiciary Committee, and the President* (New York: Nova Science, 2007), Table 1.

116. Abraham, *Justices, Presidents, and Senators*, pp. 71–73.

117. Yarborough, *David Hackett Souter*, pp. 94–109; and Dean, *The Rehnquist Choice*, pp. 138–139, 212–213, 226–234.

118. Memorandum for the President from Lloyd Cutler, Joel Klein, and Victoria Radd, "Additional Information on Supreme Court Candidate," April 29, 1994, Victoria Radd, Counsel–Supreme Court 1994/Supreme Court Potential Judges: Stephen Breyer, Box 95, William J. Clinton Presidential Library.

119. "Clark Clifford Oral History Interview, February 4, 1975," John F. Kennedy Library Oral History Program, John F. Kennedy Presidential Library.

120. Memorandum to the President from McGeorge Bundy, March 30, 1962, and Memorandum to the President from Theodore Sorensen, March 29, 1962, "Supreme Court," Papers of John F. Kennedy, Presidential Papers, President's Office Files, at *http://www.jfklibrary.org/Asset-Viewer/Archives/JFKPOF-088a-011.aspx*. Accessed March 21, 2016.

121. Kalman, *Fortas*, pp. 327–328.

122. Oral History Interview with Sherman Adams, #4, June 19, 1970, Columbia University Oral History Project, Dwight D. Eisenhower Library.

123. For a discussion of the process of choosing Stevens, see Victor H. Kramer, "The Case of Justice Stevens: How to Select, Nominate, and Confirm a Justice of the United States Supreme Court," *Constitutional Commentary*, 7 (1990): 325–340.

124. Memorandum from Douglas P. Bennett to the President, undated, at *https://www.fordlibrarymuseum.gov/library/document/0005/1561576.pdf*. Accessed May 2, 2016.

125. "Memorandum for the President" from Edward H. Levi, Attorney General, November 10, 1975, at *https://www.fordlibrarymuseum.gov/library/document/0005/1561577.pdf*.

126. Letter to Justice Felix Frankfurter from Howard B. Gotlieb, Librarian of the Historical Manuscripts and the Edward M. House Collection, October 23, 1961, White House Central Files, Supreme Court of the United States Executive File, FG535, Box 194, John F. Kennedy Presidential Library.

127. Brannon P. Denning, "The Judicial Confirmation Process and the Blue Slip," *Judicature*, 85 (March–April 2002): 218–226.

128. "US Senate Roll Call Votes 109th Congress—2nd Session, On the Cloture Motion (Motion to Invoke Cloture on the Nomination of Samuel A. Alito Jr. of New Jersey, to Be an Associate Justice of the Supreme Court," at *http://www.senate.gov/legislative/LIS/roll_call_lists/roll_call_vote_cfm.cfm?congress=109&session=2&vote=00001*. Accessed July 25, 2016; and "US Senate Roll Call Votes 109th Congress—2nd Session, On the Nomination (Confirmation of Samuel A. Alito Jr. of New Jersey, to Be an Associate Justice)," at *http://www.senate.gov/legislative/LIS/roll_call_lists/roll_call_vote_cfm.cfm?congress=109&session=2&vote=00002*. Accessed July 25, 2016.

129. Memo from Maggie to Fred Graham, undated. George Harrold Carswell file, Papers of Fred Graham, Manuscript Division, Library of Congress, Washington, DC.

130. See Leuchtenberg, *The Supreme Court Reborn*, p. 183; and Memorandum from Chuck Colson to Bryce Harlow, April 20, 1970, White House Special Files, Staff Member Office Files—Charles W. Colson, Box 43, Nixon Presidential Library.

131. "LBJ's Nomination of Abe Fortas to the Supreme Court, July 1965 and Chief Justice, 1968," Miller Center, University of Virginia, at *http://millercenter.org/presidentialclassroom/exhibits/lbjs-nomination-of-abe-fortas*. Accessed 9 May 9, 2016.

132. "LBJ's Nomination of Abe Fortas to the Supreme Court, July 1965 and Chief Justice, 1968."

133. "LBJ's Nomination of Abe Fortas to the Supreme Court, July 1965 and Chief Justice, 1968."

134. "LBJ's Nomination of Abe Fortas to the Supreme Court, July 1965 and Chief Justice, 1968."

135. Memorandum from William L. Ball, III to Kenneth M. Duberstein, November 2, 1987, Thomas Griscom Files, Series III: Subject File, Box 3, Reagan Presidential Library.

136. Denis Steven Rutkus, "Supreme Court Appointment Process: Roles of the President, Judiciary Committee, and Senate," Congressional Research Service, CRS Report RL31989, February 19, 2010, p. 15.

137. Author interview with Senator Harry Reid, July 21, 2015.

138. Memorandum from Ron Klain to Bruce Lindsey, Bernie Nussbaum, and Vince Foster, "Supreme Court Vacancy: Timing and Process," March 19, 1993, Previously Restricted Material—Batch 6, William J. Clinton Presidential Library.

139. Memorandum from Mike Manatos to the President, June 25, 1968, Chron File: 6/13/68–6/25/68, Files Pertaining to Abe Fortas & Homer Thornberry, Papers of Lyndon Baines Johnson President, 1963–1969, Lyndon Baines Johnson Library.

140. Abraham, *Justices, Presidents, and Senators*, p. 227.

141. Ellis, *The Jefferson Crisis*, pp. 239–240.

142. Yarborough, *David Hackett Souter*, pp. 100–110; and Letter from Senator Edward Kennedy to the President, April 26, 1993, Cliff Sloan, 2006-1067-F, Box 96, William J. Clinton Presidential Library.

143. Letter from Senator Edward Kennedy to the President, April 26, 1993, Cliff Sloan, 2006-1067-F, Box 96, William J. Clinton Presidential Library.

144. Anonymous interview with a Democratic Judiciary Committee staff member, July 24, 2015.

145. Carmen, "The President, Politics, and the Power of Appointment."

146. "Letter of John Rutledge to George Washington, June 12, 1795," in Maeva Marcus et al., eds., *The Documentary History of the Supreme Court of the United States, 1789–1800*, Volume 1, Part 1: *Appointments and Proceedings* (New York: Columbia University Press, 1985), pp. 94–95.

147. Quoted in Henry F. Pringle, *The Life and Times of William Howard Taft: A Biography* (Hamden, CT: Archon Books, 1964), p. 957.

148. Pringle, *The Life and Times of William Howard Taft*, pp. 957–959.

149. Ronald C. White Jr., *A. Lincoln: A Biography* (New York: Random House, 2009), p. 649.

150. Quoted in Albert Bushnell Hart, *Salmon Portland Chase* (New York: Houghton Mifflin, 1899), p. 319.

151. Quoted in Frederick J. Blue, *Salmon P. Chase: A Life in Politics* (Kent, OH: Kent State University Press, 1987), p. 243.

152. Quoted in Blue, *Salmon P. Chase*, p. 243.

153. Carmen, "The President, Politics, and the Power of Appointment."

154. Letter from Herma Hill Kay to President Bill Clinton, April 24, 1993; Letter from Michael Sovern to President Clinton, April 26, 1993; Letter from Gerhard Casper to President Bill Clinton, May 12, 1993; Letter from Kathleen Peratis to President Bill Clinton, May 5 1993; Letter from Janet Benshoof to President William Clinton, May 13, 1993; Letter from Susan Penry-Williams to Bernard Nussbaum, Counsel to the President, May 18, 1993; Letter from Governor Ann Richards to Bruce Lindsey, special assistant to the president, May 31, 1993, Letter from Sargent Shriver to President Bill Clinton, May 3, 1993, Alpha Project 24778 [Ruth Bader Ginsburg], 2006-1067-F, Box 1, William J. Clinton Presidential Library.

155. "Remarks by the President: Announcement of Supreme Court Nomination of Judge Ruth Bader Ginsburg," press release, June 14, 1993, Alpha Project 24778 [Ruth Bader Ginsburg], 2006-1067-F, Box 2, William J. Clinton Presidential Library.

156. Letter from Lloyd N. Cutler to Bernard Nussbaum, Counsel to the President, on April 8, 1993, Doug Band, Breyer Misc., 2006-1067-F, Box 91, William J. Clinton Presidential Library.

157. Letter from Milton Handler to Bernard Nussbaum, Counsel to the President, April 1, 1993 and Letter from Arthur R. Miller to President William J. Clinton, June 2, 1993, Doug Band, Breyer Misc., 2006-1067-F, Box 91, William J. Clinton Presidential Library.

158. Walter F. Murphy, "In His Own Image: Mr. Chief Justice Taft and Supreme Court Appointments," *Supreme Court Review*, 1961 (1961): 159–193; and Ragan, *Chief Justice Taft*, p. 107.

159. Abraham, *Justices, Presidents, and Senators*, pp. 131, 146.

160. Murphy, "In His Own Image."

161. Murphy, "In His Own Image."

162. Pringle, *The Life and Times of William Howard Taft*, pp. 1057–1058; and Murphy, "In His Own Image."

163. Murphy, "In His Own Image."

164. Carmen, "The President, Politics, and the Power of Appointment."

165. Dean, *The Rehnquist Choice*, pp. 19, 137, 178–184.

166. Letter to President Ford from Chief Justice Warren Burger, November 10, 1975, at *https://www.fordlibrarymuseum.gov/library/document/0005/1561577.pdf*. Accessed May 2, 2016.

167. Letter to President Ford from Chief Justice Warren Burger, November 10, 1975.

168. Carmen, "The President, Politics, and the Power of Appointment."

169. David Axelrod, "A Suprising Request from Justice Scalia," CNN, February 15, 2016, at *http://www.cnn.com/2016/02/14/opinions/david-axelrod-surprise-request-from-justice-scalia/index.html*. Accessed February 16, 2016.

170. "Conversations with Potter Stewart, 4/18/70," Box 11, Papers of Fred Graham, Manuscript Library Division, Library of Congress, Washington, DC.

171. Abraham, *Justices, Presidents, and Senators*, p. 224.

172. Abraham, *Justices, Presidents, and Senators*, p. 134.

173. Rutkus, *Supreme Court Nominations 1789–2005*, Table 1.

174. James Haw, *John & Edward Rutledge of South Carolina* (Athens: University of Georgia Press, 1997), pp. 245–258.

175. Haw, *John & Edward Rutledge*, p. 253.

176. Haw, *John & Edward Rutledge*, pp. 253–256.

177. Rutkus et al., *Supreme Court Nominations 1789–2005*, Table 1.

178. Abraham, *Justices, Presidents, and Senators*, pp. 80–82.

179. Abraham, *Justices, Presidents, and Senators*, p. 102.

180. Memorandum from Dick Darling to Doug Nobles, June 27, 1968, Chron File: 6/13/68–6/25/68, Files Pertaining to Abe Fortas & Homer Thornberry, Papers of Lyndon Baines Johnson President, 1963–1969, Lyndon Baines Johnson Library.

181. Memorandum from Mike Manatos to the President, June 26, 1968, Chron File: 6/13/68–6/25/68, Files Pertaining to Abe Fortas & Homer Thornberry, Papers of Lyndon Baines Johnson President, 1963–1969, Lyndon Baines Johnson Library.

182. US Congress, Senate. Executive Journal, 1789, 1st Cong., 1st sess., vol 1, pp. 29–30, at *http://memory.loc.gov/cgi-bin/ampage?collId=llej&fileName=001/llej001.db&recNum=35&itemLink=D?hlaw:16:./temp/~ammem_eEA0::%230010036&linkText=1*. Accessed March 30, 2015.

183. Rutkus and Bearden, "Supreme Court Nominations, 1789–2009."
184. Irving Brant, *James Madison, The President 1809–1812* (Indianapolis, IN: Bobbs-Merrill, 1956), pp. 169–171.
185. Gerald Gamm and Kenneth Shepsle, "Emergence of Legislative Institutions: Standing Committees in the House and Senate, 1810–1825," *Legislative Studies Quarterly*, 14 (February 1989): 39–66.
186. Rutkus and Bearden, "Supreme Court Nominations, 1789–20."
187. Denis Steven Rutkus and Maureen Bearden, "Supreme Court Nominations, 1789–2009: Actions by the Senate, the Judiciary Committee, and the President," CRS Report, RL33225, August 25, 2009, at *http://www.leahy.senate.gov/imo/media/doc/CRS-SupremeCourtNominations1789-2009.pdf.* (Accessed 13 April 2015)
188. John P. Frank, "The Appointment of Supreme Court Justices: III," *Wisconsin Law Review*, 1941 (1941): 471.
189. Harris, *The Advice and Consent of the Senate*, pp. 307–308.
190. 75th Congress, Cong. Record, 11214 (1937).
191. Harris, *The Advice and Consent of the Senate*, p. 307; and Kenneth C. Cole, "Mr. Justice Black and 'Senatorial Courtesy,'" *American Political Science Review*, 31 (December 1937): 1113–1115.
192. Abraham, *Justices, Presidents, and Senators*, p. 181.
193. Rutkus, "Supreme Court Appointment Process," pp. 18–19.
194. Douglas Jehl, "'If' Mitchell Is Nominated to Supreme Court Is Grist for Speculation at the White House," *New York Times*, April 8, 1994; at *http://www.nytimes.com/1994/04/08/us/if-mitchell-nominated-supreme-court-grist-for-speculation-white-house.html.* Accessed April 29, 2015; David Stout, "Howard H. Baker, Jr., 'Great Conciliator' of the Senate, Dies at 88," *New York Times*, June 26, 2014, at *http://www.nytimes.com/2014/06/27/us/politics/howard-h-baker-jr-great-conciliator-of-senate-dies-at-88.html.* Accessed April 29, 2015; Dean, *The Rehnquist Choice*; Irvin Molotsky, "Inside Fight Seen over Court Choice," *New York Times*, June 28, 1987, at *http://www.nytimes.com/1987/06/28/us/inside-fight-seen-over-court-choice.html.* Accessed April 29, 2015; and "Several Senators Possible as Supreme Court Nominees," *USA Today*, June 11, 2005; at *http://usatoday30.usatoday.com/news/washington/judicial/2005-06-11-senators-for-high-court_x.htm.* Accessed April 29, 2015.
195. Rutkus, "Supreme Court Appointment Process," p. 19.
196. Aaron Freiwald, "Senate May Create New Panel on Court Nominations," *Legal Times*, November 24, 1986, p. 2.
197. Rutkus et al., *Supreme Court Nominations 1789–2005*, Table 1.
198. Quoted in Joel B. Grossman and Stephen L. Wasby, "The Senate and Supreme Court Nominations: Some Reflections," *Duke Law Journal*, 1972 (1972): 563–564.
199. Letter from Senator Joseph McCarthy to Senator James O. Eastland, Chair of the Judiciary Committee, February 27, 1957, RG 46 Records of the US Senate, 85th Congress, Sen 85B-A3, Committee on Judiciary, Nominations (AR-Brennan), National Archives Building, Washington, DC.
200. Statement of Senator Joe McCarthy at Senate Committee on the Judiciary, February 26, 1957, RG 46 Records of the US Senate, 85th Congress, Sen 85B-A3, Committee on Judiciary, Nominations (AR-Brennan), National Archives Building, Washington, DC.
201. Statement of Senator Joe McCarthy at Senate Committee on the Judiciary, February 26, 1957.
202. Ruth Bader Ginsburg, "Confirming Supreme Court Justices: Thoughts on the Second Opinion Rendered by the Senate," *University of Illinois Law Review*, 1988 (1988): 113.
203. Unites States Senate, Committee on the Judiciary, Hearings on Nomination of William O. Douglas to Be an Associate Justice of the US Supreme Court, Washington, DC, March 24, 1939, in Roy M. Mersky and J. Myron Jacobstein, compilers, *The Supreme Court of the United States: Hearings and Reports on Successful and Unsuccessful Nominations of Supreme Court Justices by the Senate Judiciary Committee, 1916–1972*, vol. 4 (Buffalo, NY: William S. Hein, 1975).

204. United States Senate, Committee on the Judiciary, Hearings on Nomination of William O. Douglas to Be an Associate Justice of the US Supreme Court, Washington, DC, March 24, 1939.

205. United States Senate, Report of the Proceedings, Hearings Held before the Subcommittee of the US Senate Committee on the Judiciary on the Nomination of Harlan Fiske Stone to Be Chief Justice of the United States, June 21, 1941, in Roy M. Mersky and J. Myron Jacobstein, compilers, *The Supreme Court of the United States: Hearings and Reports on Successful and Unsuccessful Nominations of Supreme Court Justices by the Senate Judiciary Committee, 1916–1972*, vol. 4 (Buffalo, NY: William S. Hein, 1975).

206. Rutkus et al., *Supreme Court Nominations 1789–2005*, Table 1.

207. Abraham, *Justices, Presidents, and Senators*, pp. 71–72, 85–86, 90–92, 102

208. Abraham, *Justices, Presidents, and Senators*, p. 95.

209. Leuchtenberg, *The Supreme Court Reborn*, pp. 191–199.

The Transition toward Democracy

1. See D. J. Molloy, *The World of the John Birch Society: Conspiracy, Conservatism, and the Cold War* (Nashville, TN: Vanderbilt University Press, 2014); and John D. Morris, "Birch Unit Pushes Drive on Warren," *New York Times*, April 1, 1961, p. 1.

2. Gallup Poll, March 1941; and Gallup Poll, July 1968, Roper Center, Cornell University.

3. See Mark V. Tushnet, *NAACP's Legal Strategy against Segregated Education, 1925–1950* (Chapel Hill: University of North Carolina Press, 1987).

4. See, for example, Kevin T. McGuire and Gregory A. Caldeira, "Lawyers, Organized Interests, and the Law of Obscenity: Agenda Setting in the Supreme Court," *American Political Science Review*, 87 (September 1993): 715–726.

5. See Karen O'Connor and Lee Epstein, "Beyond Legislative Lobbying: Women's Rights Groups and the Supreme Court," *Judicature*, 67 (1983–1984): 134–143.

6. See Vanessa A. Baird, *Answering the Call of the Court: How Justices and Litigants Set the Supreme Court Agenda* (Charlottesville: University of Virginia Press, 2007).

7. Karen O'Connor and Lee Epstein, "The Rise of Conservative Interest Group Litigation," *Journal of Politics*, 45 (May 1983): 479–489.

8. Susan Navarro Smelcer, Amy Steigerwalt, and Richard L. Vining Jr., "Bias and the Bar: Evaluating the ABA Ratings of Federal Judicial Nominees," *Political Research Quarterly*, 65 (December 2012): 827–840.

9. Denis Steven Rutkus, "Supreme Court Appointment Process: Roles of the President, Judiciary Committee, and Senate," Congressional Research Service, CRS Report RL31989, February 19, 2010, p. 25.

10. Statement by President Bernard G. Segal of the American Bar Association, George Harrold Carswell file, Box 5, Papers of Fred Graham, Manuscript Library Division, Library of Congress, Washington, DC.

11. Letter from Edward J. Fox Jr., Chairman, Standing Committee on Federal Judiciary, American Bar Association, to Senator William Langer, Chairman, Committee on Judiciary, January 19, 1954, Sen 83B-A3, Judiciary, Executive Nominations, Warren, Box No. 52, National Archives Building, Washington, DC.

12. Letter to James O. Eastland, Chairman of the Senate Committee on the Judiciary, from Lawrence E. Walsh, Chairman of the ABA Standing Committee on the Judiciary, April 28, 1970, Appointment to Supreme Court: Background Information, Folder 6, Box 1357, Papers of Harry A. Blackmun, Manuscript Division, Library of Congress.

13. Fred P. Graham, "Bar Unit Endorses Haynsworth Again, but Vote Is Divided," "ABA Panel Again Backs Haynsworth," *New York Times*, October 13, 1969, p. 1.

14. Henry J. Abraham, *Justices, Presidents, and Senators*, 5th ed. (Lanham, MD: Rowman and Littlefield, 2008), pp. 108–109.

15. See Kenneth Goings, *The NAACP Comes of Age: The Defeat of Judge John J. Parker* (Bloomington: Indiana University Press, 1990).

16. Joseph P. Harris, *The Advice and Consent of the Senate: A Study of the Confirmation of Appointments by the United States Senate* (Berkeley: University of California Press, 1953), pp. 311–312.

17. Joel B. Grossman and Stephen L. Wasby, "The Senate and Supreme Court Nominations: Some Reflections," *Duke Law Journal*, 1972 (1972): 575; and Linda Greenhouse, "A.C.L.U., Reversing Policy, Joins the Opposition to Bork," *New York Times*, September 1, 1987, at *http:// www.nytimes.com/1987/09/01/us/aclu-reversing-policy-joins-the-opposition-to-bork.html*. Accessed April 21, 2015.

18. Mark Silverstein and William Haltom, "You Can't Always Get What You Want: Reflections on the Ginsburg and Breyer Nominations," *Journal of Law and Policy*, 12 (1996): 464–465.

19. Statement of Charles Smith, Representative of the National Liberal League, Before the Committee on the Judiciary, United States Senate, February 26, 1957, RG 46 Records of the US Senate, 85th Congress, Sen 85B-A3, Committee on Judiciary, Nominations (AR-Brennan), National Archives Building, Washington, DC.

20. Harris, *The Advice and Consent of the Senate*, p. 312.

21. Richard Davis, *Justices and Journalists: The U.S. Supreme Court and the Media* (New York: Cambridge University Press, 2011), pp. 57–68 .

22. Bob Woodward and Scott Armstrong, *The Brethren: Inside the Supreme Court* (New York: Simon and Schuster, 1979).

23. Davis, *Justices and Journalists*, p. 112; and Laura Kalman, *Abe Fortas: A Biography* (New Haven, CT: Yale University Press, 1990), pp. 319–376.

24. David W. Moore and Lydia Saad, "Public Supports Clinton's Supreme Court Nominee," *Gallup Poll Monthly*, June 1993, pp. 19–20; and Jeffrey M. Jones, "U.S. Support for Garland Average for Supreme Court Nominees," *Gallup*, March 21, 2016, at *http://www.gallup.com/ poll/190091/support-garland-average-supreme-court-nominees.aspx*.

25. John Maltese, *The Selling of Supreme Court Nominees* (Baltimore, MD: Johns Hopkins University Press, 1995), pp. 68–69.

26. 95 Cong. Rec. 11696 1949.

27. "Unfavorable," RG 46 Records of the US Senate, 85th Congress, Sen 85B-A3, Committee on Judiciary, Nominations (AR-Brennan), National Archives Building, Washington, DC.

28. Denis Steven Rutkus et al., *Supreme Court Nominations 1789–2005: Actions (including Speed) by the Senate, the Judiciary Committee, and the President* (New York: Nova Science, 2007), Table 1.

29. Denis Steven Rutkus and Maureen Bearden, "Supreme Court Nominations, 1789–2009: Actions by the Senate, the Judiciary Committee, and the President," Congressional Research Service, May 13, 2009, at *https://www.fas.org/sgp/crs/misc/RL33225.pdf*. Accessed July 23, 2016; and Rutkus et al., *Supreme Court Nominations 1789–2005*, Table 1.

30. Nomination of Louis D. Brandeis: Hearings before the Subcommittee of the Committee on the Judiciary, United States Senate, on the Nomination of Louis D. Brandeis to Be an Associate Justice of the Supreme Court of the United States Together with the Report of the Subcommittee of the Committee on the Judiciary Thereon. In 2 vols. United States. Congress. Senate. Committee on the Judiciary (Washington, DC: US Government Printing Office, 1916).

31. See Thomas Karfunkel and Thomas W. Ryley, *The Jewish Seat: Anti-Semitism and the Appointment of Jews to the Supreme Court* (Hicksville, NY: Exposition Press, 1978).

32. Rutkus and Bearden, "Supreme Court Nominations, 1789–2009."

33. Rutkus and Bearden, "Supreme Court Nominations, 1789–2009."

34. Letter from Irving Ferman, Director, Washington, DC, Office, American Civil Liberties Union, to Senator William Langer, Chair of the Judiciary Committee, February 24, 1954, RG 46 Records of the US Senate, 83d Congress, Sen 83B-A3, Judiciary, Executive Nominations, Warren, Box No. 52, National Archives Building, Washington, DC.

35. Rutkus, "Supreme Court Appointment Process," p. 35; and "Senate in Secret Sends Stone's Name Back to Committee," *New York Times*, January 27, 1925.

36. "Senate Opens Door to Discuss Stone," *New York Times*, February 5, 1925, p. 1.

37. "Stone Is Confirmed by Senate, 71 to 6; Scored on Wheeler," *New York Times*, February 6, 1925, p. 1.

38. "Senate Opens Door to Discuss Stone," *New York Times*, February 5, 1925, p. 1.
39. "Senate in Secret Sends Stone's Name Back to Committee," *New York Times*, January 27, 1925.
40. Ronald D. Rotunda, "Innovations Disguised as Traditions: An Historical Review of the Supreme Court Nominations Process," *University of Illinois Law Review*, 123 (1995): 127–128; and Paul Freund, "Appointment of Justices: Some Historical Perspectives," *Harvard Law Review*, 101 (1988): 1157–1158.
41. "Committee Approves Nomination of Stone," *New York Times*, February 2, 1925, p. 1.
42. Warren Duffee, "Senate Unit Approves Stewart in Court Job," *Washington Post and Times Herald*, April 21, 1959, A28.
43. Rutkus et al., *Supreme Court Nominations 1789–2005*, Table 1.
44. Rutkus, "Supreme Court Appointment Process," p. 21.
45. Ronald Garay, *Congressional Television: A Legislative History* (Westport, CT: Greenwood Press, 1984), pp. 36–76.
46. Garay, *Congressional Television*, pp. 85–129.
47. "Committee Approves Nomination of Stone," *New York Times*, February 2, 1925, p. 1.
48. Duffee, "Senate Unit Approves Stewart in Court Job," A28.
49. Abraham, *Justices, Presidents, and Senators*, pp. 153–154; John P. Frank, "The Appointment of Supreme Court Justices: III," *Wisconsin Law Review*, 1941 (1941): 492–495; and Grossman and Wasby, "The Senate and Supreme Court Nominations," 582–583.
50. Goings, *The NAACP Comes of Age*, pp. 29–30; and Freund, "Appointment of Justices," 1158.
51. Rotunda, "Innovations Disguised as Traditions," 128; Frank, "The Appointment of Supreme Court Justices: III," 507–510; Ginsburg, "Confirming Supreme Court Justices," 113; and United States Senate, Committee on the Judiciary, Hearings on Nomination of William O. Douglas to Be an Associate Justice of the US Supreme Court, Washington, DC, March 24, 1939, in Roy M. Mersky and J. Myron Jacobstein, compilers, *The Supreme Court of the United States: Hearings and Reports on Successful and Unsuccessful Nominations of Supreme Court Justices by the Senate Judiciary Committee, 1916–1972*, vol. 4 (Buffalo, NY: William S. Hein, 1975).
52. Committee on the Judiciary, United States Senate, Hearings on the Nomination of Stanley F. Reed as Associate Justice of the United States Supreme Court, Washington, DC, January 21, 1938, in Roy M. Mersky and J. Myron Jacobstein, compilers, *The Supreme Court of the United States: Hearings and Reports on Successful and Unsuccessful Nominations of Supreme Court Justices by the Senate Judiciary Committee, 1916–1972*, vol. 4 (Buffalo, NY: William S. Hein, 1975); Frank, "The Appointment of Supreme Court Justices: III," 510; and Freund, "Appointment of Justices," 1161.
53. Abraham, *Justices, Presidents, and Senators*, p. 195.
54. Quoted in David N. Atkinson, "From New Deal Liberal to Supreme Court Conservative: The Metamorphosis of Justice Sherman Minton," *Washington Law Review*, 1975 (1975): 379–381.
55. Harris, *The Advice and Consent of the Senate*, p. 195.
56. Albert W. Fox, "Stone Tells Senate Committee He Assumes Full Responsibility for Pressing New Wheeler Case," *Washington Post*, January 29, 1925, p. 1.
57. 95 Cong. Rec. 11695 1949.
58. Freund, "Appointment of Justices," 1162.
59. Letter from Abe Fortas to Senator James Eastland, September 13, 1968, Abe Fortas file, Box 5, Papers of Fred Graham, Manuscript Library Division, Library of Congress, Washington, DC; and Marjorie Hunter, "Fortas Refuses to Appear Again in Senate Inquiry," *New York Times*, September 14, 1968, p. 1.
60. Tom Korologos, "How to Scale the High Court," *Washington Post*, May 24, 2009, p. B1.
61. Oral History Interview with Tom Korologos, Senate Historical Office, Washington, DC, p. 174.
62. Abraham, *Justices, Presidents, and Senators*, p. 189.
63. Quoted in Roger Newman, *Hugo Black: A Biography* (New York: Pantheon Books, 1994), p. 240.
64. Abraham, *Justices, Presidents, and Senators*, pp. 167–168; and Newman, *Hugo Black*, pp. 247–248.
65. Rutkus and Bearden, "Supreme Court Nominations, 1789–2009."

66. United States Senate, Committee on the Judiciary, Hearings on Nomination of William O. Douglas to Be an Associate Justice of the US Supreme Court, Washington, DC, March 24, 1939, in Roy M. Mersky and J. Myron Jacobstein, compilers, *The Supreme Court of the United States: Hearings and Reports on Successful and Unsuccessful Nominations of Supreme Court Justices by the Senate Judiciary Committee, 1916–1972*, vol. 4 (Buffalo, NY: William S. Hein, 1975).

67. Statement of Charles Smith, Representative of the National Liberal League, Before the Committee on the Judiciary, United States Senate, February 26, 1957, RG 46 Records of the US Senate, 85th Congress, Sen 85B-A3, Committee on Judiciary, Nominations (AR-Brennan), National Archives Building, Washington, DC.

68. "Nomination of Abe Fortas," Hearing before the Committee on the Judiciary, United States Senate, Eighty-Ninth Congress, First Session, August 5, 1965 (Washington, DC: US Government Printing Office, 1965).

69. Harris, *The Advice and Consent of the Senate*, pp. 311.

70. Telegram from R. C. Hemphill Jr., undated, Sen 87B-A3, Judiciary Committee Papers Re: Nominations, Box 48, Center for Legislative Archives.

71. Wil Haygood, *Showdown: Thurgood Marshall and the Supreme Court Nomination That Changed America* (New York: Knopf, 2015), pp. 11–14.

72. Statement of Senator Joseph McCarthy, Senate Committee on the Judiciary, February 26, 1957, Records of the US Senate, 85th Congress, Sen 85B-A3, Committee on Judiciary, Nominations, Box 14, Center for Legislative Archives, Washington, DC.

73. Grossman and Wasby, "The Senate and Supreme Court Nominations," 573.

74. Haygood, *Showdown*, pp. 202–204; and Robert David Johnson, "Lyndon B. Johnson and the Fortas Nomination," *Journal of Supreme Court History*, 41 (March 2016): 110–111.

75. Haygood, *Showdown*, p. 246.

76. "Roll Calls in 84th Congress (First Session)," CQ Researcher, at *http://library.cqpress.com/cqresearcher/document.php?id=cqresrre1955081100*. Accessed July 16, 2016; "Nomination of Potter Stewart as Assoc. Justice of Supreme Court.—Senate Vote #58—May 5, 1959," GovTrack.us. 2004, at *https://www.govtrack.us/congress/votes/86-1959/s58*. Accessed July 16, 2016; Congressional Record—Senate, August 30, 1967, p. 24656, at *http://www.senate.gov/reference/resources/pdf/240_1967.pdf*. Accessed June 8, 2016.

77. Harris, *The Advice and Consent of the Senate*, p. 313.

78. William H. Rehnquist, "The Making of a Supreme Court Justice," *Harvard Law Record*, 29 (October 8, 1959), at *http://iiif.lib.harvard.edu/manifests/view/drs:45627133$1i*. Accessed July 2, 2016.

79. 95 Cong. Rec. 11696 1949.

80. 95 Cong. Rec. 11696 1949.

81. 95 Cong. Rec. 11696 1949.

82. Richard S. Beth and Betsy Palmer, "Cloture Attempts on Nominations," CRS Report RL 32878, March 30, 2009, in Denis Steven Rutkus et al., *Supreme Court Nominations: Presidential Nomination, the Judiciary Committee, Proper Scope of Questioning of Nominees, Senate Consideration, Cloture, and the Use of the Filibuster*, Washington, The Capitol.Net, 2010, p. 131.

83. Rutkus et al., *Supreme Court Nominations 1789–2005*, Table 2.

Presidential Selection

1. Ruth Marcus and Joan Biskupic, "Justice White to Retire after 31 Years," *Washington Post*, March 20, 1993, p. A1.

2. "Remarks by the President and Solicitor General Elena Kagan at the Nomination of Solicitor General Elena Kagan to the Supreme Court," May 10, 2010, White House Office of the Press Secretary, at *https://www.whitehouse.gov/the-press-office/remarks-president-and-solicitor-general-elena-kagan-nomination-solicitor-general-el*. Accessed July 13, 2016.

3. "Remarks Announcing the Nomination of Judge Warren Earl Burger to Be Chief Justice of the United States," May 21, 1969, The American Presidency Project, at *http://www.presidency.ucsb.edu/ws/index.php?pid=2063*. Accessed July 13, 2016.

4. Bruce Ackerman, "Transformative Appointments," Faculty Scholarship series, Yale Law School, Paper 143, at *http://digitalcommons.law.yale.edu/fss_papers/143/*. Accessed June 29, 2016.

5. Joan Biskupic, *American Original: The Life and Constitution of Supreme Court Justice Antonin Scalia* (New York: Sarah Crichton Books, 2009), p. 108.

6. Christopher E. Smith and Scott P. Johnson, "Newcomer on the High Court: Justice David Souter and the Supreme Court's 1990 Term," *South Dakota Law Review* 3721 (1991–1992): 21, 39–41.

7. "LBJ's Nomination of Abe Fortas to the Supreme Court, July 1965 and Chief Justice, 1968," Miller Center, University of Virginia, at *http://millercenter.org/presidentialclassroom/exhibits/lbjs-nomination-of-abe-fortas*. Accessed May 9, 2016.

8. John Lovett, Shaun Bevan, and Frank R. Baumgartner, "Popular Presidents Can Affect Congressional Attention, for a Little While," *Policy Studies Journal*, 43 (2015): 22–43.

9. "Presidential Approval Ratings—Gallup Historical Statistics and Trends," Gallup, at *http://www.gallup.com/poll/116677/presidential-approval-ratings-gallup-historical-statistics-trends.aspx*. Accessed August 5, 2016.

10. Henry J. Abraham, *Justices, Presidents, and Senators*, 5th ed. (Lanham, MD: Rowman and Littlefield, 2008), pp. 309–310.

11. Abraham, *Justices, Presidents, and Senators*, pp. 310–312.

12. Paul C. Light, *Domestic Policy Choice from Kennedy to Clinton*, 3rd ed. (Baltimore, MD: Johns Hopkins University Press, 1999); Andrew W. Barrett and Matthew Eshbaugh-Soha, "Presidential Success on the Substance of Legislation," *Political Research Quarterly*, 60 (March 2007): 100–112; and Matthew Eshbaugh-Soha, "The Politics of Presidential Agendas," *Political Research Quarterly*, 58 (June 2005): 257–268.

13. Keith E. Whittington, "Presidents, Senates, and Failed Supreme Court Nominations," *Supreme Court Review*, 2006 (2006): 414–420.

14. Whittington, "Presidents, Senates, and Failed Supreme Court Nominations," 417.

15. Memorandum from Jim Gaither to Joe Califano, June 24, 1968, Chron File: 6/13/68–6/25/68, Files Pertaining to Abe Fortas & Homer Thornberry, Papers of Lyndon Baines Johnson President, 1963–1969, Lyndon Baines Johnson Library

16. Warren Weaver Jr., "Douglas and the Court," *New York Times*, April 24, 1975, p. 10.

17. Memorandum from Ron Klain to Bruce Lindsey, Bernie Nussbaum, and Vince Foster, "Supreme Court Vacancy: Timing and Process," March 19, 1993, Previously Restricted Material—Batch 6, William J. Clinton Presidential Library.

18. Ira H. Carmen, "The President, Politics, and the Power of Appointment: Hoover's Nomination of Mr. Justice Cardozo," *Virginia Law Review*, 55 (1969): 616–659.

19. Mark Silverstein and William Haltom, "You Can't Always Get What You Want: Reflections on the Ginsburg and Breyer Nominations," *Journal of Law and Policy*, 12 (1996): 467–468.

20. Memorandum from Robert Gray to Governor Adams, "Recess Appointment of William Joseph Brennan, Jr. of New Jersey, to Be an Associate Justice of the Supreme Court of the United States," October 13, 1956, and Memorandum from Robert E. Hampton to General Parsons, "Recess Appointment of Potter Stewart of Ohio to Be Associate Justice of the Supreme Court," October 8, 1958, White House Central Files, Supreme Court Files, Box 321, Dwight D. Eisenhower Library.

21. "Alito Viewed Positively, But Libby Takes a Toll," Pew Research Center, November 8, 2005, at *http://www.people-press.org/2005/11/08/alito-viewed-positively-but-libby-takes-a-toll/*. Accessed July 30, 2016; and "Garland Nomination to Supreme Court Gets Positive Reception from Public," Pew Research Center, March 28, 2016, at *http://www.people-press.org/2016/03/28/garland-nomination-to-supreme-court-gets-positive-reception-from-public/*. Accessed July 30, 2016.

22. CNN/ORC Poll, February 24–27, 206, and CBS News/New York Times Poll, May 13–17, 2006, at *http://pollingreport.com/court.htm*. Accessed July 30, 2016.

23. CNN/ORC Poll, July 16–21, 2010, at *http://pollingreport.com/court.htm*. Accessed July 30, 2016; ABC News/Washington Post Poll, June 18–21, 2009, at *http://pollingreport.com/court.htm*. Accessed July 30, 2016; and "Miers Concerns Center on Qualifications and Cronyism," Pew Research Center, October 11, 2005, at *http://www.people-press.org/2005/10/11/miers-concerns-center-on-qualifications-and-cronyism/*. Accessed July 30, 2016.

24. "Garland Nomination to Supreme Court Gets Positive Reception from Public."

25. CNN/ORC Poll, June 28–July 1, 2012, at *http://pollingreport.com/court.htm*. Accessed July 30, 2016.

26. "Negative Views of Supreme Court at Record High, Driven by Republican Dissatisfaction," Pew Research Center, July 29, 2015, at *http://www.people-press.org/topics/2016-election/*. Accessed July 30, 2016.

27. William G. Ross, "The Role of Judicial Issues in Presidential Campaigns," *Santa Clara Law Review*, 42 (2002): 439; "Republican Party Platform of 1992," August 17, 1992, The American Presidency Project, at *http://www.presidency.ucsb.edu/ws/?pid=25847*. Accessed July 30, 2016; "2000 Republican Party Platform," July 31, 2000, The American Presidency Project, at *http://www.presidency.ucsb.edu/ws/?pid=25849*; "Republican Platform 2016," at *https://prod-static-ngop-pbl.s3.amazonaws.com/media/documents/DRAFT_12_FINAL[1]-ben_1468872234.pdf*. Accessed July 30, 2016; "2008 Democratic Party Platform," August 25, 2008, The American Presidency Project, at *http://www.presidency.ucsb.edu/ws/?pid=78283*. Accessed July 30, 2016; and "2016 Democratic Party Platform," July 21, 2016, at *https://www.demconvention.com/wp-content/uploads/2016/07/Democratic-Party-Platform-7.21.16-no-lines.pdf*, Accessed July 30, 2016.

28. Ross, "The Role of Judicial Issues in Presidential Campaigns," 433.

29. Ross, "The Role of Judicial Issues in Presidential Campaigns," 443.

30. Ross, "The Role of Judicial Issues in Presidential Campaigns," 461–462.

31. Neil A. Lewis, "Presidential Candidates Differ Sharply on Judges They Would Appoint to Top Courts," *New York Times*, October 8, 2000, at *http://www.nytimes.com/2010/05/06/us/06thomas.html*. Accessed July 15, 2016.

32. Laura Bassett, "Donald Trump Promises to Appoint Anti-Abortion Justices to Supreme Court," *Huffington Post*, May 11, 2016, at *http://www.huffingtonpost.com/entry/donald-trump-abortion-supreme-court_us_5733400be4b0bc9cb048aef2*. Accessed May 18, 2016.

33. Tessa Berenson, "Trump Offers Conservatives a Deal on Supreme Court," *Time*, March 21, 2016, at *http://time.com/4266700/donald-trump-supreme-court-nominations/*. Accessed May 18, 2016.

34. Juliet Eilperin, "McCain Says He Would Put Conservatives on Supreme Court," *Washington Post*, May 7, 2008, at *http://www.washingtonpost.com/wp-dyn/content/article/2008/05/06/AR2008050602527.html*. Accessed May 13, 2016.

35. CNN Transcript, August 16, 2008, at *transcripts.cnn.com/TRANSCRIPTS/0808/17/se.01.html*. Accessed July 14, 2016.

36. "Full Text: Hillary Clinton's DNC Speech," July 28, 2016, *Politico*, at *http://www.politico.com/story/2016/07/full-text-hillary-clintons-dnc-speech-226410*. Accessed July 30, 2016; and "Full Text: Donald Trump 2016 RC Draft Speech," *Politico*, July 21, 2016, at *http://www.politico.com/story/2016/07/full-transcript-donald-trump-nomination-acceptance-speech-at-rnc-225974*. Accessed July 30, 2016.

37. Bill Mears, "Election Could Tip Balance of Supreme Court," CNN, October 21, 2004, at *http://www.cnn.com/2004/ALLPOLITICS/10/20/election.scotus/*. Accessed May 17, 2016.

38. Ross, "The Role of Judicial Issues in Presidential Campaigns," 438–439.

39. "October 13, 1988: The Second Bush Dukakis Presidential Debate," Commission on Presidential Debates. Debates.org, at *http://www.debates.org*. Accessed June 4, 2015.

40. "October 3, 2000: The First Gore-Bush Presidential Debate," Commission on Presidential Debates. Debates.org, at *http://www.debates.org*. Accessed June 4, 2015.

41. "October 8, 2004: The Second Bush Kerry Presidential Debate," Commission on Presidential Debates. Debates.org, at *http://www.debates.org*. Accessed June 4, 2015.

42. Ross, "The Role of Judicial Issues in Presidential Campaigns," 447.

43. Joan Biskupic, "Justice Ruth Bader Ginsburg Intensifies Criticism of Trump: 'He Is a Faker,'" CNN, July 12, 2016, at *http://www.cnn.com/2016/07/12/politics/justice-ruth-bader-ginsburg-donald-trump-faker/index.html*. Accessed July 12, 2016.

44. Adam Liptak, "Ruth Bader Ginsburg, No Fan of Donald Trump, Critiques Latest Term," *New York Times*, July 11, 2016, p. A1; Eliza Collins, "Justice Ruth Bader Ginsburg Faces Criticism over Trump Attacks," *USA Today*, July 13, 2016, at *http://www.usatoday.com/story/news/politics/onpolitics/2016/07/13/scotus-ruth-bader-ginsburg-trump/87024248/*. Accessed July 14, 2016; "Ginsburg's Criticism of Trump Is Understandable but Injudicious,"

Los Angeles Times, July 14, 2016, at *http://www.latimes.com/opinion/editorials/la-ed-ginsburg-trump-20160713-snap-story.html.* Accessed July 14, 2016; and "Ruth Ginsburg Apologizes for Criticizing Trump," *New York Times,* July 14, 2016, at *http://www.nytimes.com/2016/07/15/us/politics/ruth-bader-ginsburg-donald-trump.html?&hp&action=click&pgtype=Homepage&cli ckSource=story-heading&module=first-column-region&region=top-news&WT.nav=top-news&_r=0.* Accessed July 14, 2016.

45. *Planned Parenthood v. Casey,* 505 U.S. 833 (1992).
46. "October 15, 2008: The Third McCain Obama Presidential Debate," Commission on Presidential Debates. Debates.org, at *http://www.debates.org.* Accessed June 4, 2015.
47. "The Third McCain Obama Presidential Debate," at *http://www.debates.org/index. php?page=debate-transcripts.*
48. Jeanne Cummings, John D. McKinnon, and Jess Bravin, "Bush's New Supreme Court Pick: A Loyal Aide with Scanty Record," *Wall Street Journal,* October 4, 2005, at *http://www.wsj.com/ articles/SB112833654307858362.*
49. Eli Stokols, "Sen. Graham: Obama's Supreme Court Pick Needs to Be a 'Consensus' Choice," *Politico,* February 13, 2016, at *http://www.politico.com/blogs/south-carolina-primary-2016-live-updates-and-results/2016/02/supreme-court-justice-appointment-lindsey-graham-219249;* Mike DeBonis and Juliet Eilperin, "Republican Governor of Nevada Brian Sandoval Being Considered for Supreme Court," *Washington Post,* February 24, 2016, at *https://www .washingtonpost.com/news/powerpost/wp/2016/02/24/brian-sandoval-republican-governor-of-nevada-is-being-vetted-for-supreme-court-vacancy/.* Accessed July 30, 2016; and Juliet Eilperin, "Sandoval Bows Out of Supreme Court Consideration," *Washington Post,* February 25, 2016, at *https://www.washingtonpost.com/news/powerpost/wp/2016/02/25/sandoval-bows-out-of-supreme-court-consideration/.* Accessed July 30, 2016.
50. DeBonis and Eilperin, "Republican Governor of Nevada Brian Sandoval Being Considered for Supreme Court"; Juliet Eilperin, "Sandoval Bows Out of Supreme Court Consideration," *Washington Post,* February 25, 2016, at *https://www.washingtonpost.com/news/powerpost/ wp/2016/02/25/sandoval-bows-out-of-supreme-court-consideration/.* Accessed May 2, 2016; and "GOP Gov. Sandoval Says Not Interested in Supreme Court Nomination," *Fox News,* February 25, 2016, at *http://www.foxnews.com/politics/2016/02/25/gop-gov-sandoval-says-not-interested-in-supreme-court-nomination.html.* Accessed May 2, 2016.
51. Author telephone interview with Greg Craig, July 6, 7, 2015.
52. Marcus and Biskupic, "Justice White to Retire after 31 Years," p. A1.
53. Marcus and Biskupic, "Justice White to Retire after 31 Years," p. A1.
54. Letter from Richard E. Nunez to William J. Clinton, May 9, 1994, and Letter from Nora T. Lum, President, Asia Pacific Advisory Council, to William J. Clinton, May 9, 1994, Stephen Breyer, April 29, 1993, 2006-1067-F, Box 35, William J. Clinton Presidential Library.
55. Letter from Bennie L. Thayer, Chairman/CEO, National Association for the Self-Employed, to Ronald Klain, June 8, 1993, Ruth Bader Ginsburg Questionnaire Responses—Vol. II, Clinton Presidential Records, Counsel's Office, Ginsburg, Ruth Bader Confirmation, 2006-1067-F, Box 16, William J. Clinton Presidential Library.
56. Letter from Donald A. Randall, Washington Representative, Automotive Service Association, to President William J. Clinton, June 10, 1993, Doug Band, Breyer Misc., 2006-1067-F, Box 91, William J. Clinton Presidential Library.
57. Ruth Bader Ginsburg, "Speaking in a Judicial Voice," *New York Law Review,* 67 (December 1992): 1185–1209; and Richard Davis, *Electing Justice: Fixing the Supreme Court Nomination Process* (New York: Oxford University Press, 2005), p. 110.
58. Anthony Lewis, "How Not to Choose a Justice for the Supreme Court," *New York Times,* May 11, 1993, p. B7.
59. Memorandum from Thomas L. Jipping to 721 Group & Allies, "Souter Nomination/'Red Flag' Decisions," July 24, 1990, White House Counsel's Office, Lee S. Liberman Files, Judicial Material Files, David Souter [1], Box 1, George Bush Presidential Library.
60. Richard Lacayo, "A Blank Slate," *Time,* August 6, 1990 at *http://content.time.com/time/magazine/ article/0,9171,970810,00.html.* Accessed June 30, 2016.
61. Press Briefing by Lloyd Cutler, Special Counsel to the President, White House Office of the Press Secretary press release, April 6, 1994, Victoria Radd, Ruth Bader Ginsburg

Questionnaire Responses—Volume 1, 2006-1067-F, Box 33, William J. Clinton Presidential Library.

62. Erin Miller, Lecture by Gregory Craig: "Picking Supreme Court Justices," *Scotusblog*, March 5, 2010, at *http://www.scotusblog.com/2010/03/lecture-by-gregory-craig-picking-supreme-court-justices/*. Accessed June 27, 2016; and author telephone interview with Greg Craig, July 6, 7, 2015.

63. Author telephone interview with Greg Craig, July 6, 7, 2015.

64. Davis, *Electing Justice: Fixing the Supreme Court Nomination Process*, pp. 91–92.

65. Memorandum from John C. Whitaker to John D. Ehrlichman, "Supreme Court Nominations," October 14, 1971, and Memorandum from Charles Colson to John Ehrlichman, "Senator Byrd/Supreme Court," October 15, 1971, White House Special Files, Staff Member and Office Files—David R. Young, Box 17, Nixon Presidential Library.

66. Harper Neidig, "McConnell: Don't Replace Scalia until after the Election," *The Hill*, February 13, 2016, at *http://thehill.com/homenews/senate/269389-mcconnell-dont-replace-scalia-until-after-election*. Accessed July 29, 2016; and Mike DeBonis and Paul Kane, "Republicans Vow No Hearings and No Votes for Obama's Supreme Court Pick," *Washington Post*, February 23, 2016, at *https://www.washingtonpost.com/news/powerpost/wp/2016/02/23/key-senate-republicans-say-no-hearings-for-supreme-court-nominee/*. Accessed July 29, 2016.

67. Burgess Everett, "Hatch to Obama: Don't Pick Me to Replace Scalia," *Politico.com*, February 16, 2016, at http://www.politico.com/story/2016/02/orrin-hatch-supreme-court-219314.

68. Denis Steven Rutkus, "Supreme Court Appointment Process: Roles of the President, Judiciary Committee, and Senate," Congressional Research Service, CRS Report RL31989, February 19, 2010, p. 8.

69. Davis, *Electing Justice: Fixing the Supreme Court Nomination Process*, p. 116.

70. Davis, *Electing Justice: Fixing the Supreme Court Nomination Process*, pp. 61–64.

71. Ackerman, "Transformative Appointments."

72. Biskupic, *American Original*, pp. 106–114.

73. "The 1998 Senate Vote Confirming Sotomayor to the Appeals Court," National Public Radio, May 26, 2009, at *http://www.npr.org/sections/politicaljunkie/2009/05/the_1998_senate_vote_confirmin.html*. Accessed July 10, 2015.

74. Ed Gillespie, *Winning Right: Campaign Politics and Conservative Policies* (New York: Threshold Editions, 2006), p. 217.

75. Robert David Johnson, "Lyndon B. Johnson and the Fortas Nomination," *Journal of Supreme Court History*, 41 (March 2016): 115.

76. John W. Dean, *The Rehnquist Choice: The Untold Story of the Nixon Appointment that Redefined the Supreme Court* (New York: Touchstone, 2001), pp. 270–273.

77. Author telephone interview with Greg Craig, July 6, 7, 2015.

78. "Robert H. Bork," undated memo, Thomas Griscom Files, Series III: Subject File, Box 3, Reagan Presidential Library.

79. "Douglas H. Ginsburg," Thomas Griscom Files, Series III: Subject File, Box 3, Reagan Presidential Library.

80. Memorandum from Bud Krogh to John Ehrlichman, "Supreme Court Nominations," September 24, 1971, White House Special Files, Staff Member and Office Files—David R. Young, Box 17, Nixon Presidential Library.

81. Memorandum from John W. Dean and David R. Young to Attorney General John N. Mitchell and John D. Ehrlichman, "Interview with Justice Mildred L. Lillie," October 16, 1971, White House Special Files, Staff Member and Office Files—David R. Young, Box 17, Nixon Presidential Library.

82. "Areas to Be Explored by Questioning," White House Special Files, Staff Member and Office Files—David R. Young, Box 17, Nixon Presidential Library.

83. "Due Diligence Questions Related to Confirmability," Thomas Griscom Files, Series III: Subject File, Box 3, Reagan Presidential Library.

84. Author telephone interview with Greg Craig, July 6, 7, 2015; and Bill Mears, "Memo Reveals Clinton's Difficulty over Supreme Court Choice," *CNN*, April 15, 2014, at *http://www.cnn.com/2014/02/17/politics/clinton-breyer-selection-memo/*. Accessed July 29, 2016.

85. Memorandum to Frank Donatelli and Frank Lavin from Jeffrey Lord, undated, "Judge Kennedy," Jeffrey Lord Collection, 0115548, Box 1, Reagan Presidential Library.

86. "Judge Breyer's Experience as Chief Counsel for the Judiciary Committee 1979–1980," undated, Doug Band, Breyer Misc., 2006-1067-F, Box 92, William J. Clinton Presidential Library.

87. Author telephone interview with Greg Craig, July 6, 7, 2015.

88. Memorandum from Charles F. Willis Jr. to Governor Adams, "Appointment of John Marshall Harlan to Be Associate Justice of the Supreme Court," November 8, 1954, Memorandum from Robert Gray to Governor Adams, "Recess Appointment of William Joseph Brennan Jr. of New Jersey, to Be an Associate Justice of the Supreme Court of the United States," October 13, 1956, and Memorandum from Robert E. Hampton to General Parsons, "Recess Appointment of Potter Stewart of Ohio to Be Associate Justice of the Supreme Court," October 8, 1958, White House Central Files, Supreme Court Files, Box 321, Dwight D. Eisenhower Library.

89. Letter to Herbert Brownell Jr., Attorney General, from William Langer, Chairman, Senate Judiciary Committee, Sen 83B-A3, Judiciary, Executive Nominations, Warren, Box 51, Center for Legislative Archives, Washington, DC.

90. Dean, *The Rehnquist Choice*, pp. 19–20.

91. "Document Request: Nomination of Anthony M. Kennedy," David McIntosh Files, Box 3, Reagan Presidential Library.

92. Dean, *The Rehnquist Choice*, pp. 170–172.

93. Abraham, *Justices, Presidents, and Senators*, pp. 304–309.

94. "Conversations with Potter Stewart, 4/18/70," Box 11, Papers of Fred Graham, Manuscript Library Division, Library of Congress, Washington, DC.

95. Mears, "Memo Reveals Clinton's Difficulty over Supreme Court Choice."

96. Dean, *The Rehnquist Choice*, pp. 214–218, 251.

97. "Trump Finished with Supreme Court Interviews," CNN.com, January 26, 2017.

98. "Conversations with Potter Stewart, 4/18/70," Box 11, Papers of Fred Graham, Manuscript Library Division, Library of Congress, Washington, DC.

99. Mears, "Memo Reveals Clinton's Difficulty over Supreme Court Choice."

100. Memorandum from Arthur B. Culvahouse Jr., "Meeting with Judge Anthony M. Kennedy," November 9, 1987, David McIntosh Files, Box 3, Reagan Presidential Library.

101. Memorandum from Ron Klain for Bernie Nussbaum, "Areas of Discussion for the President," June 11, 1993, Box 2, July 18, 2014, Previously Restricted Material—Batch 6, William J. Clinton Presidential Library.

102. Oral History Interview with Herbert Brownell, undated, Herbert Brownell Jr., Additional Papers, Box 2, Dwight D. Eisenhower Library.

103. Memorandum to the President from Theodore Sorensen, March 29, 1962, "Supreme Court," Papers of John F. Kennedy, Presidential Papers, President's Office Files, at *http://www .jfklibrary.org/Asset-Viewer/Archives/JFKPOF-088a-011.aspx*. Accessed March 21, 2016.

104. Memorandum to the President from Theodore Sorensen, March 29, 1962, "Supreme Court."

105. Memorandum from Bud Krogh to John Ehrlichman, "Supreme Court Nominations," September 24, 1971, White House Special Files, Staff Member and Office Files—David R. Young, Box 17, Nixon Presidential Library.

106. "Background Briefing by Senior Administration Officials," White House Office of the Press Secretary, June 15, 1993, Publications Office, Presidential Announcement—Nomination of Judge Ruth Bader Ginsburg to Supreme Court—June 1993, Box 34, William J. Clinton Presidential Library.

107. Memorandum from Joel Klein to Bernard Nussbaum, Counsel to the President, "Judge Breyer's Opinions and Legal Scholarship," June 10, 1993, Doug Band, Breyer Misc., 2006-1067-F, Box 92, William J. Clinton Presidential Library.

108. Undated confidential memo with unknown author, Ginsburg Nomination: FBI Follow-up Information, 2006-1067-F, Box 19, William J. Clinton Presidential Library.

109. See Dean, *The Rehnquist Choice*; and Richard Lacayo, "A Blank Slate," *Time*, August 6, 1990 at *http://content.time.com/time/magazine/article/0,9171,970810,00.html*. Accessed June 30, 2016

110. "Remarks by President Obama at US-ASEAN Press Conference," White House Press Release, February 16, 2016, at *https://www.whitehouse.gov/the-press-office/2016/02/16/remarks-president-obama-us-asean-press-conference*. Accessed February 17, 2016.

111. Letter to Edgar N. Eisenhower from Dwight D. Eisenhower, October 1, 1953, Dwight D. Eisenhower: Papers as President of the United States, 1953–61 (Ann Whitman File), Box 11, Dwight D. Eisenhower Library.

112. "Remarks Announcing the Nomination of David H. Souter to Be an Associate Justice of the Supreme Court of the United States and a Question-and-Answer Session with Reporters, July 23, 1990," The American Presidency Project, at *http://www.presidency.ucsb.edu/ws/index.php?pid=18699&st=souter&st1=*. Accessed May 25, 2016.

113. Abraham, *Justices, Presidents, and Senators*, p. 283.

114. "Remarks Announcing the Nomination of Ruth Bader Ginsburg to Be a Supreme Court Associate Justice," June 14, 1993, The American Presidency Project, at *http://www.presidency.ucsb.edu/ws/?pid=46684*. Accessed July 13, 2013.

115. "Clinton's 'Safe' Nominee," *Miami Herald*, June 15, 1993, p. 18A; "Ginsburg: Signs of a Centrist," *Rocky Mountain News*, June 15, 1993, p. 38A; and "Seems Safe Pick: Judge Ginsburg Doesn't Appear Likely to Cause Uproar," *Houston Chronicle*, June 15, 1993.

116. "Ginsburg: Nomination of Competence over Ideology," *Fort Worth Star-Telegram*, June 15, 1993, p. 18; and "Seems Safe Pick."

117. "Remarks by the President in Nominating Judge Sonia Sotomayor to the United States Supreme Court," White Office of the Press Secretary, May 26, 2009, at *https://www.whitehouse.gov/the-press-office/remarks-president-nominating-judge-sonia-sotomayor-united-states-supreme-court*. Accessed July 29, 2016

118. "Remarks Announcing the Nomination of Samuel A. Alito Jr., to Be an Associate Justice of the Supreme Court of the United States," The American Presidency Project, October 31, 2005, at *http://www.presidency.ucsb.edu/ws/index.php?pid=63783*. Accessed July 29, 2016; and "Address to the Nation Announcing the Nomination of John G. Roberts to Be an Associate Justice of the United States Supreme Court," The American Presidency Project, July 19, 2005, at *http://www.presidency.ucsb.edu/ws/index.php?pid=62762*. Accessed July 29, 2016.

119. Davis, *Electing Justice: Fixing the Supreme Court Nomination Process*, p. 116.

120. Silverstein and Haltom, "You Can't Always Get What You Want," 469.

121. Author telephone interview with Greg Craig, July 6, 7, 2015.

122. "Remarks Announcing the Nomination of Ruth Bader Ginsburg to Be a Supreme Court Associate Justice," June 14, 1993, The American Presidency Project, at *http://www.presidency.ucsb.edu/ws/?pid=46684*. Accessed July 13, 2016.

123. "Remarks by the President in Nominating Judge Sonia Sotomayor to the United States Supreme Court, White Office of the Press Secretary, May 26, 2009, at *https://www.whitehouse.gov/the-press-office/remarks-president-nominating-judge-sonia-sotomayor-united-states-supreme-court*. Accessed July 29, 2016

124. "Memorandum for Jim Hamilton," June 8, 1993, Cliff Sloan, 2006-1067-F, Box 128, William J. Clinton Presidential Library.

The Changing Role of the Senate

1. "Nomination of Byron R. White," Hearing before the Committee on the Judiciary, United States Senate, Eighty-Seventh Congress, Second Session, April 11, 1962 (Washington, DC: US Government Printing Office), 1962.

2. "Nomination of Arthur J. Goldberg," Hearing before the Committee on the Judiciary, United States Senate, Eighty-Seventh Congress, Second Session, September 11 and 13, 1962 (Washington, DC: US Government Printing Office), 1962.

3. Telegram to the President from Senator Barry Goldwater, August 30, 1962, White House Central Files, Supreme Court of the United States Executive File, FG535/A, Box 194, John F. Kennedy Presidential Library.

4. Henry J. Abraham, *Justices, Presidents, and Senators*, 5th ed. (Lanham, MD: Rowman and Littlefield, 2008), pp. 205–206.

5. CBS/New York Times Poll, May 13–17, 2016, at *http://pollingreport.com/court.htm*. Accessed August 1, 2016.

6. "Dangling Justice," *Washington Post*, February 19, 1959, p. 20.

7. Lyle Denniston, "Is a Recess Appointment to the Court an Option?" Scotusblog, February 14, 2016, at *http://www.scotusblog.com/2016/02/is-a-recess-appointment-to-the-court-an-option/*. Accessed August 1, 2016.

8. Joel B. Grossman and Stephen L. Wasby, "The Senate and Supreme Court Nominations: Some Reflections," *Duke Law Journal*, 1972 (1972): 583–584.

9. Laurence Tribe, *God Save This Honorable Court: How the Choice of Supreme Court Justices Shapes Our History* (New York: Random House, 1985).

10. Neil A. Lewis, "Washington Talk: Democrats Readying for Judicial Fight," *New York Times*, May 1, 2001, at *http://www.nytimes.com/2001/05/01/us/washington-talk-democrats-readying-for-judicial-fight.html*. Accessed June 16, 2016.

11. Anonymous interview with Republican Senate Judiciary Committee staff member, July 23, 2015.

12. Carl Hulse, "Senate Confirms Kagan in Partisan Vote," *New York Times*, August 5, 2010, at *http://www.nytimes.com/2010/08/06/us/politics/06kagan.html*. Accessed August 1, 2016.

13. Karoun Demirjian and Mike DeBonis, "Senate Democrats Slam Republican Blockade as Garland Visits Capitol Hill," *Washington Post*, March 17, 2016, at *https://www.washingtonpost.com/news/powerpost/wp/2016/03/17/merrick-garland-heads-to-capitol-hill-after-being-nominated-to-the-supreme-court/*. Accessed August 1, 2016.

14. Memorandum to Kenneth Duberstein from Pamela J. Turner, "Courtesy Calls for Judge Anthony Kennedy," November 12, 1987, Thomas Griscom Files, Series III: Subject File, Box 3, Reagan Presidential Library.

15. Memorandum from William L. Ball III to Howard Baker, "Activities Relating to Nomination of Judge Bork," October 15, 1987, David McIntosh Files, Box 3, Reagan Presidential Library; and Denis Steven Rutkus, "Supreme Court Appointment Process: Roles of the President, Judiciary Committee, and Senate," Congressional Research Service, CRS Report RL31989, February 19, 2010, p. 24, note 88.

16. Lois Romano and Juliet Eilperin, "Republicans Were Masters in the Race to Paint Alito," *Washington Post*, February 2, 2006, p. A1.

17. Chance Seales, "Merrick Garland Marks 50th Senate Visit as Trump Steals SCOTUS Spotlight," KQRE, May 19, 2016, at *http://krqe.com/2016/05/19/merrick-garland-marks-50th-senate-visit-as-trump-steals-scotus-spotlight/*. Accessed August 5, 2016; and Orrin Hatch, "My Meeting with Supreme Court Nominee Merrick Garland," *Deseret News*, May 26, 2016, at *http://www.deseretnews.com/article/865655108/Orrin-Hatch-My-meeting-with-Supreme-Court-nominee-Merrick-Garland.html*. Accessed August 5, 2016.

18. Denis Steven Rutkus and Maureen Bearden, "Supreme Court Nominations, 1789–2009: Actions by the Senate, the Judiciary Committee, and the President," CRS Report, RL33225, August 25, 2009, at *http://www.leahy.senate.gov/imo/media/doc/CRS-SupremeCourtNominations1789-2009.pdf*. Accessed April 13, 2015.

19. Letter from William Langer, Senate Judiciary Committee Chair, to Herbert Brownell, US Attorney General, RG 46 Records of the US Senate, 83d Congress, Sen 83B-A3, Judiciary, Executive Nominations, Warren, Box No. 52, National Archives Building, Washington, DC.

20. Anonymous interview with Judiciary Committee staff member, July 24, 2015.

21. Rutkus, "Supreme Court Appointment Process: Roles of the President, Judiciary Committee, and Senate," p. 22.

22. Letter to Christina McFadden from David H. Souter, August 10, 1990, White House Counsel's Office, Lee S. Liberman Files, David H. Souter Files, George H. W. Bush Presidential Library.

23. Paul M. Collins Jr. and Lori A. Ringhand, *Supreme Court Confirmation Hearings and Constitutional Change* (New York: Cambridge University Press, 2013), p. 38.

24. Michael Comiskey, "The Supreme Court Appointment Process: Lessons from Filling the Rehnquist and O'Connor Vacancies," *PS: Political Science and Politics*, 41 (April 2008): 355–358.

25. Anonymous interview with Judiciary Committee staff member, July 24, 2015.

26. Letter to Robert H. Bork from Joseph R. Biden, August 17, 1987, Peter D. Keisler Files, 1984–1987, Series I: Chronological File—July 29, 1987–September 15, 1987, Box 5, Reagan Presidential Library.

27. "Responses of Judge Ruth Bader Ginsburg to July 16, 1993 Questions from the Senate Judiciary Committee Concerning Her Membership in Woodmont Country Club," Clinton Presidential Records, Counsel's Office, Ginsburg, Ruth Bader Confirmation, 2006-1067-F, Box 12, William J. Clinton Presidential Library.

28. Letter to Joe Biden from Robert C. Byrd, October 3, 1991, Lee S. Liberman Files, Clarence Thomas Subject Files, Questionnaire, Box 5, George H. W. Bush Presidential Library.

29. Letter to Sheri Sweitzer from David H. Souter, September 5, 1990, White House Counsel's Office, Lee S. Liberman Files, Clarence Thomas Subject Files, Box 1, David Souter [2], and Letter to David Souter from Joseph R. Biden Jr., September 19, 1990, White House Counsel's Office, C. Boyden Gray Files, Subject File, Supreme Court Nomination of David Souter [1], George H. W. Bush Presidential Library.

30. For example, see Letter to Edwin Meese III, Attorney General, from Joseph R. Biden Jr., Chairman of the Senate Judiciary Committee, November 20, 1987, David McIntosh Files, Box 3, Reagan Presidential Library.

31. Quoted in Joseph P. Harris, *The Advice and Consent of the Senate: A Study of the Confirmation of Appointments by the United States Senate* (Berkeley: University of California Press, 1953), p. 308.

32. Collins and Ringhand, *Supreme Court Confirmation Hearings and Constitutional Change*, pp. 58–59; and Rutkus, "Supreme Court Appointment Process: Roles of the President, Judiciary Committee, and Senate," p. 28.

33. Oral History Interview with Tom Korologos, Senate Historical Office, Washington, DC, p. 172.

34. See Dion Farganis and Justin Wedeking, *Supreme Court Confirmation Hearings in the U.S. Senate: Reconsidering the Charade* (Ann Arbor: University of Michigan Press, 2014).

35. David Margolick, "Souter Hearings Won't Be Useful for Predictions, One Justice Says," *New York Times,* August 8, 1990, p. A14.

36. US Congress, Senate Committee on the Judiciary, Nomination of Ruth Bader Ginsburg to Be Associate Justice of the Supreme Court of the United States, 103rd Cong., 1st sess., July 20–23, 1993 (Washington, DC: US Government Printing Office, 1994), p. 52.

37. Ronald Rotunda, "The Role of Ideology in Confirming Federal Court Judges," *Georgetown Journal of Legal Ethics,* 15 (2001–2002): 127–141.

38. Lloyd N. Cutler, "In Justices, Mystery Is Essential," *Washington Post,* August 2, 1990, p. A31.

39. Letter to Joseph Biden Jr. from David Souter, undated, and Letter to David Souter from Joseph R. Biden Jr., September 19, 1990, White House Counsel's Office, C. Boyden Gray Files, Subject Files, Supreme Court Nomination of David Souter [1], George H. W. Bush Presidential Library.

40. Arlen Specter, "Supreme Court Nominees Must Answer the Questions," *Washington Times,* May 16, 1994, p. A21.

41. Farganis and Wedeking, *Supreme Court Confirmation Hearings in the U.S. Senate,* pp. 22–24.

42. Farganis and Wedeking, *Supreme Court Confirmation Hearings in the U.S. Senate,* pp. 5, 24–25, 59.

43. Anonymous interview with Senate Judiciary Committee staff member, July 24, 2015.

44. Romano and Eilperin, "Republicans Were Masters in the Race to Paint Alito," p. A1.

45. 111 Cong. Rec. 144–145 (2010).

46. US Congress, Senate. Committee on the Judiciary. Nomination of Ruth Bader Ginsburg to Be Associate Justice of the Supreme Court of the United States, 103rd Congress, 1st session, S. Rept. S. HRg 103–482, 1994, pp. 229–231.

47. US Congress. Senate, Committee on the Judiciary, Nomination of Samuel A. Alito, Jr. to Be an Associate Justice of the Supreme Court of the United States, 109th Cong., 2d sess. Rept. S. HRG. 109–277 (Washington, DC: US Government Printing Office, 2006).

48. US Congress. Senate. Committee on the Judiciary. Nomination of Hon. Sonia Sotomayor to Be an Associate Justice of the Supreme Court of the United States, 111th Cong., 1st sess. Rept. S. HRG. 111–503 (Washington, DC: US Government Printing Office, 2010).

49. For comprehensive treatments of the filibuster, see Richard A. Arenberg and Robert B. Dove, *Defending the Filibuster: The Soul of the Senate* (Bloomington: Indiana University Press, 2012); Gregory Koger, *Filibustering: A Political History of Obstruction in the House and Senate* (Chicago: University of Chicago Press, 2010); and Gregory J. Wawro and Eric Shickler, *Filibuster: Obstruction and Lawmaking in the U.S. Senate* (Princeton, NJ: Princeton University Press, 2006).

50. Arenberg and Dove, *Defending the Filibuster*, p. 24.

51. Arenberg and Dove, *Defending the Filibuster*, p. 27.

52. See Martin B. Gold and Dimple Gupta, "The Constitutional Option to Change Senate Rules and Procedures: A Majoritarian Means to Overcome the Filibuster," *Harvard Journal of Law & Public Policy*, 28 (2004): 205–272.

53. See Koger, *Filibustering*.

54. Abraham, *Justices, Presidents, and Senators*, pp. 228–229.

55. "Press Release—Lawyers Committee on Supreme Court Nominations," September 12, 1968, Abe Fortas File, Box 7, Papers of Fred Graham, Manuscript Library Division, Library of Congress, Washington, DC.

56. Denis Steven Rutkus et al., *Supreme Court Nominations 1789–2005: Actions (including Speed) by the Senate, the Judiciary Committee, and the President* (New York: Nova Science, 2007), Table 1.

57. Collins and Ringhand, *Supreme Court Confirmation Hearings and Constitutional Change*, p. 46; Charles Babington, "Senate to Vote on Alito Today," *Washington Post*, January 31, 2006, at *http://www.washingtonpost.com/wp-dyn/content/article/2006/01/30/AR2006013001021 .html*. Accessed February 8, 2016; and David W. Kirkpatrick, "Alito Sworn in as Justice after Senate Gives Approval," *New York Times*, February 1, 2006, at *http://www.nytimes.com/2006/ 02/01/politics/politicsspecial1/alito-sworn-in-as-justice-after-senate-gives.html*. Accessed July 12, 2016.

58. See Richard Harris, *Decision* (New York: E. P. Dutton, 1971).

59. Richard S. Beth and Betsy Palmer, "Cloture Attempts on Nominations," CRS Report RL 32878, March 30, 2009, in Denis Steven Rutkus et al., *Supreme Court Nominations: Presidential Nomination, the Judiciary Committee, Proper Scope of Questioning of Nominees, Senate Consideration, Cloture, and the Use of the Filibuster* (Washington: The Capitol.Net, 2010), p. 131. pp. 133–137.

60. Rutkus, "Supreme Court Appointment Process: Roles of the President, Judiciary Committee, and Senate," p. 44.

61. Betsy Palmer, "Changing Senate Rules or Procedures: The 'Constitutional' or 'Nuclear Option,'" in Richard S. Beth and Betsy Palmer, "Cloture Attempts on Nominations," CRS Report RL 32878, March 30, 2009, in Denis Steven Rutkus et al., *Supreme Court Nominations: Presidential Nomination, the Judiciary Committee, Proper Scope of Questioning of Nominees, Senate Consideration, Cloture, and the Use of the Filibuster* (Washington: The Capitol. Net, 2010), pp. 143–144.

62. Arenberg and Dove, *Defending the Filibuster*, pp. 138–139; and Michael Gerhardt and Richard Painter, "'Extraordinary Circumstances': The Legacy of the Gang of 14 and a Proposal for Judicial Nominations Reform," Issue Brief, The American Constitution Society, November 2011, at *https://www.acslaw.org/sites/default/files/Gerhardt-Painter_-_Extraordinary_Circumstances .pdf*. Accessed July 6, 2016.

63. Gerhardt Richard Painter, "Extraordinary Circumstances."

64. Paul Kane, "Reid, Democrats Trigger 'Nuclear' Option; Eliminate Most Filibusters on Nominees," *Washington Post*, November 21, 2013, at *http://www.washingtonpost.com/ politics/senate-poised-to-limit-filibusters-in-party-line-vote-that-would-alter-centuries-of-prec- edent/2013/11/21/d065cfe8-52b6-11e3-9fe0-fd2ca728e67c_story.html*. Accessed May 22, 2015; and "Republicans Weigh Expanding 'Nuclear Option' for Supreme Court Nominees," *Wall Street Journal*, January 24, 2015, at *http://blogs.wsj.com/washwire/2015/ 01/24/republicans-weigh-expanding-nuclear-option-for-supreme-court-nominees/*. Accessed May 22, 2015.

65. Memorandum from Harry C. McPherson Jr. for Mike Manatos, July 2, 1968, Additional Materials not included in WHCF: 7/3/68–8/31/68, Box 7, Files Pertaining to Abe Fortas &

Homer Thornberry, Papers of Lyndon Baines Johnson President, 1963–1969, The Lyndon Baines Johnson Library.

66. Memorandum from Marvin Watson to Larry Temple, September 20, 1968, 12:30 PM, Postmaster General W. Marvin Watson, Box 7, Files Pertaining to Abe Fortas & Homer Thornberry, Papers of Lyndon Baines Johnson President, 1963–1969, The Lyndon Baines Johnson Library.

67. Lincoln D. Chafee, *Against the Tide: How a Compliant Congress Empowered a Reckless President* (New York: Thomas Dunne Books, 2008), pp. 165–166.

68. Jennifer Steinhauer, "Swing State Republican Senators Hold Firm against Nominee," *New York Times*, March 16, 2016, at *http://www.nytimes.com/live/obama-supreme-court-nomination/swing-state-senators-hold-firm/*. Accessed August 1, 2016; and Seung Min Kim, "Embattled Toomey Agrees to Sit with Merrick Garland," *Politico*, March 23, 2016, at *http://www.politico.com/story/2016/03/pat-toomey-merrick-garland-meeting-221159*. Accessed August 1, 2016.

69. Memorandum from Mike Mantos to the President, June 27, 1968, Chron File: 6/13/68–6/25/68, Files Pertaining to Abe Fortas & Homer Thornberry, Papers of Lyndon Baines Johnson President, 1963–1969, The Lyndon Baines Johnson Library.

70. Harris, *The Advice and Consent of the Senate*, p. 309.

71. Donald R. Songer, "The Relevance of Policy Values for the Confirmation of Supreme Court Nominees," *Law and Society Review*, 13 (1978–1979): 927–948.

72. Specter, "Supreme Court Nominees Must Answer the Questions."

73. Eric Lipton, "Supreme Court Nomination Drives Groups from Left and Right to Fight," *New York Times*, March 16, 2016, at *http://www.nytimes.com/2016/03/17/us/politics/activists-protest-nomination-supreme-court.html?emc=eta1*. Accessed June 23, 2016.

74. Lee Epstein and Jeffrey A. Segal, *Advice and Consent: The Politics of Supreme Court Appointments* (New York: Oxford University Press, 2005), p. 106.

75. Warren Weaver Jr., "Carswell Attacked and Defended as Senate Opens Debate on Nomination," *New York Times*, March 17, 1970, at *http://www.nytimes.com/1970/03/17/archives/carswell-attacked-and-defended-as-senate-opens-debate-on-nomination.html*. Accessed July 25, 2016.

76. "Carswell and Mediocrity," Office of Senator Thomas Eagleton press release, March 24, 1970, Judge G. Harrold Carswell file, Box 5, Papers of Fred Graham, Manuscript Library Division, Library of Congress, Washington, DC.

77. "Carswell and Mediocrity."

78. Melanie Garunay, "The American Bar Association Gives Its Highest Rating to Chief Judge Garland," White House, June 21, 2016, at *https://www.whitehouse.gov/blog/2016/06/21/american-bar-association-gives-its-highest-rating-chief-judge-garland*. Accessed August 2, 2016.

79. Neil A. Lewis, "Bar Association Splits on Fitness of Thomas for the Supreme Court," *New York Times*, August 28, 1991, at *http://www.nytimes.com/1991/08/28/us/bar-association-splits-on-fitness-of-thomas-for-the-supreme-court.html*. Accessed August 2, 2016.

80. Susan Navarro Smelcer, Amy Steigerwalt, and Richard L. Vining Jr., "Bias and the Bar: Evaluating the ABA Ratings of Federal Judicial Nominees," *Political Research Quarterly*, 65 (2012): 827–840.

81. Debra Cassens Weiss, "ABA to Resume Early Review of Potential Judicial Nominees," *ABA Journal*, March 17, 2009, at *http://www.abajournal.com/news/article/aba_to_resume_early_review_of_potential_judicial_nominees/*. Accessed April 28, 2015.

82. American Bar Association, "Standing Committee on the Federal Judiciary: What It Is and How It Works," 2009, at *http://www.americanbar.org/content/dam/aba/migrated/scfedjud/federal_judiciary09.authcheckdam.pdf*. Accessed April 28, 2015.

83. Smelcer, Steigerwalt, and Vining, "Bias and the Bar," 827–840.

84. Debra Cassens Weiss, "Merrick Garland Gets ABA's 'Well-Qualified' Rating; ABA President Calls for Senate Action," *ABA Journal*, June 21, 2016, at *http://www.abajournal.com/news/article/merrick_garland_gets_a_well_qualified_rating_from_aba*. Accessed August 2, 2016.

85. "Press Release—Lawyers Committee on Supreme Court Nominations," September 12, 1968, Abe Fortas File, Box 7, Papers of Fred Graham, Manuscript Library Division, Library of Congress, Washington, DC.

86. Memorandum from Leigh Ann Metzger, Special Assistant to the President for Public Liaison, to David Demarest, Assistant to the President for Communications, Supreme Court Nominations, July 3, 1991, Clarence Thomas Nomination [2], Issues File, John Sununu Files, White House Chief of Staff, Box 87, George H. W. Bush Presidential Library; and "Nomination of Robert H. Bork to Be Associate Justice of the Supreme Court of the United States," Hearings before the Committee on the Judiciary, United States Senate, One Hundredth Congress, First Session, September 15, 16, 17, 18, 19, 21, 22, 23, 25, 28, 29, and 30, 1987, Part 1 of 5 (Washington, DC: US Government Printing Office, 1989).

87. "Urban Coalition Action Council Urges Withdrawal of Carswell Nomination," press release, February 6, 1970, and "NEA Opposes Carswell Nomination," press release, February 18, 1970, Box 5, Papers of Fred Graham, Manuscript Division, Library of Congress.

88. "AAUW Strongly Opposes Thomas for Supreme Court," American Association of University Women press release, August 7, 1991, and "Statement by Harriett Woods, President of the National Women's Political Caucus," August 7, 1991, Clarence Thomas Subject Files, Lee S. Liberman Files, Box 3, George H. W. Bush Presidential Library.

89. Letter to Senator Orrin Hatch from J. Ward Morrow, July 30, 1990, White House Counsel's Office, Lee S. Liberman Files, Judicial Material Files, Box 1, David Souter (Supreme Court Nomination) [1], George H. W. Bush Presidential Library.

90. "Senator Kennedy Opposes Bork Nomination," C-SPAN, July 1, 1987, at *https://www.c-span.org/video/?c4594844/senator-kennedy-opposes-bork-nomination*. Accessed August 2, 2016.

91. The Alliance for Justice, "Report on the Nomination of Merrick B. Garland to the United States Supreme Court," at *http://www.afj.org/wp-content/uploads/2016/05/TheGarlandRecord.pdf*. Accessed August 2, 2016; and National Association for the Advancement of Colored People, "A Report on the Nomination of Judge Clarence Thomas as Associate Justice of the United States Supreme Court," August 1, 1991, Mark Paoletta Files, Clarence Thomas Subject Files, "Potential Questions for Clarence Thomas" vol. 2, Box 20, George H. W. Bush Presidential Library.

92. People for the American Way Action Fund, "Report on the Nomination of David Hackett Souter to the United States Supreme Court," September 6, 1990, White House Counsel's Office, Lee S. Liberman Files, Judicial Material Files, Box 1, David Souter (Supreme Court Nomination) [1], George H. W. Bush Presidential Library.

93. "Douglas H. Ginsburg," Thomas Griscom Files, Series III: Subject File, Box 3, Reagan Presidential Library.

94. Alliance for Justice, "Report on the Nomination of Judge Ruth Bader Ginsburg to the United States Supreme Court," Clinton Presidential Records, Counsel's Office, Ginsburg, Ruth Bader Confirmation, 2006-1067-F, Box 12, William J. Clinton Presidential Library.

95. Ed Gillespie, *Winning Right: Campaign Politics and Conservative Policies* (New York: Threshold Editions, 2006), p. 197.

96. Washington Bureau, National Association for the Advancement of Colored People, "Bork Nomination Senate Report Form," Peter D. Keisler Files, 1984–1987, Series I: Chronological File—September 16, 1987–December 31, 1987, Box 6, Reagan Presidential Library.

97. Tony Mauro, "Souter Out of Limelight, but Still under Scrutiny," *USA Today*, August 22, 1990, p. 03A.

98. Anonymous interview with Senate Judiciary Committee staff member, July 24, 2015.

99. Anonymous interview with Senate Judiciary Committee staff member, July 24, 2015.

100. Robert David Johnson, "Lyndon B. Johnson and the Fortas Nomination," *Journal of Supreme Court History*, 41 (March 2016): 114.

101. Haynes Johnson, "Haynsworth Case: Politics of Pressure," *Washington Post*, November 20, 1969, p. A1.

102. Johnson, "Lyndon B. Johnson and the Fortas Nomination," p. 115.

103. Memorandum from William L. Ball III to Senator Baker and Kenneth M. Duberstein, "Mail Survey on Judge Bork," September 23, 1987, Thomas Griscom Files, Series III: Subject File, Box 3, Reagan Presidential Library.

104. National Organization for Women rally poster, White House Counsel's Office, Lee S. Liberman Files, Judicial Material Files, Box 1, David Souter (Supreme Court Nomination) [1], George H. W. Bush Presidential Library.

105. Kay Henderson, "Liberal Groups Stage Rallies to Back Obama's Supreme Court Pick," Reuters, March 21, 2016, at *http://www.reuters.com/article/us-usa-court-garland-idUSKCN0WN2AE*. Accessed August 3, 2016.

106. Memorandum from Mike Manatos for the President, July 15, 1968, 6:15 PM, and Letter to the President from Marvin Johnson, July 17, 1968, Chron. File—7/14/68–7/31/68, Files Pertaining to Abe Fortas & Homer Thornberry, Papers of Lyndon Baines Johnson President, 1963–1969, The Lyndon Baines Johnson Library.

107. Letter to the President from Richard B. Russell, September 26, 1968, Chron. File—9/16/68–9/30/68, Files Pertaining to Abe Fortas & Homer Thornberry, Papers of Lyndon Baines Johnson President, 1963–1969, The Lyndon Baines Johnson Library.

108. Burgess Everett, "GOP Rallies around Court Blockade," *Politico*, May 8, 2016, at *http://www.politico.com/story/2016/05/gop-supreme-court-merrick-garland-222898*. Accessed August 3, 2016.

109. "Chronological Buildup of Opposition to Carswell," CQ Fact Sheet, April 1, 1970, p. 1.

110. Interview notes with Senator Philip Hart, n.d., Judge George Harrold Carswell file, Box 5, Papers of Fred Graham, Manuscript Library Division, Library of Congress, Washington, DC.

111. "Bush Nominates Alito to Supreme Court," CNN, November 1, 2005, at *http://www.cnn.com/2005/POLITICS/10/31/scotus.bush/index.html*.

112. Memorandum from Mike Manatos for the President, June 28, 1968, Chron. File—6/26/68–6/30/68, Files Pertaining to Abe Fortas & Homer Thornberry, Papers of Lyndon Baines Johnson President, 1963–1969, The Lyndon Baines Johnson Library.

113. Memorandum from Marvin Watson to Larry Temple, September 20, 1968, 12:30 PM, Chron. File—9/16/68–9/30/68, Files Pertaining to Abe Fortas & Homer Thornberry, Papers of Lyndon Baines Johnson President, 1963–1969, The Lyndon Baines Johnson Library.

114. Spencer Rich, "Williams Opposes Nominee," *Washington Post*, November 20, 1969, p. A1.

115. "Dear Colleague" letter from Senator Richard Lugar, July 27, 1994, Chris Cerf through Beth Nolan, S. Breyer—Ethics Issues, 2006-1067-F, Box 93, William J. Clinton Presidential Library; Helen Dewar, "Breyer Wins Senate Confirmation to Top Court, 87 to 9," *Washington Post*, July 30, 1994, p. A9.

116. Letter from Audrey Colom and Lee Novick, Chairwoman and Vice Chairwoman of the National Women's Political Caucus, to Senator James Eastland and members of the Senate Judiciary Committee, December 8, 1975, John Paul Stevens file, Box 11, Papers of Fred Graham, Manuscript Library Division, Library of Congress, Washington, DC.

117. Planned Parenthood Action Fund, Inc., "Statement by Kenneth C. Edelin, M.D., Chairperson, Planned Parenthood Action Fund on Judge David Souter," press release, September 14, 1990, White House Counsel's Office, Lee S. Liberman Files, Clarence Thomas Subject Files, Box 1, David Souter [2], George H. W. Bush Presidential Library.

118. Society of American Law Teachers, "SALT Statement on the Confirmation of David H. Souter," press release, September 17, 1990, White House Counsel's Office, Lee S. Liberman Files, Clarence Thomas Subject Files, Box 1, David Souter Supreme Court Nomination [1], George H. W. Bush Presidential Library.

119. Anonymous interview with Judiciary Committee staff member, July 24, 2015.

120. Letter from Colleen Parro, Director of Government Affairs, Eagle Forum, to Joseph R. Biden Jr., Chairman, Committee on the Judiciary, July 19, 1993, Stephen G. Breyer, Folder 1, 2006-1067-F, Box 61, William J. Clinton Presidential Library.

121. Stuart Taylor Jr., "Politics in the Bork Battle," *New York Times*, September 28, 1987, p. A1.

122. David D. Kirkpatrick, "Kerry Gets Cool Response to Call to Filibuster Alito," *New York Times*, January 27, 2006, at *http://www.nytimes.com/2006/01/27/politics/politicsspecial1/27alito.html?_r=0*; and Charles Babington, "Democrats Split over Filibuster on Alito," *Washington Post*, January 27, 2006, at *http://www.washingtonpost.com/wp-dyn/content/article/2006/01/26/AR2006012601955.html*. Accessed February 8, 2016.

123. Memorandum from Howard S. Liebengood to Will Ball, "Bork Nomination," September 21, 1987, Thomas Griscom Files, Series III: Subject File, Box 3, Reagan Presidential Library.

124. Bill Bradley, "Against Judge Souter," *Washington Post*, September 28, 1990, p. A27.

125. Joan Biskupic, *American Original: The Life and Constitution of Supreme Court Justice Antonin Scalia* (New York: Sarah Crichton Books, 2009), p. 121.

126. Letter to Senator William Armstrong from Paul Weyrich, September 28, 1987, David McIntosh Files, Box 1, Reagan Presidential Library.

127. "C-SPAN Supreme Court Survey," July 9, 2009, C-SPAN, at *http://sites.c-span.org/camerasInTheCourt/pdf/C-SPAN%20Supreme%20Court%20Online%20Survey_070909_6pm.pdf*. Accessed August 3, 2016.

128. Clarence Thomas, *My Grandfather's Son: A Memoir* (New York: Harper, 2007).

129. Rutkus, "Supreme Court Appointment Process: Roles of the President, Judiciary Committee, and Senate," pp. 31–32.

130. Rutkus, "Supreme Court Appointment Process: Roles of the President, Judiciary Committee, and Senate," p. 32.

131. Anonymous interview with Senate Judiciary Committee staff member, July 24, 2015.

132. George Harrold Carswell file, Box 5, Papers of Fred Graham, Manuscript Library Division, Library of Congress, Washington, DC.

133. Letter from Richard Kleindienst, Deputy Attorney General, to Senator James Eastland, October 28, 1971, William Rehnquist file, Box 9, Papers of Fred Graham, Manuscript Library Division, Library of Congress, Washington, DC.

134. Glenn R. Simpson, "Senate Votes to Plug Leaks in Committees," *Roll Call*, October 12, 1992, p. 1.

135. "Yeas and Nays," Committee on the Judiciary, United States Senate, March 16, 1957, RG 46, Records of the US Senate, 85th Congress, Sen 85B-A3, Committee on the Judiciary, Nominations (Varn-Zavatt); and "Yeas and Nays," Committee on the Judiciary, United States Senate, April 9, 1959, Stewart Box 35, National Archives Building, Washington, D.C.

136. Farganis and Wedeking, *Supreme Court Confirmation Hearings in the U.S. Senate*, p. 22.

137. Collins and Ringhand, *Supreme Court Confirmation Hearings and Constitutional Change*, pp. 41–42.

138. Author interview with Senator Harry Reid, Washington, DC, July 21, 2015.

139. Nomination of David H. Souter to Be Associate Justice of the Supreme Court of the US. Hearings before the Committee on the Judiciary, United States Senate, One Hundred First Congress, second session, September 13, 14, 17–19, 1990 (Washington, DC: US Government Printing Office, 1991), p. 194.

140. Oral History Interview with Tom Korologos, Senate Historical Office, Washington, DC, p. 197.

141. Gregory A. Caldeira and Charles E. Smith Jr., "Campaigning for the Supreme Court: The Dynamics of Public Opinion on the Thomas Nomination," *Journal of Politics*, 58 (August 1996): 670–675.

142. Johnson, "Lyndon B. Johnson and the Fortas Nomination," 114–116.

143. Harris, "Public Backs Fortas Confirmation," *Washington Post and Times Herald*, August 12, 1968, p. A21.

144. Louis Harris, "Public Backs Fortas Confirmation," p. A21.

145. Louis Harris, "Haynsworth Opposed by 53 Percent in Poll," *Washington Post*, November 17, 1969, p. A4.

146. Robin Toner, "Poll Finds Most Undecided on Bork," *New York Times*, September 15, 1987, at *http://www.nytimes.com/1987/09/15/us/poll-finds-most-undecided-on-bork.html*. Accessed August 3, 2016.

147. For a discussion of the changes in knowledge levels about Thomas during the confirmation process, see Caldeira and Smith, "Campaigning for the Supreme Court," 655–681.

148. For correspondence from the public to the Senate Judiciary Committee, see Sen 83B-A3, Judiciary, Executive Nominations, Warren, Box No. 52, National Archives Building, Washington, DC.

149. For correspondence from the public to the Chair of the Senate Judiciary Committee regarding the John M. Harlan II nomination, see RG 46 Records of the US Senate, 84th

Congress, Sen 84B-A3, Judiciary, Nominations (East-Harlan), Box 19, National Archives Building, Washington, DC.

150. "Nomination of Arthur J. Goldberg," Hearing before the Committee on the Judiciary, United States Senate, Eighty-Seventh Congress, Second Session, September 11 and 13, 1962. (Washington, DC: US Government Printing Office), 1962.

151. "Nomination of Arthur J. Goldberg."

152. L. Marvin Overby and Robert D. Brown, "Reelection Constituencies and the Politics of Supreme Court Confirmation Votes," *American Politics Quarterly*, 25 (April 1997): 168–178. See also L. Marvin Overby et al., "Courting Constituents? An Analysis of the Senate Confirmation Vote on Justice Clarence Thomas," *American Political Science Review*, 86 (December 1992): 997–1003.

153. Caldeira and Smith, "Campaigning for the Supreme Court," 656.

154. Israel Wilkerson, "The 1992 Campaign: Congress; Illinois Senator Is Defeated by County Politician," *New York Times*, March 18, 1992, at *http://www.nytimes.com/1992/03/18/us/the-1992-campaign-congress-illinois-senator-is-defeated-by-county-politician.html.*

155. Spencer Rich, "Judge Vote Could Hurt Senators," *Washington Post*, November 9, 1969.

156. Oral History Interview with Tom Korologos, Senate Historical Office, Washington, DC, p. 201.

157. Rutkus and Bearden, "Supreme Court Nominations, 1789–2009: Actions by the Senate, the Judiciary Committee, and the President."

158. Memorandum from Mike Manatos to the President, September 16, 1968, 4:15 PM, Chron. File: 9/16/68—9/30/68, Files Pertaining to Abe Fortas & Homer Thornberry, Papers of Lyndon Baines Johnson President, 1963–1969, The Lyndon Baines Johnson Library.

159. Memorandum from Larry Temple to the President, July 26, 1968, Chron. File—7/14/68–7/31/68, Files Pertaining to Abe Fortas & Homer Thornberry, Papers of Lyndon Baines Johnson President, 1963–1969, The Lyndon Baines Johnson Library.

160. Anonymous interview with Senate Judiciary Committee staff member, July 24, 2015.

161. Jeffrey K. Tulis, "Constitutional Abdication: The Senate, the President, and Appointments to the Supreme Court," *Case Western Reserve Law Review*, 47 (Summer 1997): 1331–1360.

Presidential Management

1. Tom Korologos, "How to Scale the High Court," *Washington Post*, May 24, 2009, p. B1.

2. "Roll Call Votes of the 99th Congress on Judicial Nominees and Attorney General Appointment," Supreme Court, 1972–1987, Folder 4, Box 22, Papers of Robert H. Bork, Manuscript Division, Library of Congress.

3. Suzanne Garment, "The War against Robert Bork," *Commentary*, January 1988, p. 19.

4. "Statement of Judge Robert Bork," White House Office of the Press Secretary, October 9, 1987, Thomas Griscom Files, Series III: Subject File, Box 3, Reagan Presidential Library.

5. Letter to Morton C. Blackwell from Ronald Reagan, October 21, 1987, David McIntosh Files, Box 3, Reagan Presidential Library.

6. Memorandum from Jeffrey Lord to Frank Donatelli and Frank Lavin, "A Plan for the New Court Nominee," October 16, 1987, Jeffrey Lord Collection, 0115548, Box 1, Reagan Presidential Library.

7. Memorandum from Jeffrey Lord to Frank Donatelli, Frank Lavin, Carlyle Gregory, Judith Ann Butler, Becky McMahan, and Tom Thoren, "The Borker," October 11, 1987, Jeffrey Lord Collection, 0115548, Box 1, Reagan Presidential Library.

8. Memorandum from Gwen King to Frank J. Donatelli, "IGA Plan for Supreme Court Nominee," October 16, 1987, David McIntosh Files, Box 3, Reagan Presidential Library.

9. Memorandum, author unknown, September 25, 1989, Clarence Thomas Files, Lee S. Liberman Files, Materials, Box 4, George H. W. Bush Presidential Library.

10. Memorandum from William L. Ball III to Howard Baker, "Activities Relating to Nomination of Judge Bork," October 15, 1987, David McIntosh Files, Box 3, Reagan Presidential Library.

11. Memorandum from Arthur B. Culvahouse Jr., Counsel to the President, to John Tuck, Executive Assistant to the Chief of Staff, "Counsel's Office Activities on Behalf of Judge Bork," October 15, 1987, John C. Tuck Files, Box 1, Reagan Presidential Library.

12. Memorandum from Tom Gibson, Director of Public Affairs, to White House Chief of Staff, "Office of Public Affairs Activities in Support of Judge Bork," October 15, 1987, David McIntosh Files, Box 3, Reagan Presidential Library.

13. Memorandum from Tom Gibson, Director of Public Affairs, to White House Chief of Staff, "Office of Public Affairs Activities in Support of Judge Bork."

14. Memorandum from Tom Gibson.

15. Memorandum from Dwight L. Chapin to H. R. Haldeman, May 19, 1969, 5 PM, White House Special Files, White House Central Files, Subject Files, FG-51, Box 1, Nixon Presidential Library.

16. Denis Steven Rutkus et al., *Supreme Court Nominations 1789–2005: Actions (including Speed) by the Senate, the Judiciary Committee, and the President* (New York: Nova Science, 2007), Table 1.

17. Geoff Earle, "Senators Spar over 'Thurmond Rule,'" *The Hill*, July 21, 2004, at *http://web .archive.org/web/20040722212816/http://www.hillnews.com/news/072104/thurmond .aspx*. Accessed July 30, 2015.

18. E. J. Dionne Jr. "On Once and Future Supreme Court Nominations," *Washington Post*, June 19, 1992, p. A25.

19. Stuart Taylor Jr., "Politics in the Bork Battle," *New York Times*, September 28, 1987, p. A1.

20. Memorandum from Barefoot Sanders to the President, June 28, 1968, Chron. File— 6/26/68–6/30/68, Files Pertaining to Abe Fortas & Homer Thornberry, Papers of Lyndon Baines Johnson President, 1963–1969, The Lyndon Baines Johnson Library.

21. Memorandum from Barefoot Sanders to George Christian, October 17, 1968, Chron. File— 10/1/68–12/20/68, Files Pertaining to Abe Fortas & Homer Thornberry, Papers of Lyndon Baines Johnson President, 1963–1969, The Lyndon Baines Johnson Library.

22. Lee Epstein and Jeffrey A. Segal, *Advice and Consent: The Politics of Judicial Appointments* (New York: Oxford, 2005), pp. 108–113.

23. Epstein and Segal, *Advice and Consent: The Politics of Judicial Appointments*, p. 107.

24. Keith E. Whittington, "Presidents, Senates, and Failed Supreme Court Nominations," *Supreme Court Review*, 2006 (2006): 412–414.

25. Letter to Orrin Hatch from President Bill Clinton, July 30, 1993, "President William Jefferson Clinton: Swearing-in of Ruth Bader Ginsburg, Washington, DC, August 10, 1993," Alpha Project 24778 [Ruth Bader Ginsburg], 2006-1067-F, Box 2, William J. Clinton Presidential Library.

26. Alexander Mooney, "Hatch to Vote against Sotomayor," CNN, July 24, 2009, at *http:// politicalticker.blogs.cnn.com/2009/07/24/hatch-to-vote-against-sotomayor/*. Accessed July 14, 2016.

27. Dennis Romboy and Lisa Riley Roche, "FreedomWorks Endorses Mia Love, Dan Liljenquist," *Deseret News*, April 26, 2012, at http://www.deseretnews.com/article/865554758/ FreedomWorks-endorses-Love-Liljenquist.html?pg=all.

28. Memorandum from Frank J. Donatelli to Will Ball, "Thoughts on Bork Nomination," July 14, 1987, Elizabeth Board Files, 1985–1989, Box 10, Reagan Presidential Library.

29. Memorandum from Robert M. Teeter to C. Boyden Gray, October 23, 1991, Mark Paoletta Files, Clarence Thomas Subject Files, "Thomas-Hill Polling Charts," Box 18, George H. W. Bush Presidential Library.

30. "The President's News Conference in Kennebunkport, Maine, July 1, 1991," at *http:// www.presidency.ucsb.edu/ws/?pid=29651*. Accessed April 14, 2016.

31. Memorandum to Marvin Watson, July 18, 1968, 5:45 PM. Postmaster General W. Marvin Watson, Box 7, Files Pertaining to Abe Fortas & Homer Thornberry, Papers of Lyndon Baines Johnson President, 1963–1969, The Lyndon Baines Johnson Library.

32. Memorandum from Lloyd N. Cutler, Joel I. Klein, and Clifford M. Sloan to Mack McLarty, "Breyer Nomination," July 6, 1994, Previously Restricted Material—Batch 6, William J. Clinton Presidential Library.

33. Anthony Madonna, Richard L. Vining Jr., and James E. Monogan III, "Confirmation Wars and Collateral Damage: Assessing the Impact of Supreme Court Nominations on Presidential

Success in the U.S. Senate," paper, October 25, 2012, at *http://spia.uga.edu/faculty_pages/ ajmadonn/Presidential%20Capital.pdf.* Accessed June 27, 2016.

34. "The White House," Office of the White House Press Secretary Press Release, March 30, 1962, "Supreme Court," Papers of John F. Kennedy, Presidential Papers, President's Office Files, at *http://www.jf12klibrary.org/Asset-Viewer/Archives/JFKPOF-088a-011.aspx.* Accessed March 21, 2016.

35. "President Trump's Nominee for the Supreme Court Neil M. Gorsuch," White House Office of the Press Secretary, January 31, 2017, at *https://www.whitehouse.gov/nominee-gorsuch#page.* Accessed February 1, 2017.

36. Memorandum from Frank J. Donatelli to Will Ball, "Thoughts on Bork Nomination," July 14, 1987, Elizabeth Board Files, 1985–1989, Box 10, Reagan Presidential Library.

37. Memorandum from Frank J. Donatelli to Will Ball.

38. Memorandum from Peter D. Keisler to Arthur B. Culvahouse Jr., "List of Bork Spokesmen," August 12, 1987, Peter D. Keisler Files, 1984–1987, Series I: Chronological File—July 29, 1987–September 15, 1987, Box 5, Reagan Presidential Library.

39. "Supreme Court, Undated," Box 22, The Papers of Robert H. Bork, Manuscript Division, Library of Congress.

40. Memorandum from Warren Christopher, Deputy Attorney General, to Larry Temple, Special Assistant to the President, "Draft Statement on the Judicial Restraint Exercised by Mr. Justice Fortas, July 13, 1968," Chron. File—7/7/68–7/13/68, Files Pertaining to Abe Fortas & Homer Thornberry, Papers of Lyndon Baines Johnson President, 1963–1969, The Lyndon Baines Johnson Library.

41. "Remarks by the President Announcing Judge Merrick Garland as His Nominee to the Supreme Court," White House Office of the Press Secretary, March 16, 2016, at *https://www .whitehouse.gov/the-press-office/2016/03/16/remarks-president-announcing-judge-merrick-garland-his-nominee-supreme.* Accessed August 3, 2016.

42. "Remarks by the President Announcing Judge Merrick Garland as His Nominee to the Supreme Court"; and "Remarks by the President and Solicitor General Elena Kagan at the Nomination of Solicitor General Elena Kagan to the Supreme Court," Office of the White House Press Secretary, May 10, 2010, at *https://www.whitehouse.gov/the-press-office/remarks-president-and-solicitor-general-elena-kagan-nomination-solicitor-general-el.* Accessed August 4, 2016.

43. Epstein and Segal, *Advice and Consent: The Politics of Judicial Appointments,* p. 93.

44. " 'Judicial and Intellectual Excellence': What America's Leaders are Saying about Judge David Souter," White House Counsel's Office, Lee S. Liberman Files, Judicial Material Files, Box 1, David Souter Files [1], George H. W. Bush Presidential Library.

45. Memorandum from the President for Bob Haldeman, April 13, 1970, President's Personal File, Memoranda from the President, 1969–1974, Box 2, Nixon Presidential Library.

46. "Remarks Announcing the Nomination of Judge Warren Earl Burger to Be Chief Justice of the United States," May 21, 1969, The American Presidency Project, at *http://www.presidency .ucsb.edu/ws/index.php?pid=2063.* Accessed July 6, 2016.

47. "Address to the Nation Announcing Intention to Nominate Lewis F. Powell Jr. and William H. Rehnquist to Be Associate Justices of the Supreme Court of the United States," October 21, 1971, The American Presidency Project, at *http://www.presidency.ucsb.edu/ws/index .php?pid=3196&st=&st1=.* Accessed July 6, 2016.

48. "Ginsburg for the Supreme Court," *Baltimore Sun,* June 15, 1993, p. 12A.

49. Memorandum from Barefoot Sanders to the President, July 30, 1968, 8:45 PM, Chron. File—7/14/68–7/31/68, Files Pertaining to Abe Fortas & Homer Thornberry, Papers of Lyndon Baines Johnson President, 1963–1969, The Lyndon Baines Johnson Library.

50. Erin Miller, Lecture by Gregory Craig: "Picking Supreme Court Justices," Scotusblog, March 5, 2010, at *http://www.scotusblog.com/2010/03/lecture-by-gregory-craig-picking-supreme-court-justices/.* Accessed June 27, 2016.

51. Ronald Reagan, "Radio Address to the Nation on Independence Day and the Centennial of the Statue of Liberty," Speech, Washington, DC, July 5, 1986, Reagan Presidential Library, at *https://reaganlibrary.archives.gov/archives/speeches/1986/70586a.htm.* Accessed April 20, 2016.

52. Jesse Lee, "The President's Nominee: Judge Sonia Sotomayor," The White House Blog, May 26, 2009, at *https://www.whitehouse.gov/blog/2009/05/26/presidentrsquos-nominee-judge-sonia-sotomayor*. Accessed July 10, 2015.

53. Joan Biskupic, *American Original: The Life and Constitution of Supreme Court Justice Antonin Scalia* (New York: Sarah Crichton Books, 2009), p. 106.

54. Ronald Reagan: "Radio Address to the Nation on the United States Supreme Court Nominations," August 9, 1986, The American Presidency Project, at *http://www.presidency.ucsb.edu/ws/?pid=37723*. Accessed July 10, 2015.

55. "Presidential Radio Address," White House studio, Friday, September 6, 1991, 1:15 PM, Lee S. Liberman Files, Clarence Thomas Subject Files, POTUS Speeches, Box 5, George H. W. Bush Presidential Library.

56. Steven V. Roberts, "Selection Praised by GOP Senators," *New York Times*, June 18, 1986, p. A32.

57. Paul M. Barrett, "Backers of Clinton's Supreme Court Pick Put Robin Hood Spin on Breyer's Role," *Wall Street Journal*, May 20, p. 1994, p. B4B; Neil A. Lewis, "Nominee Has a Net Worth of $8 Million; Judge Breyer Could Be Richest on Court," *New York Times*, June 10, 1994, p. 8; "Remarks Announcing the Nomination of Stephen G. Breyer to Be a Supreme Court Associate Justice and an Exchange with Reporters," May 13, 1994, The American Presidency Project, at *http://www.presidency.ucsb.edu/ws/?pid=50164*. Accessed April 11, 2016; and "Nomination of Stephen G. Breyer to Be an Associate Justice of the Supreme Court of the United States," Hearings before the Committee on the Judiciary, United States Senate, One Hundred Third Congress, Second Session, July 12, 13, 14, and 15, 1994 (Washington, DC: US Government Printing Office, 1995).

58. "NARAL Statement on Nomination of Neil Gorsuch to Supreme Court," January 31, 2017, at *http://www.prochoiceamerica.org/media/press-releases/2017/pr01312017_trump_scotus_nominee.html*. Accessed February 1, 2017.

59. Joseph Williams, "Cyberspace Hosts a Blitzkrieg over Nominee," *Boston Globe*, May 28, 2009, p. A2.

60. "Response Prepared to White House Analysis of Judge Bork's Record," September 2, 1987, Thomas Griscom Files, Series III: Subject File, Box 3, Reagan Presidential Library.

61. Undated statement, Thomas Griscom Files, Series III: Subject File, Box 3, Reagan Presidential Library.

62. Memorandum from John Brown III to Herb Klein, April 2, 1970, and Memorandum from Jeb S. Magruder to Staff Secretary, April 7, 1970, White House Special Files, White House Central Files, Subject Files: Confidential Files, 1969–1974, Box 22, Nixon Presidential Library.

63. Memorandum from Clark B. Mollenhoff, undated, White House Special Files, Staff Member Office Files—H. R. Haldeman, Box 139, Nixon Presidential Library.

64. Memorandum from Sue Richard and Elizabeth Board to Leslye Arsht, "Media Plan for Support of Bork Nomination," July 23, 1987, Elizabeth Board Files, 1985–1989, Box 10, Reagan Presidential Library.

65. Memorandum from Jeb S. Magruder for the President, April 8, 1970, and Memorandum from John R. Brown III for Herb Klein, April 2, 1970, White House Special Files, White House Central Files, Subject Files: Confidential Files, 1969–1974, Box 22, Nixon Presidential Library.

66. R. W. Apple Jr., "Biden's Waterloo? Too Soon to Tell," *New York Times*, September 18, 1987, p. A23.

67. Apple, "Biden's Waterloo? Too Soon to Tell," p. A23.

68. Undated memorandum, Chron. File: Undated 1 of 3, Files Pertaining to Abe Fortas & Homer Thornberry, Papers of Lyndon Baines Johnson President, 1963–1969, The Lyndon Baines Johnson Library.

69. Memorandum from Jeffrey Lord to Frank Donatelli, Frank Lavin, Carlyle Gregory, Judith Ann Butler, Becky McMahan, and Tom Thoren, "The Borker," October 11, 1987, Jeffrey Lord Collection, 0115548, Box 1, Reagan Presidential Library.

70. Anonymous interview with George W. Bush administration official, August 7, 2015.

71. Memorandum from Joe Rodota to David Chew, "Tracking of Bork Editorials and Reports," July 24, 1987, Thomas Griscom Files, Series III: Subject File, Box 3, Reagan Presidential Library.

72. Memorandum from George Christian to the President, June 27, 1968, 9:35 AM, WHCF: Ex FG 535/A 6/25/68–6/30/68, Chron File: Undated 3 of 3, Files Pertaining to Abe Fortas & Homer Thornberry, Papers of Lyndon Baines Johnson President, 1963–1969, The Lyndon Baines Johnson Library.

73. Memorandum from Ken Cole to John Ehrlichman, undated, White House Special Files, Staff Member Office Files: John D. Ehrlichman, Box 23, Nixon Presidential Library.

74. For an example, see Memorandum from Peter Keisler to Arthur B. Culvahouse, "Op-Ed on Bork," September 11, 1987, Peter D. Keisler Files, 1984–1987, Series III: Supreme Court Nominations, Box 24, Reagan Presidential Library.

75. Memorandum from Sue Richard and Elizabeth Board to Leslye Arsht, "Media Plan for Support of Bork Nomination," July 23, 1987, Elizabeth Board Files, 1985–1989, Box 10, Reagan Presidential Library.

76. Author telephone interview with Greg Craig, July 6, 7, 2015.

77. Gillespie, *Winning Right*, p. 196.

78. Memorandum from William E. Timmons to H. R. Haldeman, April 10, 1970, and Presidential Statement Report, April 9, 1970, 11 PM, White House Special Files, Staff Member Office Files: H. R. Haldeman, Box 67, Nixon Presidential Library.

79. Author interview with Peter Keisler, August 27, 2014.

80. Anonymous interview with George W. Bush administration official, August 7, 2015.

81. Author telephone interview with Greg Craig, July 6, 7, 2015.

82. See, for example, Memorandum for Kenneth Duberstein from Pamela J. Turner, "Judge Kennedy's Courtesy Calls, December 3rd," December 4, 1987, Thomas Griscom Files, Series III: Subject File, Box 3, Reagan Presidential Library.

83. Memorandum from Frederick D. McClure to Fred Nelson, "Issues for Background Briefing Book," July 26, 1990, White House Counsel's Office, Lee S. Liberman Files, David H. Souter Files, Box 1, David H. Souter—Hearings, George H. W. Bush Presidential Library.

84. Oral History Interview with Tom Korologos, Senate Historical Office, Washington, DC, p. 147.

85. Undated memo to Ken Duberstein, author unclear, Peter D. Keisler Files, 1984–1987, Series III: Supreme Court Nominations, Box 24, Reagan Presidential Library.

86. Charles Babington, "After the Home Run, a White House Balk?" *Washington Post*, October 21, 2005, p. A04.

87. "Interview Requests for Stephen G. Breyer," June 8, 1994, Cliff Sloan, 2006-1067-F, Box 96, William J. Clinton Presidential Library.

88. "Interview Requests for Stephen G. Breyer."

89. Memorandum from Thomas C. Griscom to Senior Administration Officials, "Judge Robert H. Bork," Thomas Griscom Files, Series III: Subject File, Box 3, Reagan Presidential Library.

90. "Supreme Court Nomination: David H. Souter—Talking Points," Mark Paoletta Files, Judicial Nomination Files, Box 1, George Bush Presidential Library.

91. Letter to Chris Fabry, Openline, from Peter D Keisler, Associate Counsel to the President, August 14, 1987, Peter D. Keisler Files, 1984–1987, Series I: Chronological File—July 29, 1987–September 15, 1987, Box 5, Reagan Presidential Library; and Memorandum from Sue Richard and Elizabeth Board to Leslye Arsht, "Media Plan for Support of Bork Nomination," July 23, 1987, Elizabeth Board Files, 1985–1989, Box 10, Reagan Presidential Library.

92. Memorandum from John C. Tuck to Senator Baker, September 17, 1987, John C. Tuck Files, Box 1, Reagan Presidential Library.

93. Memorandum from Elizabeth Board to Tom Griscom, "Regional Media Activities #1," November 6, 1987, Thomas Griscom Files, Series III: Subject File, Box 3, Reagan Presidential Library.

94. Memorandum from Lloyd N. Cutler, Joel I. Klein, and Clifford M. Sloan to Mack McLarty, "Breyer Nomination," July 6, 1994, Previously Restricted Material—Batch 6, William J. Clinton Presidential Library.

95. Memorandum from Elizabeth Board to Chris Cox, November 3, 1987, Elizabeth Board Files, 1985–1989, Box 10, Reagan Presidential Library; and Memorandum from Tom Gibson to Tom Griscom and Chris Cox, "Status Report on Bork Advocates," July 12, 1987, Elizabeth Board Files, 1985–1989, Series II: Subject File—Bork Nomination, Box 7, Reagan Presidential Library.

96. Memorandum from Warren Christopher, Deputy Attorney General, to Larry Temple, Special Assistant to the President, "Honorable Homer Thornberry," June 26, 1968, Thornberry: Chronological Order 2 of 2, Box 10, Files Pertaining to Abe Fortas & Homer Thornberry, Papers of Lyndon Baines Johnson President, 1963–1969, The Lyndon Baines Johnson Library; and Memorandum from Irv Spraque to Barefoot Sanders, July 2, 1968, 11 AM, Chron. File—7/1/68–7/6/68, Files Pertaining to Abe Fortas & Homer Thornberry, Papers of Lyndon Baines Johnson President, 1963–1969, The Lyndon Baines Johnson Library.

97. Memorandum from Arthur B. Culvahouse Jr., Counsel to the President, to John Tuck, Executive Assistant to the Chief of Staff, "Counsel's Office Activities on Behalf of Judge Bork," October 15, 1987, and Memorandum from Joe Rodota to Peter Keisler, "Draft Op-Ed by Dinesh D'Souza," August 11, 1987, John C. Tuck Files, Box 1, Reagan Presidential Library.

98. Memorandum from Elizabeth Board to Tom Griscom, "Judge Ginsburg," November 2, 1987, Elizabeth Board Files, 1985–1989, Box 10, Reagan Presidential Library.

99. Memorandum from Dorrance Smith for the President, October 17, 1991, Clarence Thomas Nomination [1], Issues File, John Sununu Files, Box 87, White House Chief of Staff, George H. W. Bush Presidential Library.

100. Memorandum from Charles Colson to Jon Huntsman, "Court Confirmation Controversy," October 27, 1971, White House Special Files, Staff Member Office Files: Charles Colson, Box 110, Nixon Presidential Library.

101. Memorandum from Herb Klein to Ken Cole, October 8, 1969, White House Special Files, White House Central Files, Subject Files: Confidential Files, 1969–1974, Box 22, Nixon Presidential Library.

102. Memorandum from Larry Temple to the President, July 1, 1968, 5:45 PM, Memorandum from Larry Temple to Mike Manatos, July 1, 1968, Memorandum from Leo Janos to Jim Gaither, July 2, 1968, Chron. File—7/1/68–7/6/68, and Memorandum from Warren Christopher, Deputy Attorney General, to Larry Temple, Special Assistant to the President, "Answer to Criticism Raised by Senator Griffin with Respect to a Recent Opinion of Judge Thornberry," Thornberry: Chronological Order 2 of 2, Box 10, Files Pertaining to Abe Fortas & Homer Thornberry, Papers of Lyndon Baines Johnson President, 1963–1969, The Lyndon Baines Johnson Library.

103. "A Four-Part Dialogue," Chron. File—6/26/68–6/30/68, Files Pertaining to Abe Fortas & Homer Thornberry, Papers of Lyndon Baines Johnson President, 1963–1969, The Lyndon Baines Johnson Library.

104. Memorandum from William E. Timmons to H. R. Haldeman, April 10, 1970, and Presidential Statement Report, April 9, 1970, 11 PM, White House Special Files, Staff Member Office Files: H. R. Haldeman, Box 67, Nixon Presidential Library; and Memorandum from Joe Rodota to Tom Griscom, "Floor Speeches in Support of Robert Bork," October 6, 1987, David McIntosh Files, Box 1, Reagan Presidential Library.

105. Oral History Interview with Tom Korologos, Senate Historical Office, Washington, DC, p. 199.

106. Lois Romano and Juliet Eilperin, "Republicans Were Masters in the Race to Paint Alito," *Washington Post*, February 2, 2006, p. A1.

107. Memorandum from Terry Eastland to William Bradford Reyolds, "Ginsburg Confirmation," October 30, 1987, Thomas Griscom Files, Series III: Subject File, Box 3, Reagan Presidential Library.

108. Memorandum: "Issues and Questions of Interest from the Senate Confirmation Hearings of Judge Robert H. Bork and Justices Kennedy, O'Connor, Souter, and Thomas," June 27, 1993, Alpha Project 24778 [Ruth Bader Ginsburg], 2006-1067-F, Box 8, William J. Clinton Presidential Library.

109. Memorandum for Howard Paster from Ron Klain—"Likely Areas of Committee Questioning," July 19, 1993, Clinton Presidential Records, Counsel's Office, Ginsburg, Ruth Bader Confirmation, 2006-1067-F, Box 12, William J. Clinton Presidential Library.

110. Letter from Larry Pressler to Ruth Bader Ginsburg, July 12, 1993, Clinton Presidential Records, Counsel's Office, Ginsburg, Ruth Bader Confirmation, 2006-1067-F, Box 12, William J. Clinton Presidential Library.

111. Letter from Orrin G. Hatch, Ranking Minority Member, to Stephen G. Breyer, June 28, 1994, Doug Band, Breyer Confirmation Material, 2006-1067-F, Box 87, William J. Clinton Presidential Library.

112. Anonymous interview with George W. Bush administration official, August 7, 2015.

113. Undated Notes, Doug Band, Breyer Confirmation Material, 2006-1067-F, Box 86, William J. Clinton Presidential Library.

114. Memorandum from Preeta D. Bansal to Clifford M. Sloan, "Senator's Likely Questions for Breyer Hearings," July 7, 1994, Doug Band, Breyer Confirmation Material, 2006-1067-F, Box 87, William J. Clinton Presidential Library.

115. Anonymous interview with George W. Bush administration official, August 7, 2015.

116. "Notes from Meeting of June 25, 1993," Clinton Presidential Records, Counsel's Office, Ginsburg, Ruth Bader Confirmation, 2006-1067-F, Box 12, William J. Clinton Presidential Library.

117. Memorandum from Don Verrilli to Joel Klein, Deputy Counsel to the President, July 19, 1994; Doug Band, Breyer Confirmation Material, 2006-1067-F, Box 86, William J. Clinton Presidential Library.

118. Office of Legal Policy, Department of Justice, "Briefing Materials Relating to Past Supreme Court Confirmation Hearings," October 1986, Supreme Court Nominees (Background Information), White House Counsel's Office, Lee S. Liberman Files, Supreme Court Files, Box 3, George H. W. Bush Presidential Library.

119. Ruth Marcus, "As Thomas Hearings Wrap Up, Democrats Question the Process," *Washington Post*, September 21, 1991, p. A7.

120. Anonymous interview with George W. Bush administration official, August 7, 2015.

121. "Hearing Assignments 7/13/93," Clinton Presidential Records, Counsel's Office, Ginsburg, Ruth Bader Confirmation, 2006-1067-F, Box 12, William J. Clinton Presidential Library.

122. "Suggested Topics for Tuesday Prep Session," undated, Peter D. Keisler Files, 1984–1987, Series III: Supreme Court Nominations, Box 25, Reagan Presidential Library.

123. Oral History Interview with Tom Korologos, Senate Historical Office, Washington, DC, p. 149.

124. Memorandum from Arthur B. Culvahouse Jr., Counsel to the President, to John Tuck, Executive Assistant to the Chief of Staff, "Counsel's Office Activities on Behalf of Judge Bork," October 15, 1987, John C. Tuck Files, Box 1, Reagan Presidential Library.

125. Memorandum from C. Christopher Cox, Patricia M. Bryan, Peter D. Keisler, and Benedict S. Cohen to Arthur B. Culvahouse Jr., "Outline of Recommended White House Support for Confirmation of Judge Bork," August 21, 1987, Peter D. Keisler Files, 1984–1987, Series I: Chronological File—July 29, 1987–September 15, 1987, Box 5, Reagan Presidential Library.

126. Anonymous interview with George W. Bush administration official, August 7, 2015.

127. Memorandum from Ron Klain to David Gergen, "Judge Ginsburg: Performance Pitfalls," July 14, 1993, Previously Restricted Material—Batch 6, William J. Clinton Presidential Library.

128. Korologos, "How to Scale the High Court," p. B1.

129. Oral History Interview with Tom Korologos, Senate Historical Office, Washington, DC, p. 160.

130. Memorandum from Ron Klain to David Gergen, "Judge Ginsburg: Performance Pitfalls," July 14, 1993, Previously Restricted Material—Batch 6, William J. Clinton Presidential Library.

131. Memorandum from Charles Colson to Bryce Harlow, April 20, 1970, White House Special Files, Staff Member Office Files—Charles W. Colson, Box 43, Nixon Presidential Library.

132. Memorandum from William L. Ball, III to Kenneth M. Duberstein, "Legislative Strategy for Ginsburg Nomination," November 2, 1987, Thomas Griscom Files, Series III: Subject File, Box 3, Reagan Presidential Library.

133. Memorandum from Mike Manatos to the President, June 26, 1968, Chron File: 6/13/68–6/25/68, Files Pertaining to Abe Fortas & Homer Thornberry, Papers of Lyndon Baines Johnson President, 1963–1969, The Lyndon Baines Johnson Library.

134. Memorandum from Charles Colson to Bryce Harlow, April 20, 1970, White House Special Files, Staff Member Office Files—Charles W. Colson, Box 43, Nixon Presidential Library.

135. Anonymous interview, July 24, 2015.

136. Memorandum from Charles Colson to Bryce Harlow, April 20, 1970, White House Special Files, Staff Member Office Files—Charles W. Colson, Box 43, Nixon Presidential Library.

137. Memorandum from Frank Donatelli to Ken Duberstein, "Judge Ginsburg," November 2, 1987, Jeffrey Lord Collection, 0115548, Box 1, Reagan Presidential Library.

138. Memorandum from Sue Richard and Elizabeth Board to Leslye Arsht, "Media Plan for Support of Bork Nomination," July 23, 1987, Elizabeth Board Files, 1985–1989, Box 10, Reagan Presidential Library.

139. "LBJ's Nomination of Abe Fortas to the Supreme Court, July 1965 and Chief Justice, 1968," Miller Center, University of Virginia, at *http://millercenter.org/presidentialclassroom/exhibits/lbjs-nomination-of-abe-fortas*. Accessed May 9, 2016.

140. "Recommended Telephone Call for the President—Senator David Boren," October 2, 1987, Presidential Handwriting File, Series IV: Presidential Telephone Calls—3/12/87–2/1/88, Box 10, Reagan Presidential Library.

141. Memorandum from Barefoot Sanders to the President, June 28, 1968, Friday, 11:20 AM, Chron. File—6/26/68–6/30/68, Files Pertaining to Abe Fortas & Homer Thornberry, Papers of Lyndon Baines Johnson President, 1963–1969, The Lyndon Baines Johnson Library; List of Cabinet Members, unknown author, June 29, 1968, Chron. File—6/26/68–6/30/68, Files Pertaining to Abe Fortas & Homer Thornberry, Papers of Lyndon Baines Johnson President, 1963–1969, The Lyndon Baines Johnson Library.

142. "LBJ's Nomination of Abe Fortas to the Supreme Court, July 1965 and Chief Justice, 1968," Miller Center, University of Virginia, at *http://millercenter.org/presidentialclassroom/exhibits/lbjs-nomination-of-abe-fortas*. Accessed May 9, 2016.

143. "Table. Ginsburg Cases" and "Published Opinions with a Dissent," Alpha Project 24778 [Ruth Bader Ginsburg], 2006-1067-F, Box 8, William J. Clinton Presidential Library.

144. Memorandum from Arthur B. Culvahouse Jr., Counsel to the President, to John Tuck, Executive Assistant to the Chief of Staff, "Counsel's Office Activities on Behalf of Judge Bork," October 15, 1987, John C. Tuck Files, Box 1, Reagan Presidential Library.

145. Memorandum from Larry Temple to the President, June 29, 1968, 7:07 PM, and Memorandum from Warren Christopher, Deputy Attorney General, to Larry Temple, Special Assistant to the President, July 2, 1968, Thornberry: Chronological Order 2 of 2, Box 10, Files Pertaining to Abe Fortas & Homer Thornberry, Papers of Lyndon Baines Johnson President, 1963–1969, The Lyndon Baines Johnson Library.

146. Memorandum from Mike Manatos to the President, June 26, 1968, Chron File: 6/13/68–6/25/68, Files Pertaining to Abe Fortas & Homer Thornberry, Papers of Lyndon Baines Johnson President, 1963–1969, The Lyndon Baines Johnson Library.

147. Memorandum from Doug Nobles to the Postmaster General, "Senator Russell Long," July 9, 1968, Postmaster General W. Marvin Watson, Box 7, Files Pertaining to Abe Fortas & Homer Thornberry, Papers of Lyndon Baines Johnson President, 1963–1969, The Lyndon Baines Johnson Library.

148. Memorandum from Larry Temple to Jim Jones, July 13, 1968, Additional Materials not included in WHCF: 7/3/68–8/31/68, Box 7, Files Pertaining to Abe Fortas & Homer Thornberry, Papers of Lyndon Baines Johnson President, 1963–1969, The Lyndon Baines Johnson Library.

149. Memorandum from Bryce Harlow for the President, "Meeting with Senator Marlow Cook," April 6, 1970, White House Special Files, White House Central Files, Subject Files: Confidential Files, 1969–1974, Box 22, Nixon Presidential Library.

150. Letter from Richard B. Russell to the President, July 1, 1968, Thornberry: Chronological Order 2 of 2, Box 10, Files Pertaining to Abe Fortas & Homer Thornberry, Papers of Lyndon Baines Johnson President, 1963–1969, The Lyndon Baines Johnson Library.

151. Letter to Richard B. Russell from the President, July 2, 1968, Thornberry: Chronological Order 2 of 2, Box 10, Files Pertaining to Abe Fortas & Homer Thornberry, Papers of Lyndon Baines Johnson President, 1963–1969, The Lyndon Baines Johnson Library.

152. Memorandum from Bryce Harlow to Staff Secretary, April 2, 1970, White House Special Files, Staff Member Office Files, Memoranda for the President, Box 80, Nixon Presidential Library.

153. "Notes from Meeting of June 25, 1993," Clinton Presidential Records, Counsel's Office, Ginsburg, Ruth Bader Confirmation, 2006-1067-F, Box 12, William J. Clinton Presidential Library.

154. See, for example, "Action Items—Carswell Nomination," April 2, 1970, White House Special Files, White House Central Files, Subject Files: Confidential Files, 1969–1974, Box 22, Nixon Presidential Library.

155. Memorandum from C. Christopher Cox, Patricia M. Bryan, Peter D. Keisler, and Benedict S. Cohen to Arthur B. Culvahouse Jr., "Outline of Recommended White House Support for Confirmation of Judge Bork," August 21, 1987, Peter D. Keisler Files, 1984–1987, Series I: Chronological File—July 29, 1987–September 15, 1987, Box 5, Reagan Presidential Library.

156. "Questions to Thomas: Natural Law," Lee S. Liberman Files, Clarence Thomas Subject Files, Questionnaire, Box 5, George H. W. Bush Presidential Library.

157. Memorandum from Barefoot Sanders to the President, July 30, 1968, 8:45 PM, Chron. File—7/14/68–7/31/68, Files Pertaining to Abe Fortas & Homer Thornberry, Papers of Lyndon Baines Johnson President, 1963–1969, The Lyndon Baines Johnson Library.

158. Memorandum from Jay B. Stephens, Deputy Counsel to the President, to Arthur B. Culvahouse Jr., "Bork," July 31, 1987, Thomas Griscom Files, Series III: Subject File, Box 3, Reagan Presidential Library.

159. Note to the President, October 13, 1969, President's Office Files, President's Handwriting, September 1969 to November 1969, Box 3, Nixon Presidential Library.

160. Memorandum from David Dreyer, Office of Communications, to Patricia A. McHugh and Paul A. Toback, "Breyer Nomination," May 14, 1994, Box 2, July 18, 2014, Previously Restricted Material—Batch 6, William J. Clinton Presidential Library.

161. Memorandum from Lloyd N. Cutler, Joel I. Klein, and Clifford M. Sloan to Mack McLarty, "Breyer Nomination," July 6, 1994, Previously Restricted Material—Batch 6, William J. Clinton Presidential Library.

162. Notes from meeting on June 23, 1993, Victoria Radd, Ruth Bader Ginsburg Questionnaire Responses—Volume 1, 2006-1067-F, Box 33, William J. Clinton Presidential Library.

163. Letter to Senator James Eastland from Joshua M. Morse III, Dean, School of Law, July 8, 1968, Chron. File—7/7/68–7/13/68, Files Pertaining to Abe Fortas & Homer Thornberry, Papers of Lyndon Baines Johnson President, 1963–1969, The Lyndon Baines Johnson Library.

164. Memorandum from Dick Darling to Doug Nobles, June 28, 1968, Chron. File—6/26/68–6/30/68, Files Pertaining to Abe Fortas & Homer Thornberry, Papers of Lyndon Baines Johnson President, 1963–1969, The Lyndon Baines Johnson Library.

165. Memorandum from Larry Temple to the President, July 2, 1968, 7:45 PM, Chron. File—7/1/68–7/6/68, Files Pertaining to Abe Fortas & Homer Thornberry, Papers of Lyndon Baines Johnson President, 1963–1969, The Lyndon Baines Johnson Library.

166. Draft Form letter to Republican State Chairman from Frank Donatelli, Assistant to the President for Political and Intergovernmental Affairs, November 3, 1987, Jeffrey Lord Collection, 0115548, Box 1, Reagan Presidential Library.

167. Joan Biskupic, *Sandra Day O'Connor: How the First Woman on the Supreme Court Became Its Most Influential Justice* (New York: Harper Perennial, 2006), p. 194.

168. "Index to Endorsement Letters," Clinton Presidential Records, Counsel's Office, Ginsburg, Ruth Bader Confirmation, 2006-1067-F, Box 12, William J. Clinton Presidential Library.

169. Memorandum from Barefoot Sanders to the President, June 29, 1968, 4:45 PM, WHCF: Ex FG 535/A 6/25/68–6/30/68, Chron File: Undated 3 of 3, Files Pertaining to Abe Fortas & Homer Thornberry, Papers of Lyndon Baines Johnson President, 1963–1969, The Lyndon Baines Johnson Library.

170. Unauthored memo, June 29, 1968, Chron. File—6/26/68–6/30/68, and Memorandum from Jim Gaither to Joe Califano, July 2, 1968, Chron. File—7/1/68–7/6/68, Files Pertaining to Abe Fortas & Homer Thornberry, Papers of Lyndon Baines Johnson President, 196—1969, The Lyndon Baines Johnson Library.

171. Memorandum from Jim Gaither to Joe Califano, June 29, 1968, Chron. File—6/26/68–6/30/68, Memorandum from Jim Gaither to Joe Califano, Chron. File—7/1/68–7/6/68, and Memorandum from Larry Levinson to Larry Temple, July 10, 1968, Chron. File—7/7/68–7/13/68, Files Pertaining to Abe Fortas & Homer Thornberry, Papers of Lyndon Baines Johnson President, 1963–1969, The Lyndon Baines Johnson Library.

172. Memorandum from Harry S. Dent to the Attorney General and Bryce Harlow, October 27, 1969, White House Special Files, Staff Member Office Files—H. R. Haldeman, Box 139, Nixon Presidential Library.

173. Memorandum from Harry S. Dent to the Attorney General and Bryce Harlow, October 27, 1969.

174. Memorandum from Peter D. Keisler to Arthur B. Culvahouse Jr., "Draft Op-Ed Pieces on Bork by Gary Bauer," August 17, 1987, Peter D. Keisler Files, 1984–1987, Series I: Chronological File—July 29, 1987–September 15, 1987, Box 5, Reagan Presidential Library.

175. Ruth Marcus and David Hoffman, "White House Looks Past Judge Bork," *Washington Post*, October 11, 1987, at *https://www.washingtonpost.com/archive/politics/1987/10/11/white-house-looks-past-judge-bork/d56a958e-3e8a-4614-b392-8a3e8689ea77/*. Accessed June 20, 2016; and Linda Greenhouse, "Bork's Nomination Is Rejected, 58-42; Reagan 'Saddened,'" *New York Times*, October 24, 1987, at *http://www.nytimes.com/1987/10/24/politics/24REAG.html?pagewanted=1*. Accessed June 20, 2016.

176. Memorandum from Edward E. McNally to the President through Chriss Winston, "International Appellate Judges Conference," September 13, 1990, C. Boyden Gray Files, Subject Files, Supreme Court Nomination of David Souter [1], George H. W. Bush Presidential Library.

177. Memorandum from Mike Manatos for the President, June 26, 1968, and Memorandum from Barefoot Sanders to the President, June 28, 1968, Chron File: 6/13/68–6/25/68, Files Pertaining to Abe Fortas & Homer Thornberry, Papers of Lyndon Baines Johnson President, 1963–1969, The Lyndon Baines Johnson Library.

178. Memorandum from William L. Ball III to Senator Baker and Kenneth M. Duberstein, "Early Reaction to Kennedy Nomination," November 11, 1987, Thomas Griscom Files, Series III: Subject File, Box 3, Reagan Presidential Library.

179. "International Drug Officers Support Souter," news release undated, White House Counsel's Office, Lee S. Liberman Files, David H. Souter Files, Box 1, David H. Souter—Analysis [1], George H. W. Bush Presidential Library.

180. NRA-ILA, "NRA Opposes Nomination of Merrick Garland to the U.S. Supreme Court," March 16, 2016, at *https://www.nraila.org/articles/20160316/nra-opposes-nomination-of-merrick-garland-to-the-us-supreme-court*. Accessed June 23, 2016.

181. Mark Silverstein and William Haltom, "You Can't Always Get What You Want: Reflections on the Ginsburg and Breyer Nominations," *Journal of Law and Policy*, 12 (1996): 471–472.

182. Katie Ackley, "Interest Groups Swing into Action on Supreme Court Pick," *Roll Call*, March 16, 2016, at *http://www.rollcall.com/news/policy/interest-groups-swing-into-action-on-supreme-court-pick*. Accessed June 23, 2016; "Statement by NOW President Terry O'Neill on the Supreme Court Justice Selection," March 16, 2016, at *http://now.org/media-center/press-release/statement-by-now-president-terry-oneill-on-the-supreme-court-justice-selection/*. Accessed July 20, 2016; and Arlane de Vogue, "Some Liberals Disappointed with Merrick Garland Pick," *CNN*, March 16, 2016, at *http://www.cnn.com/2016/03/16/politics/liberals-disappointment-merrick-garland-supreme-court/index.html*. Accessed July 20, 2016.

183. "RR's 'Mystery Man' Jolts Anti-aborts: Is He 'Ginsbork'?" Lifeletter '87, #11, David McIntosh Files, Box 3, Reagan Presidential Library.

184. "The Confirmation of Judge Anthony Kennedy," List of participants, Jeffrey Lord Collection, 0115548, Box 1, Reagan Presidential Library.

185. Memorandum: Clarence Thomas Meeting, July 11, 1991, Roosevelt Room—10:00 AM, Lee S. Liberman Files, Clarence Thomas Subject Files, Various Meetings, Box 7, George H. W. Bush Presidential Library.

186. "Confirmation Projects," undated memo, Confirmation Materials, Binder, 2006-1067-F, Box 42, William J. Clinton Presidential Library.

187. Memorandum from Jeff Vogt to Bobbie Kilberg, July 30, 1991, White House Office of Public Liaison, Bobby Kilberg Files, "Clarence Thomas," George H. W. Bush Presidential Library.

188. Memorandum from Rebecca G. Range to Tom Griscom, "Weekly Report on Public Efforts to Support Judge Ginsburg," November 6, 1987, Thomas Griscom Files, Series III: Subject File, Box 3, Reagan Presidential Library.

189. Memorandum from Rebecca G. Range to Tom Griscom, "Weekly Report on Public Efforts to Support Judge Ginsburg."

190. Charles Babington, "After the Home Run, a White House Balk?" *Washington Post*, October 21, 2005, p. A04.

191. Letter from Paige Patterson, President, The Criswell College, to Arthur Culvahouse Jr., August 6, 1987, Peter D. Keisler Files, 1984–1987, Series III: Supreme Court Nominations, Box 24, Reagan Presidential Library.

192. Memorandum from Jim Gaither to Joe Califano, July 2, 1968, Chron. File—7/1/68–7/6/68, Files Pertaining to Abe Fortas & Homer Thornberry, Papers of Lyndon Baines Johnson President, 1963–1969, The Lyndon Baines Johnson Library.

193. Undated memorandum, author unknown, September 9, 1987, Peter D. Keisler Files, 1984–1987, Series III: Supreme Court Nominations, Box 26, Reagan Presidential Library.

194. Memorandum to Carl A. Anderson, Acting Director of Public Liaison, to T. Kenneth Cribb, Assistant to the President for Domestic Affairs, July 24, 1987, David McIntosh Files, Box 1, Reagan Presidential Library.

195. Memorandum from Jeff Vogt to Bobbie Kilberg, July 30, 1991, White House Office of Public Liaison, Bobby Kilberg Files, "Clarence Thomas," George H. W. Bush Presidential Library.

196. "Statement by National Right to Life Committee on the Nomination of Judge Clarence Thomas to the US Supreme Court," press release, July 1, 1991, Clarence Thomas Nomination [4], Issues File, John Sununu Files, White House Chief of Staff, Box 87, George H. W. Bush Presidential Library.

197. NRA-ILA, "NRA Opposes Nomination of Merrick Garland to the U.S. Supreme Court," March 16, 2016, at *https://www.nraila.org/articles/20160316/nra-opposes-nomination-of-merrick-garland-to-the-us-supreme-court*. Accessed June 23, 2016.

198. Memorandum from Charles W. Colson for H. R. Haldeman, March 25, 1970, White House Special Files, Staff Member Office Files: Charles Colson, Box 43, Nixon Presidential Library.

199. "125 Days—and No Hearing," Organizing for Action, July 25, 2016, at *https://www.barackobama.com/news/past-time-for-action/*. Accessed August 5, 2016.

200. "Women for Judge Thomas," press release, undated, and "Citizens Group Launches Pro-Thomas Media Campaign," press release, September 4, 1991, White House Office of Public Liaison, Bobby Kilberg Files, "Clarence Thomas," George H. W. Bush Presidential Library.

201. Ruth Marcus and Joan Biskupic, "Justice White to Retire after 31 Years," *Washington Post*, March 20, 1993, p. A1.

202. "Final Report on the Confirmation Process for Ruth Bader Ginsburg, June–August 1993," Ruth Bader Ginsburg Questionnaire Responses—Vol. II, Clinton Presidential Records, Counsel's Office, Ginsburg, Ruth Bader Confirmation, 2006-1067-F, Box 16, William J. Clinton Presidential Library.

203. Author telephone interview with Greg Craig, July 6, 7, 2015.

204. Anonymous interview with George W. Bush administration official, August 7, 2015.

Conclusion

1. Denis Steven Rutkus et al., *Supreme Court Nominations 178–2005: Actions (including Speed) by the Senate, the Judiciary Committee, and the President* (New York: Nova Science, 2007), Table 1.

2. Holly Idelson, "Breyer's Bipartisan Appeal Extinguishes Fireworks," *Congressional Quarterly Weekly Report*, July 9, 1994, p. 186.

3. "Statement on Confirmation of Ruth Bader Ginsburg," August 3, 1993, Alpha Project 24778 [Ruth Bader Ginsburg], 2006-1067-F, Box 2, William J. Clinton Presidential Library.

4. See Sarah A. Binder, "The Senate as a Black Hole? Lessons Learned from the Judicial Appointments Experience," in G. Calvin Mackenzie, ed., *Innocent until Nominated: The Breakdown of the Presidential Appointments Process* (Washington: Brookings, 2001), pp. 173–195; and Benjamin Wittes, *Confirmation Wars* (Lanham, MD: Rowman and Littlefield, 2006).

5. "Nomination of Judge Clarence Thomas to Be Associate Justice of the Supreme Court of the United States," Hearings before the Committee on the Judiciary, United States Senate, One Hundred Second Congress, First Session, October 11, 12, and 13, 1991, Part 4, Washington: Government Printing Office, 1993.

6. "Scalia: Constitution Shouldn't Change with Times," Tennessee Bar Association, December 18, 2007, at *http://www.tba.org/tbatoday/2007/TBAtoday12-18-2007.htm*. Accessed August 5, 2016.

7. Jamie Stengle, "Ruth Bader Ginsburg Speaks at SMU," August 30, 2011, at *https://www.smu.edu/News/2011/ruth-bader-ginsburg-30aug2011*. Accessed June 8, 2016.

8. Adam Liptak, "John Roberts Criticized Supreme Court Confirmation Process, Before There Was a Vacancy," *New York Times*, March 21, 2016, at *http://www.nytimes.com/2016/03/22/us/politics/john-roberts-criticized-supreme-court-confirmation-process-before-there-was-a-vacancy.html?_r=0*. Accessed August 5, 2016.

9. "Statement by the President," press release, Office of the White House Press Secretary, October 10, 1968, Chron. File—10/1/68–12/31/68, Files Pertaining to Abe Fortas & Homer Thornberry, Papers of Lyndon Baines Johnson President, 1963–1969, The Lyndon Baines Johnson Library.

10. "Statement by the President," White House Office of the Press Secretary, October 9, 1987, Thomas Griscom Files, Series III: Subject File, Box 3, Reagan Presidential Library; and "Announcement by the President of Supreme Court Justice Nominee Judge Douglas Ginsburg," White House Office of the Press Secretary, October 29, 1987, David McIntosh Files, Box 3, Reagan Presidential Library.

11. "Remarks by the President Announcing Judge Merrick Garland as His Nominee to the Supreme Court," White House Office of the Press Secretary, March 16, 2016, at *https://www.whitehouse.gov/the-press-office/2016/03/16/remarks-president-announcing-judge-merrick-garland-his-nominee-supreme*. Accessed August 5, 2016.

12. Richard Davis, *Electing Justice: Fixing the Supreme Court Nomination Process* (New York: Oxford University Press, 2005); and Steven G. Calibresi and James Lindgren, "Term Limits for the Supreme Court: Life Tenure Reconsidered," *Harvard Journal of Law and Public Policy*, 29 (2005–2006): 769–877. For other views, see Kevin T. McGuire, "An Assessment of Tenure on the U.S. Supreme Court," *Judicature*, 89 (July–August 2005): 8–15; and John Gruhl, "The Impact of Term Limits for Supreme Court Justices," *Judicature*, 81 (September–October 1997): 66–72.

13. Lee Epstein, Jack C. Knight, and Olga Svetsova, "Comparing Judicial Selection Systems," *William & Mary Bill of Rights Journal*, 10 (2001): 7–36; and David J. Garrow, "Mental Decrepitude on the U.S. Supreme Court: The Historical Case for a 28th Amendment," *University of Chicago Law Review*, 67 (Autumn 2000): 995–1087.

14. Garrow, "Mental Decrepitude on the U.S. Supreme Court."

15. Sarah A. Binder and Forrest Maltzman, *Advise & Dissent: The Struggle to Shape the Federal Judiciary* (Washington: Brookings, 2009), chapter 7.

16. Tuan Samahon, "The Judicial Vesting Option: Opting Out of Nomination and Advice and Consent," *Ohio State Law Journal*, 67 (2006): 783–847.

17. Memorandum from David R. Young to John D. Ehrlichman, "Supreme Court Nominations," October 21, 1971, White House Special Files, Staff Member and Office Files—David R. Young, Box 17, Nixon Presidential Library.
18. Carl Tobias, "Senate Gridlock and Federal Judicial Selection," *Notre Dame Law Review*, 88 (2012–2013): 2233–2266.
19. Binder and Maltzman, *Advise & Dissent*, chapter 7.
20. John P. Frank, "The Appointment of Supreme Court Justices: III," *Wisconsin Law Review*, 1941 (1941): 508.
21. Benjamin Wittes, *Confirmation Wars* (Lanham, MD: Rowman and Littlefield, 2006), pp. 119–131.
22. Paul Freund, "Appointment of Justices: Some Historical Perspectives," *Harvard Law Review*, 101 (1988): 1146–1163.
23. David A. Strauss and Cass R. Sunstein, "The Senate, the Constitution, and the Confirmation Process," *Yale Law Journal*, 101 (May 1992): 1518.
24. Ludmilla Savelieff, "Hyper-Partisanship's Impact on the Supreme Court Nomination and Confirmation Process," *Georgetown Journal of Law & Public Policy*, 10 (2012): 586.
25. Freund, "Appointment of Justices: Some Historical Perspectives," 1146–1163.
26. "Three Hundred and Fifty-Four Former Presidential Appointees Endorse 'Nominee's Bill of Rights,'" Brooking Institution press release, June 14, 2001.
27. Michael Gerhardt and Richard Painter, "'Extraordinary Circumstances:' The Legacy of the Gang of 14 and a Proposal for Judicial Nominations Reform," Issue Brief, The American Constitution Society, November 2011, at *https://www.acslaw.org/sites/default/files/Gerhardt-Painter_-_Extraordinary_Circumstances.pdf*. Accessed July 6, 2016.
28. Nadine Cohodas, *Strom Thurmond and the Politics of Southern Change* (New York: Simon and Schuster, 1993), pp. 294–297.
29. Aaron Blake, "Where Ted Cruz' Marathon Speech Stands in History," *Washington Post*, September 25, 2013, at *http://www.gallup.com/poll/139880/election-polls-presidential-vote-groups.aspx*. Accessed April 29, 2015.
30. Richard A. Arenberg and Robert B. Dove, *Defending the Filibuster: The Soul of the Senate* (Bloomington: Indiana University Press, 2012), pp. 142–152.
31. Arenberg and Dove, *Defending the Filibuster*, pp. 137–138.
32. Author interview with Senator Harry Reid, Washington, DC, July 21, 2015.
33. Stuart Taylor Jr., "Justice Stevens, in Unusual Move, Praises Bork as Nominee to Court," *New York Times*, August 31, 1987, at *http://www.nytimes.com/1987/08/01/us/justice-stevens-in-unusual-move-praises-bork-as-nominee-to-court.html*. Accessed July 2, 2016.
34. Adam Liptak, "Ruth Bader Ginsburg, No Fan of Donald Trump, Critiques Latest Term," *New York Times*, July 11, 2016, p. A1.
35. David Margolick, "Souter Hearings Won't Be Useful for Predictions, One Justice Says," *New York Times*, August 8, 1990, p. A14.
36. *NFIB v. Sebelius*, 567 U.S. (2012); *District of Columbia v. Heller*, 554 U.S. (2008); *Citizens United v. Federal Election Commission*, 558 U.S. 310 (2010); *Gonzales v. Carhart*, 550 U.S. 124 (2007).
37. "Fetal Homicide State Laws," National Conference of State Legislatures, March 4, 2015, at *http://www.ncsl.org/research/health/fetal-homicide-state-laws.aspx*. Accessed August 4, 2016.
38. Emma Green, "Why Are Fewer American Women Getting Abortions?" *Atlantic*, June 17, 2015, at *http://www.theatlantic.com/politics/archive/2015/06/american-abortion-rate-decline/395960/*. Accessed June 24, 2016; Lydia Saad, "Generational Differences on Abortion Narrow," *Gallup.com*, March 12, 2010, at *http://www.gallup.com/poll/126581/generational-differences-abortion-narrow.aspx*. Accessed June 20, 2016; and Gallup, In Depth: Topics A to Z, "Abortion," at *http://www.gallup.com/poll/1576/abortion.aspx*. Accessed June 24, 2016.

INDEX